# Community Policing in a Community Era

## An Introduction and Exploration

**Quint Thurman**
*Wichita State University*

**Jihong Zhao**
*University of Nebraska at Omaha*

**Andrew Giacomazzi**
*Boise State University*

**Roxbury Publishing Company**
Los Angeles, California

**Library of Congress Cataloging-in-Publication Data**

Thurman, Quint.

Community policing in a community era: An introduction and exploration/ Quint Thurman, Jihong Zhao, Andrew L. Giacomazzi

p. cm.

Includes bibliographical references and index.

ISBN 1-891487-31-0

1. Community policing—United States. 2. Police-community relations—United States. I. Zhao, Jihong. II. Giacomazzi, Andrew L., 1966– . III. Title.

HV7936.C83T58 2001

363.2'3–dc21                                                        99-35822

                                                                    CIP

**Community Policing in a Community Era: An Introduction and Exploration**

Publisher: Claude Teweles
Managing Editor: Dawn VanDercreek
Production Editor: James Ballinger
Assistant Editor: Kate Sterner
Copy Editors: Susan Converse-Winslow, David Marion, and Roger Mensink
Typography: Synergistic Data Systems
Cover Design: Marnie Kenney

Printed on acid-free paper in the United States of America. This paper meets the standards for recycling of the Environmental Protection Agency.

ISBN 1-891487-31-0

**Roxbury Publishing Company**
P.O. Box 491044
Los Angeles, California 90049-9044
Tel: (310) 473-3312 • Fax: (310) 473-4490
Email: roxbury@roxbury.net
Website: www.roxbury.net

# Contents

# Foreword

*Anthony V. Bouza*

American policing has long displayed greater fondness for slogans than Madison Avenue. The latest shibboleth is community policing and its meaning ranges the rough peaks of individual chiefs' proclivities and biases. None (or at least very few) of previous catch phrases, whether team policing, neighborhood crime watch, local offices, or whatever, made much of an impact on a public frustrated by a losing drug war, escalating crime rates, and a general sense of expanding violence and malaise.

Suddenly, failure's orphan has acquired a thousand parents by the serendipitous and rather miraculous (and indubitably accurate) sharply declining crime rates, now spanning a brace of years. With utter and fatal predictability, every police chief has trotted out the clutch of programs he or she has uniquely devised to bring about this marvelous result. Fashions being what they are, whatever the program, it now has to be attributed to a framework of community policing. But what is community policing really?

Essentially community policing involves a police-community partnership, in which the police participate with the people they serve in attempts to solve problems troubling the community. The problems may be of the "police" variety, i.e., the prevention of crime, detection and arrest of offenders, preservation of the peace, enforcement of the law, or protection of life and property, or—and this is where tradition is broken—any problem in which the police may intervene on behalf of the people. Thus, a tree across the road, a clogged sewer, a flood emergency, or any of the thousand other ills that may beset a neighborhood become fair game for the interventions of the police, following discussions with the persons affected.

One of the great problems with the concept of community policing is that the police have jealously guarded their power and secrets and have been historically reluctant to include the public in their activities, notwithstanding giving fervent lip service to the notion. Another problem is that the police often undertake "touchy-feely" community police programs, in attempts to gain the popular support (which they already have in abundance, at least in the white community) without altering their essentially autonomous approach to policing. Police chiefs have long known that citizens love to see cops on foot patrolling a beat. Few images are more reassuring to a public who the chiefs well know cannot really distinguish between being well served and being well pleased.

As a consequence, community policing has become a way of "escaping the tyranny of 911" and getting the cops out of their cars and schmoozing with the public. Forgotten in this equation are the decades of soaring crime rates, the police's frantic attempts to respond, and the fundamental futility of that response. Exacerbating this frustration—in which it becomes historically clear that the police are essentially irrelevant to crime rates and arrive only when the criminal is formed and the crime has occurred—is the growth of black political power in core cities that has indirectly (and, in such cases as Detroit, directly) resulted in the atrophying or disappearance of really aggressive police tactics such as stakeouts, stings, decoys, and other proactive police operations that frequently resulted in the disproportionate arrests of black males, centering on the 15- to 24-year-old population of the underclass. Policing's dirty little secret is that, at the very time they are being credited with prodigious achievements, they have never been in fuller retreat from what any observer would label "aggressive policing," which, it must be said, is not in any way inconsistent with either the Constitution or racial injustice.

Crime is declining but, despite outlandish claims being made, the truth is that no one knows why. There is a trough in the "at risk" population, which will fill, like a creeping malignant tide, in about four or five years. The crack epidemic that hooked so many women, especially in the ghetto, creating true anomie, seems to have peaked in 1985 and appears to be in decline since, restoring a semblance of cohesion to ghetto life. Unemployment, though still substantially higher for black males than for white, has dropped dramatically in the "at risk" group. The swelling tide of American prosperity has, indeed, lifted even many of the oppressed and excluded. For all we know, there may be an as yet unmeasured and unanalyzed shift in underclass attitudes about family, work, and child rearing that is having an as yet unrecognized impact. The Million Man March may have tapped into a resurgent spirit of responsibility that no one has yet recognized, measured, or acknowledged.

To understand crime and policing, we must return to Aristotle: "Poverty is the parent of revolution and crime." Were he alive today he likely would have added "riots."

So, then, is the notion of community policing a bankrupt idea, another hustle from our trusty servants? Not really. All police programs, over history, have had their *raison d' être*.

If the police really want to professionalize their approach to community problems, why is it that they ignore the simple expedient of requiring a bachelor's degree from every employee at a time when everyone knows they would get all the qualified candidates they want?

And we have to remember that 911, introduced in the President's Commission on Crime Report of March 1967, has proven an enormous boon to the public's emergency needs, as well as being one of the few genuine invitations to the public to reach the police.

The physical environment matters. An ambience of "anything goes" and decay will produce predictable, and lamentable, behavior responses. Law and order have a genuine place in American society. The Founding Parents never envisioned—nor should they have—that the Constitution would prove an impediment to aggressive police approaches, including those so regrettably abandoned under political pressure.

The notion of the police and the public (whatever its makeup) coming together to solve a neighborhood problem has a lot of merit. Lawrence W. Sherman, in one of his landmark experiments, found that fewer than 10 percent of the locations in Minneapolis generated about two-thirds of police responses. Clearly there were hot spots that produced chronic, serious, and treatable police problems that were bedeviling the community.

Community policing has to be a substantive approach to serious community problems and their solutions. Problem families can be a cancer on the block; "bucket-of-blood" bars may have to be shuttered to prevent further acts of violence; drug houses have to be attacked. In short, the nagging, chronic, terrifying sores on the body politic cannot be cured on an ad hoc, isolated, and individual-case basis but must be regarded as difficulties that require analysis, prescription, and treatment. The people can identify the problems in the neighborhood and the police can marshal the resources necessary to their solution; this is the real promise of community policing—to be responsive to the needs of the people! ✦

# Acknowledgments

The list of persons whom the authors wish to acknowledge grows long in the process of writing and rewriting a book. Certainly each of us owes a great debt of gratitude to our wives and children, for without their support and encouragement this enterprise would not have been possible or as meaningful.

A second set of persons whom we wish to thank includes 10 excellent reviewers, whose suggestions have strengthened this work. We graciously acknowledge the contributions made in this regard by Michael Blankenship (East Tennessee State University), David Carter (Michigan State University), Dean Champion (Minot State University), Brant Forst (American University), Randy Garner (Sam Houston State University), Ronald Hunter (Jacksonville State University), Clinton Terry (Florida International University), Lawrence Travis III (University of Cincinnati), Gennaro Vito (University of Louisville), and Gerald L. Williams (University of Colorado-Denver).

A third set of persons we wish to thank are the great number of people who submitted supplemental materials ranging from short essays and articles to photos. Most have brief identifying biographies. Some, however, provided invaluable behind-the-scenes help in acquiring needed material. Paul Cromwell worked every step of the way with the senior author helping to provide publishing tips, perspective, and most important, his friendship. Sergeant Allen Wolf and Lieutenant Max Tenbrook of the Wichita Police Department, Carl Koster, mayor of Cheney (KS), and Debbie Phelan of the Boise Police Department contributed key photos that help tell a more complete story.

Last, but not least, we express our deep gratitude to the staff and graduate students of the School of Community Affairs at Wichita State University who put up with great demands on their time by the senior author. Cathy Blackmore on numerous occasions kept the project from stalling by lending her extensive computer skills scanning documents and converting files from Word to WordPerfect: Jason Curtis and Kathleen McLean pitched in at much needed times to read and correct bad prose. Finally, much appreciation is owed to Brenda Vose, who learned firsthand about the crazy pace of the publishing process from library research to Ventura coding—skills that we expect she will put to good use as she eventually enters the academic world as a doctoral student and later as a professor of criminal justice. ✦

# Preface

Legend has it that the Anatolian sheepdog is a formidable force against larger and more predatory adversaries. Mountain lions, with their sharp teeth and razor-sharp claws, seldom are so bold as to take on this loyal guard dog, for experience has taught them respect for its ferocity. A deep, resonant growl ordinarily is enough to frighten away the most curious beast. Odd as it may seem, this sheepdog has made quite a name for itself as a family pet and watchdog in the western United States (the actress Andie MacDowell reportedly has one to protect her children from cougars who stray onto their Montana ranch), for the Anatolian sheepdog is as gentle as it is intelligent and fierce. This complex canine truly is a remarkable and multifaceted friend of humankind.

Two-legged predators pose a similar threat to individuals, families, property, and society, all of which need protection. Although Americans generally take for granted that protection is the role of local, state, and federal law enforcement authorities, the trend until quite recently has been less toward a multifaceted, full-service approach than to one primarily limited to the traditional enforcement of laws. To continue the analogy, we have bred our police department to become more guard dog than family member and protector of public safety. At the same time, American citizens have relinquished a great deal of their own responsibility for crime prevention and public safety, although they have not entirely given up their rights to criticize legal authorities for the services they provide and the way they do their jobs.

Community policing, for many of the reasons explained in this book, attempts to knit together a complete and comprehensive partnership of police, other public officials, and the public to improve community safety and the quality of life. How it does so, of course, varies from place to place, but it usually involves community engagement, organizational change, problem solving, and innovative fieldwork.

Many of the examples featured in the chapter supplements originate from research sponsored by the National Institute of Justice, among other sources. Some examples are of local origin, provided by the uniformed descendants of O. W. Wilson's original shop, the Wichita Police Department. It is notable that the National Civic League selected Wichita as one of 10 All American Cities this year (an honor it has received twice before) based upon its demonstrated success in problem solving and grassroots community organization. We believe that behind every good city can be found a sterling public safety component and Wichita is a case in point. Of course, we also acknowledge that the local examples often were more convenient to collect than some of the others. Ultimately, we think that all the examples chosen provide good illustrations of the points we are trying to make.

As I close this brief introductory note I would like to share an anecdote that I think illustrates where the development of community policing is in this country.

I was having lunch with an old friend of my father's, whom I had known quite well to be a long-time carouser. I chided him for continuing to drink way too hard and too heavy. I pointed out that his life's habits had destroyed his health, and if he did not drastically change his ways, his doctor had predicted that his poor health choices would lead to an early death. I also took the opportunity to suggest to him how much better he might feel waking each day without a painful hangover if only he could break out of his cycle of addiction. He looked at me for a moment, and in a gravelly voice stoically replied, "Son, when you've drank as long and as hard as I have, a hangover is as good as you ever feel."

I would submit that from my experience, and that of my fellow authors, police departments (really, any organizations) that continue to do things the way they have always done them are like my father's friend. Not confident that they can change or at all convinced that change would make them better off or more effective, they simply refuse to even try, preferring to endure the pains with which they are familiar. And yet we ask the question, How is it possible for people who chose their profession expecting that they might have to put their lives in the line of fire in service to their communities, to lack the moral courage to make changes that ultimately will better themselves, their departments, and their communities?

We have tried in this book to present useful information for those students curious about modern policing in a community era and, particularly, for those persons courageous enough to take up the challenges of community policing in the twenty-first century. We expect that the career experiences of the students who read this book will tell much about the extent to which we have succeeded.

—Quint Thurman

# Chapter One

# An Introduction to Community Policing

❖ ❖ ❖ ❖

*The good of the people is the chief law.*

—Marcus Tullius Cicero

This book presents an approach to policing that differs from the one most police and sheriff's departments in the United States have relied on over the past 60-odd years. As a background to community-oriented policing (COP), or what some refer to as community-oriented public safety (COPS), or what this text will simply call community policing, the authors will introduce students to a brief history of American policing, the emergence of professional policing in the last 50 years, and the change to a more community-oriented approach. In addition, they will discuss the meaning behind the term *community*, the internal changes and obstacles that police departments face when they try to adopt community policing, how police operations and personnel are affected, and the benefits of community policing where it has been tried.

## Setting the Stage

One way to set the stage for understanding how community policing differs from earlier forms of policing is to look at a real-life example, such as the crime-related problem faced by the local chief of police of Mountlake Terrace, Washington, in August 1992.

When two of the four strip malls that made up the town's entire business district burned to the ground during the early morning hours within two weeks of each other, residents of this Seattle suburb who witnessed the scene were stunned to see so many youths out on the streets watching firefighters at work. Few people were aware that so many of the city's young people hung

*Despite their mandate to use deadly force, there are limits to police power. (Photo: Mark C. Ide)*

out so late. They voiced their concerns to the Mountlake Police Department about the potential for unsupervised youths to join gangs or otherwise get into trouble. Chief John Turner initially suggested imposing a curfew for youths under 18. After all, that's what all the other chiefs in the surrounding areas were doing—curfews were the traditional police response to too many kids on the streets too late at night.

The Mountlake Terrace story provides one example of the kinds of challenges that American police chiefs and sheriffs faced in the 1990s. However, whether the problem is youths out too late, speeding cars, or drive-by shootings, the ability of the police (a term that includes sheriff's deputies throughout the book) to respond to issues raised by citizens is constrained by legal, social, and political considerations. By law, the police are limited as to the amount of force they can apply and by the policies and procedures they must follow in any particular situation. Similarly, citizen expectations may further reduce what the police can do according to what citizens believe is acceptable police behavior. In addition, police leaders may have to consider their possible actions in terms of the support or resistance from certain interested and organized groups.

Economic forces also interact with legal, social, and political systems to play an important role in the delivery of criminal justice. On the one hand there is poverty, which Aristotle once referred to as the "parent of revolution and crime." On the other hand, there are expectations about the economic standards of living that we as Americans should aspire to regardless of our financial circumstances. Americans seem to believe that the United States is the land of opportunity and that anyone who wants to can succeed economically. But when poverty, lack of education, or other social conditions block access to jobs and salaries that can support a desired standard of living, people may be tempted to resort to illegal means to gain highly valued goods.

Americans have greater access to material goods than most other nationalities have and are more constantly being encouraged through marketing and advertising to believe that life is not complete unless you drive the best car, wear the best clothes, or vacation in the most exotic places. Unfortunately, all this emphasis on material success comes without much attention being paid to the price of success in terms of rules and legal obligations. The result is that Americans seem to have incredibly large appetites for enjoying themselves, a large menu from which to choose, and the ability to ignore the known complications that result from making unwise or illegal choices. Thus, the individual freedoms that we enjoy as citizens of the United States also give rise to perplexing social problems. For example, such freedom of choice lends itself to greater opportunity for crime in a variety of ways—more things to steal, more people to steal from, and more people willing to consider stealing an appropriate way to obtain the things they want.

## America Is Organized for Crime

Steven Messner and Richard Rosenfeld have suggested that American society in particular is organized for crime and disorder.[1] At no other time in the history of this country have civil liberties been so high, extending through nearly all age groups. At no other time have people felt that it is their right as American citizens to enjoy life and all that it may offer in terms of expressing

❖ ❖ ❖ ❖  themselves and feeding their appetites for material goods. Simultaneously, Messner and Rosenfeld note that Americans are all too willing to downplay the means that people use to get what they want. So not only are many Americans organized for crime, they also are relatively unorganized for controlling it. This makes policing more difficult in the United States than in many other countries.

Traditionally, ensuring that people obey the law has been attended to by instruction from families, churches, schools, friends, and coworkers. People learn what to do and what not to do from those who are closest to them during their adolescent years, when they are being socialized. However, when they do not receive adequate instruction from these institutions, their unruly behavior may attract disapproval and, ultimately, the police, as in the example of the teens out on the streets too late at night in Mountlake Terrace.

Public expectations about who should take the lead in handling crime and crime-related matters have not changed all that much over time, except for one subtle difference. Although American citizens still fundamentally believe that it is the police who can make people obey the law by issuing citations or using arrests or punishments if they refuse, the public also has begun to recognize that the police cannot solve crime problems alone. Both the public and police departments around the world are starting to realize that by working together they can do more to improve the quality of life in their communities than when the police concentrate only on basic law enforcement.

Pleas from the public for the police to do something about crime and delinquency sometimes require more complex solutions than first thought. For example, in the state of Washington, curfews offer little hope for solving late-night teen problems. By state law, juveniles as young as 13 can be detained by police no longer than two hours at a time, and they cannot be forced to stay at home under parental supervision if they don't want to. Washington municipalities, like their counterparts in other states, usually do not have the facilities or the personnel to detain and supervise all of the teenagers they see who simply are guilty of being out on the streets too late at night.

## Community Policing: A Sensible Response to Social Problems

Sometimes social problems are best solved by bringing the public and the police together to work on them. In the case of Mountlake Terrace, Chief Turner first began working on this problem by getting residents older than 17 to endorse the traditional police response of a curfew (he actually went to the high school and asked 18-year-olds what they thought about keeping 17-year-olds and younger teens off of the streets after 10 P.M.). But as the idea of a curfew was debated around town, this not-so-typical chief began to see that local residents were taking a harder look at the problem. They seemed determined to try to reach its root cause rather than just allow the police to employ a typical police response that only dealt with one symptom of the larger problem. Researchers David Mueller and Cary Heck describe what happened next.

> Instead of resorting to a quick-fix solution to the problem, Chief Turner decided to hold public meetings on the issue to allow residents to vent their frustrations and air their opinions about possible alternatives. Out of these meetings arose the idea that perhaps a better way to control juvenile delin-

## The Career of John Turner

❖ ❖ ❖ ❖

*Mountlake Terrace (WA) Police Chief John Turner.*

After completing a Bachelor of Science degree in police science at Washington State University, John Turner began a career in law enforcement as a sheriff's deputy in 1971. Since then, he has risen through the ranks to the position of chief of police in Mountlake Terrace, Washington, a position he has held since 1989. He currently directs 31 uniformed officers and manages a budget of $3 million for the 20,000 citizens of his community. Chief Turner is known throughout the Pacific Northwest as an energetic and innovative leader. His efforts to create the Neutral Zone were a result of his collaboration with 16 different community agencies. Chief Turner also played a key role in lobbying state legislators to change Washington laws to extend insurance liability coverage to public buildings used after regular business hours for extracurricular community-service projects.

In addition to his involvement with the Neutral Zone, Chief Turner's commitment to community policing in Mountlake Terrace is evident in various forms. He employs citizen surveys to keep informed of community needs and opinions of policing services; he maintains a citizens' advisory board to provide him with steady input about community problems; he regularly holds citizen academies for

*A popular event at Mountlake Terrace's Neutral Zone program is meal time. The midnight meal halfway through the evening's operating hours is the only hot meal that many of the participants get during the weekend. (Photo: Courtesy of the Mountlake Terrace Police Department)*

❖ ❖ ❖ ❖    ☞

*Youths and law enforcement mingle in the break room during the Neutral Zone in Mountlake Terrace (WA). Interacting with teens helps build cooperation, as well as promote informal social control. (Photo: Courtesy of the Mountlake Terrace Police Department)*

Mountlake Terrace residents who want to learn more about how his department works; and he teaches a criminal justice class to students at Edmonds/Woodway High School.

quency would be to involve area youth in a sports-related program that would simply keep them busy and off public streets on weekend nights when problems seemed to be at their worst. The idea was that youths would be forced to choose between attending the late-night program or be escorted home after curfew by the local police department. But would a 'midnight basketball program' really produce the outcomes that local residents were hoping for? After holding several of these meetings, the suggestion was made to offer the participants free food to increase their participation and turnout. Slowly, but surely, a grass roots movement was set in motion that eventually led to the establishment of the Mountlake Terrace Community Action Resource Team (CART). Rather than dealing with the symptoms of juvenile problems in a revolving-door fashion, Chief Turner and CART sought solutions that would get at the root of juvenile crime and gang delinquency.

After reviewing a number of alternative strategies in various cities around the nation, Turner and CART established a collaborative, nontraditional crime prevention program in Mountlake Terrace in June, 1992, called the Neutral Zone. As originally designed, the Neutral Zone was created to: (1) reduce the likelihood of youth involvement in, as victims or as perpetrators, crimes or violence on Mountlake Terrace streets specifically during the most active portions of the week; (2) make inroads into the youth gang culture for purposes of prevention, intervention, and suppression of youth gang activity; (3) provide an arena where recreation and services were available to high-risk youth during the most crucial hours; and (4) allow youth, community volunteers, police, and other helping professionals to work together in seeking more positive outcomes for high-risk youth.

Designed and implemented as a community-based response to the problem of youth crime, the Neutral Zone offers juvenile participants, ages 13 to 20, an alternative environment in which to more productively pass their time during the most crime-prone hours of the weekend on Fridays and Saturdays from 10:00 P.M. to 2:00 A.M. Though originally designed to act as a late-night sports program, the Neutral Zone has since evolved into an educational and

social services-oriented outreach program that has substantially reduced juvenile crime in the area (by some estimates, as much as 63 percent).[2]

❖ ❖ ❖ ❖

## Defining Community Policing

Many definitions of community policing exist. In one of the earliest ver-
sions of this concept, John Angell coined the term *democratic policing* to distinguish current practices of the time from those which he thought would
better fit the American political system.[3] Angell suggested that American
policing had become too far removed from its initial purpose of creating a
safe society that would maximize freedom regarding the exchange of ideas,
movement across jurisdictions, and religious practices. He called for a
change from police who are the crime experts, solely oriented toward enforcing criminal laws to a situation where citizens have a voice in deciding how
police services should be carried out in the community. After all, it is the citizens who pay the taxes that support policing services and the public has a
right to expect accountability from the police whenever tax dollars are spent.

Perhaps the most frequently used definition of community policing is the
one that was developed by the late Robert Trojanowicz and Bonnie
Bucqueroux. For these authors, community policing, unlike previous
attempts to reform the police, is a set of values rather than a complete pack-
age of strategies. In their book, *Community Policing: A Contemporary Perspective*, they offer this definition of community policing:

> [A] new philosophy of policing, based on the concept that police officers and
> citizens working together in creative ways can help solve contemporary
> community problems related to crime, fear of crime, social and physical dis-
> order, and neighborhood decay.[4]

More recently, William A. Geller and Guy Swanger's views have expanded
the definition of community policing even further to clarify not only what
community policing is but also what it is not:

> Community policing is a reorientation of policing philosophy and strategy
> away from the view that police alone can reduce crime, disorder and fear.
> The strategy is based on the view that police don't help their communities
> very much by placing primary reliance on random preventive patrolling,
> rapid response to calls for service irrespective of their urgency, post-incident
> investigations to identify and arrest offenders, and other primarily reactive
> criminal justice system tactics. [5]

Perhaps the definition that explains community policing in the fewest
words is one expressed by a former police superintendent of Edmonton, Canada. Police Superintendent Chris Braiden defines community policing in
light of the golden rule for getting along well with other people: "Police others
as you would have them police you."[6]

## Defining Community Policing According to
## Four Dimensions

Despite some of the best efforts to define the concept of community policing, there remain differences of opinion about what exactly community
policing is or is not. As Gary Cordner points out, "Community policing

❖ ❖ ❖ ❖ remains many things to many people."[7] He observes that four major dimensions help to identify the shape of community policing.[8]

First, the philosophical dimension of community policing contains the values of the department and what its membership thinks it ought to be doing. Central ideas and beliefs about the role of citizen input, the police mission, and how best to serve the public say a lot about a department's philosophy. Community-oriented police departments value citizen input, define their mission more broadly than just law enforcement, and believe that policing must be tailored to the needs of the community.[9]

Second, the strategic dimension represents a more "operational" version of a department's philosophy. The strategic dimension has to do with translating the philosophical side into practice through planning. Here the department thinks through how best to reorient its operations, geographic focus, and emphasis on crime prevention. Reexamining the way it investigates crimes, assigning officers to cover beats rather than neighborhoods, and allocating resources to prevent crimes in the first place are examples of issues addressed strategically.[10]

The third dimension is tactical, concerned with that part of the department involving daily operations that currently are in place. Moving from ideas to planning to daily operations indicates a clear progression from the abstract to the concrete, from what the department might imagine to what it actually does to what the public actually sees. Community-oriented police departments will stand out from more traditionally focused departments in that the former emphasize positive citizen interactions, police-community partnerships, and problem-solving activities.[11]

The fourth and final dimension is organizational. It concerns the structure of the department and its personnel, the department's management practices, and how the department maintains and distributes information related to evaluating employees, policies, and procedures. Cordner points out that community policing favors a work environment where employee input is highly valued, mentoring is encouraged, and systematic evaluation methods are in place.[12]

## PERF's Five Perspectives of Community Policing

A closer look at the various definitions of community policing and the police programs that are said to be community oriented reveals common features. For example, the Police Executive Research Forum (PERF) categorizes the various approaches to community policing it has observed according to five perspectives.[13] First, is the *deployment* perspective, that is, community policing is seen as a way to move officers closer to citizens on the streets, whether by foot patrol, police substations, or some other means that increases the familiarity of officers with the persons and places they police. As citizens and police get to know each other better, levels of trust between them should rise and there should be more sharing of information.

A second perspective identified by PERF is *community revitalization*. This view focuses on preventing neighborhood decay and fighting the fear of crime by eliminating those features of a neighborhood setting that cause people who live there to feel afraid. This approach fits well with the idea that turning a neighborhood or community around, or preventing it from going

downhill in the first place, requires maintaining the upkeep of property so
that residents seem to be keeping a watchful eye on the area. Allowing things
to run down to a state of disrepair or neglect invites crime and disorder since
those who sell illegal drugs or engage in other criminal activity will view such
places as uncontrolled space that can readily be used to carry out illegal acts.
This view fits James Wilson and George Kelling's notion of "broken windows":

> That link [between order maintenance and crime prevention] is similar to
> the process whereby one broken window becomes many. The citizen who
> fears the ill-smelling drunk, the rowdy teenager, or the importuning beggar is
> not merely expressing his distaste for unseemly behavior, he is also giving
> voice to a bit of folk wisdom that happens to be a correct generalization—
> namely, that serious street crime flourishes in areas in which disorderly con-
> duct goes unchecked. The unchecked panhandler is, in effect, the first bro-
> ken window. Muggers and robbers, whether opportunistic or professional,
> believe they reduce their chances of being caught where potential victims are
> already intimidated by prevailing conditions. If the neighborhood cannot
> keep a bothersome panhandler from annoying passersby, the thief may rea-
> son, it is even less likely to call the police to identify a potential mugger or to
> interfere if the mugging actually takes place.[14]

PERF identifies *problem solving* as a third perspective. In this view, community policing may be seen as a focused approach to a crime problem that
involves both the police and the community in identifying a problem, analyzing its scope, developing a proactive response, and then assessing how well
their solution worked. This approach, which students might recognize from
the example of Mountlake Terrace's Neutral Zone, was developed by Herman
Goldstein as "problem-oriented policing."[15]

A fourth perspective recognized by PERF is the *customer*, which emphasizes the importance of listening to the needs of citizens. Citizen priorities
would help determine the importance that police leadership places upon the
various crime and crime-related issues that the community would like
addressed before any others. An important feature of this perspective is the
emphasis on open lines of communication with local residents, frequently
involving the use of citizen advisory groups and citizen surveys to provide
feedback on police performance and insight into the priorities that the public
assigns to various problems.

The fifth and final perspective recognized by PERF is *legitimacy*, which
emphasizes establishing the credibility of the police as a fair and equitable
public-service organization that dispenses resources evenly and effectively
throughout the community. Of particular importance for this perspective is
the just treatment of the concerns of racial minorities and other groups that
historically have suffered from poor police-community relations.

## A New Definition of Community Policing

Some scholars believe that community policing should remain a loosely
defined concept. For example, Mark Moore suggests that concepts such as
community policing and problem-oriented policing should be viewed "not as
new programmatic ideas or administrative arrangements but as ideas that
seek to redefine the overall goals and methods of policing."[16] Moore suggests
that such ambiguity allows police departments more flexibility to try any of a

❖ ❖ ❖ ❖      wide variety of "community-policing" approaches they think might work to control and prevent crime. As long as the public approves of the community-policing concept, virtually anything that police departments try that they might label community policing is bound to be given some initial community support.

> In short, it is partly the ambiguity of the concept that is stimulating the wide pattern of experimentation we are observing. In this sense, it is important that the concept mean something, but not something too specific. Ambiguity is a virtue.[17]

For the purposes of this book, the authors define community policing as *the guiding philosophy for the delivery of police services that relies upon positive interactions among police, other public servants, and community representatives to serve local needs regarding crime control, crime prevention, and crime-related quality-of-life issues*. This definition stresses three elements.

## Positive Interactions

First, it emphasizes *positive interactions* between the police and others who are not specially equipped to deal with the problems of crime in society. Crime is seen as a problem that is larger than the police can handle by themselves. Greater resources than the police can muster by themselves must be brought to bear to deal with crime and related issues.

Positive interactions, as the term is used here, also implies a partnership of an unusual or extraordinary nature. A key partnership that can be expected from community policing is between the police department and the public it serves, who do not necessarily have any policing expertise at all. As one of the authors suggests, such a role for the public is unusual because citizen involvement in policing during the professional era was limited to that of victim, bystander, or criminal.[18] Community policing gives ordinary citizens a primary role that does not require them to become involved in a criminal matter until the police can show interest in their concerns, their ideas about what to do, and their willingness to participate in a solution. Citizens who wish to be involved with helping the police in this way can be proactive before any particular crime occurs, just like police who might invest time in crime prevention strategies rather than waiting to react to crimes that already have occurred.

Community policing changes the very nature of the usual interactions between police and residents of the communities they patrol. Consider officers assigned to the 11:00 P.M. to 7:00 A.M., or "graveyard," shift. They have little opportunity to meet the average, law-abiding citizens whose homes, businesses, and streets they protect. Instead, the graveyard officers usually receive calls for service that mainly involve domestic violence, public drunkenness, and bar fights. Exposed to the worst side of human nature, they run the risk of losing sight of the good citizens they serve.

Similarly, the kinds of situations that face patrol officers assigned to high-crime areas can lead to poor police perceptions of the public. William Bratton, a former police commissioner in Boston and New York City, writes that "A cop will try to stay within the bounds of acceptable behavior, but sometimes, when he gets immersed in the job, he begins to identify more with the people in the street than with his own family and friends."[19] When fre-

## I Would Not Talk to Police

### Myle Nguyen, age 15

Usually I would not talk to police officers. You don't think of them as one of us. It's them and us. They're just the people out there giving us tickets. [But] . . . getting to know them you learn to trust them more. I have more respect for people I know.

We see them everywhere, everyone knows who they are, and everyone has a different opinion on them. Some opinions are reasonable but some are so outrageous. Well this is my opinion on cops.

Lt. Max Tenbrook talks with Myle and her cousin Natalie on the steps of their school. (Photo: Courtesy of the Wichita Police Department)

In the early parts of my life, I didn't really think much of them, but I had a pretty good impression towards them. It seems like whenever someone needed help they were there willing and ready to do whatever they can. I knew they were cool, and they just wanted the best for everybody.

In the past year I've gotten to know a lot of cops personally, because I worked with them in several community service activities. They seemed like normal people to me, I saw them as my friends. But not too long ago, I did something that was somewhat bad, and one of my cop friends caught me. I was scared, but I thought I was gonna have it easy and he would just give me a warning. To my surprise, he transformed [in]to another person, or so it seemed. He was yelling at me, and did not tolerate any of my foolish acts. I was mad, I thought he was my friend. We went through the whole procedure like anyone who did what I did would.

After that incident I did not have a very nice opinion towards cops. I had a few more negative encounters with them later on, so now I just despised them. I felt like everything I did they would just be in my business. They would never leave me and my friends alone. They were like Freddy Krueger . . . they kept coming back. We treated them like dirt, everything they had to say would go in one ear and come out the other, and all suggestions they made, no matter if it was good or bad, we would not take it and do the exact opposite.

I didn't get it . . . why did we have them—they are such a pain in the butt! But not too long ago I realized what it was to feel and be a cop. It's not all that easy. I thought they are there to make other people's lives miserable, but no. They sure do things that make us miserable, but whose fault is it? I thought about that question for a while. If I didn't do it [break the law] then they wouldn't bother me.

Why do people hate cops so much? Because mostly when we see them is when we are getting a traffic ticket or about to get arrested. It seems like whenever "bad" things happen they are there. So we misunderstand the real reason why they do what they do. It's harder blaming a traffic ticket on yourself than blaming the cop that pulled you over for it.

It's hard being a cop. A lot of people, like me for example, take them for granted. They help and serve our community loyally. We need to start putting ourselves in their shoes before we start whining.

quent and negative interactions with the public become the norm, it is the "bad guys" who become a police officer's reference point for judging all of society. "In high-crime precincts, cops spend a lot of their time dealing with hard-core criminals, sociopaths, and psychopaths."[20] As a result, Bratton concludes that these negative experiences encourage officers to develop a

❖ ❖ ❖ ❖  "street morality" when dealing with citizens, that in turn creates public mistrust of the police. And the police can ill afford to risk further mistrust by its citizens in light of sensational accounts of brutality and excessive force in 1990s cases such as those of Abner Louima and Amadou Diallo.

Bratton has argued that policing in New York City could not succeed without public support. This same statement applies just as well outside New York. Negative experiences with the public can reinforce impressions of the public as untrustworthy and fickle and create barriers to police-citizen partnerships and problem solving. It is through positive interactions with the great majority of law-abiding citizens who appreciate police services that the police are brought into favorable contact with those persons who they are called upon to "protect and serve."

## Contacts With Other Groups

The second element in the definition is contact between the police, who ordinarily are seen as the experts in criminal matters, and other groups in the community. Sometimes this contact may mean the involvement of other public-service agencies such as the courts, social-welfare agencies, and sanitation departments, depending on the role that each might contribute to helping a police-community partnership work through a crime or crime-related problem. Effective contact requires the participation of local citizens who either formally or informally represent identifiable groups or the community-at-large in a deliberate effort to resolve crime or crime-related matters that affect the local quality of life.

The way citizens are included in a police-community partnership is an important issue that may distinguish community policing from more traditional policing approaches that are passed off as community policing in smaller towns and jurisdictions . Although "small-town" police administrators may be practicing community policing by virtue of their familiarity with the needs of the citizens whom they police, a genuine effort to implement community policing requires the inclusion of a broad representation of all the citizens of a community. Coffee shop discussions with mayors, business leaders, and close friends in order to keep a pulse on the needs of the community do not by themselves provide a good foundation for forming police-community partnerships. Representation from all (or as many as possible) of the diverse ethnic, social, and economic groups that make up the community has to be undertaken in a systematic and deliberate way. Obtaining input from the broad cross section of people who live in a community and then getting them involved in police-community partnerships is a continuous challenge for police departments that are committed to community policing.

## Expanded Mission

The third element in the definition is an expanded mission of the police to include whatever issues the community believes are crimes or related to crime. Instead of the police deciding what are the most significant issues of the day, they set priorities in consultation with the public about what their concerns are. Research shows that the police believe that most citizens share their concern for better protection against serious and violent crimes that occur fairly infrequently. When asked directly, however, about what issues cause them most concern or which crimes make them most fearful, citizens, according to surveys, are more interested in controlling the less serious law violations that occur more frequently. In most communities, it is barking dogs, noisy neighbors, and speeding cars that trouble citizens the most, because these are the "crimes" that citizens usually see.

❖ ❖ ❖ ❖

*Other municipal partners can play an important role in a community's public safety. Here a police officer and a fire department representative use a firetruck to capture the attention of two local youths. (Photo: Courtesy of the Omaha Police Department)*

When the police begin asking citizens about which issues deserve more police attention, they also create an opportunity to begin discussions with citizens about what steps should be taken to develop likely solutions. Without this type of interaction, police departments can be out of touch with citizen concerns and unaware of how citizens might be willing to participate in finding a solution. Similarly, the public cannot understand the perspective of the police or the police's lack of awareness of the everyday problems that concern most citizens. The public also will not know the limitations of the police in terms of their resources or how the public might contribute to problem solving. Keeping citizens and the police apart only ensures that understanding will not occur, needs will go unheard, and problem solving partnerships will not develop. In short, without these partnerships, crime control will prove more difficult.

## Limitations in Defining Community Policing

One drawback of such a broad definition of community policing as the one just proposed is that it is not particularly useful for telling students how to do community policing. A simpler definition may be to move from the abstract, conceptual level to one that is more concrete or operational. For

❖ ❖ ❖ ❖  example, the Community Policing Consortium identifies two key components of community policing: community engagement and problem solving. Refining these terms, David Bayley suggests that the police must consult with communities to understand their needs, mobilize resources that address citizen concerns, and pay particular attention to the underlying conditions that cause crime and its symptoms to occur.[21] A third key component of community policing that will be discussed throughout this book is organizational change.

One might conclude that the definition of community policing is still evolving and that no one definition will be agreeable to everyone. Whatever the definition, however, it is clear that community policing remains a popular alternative to the professional model of policing. Quint Thurman and Edmund McGarrell write that "While community policing can be many things to many people, the fuzziness of this concept has not slowed the enthusiasm for it among law enforcement executives in the United States."[22] They cite results from a recent National Institute of Justice study indicating that "over 80 percent of the police chiefs surveyed were either practicing community policing or had plans to do so in the near future. The problems begin when agencies start asking what it looks like, how to do it, and where to start."[23] This book was written to help answer these questions.

## Criticisms of Community Policing

Community policing has it critics. For example, Roy Roberg and Jack Kuykendall question whether community policing is truly a welcome change or is just seen by police administrators as a continuation of the public relations campaigns begun by the police in the 1950s and 1960s that ultimately led to the introduction of team policing in the 1970s.[24] At that time, team-policing strategies were based on the ideas of decentralizing police forces throughout a jurisdiction and having officers assigned to a beat provide personalized services to the citizens with whom they came into contact. Team policing, like community policing, assumed that more familiarity between officers and citizens would result in officers developing a greater sense of responsibility for what went on in a neighborhood. In turn, increased trust and cooperation with the police would make neighborhood residents want to do more on their own to prevent crime.

Summarizing the studies of team policing, Moore concluded that this "first modern model of what is becoming community policing" showed many positive results, including favorable reactions to it by both citizens and the police, decreases in crime, and improvements in the quality of neighborhood life.[25] Nevertheless, team policing died out by the late 1970s. Although there may be many reasons, one likely explanation is that team policing failed because it required too much change in the formal and informal organization of the police. Critics of community policing wonder if it too expects policing to change in too many ways.

Other criticisms of community policing can be found in Jack Greene and Stephen Mastrofski's book *Community Policing: Rhetoric or Reality?*[26] Several contributors to that book questioned whether or not community policing actually exists, whether or not it has really been tried, and whether or not it really works. Mastrofski notes that it is difficult in modern cities to even iden-

❖ ❖ ❖ ❖

tify what a community is in the first place.[27] Similarly, Peter Manning asks about the nature of police-community partnerships and questions how we can know them to be real.[28] Still other criticisms raised in Greene and Mastrofski's book draw attention to the potential for resistance to community policing by the police subculture, the possibility that closer ties with the public might result in illegal policing or corruption, and the difficulty of controlling the discretionary behavior of officers who are authorized to do community policing. Finally, there remain some questions as to whether all neighborhoods within a community actually want increased contact with the police[29] or if those who do will necessarily get it.[30]

The criticisms found in Greene and Mastrofski's book raise many valid questions. Undoubtedly for some police departments, community policing may be little more than a popular fad that police chiefs seem to support for the sake of good public relations. For many other police departments, community policing may simply represent a goal that will not be quickly realized. Still, quite a few departments can be held up as examples where great progress is being made.

All good ideas generally meet with skepticism in the beginning. Wesley Skogan notes that the rhetorical nature of community policing is a necessary preliminary step to becoming a reality. First, community policing reflects a new philosophy for conducting police business that differs from the professional approach departments usually employ. For community policing to be accepted by police personnel it must be presented to them as a desirable alternative that offers them attractive features. Second, community policing has to draw favorable support from the taxpayers whose dollars pay for it. For the public to accept it, community policing must benefit the community in ways that they ordinarily would not experience if policing styles remain unchanged.[31]

Viewed in another way, however, one might conclude that if everyone were happy with a professional model of policing, then there would be little room for the rhetoric of community policing. Community policing by its nature necessarily must start out as rhetoric that promises something new and different from the old way of enforcing laws. If change were not needed, then the rhetoric of community policing would not appear so promising.

## Organization of This Book

The example chosen to begin this book illustrates how community policing might look in one community that was forced to deal with a crime-related issue that was brought to the attention of the police chief by local residents. Other examples will be presented in the chapters that follow. But first it is necessary to examine the history of policing and the concept of community that has led up to recent changes and plays an important role in shaping the future of community policing.

Chapter 2 provides a brief history of modern policing from its British roots, its introduction to the United States at the start of the 20th century, and its development through the 1930s into the professional model with which most recent students of policing are familiar.

Chapter 3 introduces the reader to the idea of community. Most people are familiar with the community or communities in which they grew up but

❖ ❖ ❖ ❖          are somewhat less able to discuss in any systematic way how one community resembles or differs from another. This chapter defines what a community is and how communities change over time.

Chapter 4 discusses more broadly the three eras of American policing—the political era, the professional era, and the community era—and the driving forces that led to changes from one era to another. This chapter pays particular attention to the needs of American policing that change has tried to address and the effects of change on police departments and the police subculture.

Chapter 5 offers an analysis of police organizational change and reviews how the environment outside of a police department interacts with conditions inside the department. It discusses how organizational change is influenced by political pressures, crime trends, and public expectations about the appropriate level of government services.

Chapter 6 considers how far police departments have moved toward reinventing themselves as community policing departments. Survey results comparing departments across the country are presented to help mark the amount of change that has occurred. Specific community policing operational approaches are described to illustrate the many ways that community policing is taking shape.

Chapter 7 describes how successful community policing approaches and programs are received by the employees of the departments who implemented them. Support and resistance among line staff, mid-level managers, and chief executives are examined for the part they might play in a department's acceptance or rejection of community policing.

Chapter 8 discusses the idea that departments which want to do community policing must consider changing their recruitment, selection, and training procedures. Traits that make for good community policing officers are discussed along with procedures for hiring community-oriented officers and ways to retrain those who may not be enthusiastic supporters of change.

Chapter 9 examines motivation and management strategies that make possible the implementation of community policing. It considers how change requires more up-to-date motivation and management strategies.

The potential success of police departments in adopting community policing is discussed in chapter 10. Important tools for measuring departmental preparedness and citizen support for change are presented, along with ideas for monitoring progress.

Chapter 11 addresses the issue of the effectiveness of community policing. Does it work? It considers indicators of success such as reduced fear of crime, crime reduction, and increased citizen satisfaction.

Chapter 12 looks at the long-term success of community policing in the United States. It pays particular attention to understanding the permanence of community policing as a replacement for the professional style and examining unsettled issues such as measuring police performance.

Finally, chapter 13 considers the future of community policing in a changing world. It looks at crime trends, technological change, and geographic mobility in the context of policing in the twenty-first century. Where will community policing be then?

## Study Questions

1. How is America "organized" for crime?

2. What five perspectives does PERF use to define community policing?

3. List the various definitions of community policing found in the chapter.

## Endnotes

1. Steven F. Messner and Richard Rosenfeld, *Crime and the American Dream* (Belmont, CA: Wadsworth, 1994).

2. David G. Mueller and Cary Heck, "The Neutral Zone as One Example of Police-Community Problem Solving," in *Community Policing in a Rural Setting*, eds. Quint C. Thurman and Edmund F. McGarrell (Cincinnati: Anderson, 1997), pp. 115–121.

3. John E. Angell, "Toward an Alternative to the Classic Police Organizational Arrangement: A Demographic Model," *Criminology* 8 (1971): 185–206.

4. Robert Trojanowicz and Bonnie Bucqueroux, *Community Policing: A Contemporary Perspective* (Cincinnati: Anderson, 1990).

5. Quotation appearing in William A. Geller and Guy Swanger, *Managing Innovation in Policing: The Untapped Potential of the Middle Manager* (Washington, DC: Police Executive Research Forum, 1995).

6. *Ibid.*

7. Gary W. Cordner, "Community Policing: Elements and Effects," in *Critical Issues in Policing: Contemporary Readings*, 3rd ed., ed. Roger Dunham and Geoffrey Alpert (Prospect Heights, IL: Waveland, 1997), pp. 451–468.

8. Gary W. Cordner, "Elements of Community Policing," in *Policing Perspectives: An Anthology*, eds. Larry K. Gaines and Gary W. Cordner (Los Angeles: Roxbury, 1999), pp. 137–149.

9. *Ibid.*

10. *Ibid.*

11. *Ibid.*

12. *Ibid.*

13. Police Executive Research Forum, *Themes and Variations in Community Policing*, (Washington, DC: Police Executive Research Forum, 1996).

14. James Q. Wilson and George L. Kelling, "Broken Windows: The Police and Neighborhood Safety," *Atlantic Monthly* (March, 1982): 29–38, [p. 33].

15. Herman Goldstein, "Improving Policing: A Problem-Oriented Approach," *Crime and Delinquency* 25 (1979): 236–258.

16. Mark H. Moore, "Problem Solving and Community Policing," in *Modern Policing*, vol. 15, eds. Michael Tonry and Norval Morris (Chicago: University of Chicago Press, 1992), pp. 99–158.

17. Mark H. Moore, "Research Synthesis and Policy Implications," in *The Challenge of Community Policing*, ed. Dennis Rosenbaum (Thousand Oaks, CA: Sage, 1994), pp. 285–299.

18. Quint C. Thurman, "The Police as a Community-Based Resource," in *Reinvesting Human Services: Community and Family-Centered Practice*, eds. Paul Adams and Kristine Nelson (New York: Aldine de Gruyter, 1995), pp. 175–187.

19. William Bratton and Peter Knobler, *Turnaround: How America's Top Cop Reversed the Crime Epidemic* (New York: Random House, 1998), p. 241.

20. *Ibid.*

21. David H. Bayley, *Police for the Future* (New York: Oxford University Press, 1994).

❖ ❖ ❖ ❖     22. Quint C. Thurman and Edmund F. McGarrell, "Community Policing in a Rural Setting: Innovations and Organizational Change," in *Community Policing in a Rural Setting*, eds. Quint C. Thurman and Edmund F. McGarrell (Cincinnati: Anderson, 1997), pp. 1–8 [p. 1].

23. *Ibid.*

24. Roy R. Roberg and Jack Kuykendall, *Police Organization and Management: Behavior, Theory, and Process* (Pacific Grove, CA: Brooks/Cole, 1990).

25. Moore, "Problem Solving and Community Policing."

26. Jack R. Greene and Stephen D. Mastrofski, *Community Policing: Rhetoric or Reality?* (New York: Praeger, 1988).

27. Stephen D. Mastrofski, "Community Policing as Reform: A Cautionary Tale," in *Community Policing: Rhetoric or Reality?*, eds. Jack R. Greene and Stephen D. Mastrofski (New York: Praeger, 1988), pp. 47–68.

28. Peter K. Manning, "Community Policing as a Drama of Control," in *Community Policing: Rhetoric or Reality?*, eds. Jack R. Greene and Stephen D. Mastrofski (New York: Praeger, 1988), pp. 27–46.

29. Michael E. Buerger, "The Limits of Community Policing," in *The Challenge of Community Policing: Testing the Promises*, ed. Dennis P. Rosenbaum (Thousand Oaks, CA: Sage, 1994), pp. 270–273.

30. Hubert Williams and Patrick V. Murphy, "The Evolving Strategies on Policing: A Minority View," in *The Police and Society: Touchstone Readings*, ed. Victor E. Kappeler (Prospect Heights, IL: Waveland), pp. 29–52.

31. Wesley G. Skogan, "The Impact of Community Policing on Neighborhood Residents: A Cross-Site Analysis," in *The Challenge of Community Policing: Testing the Promises*, ed. Dennis Rosenbaum (Thousand Oaks, CA: Sage, 1994), pp. 167–181. ✦

# Chapter Two

# A History of
# American Policing

❖ ❖ ❖ ❖

> *The police at all times should maintain a relationship with the public*
> *that gives reality to the historic tradition that the police are the public*
> *and that the public are the police; the police are the only members of the*
> *public who are paid to give full-time attention to duties which are*
> *incumbent on every citizen in the interest of the community welfare*
> *and existence.*

—Sir Robert Peel

Policing in the United States, like our common law legal system itself, can be traced to British policing some one and three-quarters centuries ago. This chapter provides an overview of some of the more important themes and ideas from the British experience that led to the development of policing in the United States during the nineteenth century and even today as we reorient ourselves to community policing. This brief history also will set the stage for a deeper understanding of organizational change in American policing during the three eras that are detailed in this chapter and chapter 4.

## The Concept of Policing in the United States

Policing varies around the world in a number of ways. To a large extent, styles of policing are the result of the local, state, or national political structure within which policing exists. Before looking more closely at the influence of politics on policing as chapter 4 does, it is helpful to ask what policing is and from where it comes.

Roberg, Crank, and Kuykendall define police as those

> nonmilitary individuals or organizations who are given the general right by government to use coercive force to enforce the law and whose primary purpose is to respond to problems of individual and group conflict that involve illegal behavior.[1]

But as will be seen, policing throughout history has been much broader than this definition suggests.

The word *police* comes from the Greek word *polis*, meaning "city." The Greek word includes the idea of the city's "government." Government, also referred to as the state, can take a variety of forms, from a totalitarian regime at one end of the spectrum, to a democracy at the other. Totalitarian governments make and enforce laws to regulate all aspects of life for the benefit those who are in power (e.g., a dictator or the ruling elite). In a totalitarian regime, individual rights and civil liberties are sacrificed to ensure that those in power stay powerful. By contrast, democratic governments value citizen participation in the governing process and do not attempt to control everything. Citizens either directly make laws and choose methods of enforcement, or they elect representatives to make informed decisions on their behalf.

## The Constitution                                                    ❖ ❖ ❖ ❖

When the U.S. Constitution was ratified in 1789, it embraced the ideas of John Locke, Cesare Beccaria, and others who believed that a limited government is the best way to ensure the liberties of its citizens. As such, many of the first 10 amendments to the U.S. Constitution—the Bill of Rights, adopted in 1791—strike broadly at the activities of criminal justice agencies. In particular, the Fourth Amendment, the right of individuals not to be subject to unreasonable searches and seizures, has become a cornerstone of American policing:

> The right of the people to be secure in their persons, houses, papers, and effects, against unreasonable searches and seizures, shall not be violated, and no warrants shall issue, but upon probable cause, supported by oath or affirmation, and particularly describing the place to be searched, and the persons or things to be seized.

Along with the other amendments to the U.S. Constitution, the Fourth Amendment depicts the problem of trying to maintain an important balance in a democracy: the necessity for government to enforce substantive criminal laws and ensure that violators are punished (the social contract) versus the concern for procedural safeguards to ensure the liberties of individuals, including those accused of committing crimes.

The U.S. Constitution also established three branches of government at the national level as a system of checks and balances. For example, Congress has the power to make laws, the presidency has the power to oversee the execution and enforcement of the laws, and the courts have the power to hear and settle disputes originating from the law. In addition, the Constitution established two layers of government according to the principle of *federalism*, which distributes power between the national and state governments. Although the Bill of Rights was adopted in 1791, it was not until the due-process revolution in the 1960s under Chief Justice Earl Warren that the amendments dealing with the administration of justice were applied to individuals involved in state cases. For instance, the Fourth Amendment against unreasonable searches and seizures was first applied to state police forces as a result of the U.S. Supreme Court decision of *Mapp v. Ohio* in 1961.

This distribution of power has resulted in a decentralized and fragmented system of policing in the United States that goes well beyond the division into federal and state police forces. In fact, the majority of sworn police officers are employed either in municipal or county police forces. The bulk of police powers, then, are reserved to the states, which authorize the enforcement of their laws by state, county, and municipal police. Fewer police forces operate at the federal level, mainly to enforce federal substantive criminal laws. The federal police agency with the broadest mandate is the *Federal Bureau of Investigation* (FBI), which is charged with the enforcement of federal laws not specifically delegated to other federal agencies, such as the *U.S. Secret Service* and the *Bureau of Alcohol, Tobacco and Firearms*, among others.

## The Difficulty of Policing in a Democracy

Perhaps the quintessential description of a totalitarian government is "a police state." But aggressive policing poses a problem for a democratic form

❖ ❖ ❖ ❖ of government. Democracies in their various forms rely on consensus of opinion, liberty, and citizen participation to make and even enforce laws. Yet policing, by its very nature, involves power, authority, and in some cases the restriction of freedom. Herman Goldstein describes this tension as the *democracy-police conflict*. In a democracy, policing must be sensitive to the needs of all citizens, not just the politically powerful ones.

Goldstein illustrates this tension in a number of ways. For example, although government exists to serve and represent its citizens, at times the police provide services that some people do not want. For example, you might ask yourself, when was the last time you wanted a traffic citation? Because police provide service by enforcing laws, individuals might resist governmental intervention because of possible negative consequences for themselves. In addition, although a democracy is founded upon the idea of "freedom for all," it is unrealistic that in any society, even a democratic one, citizens truly are free to do anything they want. The police are a constant reminder that a "free society" really is not completely free; the exercise of police authority in enforcing the law is a clear indication of this truth.

The concept of policing in the United States, formally defined by the structure of our government as spelled out in the U.S. Constitution, tells only half the story. The development of formal police institutions has a long history, to which this chapters now turns.

## Policing From an Historical Perspective

### The English Origins of Policing

Throughout much of England's history, policing truly was a community effort. Until the nineteenth century, England had a loose system of citizen policing, stemming from the *feudal* system of government that prevailed in the Middle Ages.

In feudal England the king appointed a *reeve* for each *shire* (district), who was known as the shire-reeve (or *sheriff*). He was officially charged with law enforcement throughout his jurisdiction and attended to other duties as well, such as the collection of taxes.

There were also more localized forms of policing. By the twelfth century, sheriffs were given the responsibility to ensure the functioning of the *frankpledge* system. According to this system, which had existed for hundreds of years prior to the sheriff's involvement, groups of 10 families formed a tithing. Ten tithings were known as a hundred, and several hundreds formed a shire. The frankpledge system required that every male over the age of 12 come into service to help maintain law and order; indeed, if one tithingman committed a crime, the entire tithing was punished. In addition, if one tithingman happened upon a crime, he was to raise a *hue and cry*, and all other members of the tithing were required to come to his aid. This form of citizen policing, however, was not effective in dealing with the growing problems caused by transients, vagrants, and beggars in the late thirteenth century, for these individuals were outsiders who were not bound to a tithing or its rules.

The Statute of Winchester replaced the frankpledge system with a *parish constable system* of policing, which, in reality, differed little from the previous system. T. A. Critchley described the new policing system as one in which it was the duty of everyone to maintain the king's peace.[2] However, it was the part-time, unpaid constable serving a one- year term who had a special duty to do so. The constable was assisted in his duty during the night by "inferior" officers known as *watchmen*. In addition, if the offender was not caught red-handed, hue and cry was to be raised, and all able-bodied men were required to come to the constable's or watchman's aid. Finally, the law also required individuals to keep arms with which to answer the hue and cry when required. As such, the parish constable system simply established yet another system of citizen policing. The position of constable—a position that was dreaded by most—involved chiefly organizing and officiating.

After the office of *justice of the peace* was created in the fourteenth century, constables became assistants to the justice of the peace in English cities and played a more important role. In addition to supervising the night watchmen, constables conducted investigations, served summons and warrants, and took charge of prisoners. This justice-constable-night watchman system of policing remained fairly stable, yet increasingly ineffective, well into the 1800s.

By the end of the 1700s, as the Industrial Revolution took hold, impoverished farmers were migrating to cities and towns in search of jobs. Many found them in the newly built factories, but others ended up unemployed and homeless. They had to steal to survive. Faced with these new problems of unemployment, social unrest, and crime, entrepreneurially minded citizens devised new, supplemental forms of policing.

In larger cities such as London, for example, the constable was usually unable to gain citizen assistance when raising a hue and a cry. As a result, those citizens who could afford it hired private police or bodyguards. Others hired *thief takers*, many of whom were former constables, who were now in the thief-taking business for the money. Thief takers would be paid a fee to secure stolen property. But this type of policing was of little use to the poor, who could not afford to pay for it. In addition, thief takers often were corrupt; they would routinely keep a share of the stolen property—if found—for themselves.

*Sir Robert Peel.*

By the early 1800s, civic organizations such as the Bow Street Horse and Foot Patrol were providing police services in some areas of England. Unlike the thief takers, their goal was to detect and apprehend law breakers. Despite these efforts, however, policing in England remained largely citizen-based, uncoordinated, and ineffective until 1829.

## Modern Policing in Britain

Modern public policing began in Britain in the early nineteenth century. Sir Robert Peel is credited with much of the work that led to the appointment of the first public police officers in London in 1829. Peel had a long and impressive career in politics. He was a member of the House of Commons,

❖ ❖ ❖ ❖   later served as chief secretary for Ireland, was Parliamentary member for Oxford University, and served as home secretary and two terms as prime minister.[3]

As home secretary, Peel introduced legislation in Parliament outlining a plan to replace a loose system of citizen police with a well-trained and highly disciplined body of public police officers. Although such a force undoubtedly would have been more effective than citizen policing in dealing with the civic problems caused by the Industrial Revolution, many members of Parliament and citizens alike saw it as a potentially powerful arm of the state that could threaten the liberties and freedoms of its citizens. Their criticism delayed action for years. Finally, in the face of rising crime rates and increased victimization, Parliament was forced to choose the lesser of two evils. It passed Peel's Metropolitan Police Act in 1829, despite the continued fear that a public police force could turn malevolent and ultimately suppress the rights and freedoms of British citizens. Such fear resulted in the carefully worded principles of British policing. According to Peter Manning, these principles had four common themes:

- To prevent crime without using repressive force.

- To maintain public order through nonviolent means, using force only as a last resort.

- To reduce conflict between the police and the public.

- To demonstrate police efficiency through the absence of crime and disorder, rather than through visible police actions.[4]

Above all, crime prevention was the ultimate goal of Peel's police force, which represented, at least symbolically, a benevolent government. It would use physical force only sparingly and it lacked a mandate to "fight crime" in a repressive manner. The public gradually came to accept Peel's police force mainly because of Peel's insistence that his *bobbies* be highly qualified for the position. He recruited a select group of men for the job. Above all, potential bobbies were required to be able to read, write, and take orders. Modest pay ensured that those who ultimately were hired were similar to those with whom they would interact on the streets. In addition, Peel wanted a highly visible police force but one that would not be confused with the military, which had a similar structure. As such, the dark blue uniforms and shiny police badges distinguished British bobbies from the red-coated British soldiers.[5]

Over the years, fears of a centralized and potentially malevolent police force dissipated. Citizens were encouraged to keep bobbies in check by reporting instances of discourtesy by officers. According to Randy LaGrange, the public monitoring of police had the dual benefit of holding officers accountable to the public and, at least symbolically, allowing citizens to have some control over the police. Elements of Peel's "ideal" police force ultimately made their way into American policing in the middle of the nineteenth century.

# Policing in Early America

During the colonial era in America (roughly the early 1600s to the late 1700s), policing, as in England during this time, was primarily a citizen function. Throughout the colonies, variations of the justice of the peace-sheriff-constable-night watchman system existed. For example, in New England, settlers adopted the constable-night watchman system, but in the South and West, constables, sheriffs, and town marshals were responsible for policing.

According to Samuel Walker, the office of the sheriff was the most important law enforcement agency in the colonial era and later, especially in the West and Southwest. The sheriff, however, was often ineffective; he reacted only to complaints of known crimes, and he often had to travel long distances on poor roads. In addition, the sheriff was paid fixed fees for making arrests, serving subpoenas, and appearing in court. Furthermore, enforcing the law was only one of many duties of the sheriff. Others included collecting taxes and supervising elections.[6]

Because of the ineffectiveness of the sheriff in more formalized societies and in places where settlement was too sparse to permit formal institutions of authority, settlers took the law into their own hands. They formed *vigilante* groups to enforce the law. According to Roberg, Crank, and Kuykendall, vigilante groups were primarily groups of men who organized to protect their property or power, to seek revenge, or to respond to threats to their personal safety. Vigilante groups gained prominence throughout America's early history but became most common in the West during the nineteenth century.[7]

By the mid 1700s in the South, a different kind of policing began to develop: *slave patrols*. Slave patrols were primarily a citizen function directed at capturing runaway slaves. They also performed a preventive function by attempting to ensure that slaves would not revolt against their masters.

Despite the variety of forms of policing in early America, the developments in policing that took place in the Northeast in the mid-1800s ultimately served as a model for local policing across the country. Although the offices of constable and the night watch became paid, professional occupations in many cities in the 1800s, they were typically ineffective in dealing with the riots and general social unrest that occurred as a result of urbanization, immigration, and industrialization.[8]

The precursors of modern, public police forces were established in some northeastern cities by the 1830s. For example, in 1833 in Philadelphia a daytime force was created to supplement the night watchman. In 1838, the first police force based on Peel's London model was created in Boston. Soon thereafter (e.g., New York in 1844 and Philadelphia in 1854), other cities adopted a police system similar to Peel's. By the 1880s, Peel's modern, public police force was adopted in most cities and towns across the United States.

Although the new, modern police forces in America were similar to the London model, important differences existed, based largely on the federal structure of U.S. government. LaGrange outlines a number of the similarities between cops in the United States and bobbies in Britain:

- Common legal and historical tradition.

- Civilian police for domestic order (not soldiers).

- Military-style command structure.

❖ ❖ ❖ ❖
- Main mission—crime prevention.

- Main strategy—random patrol over fixed beats.

- Twenty-four hours a day, seven days a week availability.

- Restrained police powers.

- Combined crime-control and order-maintenance duties.

- Paid, uniformed police force.[9]

Despite these similarities, however, there exist important differences between modern U.S. and British police forces. In particular, the political structures differ in the two countries. The British system of government is highly centralized; U.S. citizens are governed by a system that is fragmented and decentralized. Just like the U.S. government, American policing is the result of a complex system of federalism in which policing powers are shared among different levels of government. In contrast to Great Britain, police forces across the United States are scattered and at times have overlapping jurisdictions. In fact, there was no overall plan for the development of policing in the United States, nor for other government services, for that matter. Instead, these services were established at all levels of government as the need arose, through a process sometimes labeled "chinking-in."[10]

Although policing in Britain was never completely centralized, in comparison to the United States, where local autonomy prevails, there is considerably less variation of policing styles and practices in Britain. As was true

---

### The Roots of Community Policing

#### *Bryan Vila and Cynthia Morris*

When Los Angeles Police Chief Alexander Galloway presented the city's first full-time woman police officer, Alice Stebbins Wells, with her badge in 1910, he joked that "he was sorry to offer a woman so plain an insignia of office; that when he had a squad of Amazons he would ask the police commission to design a star edged with lace ruffles."[1] Perhaps Chief Galloway would have taken Wells a bit more seriously if he had known that by the end of the century, many of her ideas about the role of police would be embraced by police departments and sheriff's offices across the United States.

Many of the types of crime-prevention and community-service duties associated with community policing today were championed by pioneering women police officers such as Alice Stebbins Wells. For example, Wells was responsible for patrolling such places as "penny arcades, moving picture shows, skating rinks, dance halls, and other places of public amusement, including the parks on Sunday"[2] to discover "places and people with immoral tendencies."[3] She also gave aid to lost children, assisted juvenile and female crime victims and lawbreakers, and counseled families with problem children.

Wells discussed her views on the importance of social intervention to crime prevention in a 1911 *Good Housekeeping* interview:

> The thinking world is more and more recognizing the causes of crime as a vital part of the problem of crime. Since many of these causes arise from improper home conditions, their correction necessarily depends in a large measure upon the intelligent cooperation of women. As all the world knows, the perfect home training of every child would largely eliminate the need of police work. . . .

☞

❖ ❖ ❖ ❖

. . . As all who deal with the erring know, a multitude of young people know no law but that of their own imperious wills. These things, together with wrong ideals, bad blood, poorly nourished bodies, and industrial strife, produce a large part of the tide endlessly sweeping into the precincts of the police.

Under modern conditions, much of the remedy must be applied directly or indirectly by women....One or more women in the police department of every city can learn much concerning the need of changes in worn-out and ineffective laws, and the practical handling of wrongdoers, which other women can embody in their manifold labors for the city's good. This is more important than may be obvious. The police department is the organized, empowered body, and all other upbuilding social agencies should work in harmony with it.

Looking beyond the language and mores of a bygone era, it appears that one of the main differences between Wells' 1910 duties and views on policing and present-day community policing is that such police activities are no longer divided along gender lines. Today, police officers of either sex typically juggle several roles: peacekeeping (order maintenance and crime prevention), crime fighting (law enforcement), and community service (the "social work" role formerly assigned to woman officers).

In addition to Wells, other police reformers of the early twentieth century who advocated many of the tenets of what is now considered to be community policing included August Vollmer and Orlando W. Wilson. In a 1919 speech, "The Policeman as a Social Worker,"[4] Vollmer, one of the most influential and innovative American police chiefs of all time, challenged all police officers to take responsibility for prevention efforts that attack the sources of crime and work with community organizations to do so.

[Police officers are] fast learning that dealing with criminals after the evil habits have been formed is a hopeless task as far as the eradication, or even lessening of crime is concerned.

If he would serve his community by reducing crime he must go up the stream a little further and dam it up at its source, and not wait until it is a rushing torrent, uncontrollable and resistless. Moreover, if he would succeed in his efforts he must utilize to the fullest extent every helpful agency in the community, such as schools, churches, recreation and juvenile departments, public welfare and employment bureaus, clinics, dispensaries, hospitals and fraternal and labor organizations. Cooperation is also necessary with character forming organizations, such as Boy Scouts, Campfire Girls, well organized boys' clubs, community social centers and auxiliary and junior police forces. . . .

. . . No single individual in the community has more opportunities to do good, solid, constructive social service than the intelligent, sympathetic and trained policeman.

Three decades later, Vollmer's protégé, Orlando W. Wilson, also advocated an expanded role for the police that included a "broader social concept":

The old police philosophy of "throw 'em in jail" has changed to a new philosophy of keeping people out of jail. Police service has broadened to include certain aspects of social service for which the police are particularly well suited; some cases have more than ordinary social-welfare significance, notably those involving the mentally defective, the very young, the very old, and family relationships. Police service today extends beyond mere routine investigation and disposition of complaints; it also has as its objective the welfare of the individual and of society. If society is to be effectively safeguarded against crime, the police must actively seek out and destroy delinquency-inducing influences in the community and assist in providing suitable treatment for the maladjusted.[5]

☞

❖ ❖ ❖ ❖     ☞

> Seen from this perspective, community policing can hardly be considered an in-
> novation. Rather, it is the natural outgrowth of reforms set in motion since the
> turn of the century by people such as Wells, Vollmer, and Wilson who recognized
> the unique, constructive potential of police work.

---

Bryan Vila, is associate professor of political science and administration of justice at the University of Wyoming. Previously, he spent 17 years in local, national, and international law enforcement. Cynthia Morris is a writer and editor
living in Laramie, Wyoming. Vila and Morris have coauthored *Capital Punishment in the United States* (Greenwood Press, 1997) and *The Role of Police in
American Society* (Greenwood Press, 1999), which traces the development of policing in the United States from colonial times to the present using excerpts from
95 key historical documents.

### Endnotes

1. Bertha H. Smith, "The Policewoman," in *Good Housekeeping*, February, 1911: pp. 296–298.
2. *Ibid*.
3. *Los Angeles Times*, September 13, 1910: Part II, p. 9.
4. Address before the International Association of Chiefs of Police 26th Convention, New Orleans, April 14–16, 1919.
5. From *Police Administration* (New York: McGraw-Hill, 1950), pp. 3–4.

during Peel's efforts to pass the Metropolitan Police Act, the British home secretary is still responsible for the police throughout Britain. Consequently, in
practice there is much less variation in British policing because central
authorities have considerable say over how police forces at the local level
operate. This situation is in direct contrast to the way in which policing operates in the United States. As the London model of policing gradually was
established in U.S. cities and towns in the 1800s, the detrimental effects of
local autonomy were beginning to be realized.

## Police Corruption During the Political Era

The period of policing in the United States from about 1840 to 1920 is
known as the *political era* of policing. The name reflects the inextricable link
that existed between police forces and local politics. Although policing continues to be closely tied to local politics even today, the next section will discuss the reasons why progressive reformers of the twentieth century
attempted to curtail the influence of local politics on policing and the ways
they went about it.

As police departments became more formalized in the nineteenth century, close ties between the police and local political leaders developed. In
many cities, police forces were administered by *police commissions*, whose
membership often included the city mayor, a recorder, a city judge, and sometimes even citizens. The police commissions were in an ideal position to control local police policy since it was the police commissioners who hired and
fired police officers, including the chief of police.

In the 1800s, local political leaders (*political machines*) controlled every
aspect of the city's government. In order to stay in office, however, they had to
rely on the support of voters. The upper and middle classes tended to have the
influence to ensure that their needs were heard and met. But newly arriving

*Pennsylvania State Police Officers, circa 1900. (Courtesy of Pennsylvania State Police)*

immigrants to the city did not. A large part of politics during the 1800s was an attempt to retain the support of the middle and upper classes and to gain the support of others.

One of the promises typically made by local political leaders was to reduce unemployment. They freely gave government jobs to those whose support they wanted. The *patronage system,* or *spoils system,* describes this practice. Police jobs were no exception; they were viewed as particularly attractive because they were relatively well paid and required only minimal skill.[11]

The patronage system, however, resulted in a number of practices that seem incompatible with the ideal that government should provide efficient and effective service to all. The first and foremost problem had to do with the selection of police officers. Since police officers were hired under patronage, the only qualification was an individual's political support. As Walker notes:

> Ignorance, poor health, or old age was no barrier to employment. An individual with the right connections could be hired despite the most obvious lack of qualifications. Recruits received no formal training. A new officer would be handed a copy of the police manual (if one could be found) containing the local ordinances and state laws, and sent out on patrol.[12]

The second major problem related to policing in the political era concerned the police use of discretion within the patronage system. As is generally true even today, patrol officers in the political era spent most of their day unsupervised. But because of a lack of even minimum qualifications, many police officers did little in the way of policing. According to Walker, officers spent hours drinking in saloons and gossiping in barbershops. And when a police officer worked his fixed beat, police corruption and brutality were rampant.[13]

Because police officers primarily were tools used to keep local politicians in office, they were anything but ideal, impartial public servants. One activity that was common was to "help get the word out" for a political leader. After all, the future of the police officer's job depended highly on the ability of the

❖ ❖ ❖ ❖    political leader to get reelected. At times, this meant that a police officer used intimidation and bribery toward citizens on behalf of his political boss. According to Roberg, Crank, and Kuykendall,

> The police were particularly useful during elections because they maintained order at polling booths and were able to determine who voted and who did not. Individuals who became police officers were often avid supporters of the political machine and would do anything to help keep it in power.[14]

During the 1800s, police officers were expected to work long hours, mostly patrolling their beats on foot. Because of their wide use of discretion, laws related to keeping order and more serious crime were only haphazardly enforced. Citizens who were arrested for public drunkenness or disorderly conduct often were disrespectful to the police and at times were aided by other citizens. Police brutality developed from this citizen disrespect as officers resorted to physical force in an attempt to gain the respect that was not freely given.[15]

The middle and upper classes tended to support such police actions as long as they were directed against the lower-class. In addition, Samuel Walker notes that as immigrants gained police employment through the patronage system by the late 1800s, laws that were directed at keeping the lower classes in check (including laws against gambling and prostitution) were systematically overlooked. Indeed, many of these police officers not only tolerated such illegal behaviors but also participated in them. Other police officers ignored these crimes in return for regular payoffs.[16]

By the close of the nineteenth century, policing in the United States was far removed from the ideal, public police force envisioned by Sir Robert Peel across the Atlantic only a few decades earlier. Although U.S. police in the political era provided some social services such as operating soup kitchens and temporarily housing the homeless, they were openly corrupt, brutal, and inefficient at combating a growing crime problem facing most American cities by the turn of the century.

## Police Reform During the Professional Era

In the few years prior to the start of the twentieth century, government at all levels was being criticized for its lack of efficiency in providing needed services to citizens; policing was no exception. This Progressive Movement in government (from approximately 1900 to 1920) set the stage for the professional era of policing. The Progressive Movement was dominated by middle-class and upper-class reformers who wanted to see a number of changes in the way government operated. According to Walker, two main themes dominated the Progressive Movement—efficiency in government and social justice; the former ultimately won out.[17]

Civic-minded reformers sought ways to make government (including policing) more efficient. According to Johnson, the Progressive Movement was based on three principles: (1) honesty and efficiency in government, (2) more authority for public officials, and (3) the use of experts to respond to problems. These and other related ideas dominated policing during the professional era.

One of the more prominent strategies of reform in the early 1900s was the establishment of special commissions at the local, state, and federal level. The commissions often included noted experts in the field of criminal justice, and they were charged with recommending improvements to the existing system of criminal justice. At the national level, one of the most noted commissions was established in 1929 by President Herbert Hoover: the National Commission on Law Observance, also known as the *Wickersham Commission*, named after its chair, former Attorney General George Wickersham.

The Wickersham Commission published its final report in 14 separate volumes in 1931; the most publicity was directed at Volume 11, *Lawlessness in Law Enforcement*. This volume documented widespread occurrences of police corruption, brutality, and violations of individual rights, and through widely published excerpts, resulted in a growing public intolerance for police misconduct.

The principal police consultant to the Wickersham Commission was August Vollmer, a progressive reformer and leading advocate of the police professionalism movement. In the decade prior to joining the commission, Vollmer listed several essential elements of professional policing at the International Association of Police Chiefs (IACP), in what later became known as Volume 14. Walker describes the most important elements of professional:

- Professional policing is efficient, nonpartisan, and committed to high standards of public service.

- Police departments should be led by trained experts, selected on proven ability, not by political favoritism.

- Police executives should be given a great deal of job security.

- Police command should be centralized for the sake of consistent policy and efficient public service.

- Standards for personnel should be raised: entrance exams should be given to applicants, and formal training and discipline should be given to recruits; competitive exams should be given for promotions.

- Substantive criminal laws should be evenly enforced and consistently applied.

- Police should take advantage of technological developments in an effort to do their job more efficiently.

- Promotions should be based on merit.

- The primary goal of policing should be that of crime fighting.[18]

O. W. Wilson, a reformer who was a student of Vollmer's, added several key operational dimensions to the professional model of policing. He advocated the use of motorized patrols and two-way radios, the assignment of "beats" on a rotated schedule (so that the police would not get too close to citizens), and the breaking up of pairs of police officers in favor of single patrols.

The ideas and strategies of both Vollmer and Wilson were adopted in cities and towns by the end of the 1930s and continued with little opposition until the 1960s. Although the proponents of the professional style of policing intended to improve police operations substantially by making them more efficient, they did so at the expense of those they served—the public. Because

❖ ❖ ❖

# O. W. Wilson, A Brief History

### *Jason Jolicoeur*

*O. W. Wilson shortly after his arrival in Chicago in 1961 to take over the Chicago police force.*

Orlando W. Wilson was born into a middle-class family in Veblen, South Dakota, in 1900. His father tried to convince his young son to follow him into the business world. These efforts seemed to pay off when Wilson enrolled at the University of California at Berkeley to obtain a business degree. A depression following World War I, however, forced Wilson's future career to take a new direction. His father found himself unable to continue to pay for his son's education, so Wilson was forced to look for a job. He answered a classified ad for police officers with the Berkeley Police Department and was subsequently interviewed by the Berkeley chief of police, August Vollmer. Vollmer took an immediate liking to Wilson and hired him, thus launching one of the most successful and productive policing careers in the history of American law enforcement. Eventually, Wilson's career would span nearly 50 years, and upon his death he would be heralded as the father of professional policing and one of the most outstanding leaders in the field of criminal justice.

The new recruit, however, got off to a rocky start. After a few years of service as an officer in Berkeley, in 1925 he accepted a position as chief of police in Fullerton, California. He immediately went about trying to implement widespread change within the small department. Whether it was the changes themselves or the aggressive way in which he pursued them, his tenure was short-lived and he asked to resign approximately six months later. After leaving Fullerton, he returned to his original career plan and spent two years in the business world.

In 1928 Wilson was offered the post of chief of police with a medium-size department in Wichita, Kansas. Hesitant at first, he was eventually persuaded to accept the position by his old boss and mentor, August Vollmer. It was fortunate that he accepted, for his years as chief of the Wichita Police Department proved to be some of the most productive in his entire career. Wilson's tenure in Wichita enabled him to implement many of the innovations that have since made him famous. Although many scholars and police officers associate his ideas with the years he later spent as a police chief in Chicago, many of his most important contributions were actually introduced and tested many years earlier in Wichita.

After serving for 11 years in Wichita, Wilson came up against bitter criticism over the aggressive manner in which his department pursued the local prostitution industry. As political pressure mounted, he decided the time was right to leave Wichita and accepted a position with the Public Administration Service (PAS) in Chicago. During his short period there, he was very productive. He had two primary duties: to conduct evaluations of various American police departments and to write monographs on a wide variety of policing subjects. It was his departmental evaluations that proved to be his most noticeable achievements during this period. In a brief three months, he studied police departments in Peoria, Illinois; Hartford, Connecticut; and San Antonio, Texas, just to name a few. Despite his excellent work, he was lured back to Berkeley, this time as an educator instead of an officer.

The University of California at Berkeley had been offering police science courses for quite some time, but in 1939 it decided to expand the program and hire a full-time faculty member. Vollmer recommended Wilson for the position and eventually convinced him to take it. Wilson thus had the distinction of becoming the first full-time professor of police administration in the country.[1] He quickly began upgrading the fledgling police-administration program at Berkeley shortly after his arrival in August, 1939. Although he had some initial successes, his long-term plans for the program were supplanted by the country's entry into World War II. Millions of American men began to enlist, including many college students and professors. Wilson, who also felt the need to serve in the war effort, enlisted in the army in Jan-

☞  uary, 1943. He served in a number of capacities but was primarily responsible for helping to restore order in countries captured by the Allied forces, by overseeing the creation of local civilian police forces. Initially sent to Italy, he was later moved to Germany, where he helped reshape the German system of policing. He enjoyed his army service so much that he stayed on, in a civilian capacity, as a military adviser for a year after the war ended.

In 1947 Wilson returned to Berkeley and continued where he had left off four years earlier. He began improving and expanding the police administration program until it was formally recognized as the School of Criminology in 1950. During this period Wilson also wrote extensively, publishing the seminal book *Police Administration* in 1950. He continually sought to improve the program and by 1960 had succeeded in creating one of the best-respected and largest criminology programs in the country, despite efforts by many at the university to have the program eliminated. In 1960 Wilson was asked to serve on a search committee to select a new chief for the Chicago Police Department. He accepted the invitation that would eventually bring him back into law enforcement.

The committee was charged by Mayor Richard Daley with finding a candidate capable of restoring public faith in the corrupt, embattled police department. The committee quickly became dissatisfied with the list of potential applicants, and several members approached Wilson about taking the position. Hesitant at first, he was eventually persuaded to accept the awesome task of rebuilding the Chicago Police Department. In the next seven years he began a program of reorganization and modernization that was unprecedented in the history of policing. He also undertook a massive effort aimed at rooting out corruption within the department. When he retired in 1967 he had succeeded in restoring public confidence in the department and making it into one of the premier law enforcement bodies in the country.

Wilson returned to California in order to spend more time with his family. On October 18, 1972, Orlando Wilson died of a stroke in his California home. He was gone, but he left behind a lengthy list of contributions to modern law enforcement.

Wilson was one of the first to develop and implement a comprehensive system of police record keeping. The system he created in Wichita became the standard by which all others were measured, and it is still the basis for most current systems. Wilson also changed the way police officers are selected and trained. He was one of the first to use a system of psychological, mental, and physical tests in the selection process. He was one of the first to establish in-service training for officers in the form of crab or roll call meetings. Furthermore, he was a strong supporter of higher education for officers. He created the first police cadet program, which helped college students earn degrees while working part time for the local police department. He helped create the criminology programs at both Wichita State University and the University of California at Berkeley.

In addition to the accomplishments noted above, Wilson was a champion of integrity and honesty in police practices. During his career he was called on twice to clean up very troubled departments, and on both occasions he succeeded. He created the first police code of ethics during his Wichita tenure, and all later codes were largely based on his original Square Deal Code. Wilson changed the patrol system by introducing the one-man patrol car and surveys to determine beat size. A pioneer in the area of police public relations, he created one of the nation's first police newsletters and police speaker's bureau. Finally, he was one of the first police administrators to support the idea of crime prevention. At Wichita he established one of the earliest crime-prevention bureaus and then went on to assign the nation's first female police captain to run the bureau.

Although Wilson will always be remembered for the revolutionary changes that he introduced to American law enforcement, many of his most impressive accomplishments were the result of applying common sense to complicated problems. For example, during his military service in Germany, he was assigned the task of selecting administrators for all the newly created local German police departments. The army's one restriction was that none could be former or active members of the Nazi Party. In the confusion that existed after World War II, few thought that  ☞

❖ ❖ ❖ ❖    ☞

> Wilson would be capable of carrying out such a formidable task. After considering various options, he came up with the ingenious solution of having local boards select the candidates. To ensure that no former Nazis were chosen, he recommended that the boards be made up only of German Jews who had suffered the brunt of the Nazi wrath. He correctly judged that such men would be extremely vigilant in uncovering the wartime backgrounds of prospective applicants. The development of modern policing today owes much to the wisdom and integrity of leaders such as Orlando W. Wilson.
>
> ---
>
> Jason Jolicoeur is a doctoral student in criminal justice at the University of Nebraska at Omaha. He has B.S. and M.A. degrees in criminal justice from Wichita State University. He is also a former police officer.
>
> **Endnote**
>
> 1. William Bopp, *O. W. Wilson and the Search for a Police Profession* (Port Washington, NY: Kennikat Press, 1977).

of the professional style's mission of "fighting crime," other important aspects of the police role were deemphasized, including maintaining order and providing service. By the 1960s, professional policing in the most economically disadvantaged neighborhoods of American cities appeared anything but "professional."

## The Effects of the Police Professionalization Movement

Although progressive reformers such as Vollmer and Wilson attempted to increase the efficiency of the police as crime fighters during the professional era of policing, many of these innovations and patrol practices had detrimental consequences for police-community relations. For example, the increased use of the patrol car tended to isolate officers from those whom they served. Despite the barriers it created between the police and the public, the police justified its increased use as a necessary response to the problems of inefficient beat coverage by foot patrol.

In addition, with the creation of the FBI's *Uniform Crime Reports* in the 1930s, the police mission of crime fighting was solidified. As police departments adopted the UCR as their measure of productivity, they were continually preoccupied with the FBI's Part 1 crimes (serious offenses) and Part 2 crimes (by comparison, less serious offenses) and less concerned about maintaining order and providing service, which simply were not counted in the UCR. Despite the fact that service and order were a large part of a police officer's job, many officers considered them outside the realm of law enforcement, and thus simply nuisances.

The professional era also witnessed a solidifying of the police subculture. A *subculture* is comprised of the symbols, values, and beliefs of members of a group in a larger society. Although police reform initially brought about opportunities to reduce corruption and brutality and improve effectiveness, thereby enhancing the public image of the police, the new professionalism of the police created a subculture set apart from the citizens it served and therefore a stain on police-community relations. Police professionalization encouraged a police subculture with the following values:

- Police generally distrust the public.

- Police officers are in the best position to fight crime and identify criminals.

- Most people dislike police officers.

- Ordinary citizens are potentially dangerous individuals.

In sum, police departments across the country were driven by a desire to reduce serious crimes identified in the FBI's *Uniform Crime Reports*, and in so doing, produced an "us versus them" mentality, which further strained police-community relations, especially in the most economically disadvantaged areas of American cities.

## Urban Racial Violence

During the professional era, large city police departments such as the Los Angeles Police Department initiated aggressive patrol strategies designed to control and prevent crime by stopping, questioning, and frisking individuals in high-crime areas. Invariably, this approach led to tension in the urban ghettos, where a large percentage of the inhabitants were African American. These and other minority groups viewed the aggressive police tactics as harassment, and relations between the police and minority groups steadily deteriorated.

The civil rights movement in the 1960s resulted in a number of outward demonstrations by African American groups demanding equality under the law. In large cities across the United States, demonstrations turned to violence. In one incident in Birmingham, Alabama, police attempted to disband a civil rights demonstration by setting police dogs and fire hoses on demonstrators.[19]

The summers of 1964 through 1967 witnessed increasing violence as a result of what was considered "institutional racism." Rioting continued, mostly as a result of aggressive police tactics directed against African Americans, leaving thousands dead or injured and millions of dollars in property damage in cities such as Philadelphia, New York, Los Angeles, Chicago, San Diego, and San Francisco. Clearly, the police were viewed as a primary source of institutional racism, given their mostly white, middle-class composition and the overwhelming support of white, middle-class America for their aggressive tactics.

While rioting once again flared up in 1968 over the assassination of Martin Luther King, Jr., the National Advisory Commission on Civil Disorders (commonly known as the Kerner Commission) issued its report. The Kerner Commission, in essence, took exception to police policies and patrol tactics during the professional era of policing. Its position is summarized by noted historian Samuel Walker:

> A half century of professionalization had created departments that were vast bureaucracies, inward-looking, isolated from the public, and defensive in the face of any criticism. Automobile patrol had further isolated the police officer against routine face-to-face contact with much of the public. Finally, aggressive stop-and-frisk tactics designed to suppress crime aroused resentment among the most common target population: young blacks.[20]

❖ ❖ ❖ ❖   # Improving Police-Community Relations Through Team Policing

The events in the late 1960s and early 1970s triggered a movement by many U.S. police departments to improve the relations between the police and the public. This movement, *team policing*, had its origins in a set of activities undertaken in Aberdeen, Scotland, in the late 1940s in an effort to reduce the boredom of police on single patrol, and to increase morale. Essentially, the Aberdeen project called for teams of five to 10 police officers, on foot or in cars, to respond to calls for service in distinct areas of the city. As the workload shifted from one area of the city to another, so too did the police teams.

Another type of team policing was established in the County of Coventry, England in 1966. Unit beat policing, as it was called, brought constables together to work as a team in one specific area. Although constables in each area did not work as one team *per se*, an information facilitator, known as a collator, passed on various pieces of information collected from the beat constables to the other constables in the area.[21]

A number of U.S. cities—most notably Tucson, Arizona, and Richmond, California—began experimenting with team policing in the 1960s. The events that triggered the team policing movement included the riots described above, and the general negative effects of the police professionalization movement on police-community relations. Other contributing factors were the Kerner Commission Report in 1968, the President's Commission on Law Enforcement and the Administration of Justice in 1967, funded through the Law Enforcement Assistance Administration (described below).

## The President's Commission on Law Enforcement and the Administration of Justice and the Availability of Federal Funding for Team Policing

In late 1967, after two years of work, the President's Commission on Law Enforcement and the Administration of Justice issued its final report, *The Challenge of Crime in a Free Society*. The report and corresponding "task-force" reports dealt with a number of issues regarding the administration of criminal justice and juvenile justice. For example, the report spoke of the need to divert cases out of the juvenile and criminal justice system if formal prosecution was not warranted. In the area of corrections, it emphasized the need to strengthen an offender's ties with the community. Many of the some 200 recommendations offered by the report were provocative and corresponded closely to the Office of Economic Opportunity's mission of attacking crime at its root by reducing poverty and unemployment.

The President's Commission also recommended that policing decentralize in an effort to improve police-public relations:

> Police departments should commence experimentation with a team policing concept that envisions those officers with patrol and investigative duties combining under unified command with flexible assignments to deal with the crime problem in a defined sector.[22]

Historically, police have been used to control crowds and disperse riots. (Photo: The Feminist Majority Foundation)

By 1970, the federal government had made funds available through the Law Enforcement Assistance Administration to develop team policing projects in cities throughout the United States.[23]

## A Definition of Team Policing

Despite its popularity with police administrators in the early 1970s, team policing was, and still is, a very elusive and ambiguous term that meant different things depending on where it was implemented. One of the few in-depth studies on team policing was conducted in the early 1970s by Lawrence Sherman and his associates. In all but one of the seven cities they studied, Richmond, California, there were three common elements to the team policing programs: geographic stability of patrol, maximum interaction among team members, and maximum communication among team members and the community.[24]

*Geographic stability of patrol.* In six of the seven cities studied by Sherman, teams of police were permanently assigned to small neighborhoods. This geographic stability resulted in decentralization of command and allowed police teams to provide localized, neighborhood service.[25]

*Maximum interaction among team members.* According to Sherman, all seven of the cities studied attempted to increase communication among police officers through team policing programs. Interaction and communication were sought from all team police officers assigned to a particular area during a 24-hour period. Information exchange was facilitated by team conferences at regular intervals in some cities or, less formally, through the use of a team leader. Sherman points out that when the team leader was able to instill a sense of teamsmanship, team members communicated more often.[26]

❖ ❖ ❖ ❖          ***Maximum communication among team members and the commu-***
***nity.*** Communication of police with the community was facilitated through
regular meetings between the two groups, through participation of neighborhood residents in some aspects of police work, and/or through referral systems for nonpolice problems.[27]

According to Sherman, those cities that were most successful at team
policing also had several common organizational supports in place, including the following: (1) unity of supervision, in which one supervisor was
responsible for team members assigned to a given area; (2) lower-level flexibility in policy making so that team officers could decide the best strategies
for delivering police services in their assigned area; (3) unified delivery of services, which further extended team decision making so that team members
could decide when specialized police units were necessary; and (4) combined
investigative and patrol functions with the presumption that there is a
greater likelihood of clearing crimes by arrest when investigative units also
are familiar with area residents and neighborhood conditions.[28]

### The Demise of Team Policing

Although the goal of team policing was to improve public relations
through the decentralization of police services, team policing is best known
as a fad of the 1970s. Why did it ultimately fail? Roberg and Kuykendall suggest that "team policing" in most cities did not differ substantially—or at all—
from policing in the professional era.[29] It was in effect simply a ploy to
improve public relations while police practices and strategies remained virtually unchanged. In addition, Walker and Sherman point toward a number
of problems that surfaced in those cities that attempted real change.[30]

First, in some cities mid-level police managers felt that their authority
was threatened by team policing and therefore either subverted or actively
sabotaged team policing projects. Second, although team policing projects
were intended to decentralize police into defined areas (e.g., geographic stability through the team concept), in reality dispatching technology remained
centralized, thereby often forcing police officers to leave their designated
areas. Third, the objectives of team policing were never clearly defined, and
thus the police role was ambiguous. Finally, team policing also seemed to
have suffered from poor planning. Such a large organizational change—from
centralized to a decentralized command—would have taken years to complete successfully. Because team policing appeared in U.S. cities almost
"overnight," it appeared doomed for failure from its very beginnings.

## Conclusion

Despite the failures of team policing, many of its important features
remained on the minds of police administrators, academics, and citizens
alike. The need to improve the quality of police services, to be responsive to
the public, and to improve police-community relations were top priorities in
the 1970s and 1980s. As later chapters will show, these themes manifest
themselves once again in the forms of problem-oriented policing and community policing, but this time with important lessons that had been learned
from the failure of team policing in the early 1970s.

# Study Questions                                        ❖ ❖ ❖ ❖

1. What were the problems related to policing during the political era?

2. What triggered the team policing movement?

3. What factors contributed to the demise of team policing?

4. What was the relationship between the police and the community in the professional era of policing?

# Endnotes

1. Roy R. Roberg, John Crank, and Jack Kuykendall, *Police and Society*, 2nd ed. (Los Angeles: Roxbury, 2000).
2. T. A. Critchley, *A History of Police in England and Wales*, 2nd ed. (Montclair,, NJ: Patterson Smith, 1967).
3. Edward Eldefonso, Alan Coffey, and Richard C. Grace, *Principles of Law Enforcement*, 2nd ed. (New York: Wiley, 1974).
4. Peter K. Manning, *Police Work: The Social Organization of Policing* (Cambridge, MA: MIT Press, 1977).
5. Randy L. LaGrange, *Policing American Society* (Chicago: Nelson-Hall, 1993).
6. Samuel Walker, *Popular Justice* (New York: Oxford University Press, 1980).
7. Roberg, Crank and Kuykendall, *Police and Society*.
8. Walker, *Popular Justice*.
9. LaGrange, *Policing American Society*.
10. Richard J. Stillman, *Preface to Public Administration: A Search for Themes and Direction* (New York: St. Martin's, 1991).
11. *Ibid.*
12. Walker, *Popular Justice*.
13. *Ibid.*
14. Roberg, Crank, and Kuykendall, *Police and Society*, p. 43.
14. Walker, *Popular Justice*.
16. *Ibid.*
17. *Ibid.*
18. *Ibid.*
19. *Ibid.*
20. *Ibid.*, p. 52.
21. Lawrence W. Sherman, Catherine H. Milton, and Thomas V. Kelly, *Team Policing: Seven Case Studies* (Washington, DC: Police Foundation, 1973).
22. Report of the National Advisory Commission on Civil Disorders: President's Commission on Law Enforcement and Administration of Justice, *The Challenge of Crime in a Free Society* (New York: Avon, 1968).
23. Sherman, Milton, and Kelly, *Team Policing*.
24. *Ibid.*
25 *Ibid.*
26. *Ibid.*
27. *Ibid.*
28. *Ibid.*
29. Roberg, Crank, and Kuykendall, *Police and Society*.
30. Walker, *Popular Justice*; Sherman, Milton, and Kelly, *Team Policing*. ✦

**Chapter Three**

# The Community

❖ ❖ ❖ ❖

*Success in life has nothing to do with what you gain or accomplish for yourself. It's what you do for others.*

—Danny Thomas

This chapter examines the term *community*. It will explore definitions of community and consider how communities might differ over time and from one another.

## The Difficulty of Defining 'Community'

One obvious feature of the term *community policing* that tends to be ignored completely or dismissed as very unimportant is the definition of community. What is, or who is, the community that the term refers to? Is it the place that the police are responsible for patrolling or is it the people who live in a particular police jurisdiction? Or is it both, something else, or something more?

Defining just what a community is proves to be no easy task. Although the term has been used increasingly in the last 10 years, few scholars have bothered to stop and explain what it means. Most people seem to recognize "community" as having positive connotations without giving much thought to what exactly it is. The lack of a precise definition, however, is not necessarily a drawback. As Larry Lyon has observed, "in the social sciences the most important concepts are often among the most imprecise."[1]

Like Lyon, Jayne Seagrave, acknowledges that "the concept of community defies exact definition." She suggests, however, that we might get a better idea of what it is by seeing how the term has been used by writers on the subject. Seagrave identifies five such ways. First, the term *community* has been used throughout the history of the social sciences without much effort to define it. Second, it has nearly always been used with positive connotations despite its vagueness. Third, it has often been used to add credibility to the launching of a new reform, program, or policy. Fourth, it has been allowed to remain underdeveloped rather than being developed into a theoretical concept. And fifth, it has been embraced throughout American history by both political conservatives and liberals, both Republicans and Democrats.[2]

To look at specific definitions of community is to see how difficult it is to define a concept that most people take for granted. For example, Eric Rothenbuhler suggests that while to many, "community" may refer to a place, this definition fails to capture what the full concept of community entails. "A community is an aggregate of individuals, in a group, in a place, engaged in patterns of activity, holding ideals they hope govern that activity, identifying themselves with this constellation, with feelings about the happiness of it all."[3]

One of the earliest American sociologists to define community was Robert Park. Writing in the 1930s, he noted three important features of a community that most definitions have included ever since. They are "a population territorially organized, [that is] more or less completely rooted in the soil it occupies, [with] individual units living in a relationship of mutual interde-

❖ ❖ ❖ ❖

pendence."[4] More simply put, Park recognizes a community as people living in a place who are mutually interdependent.

Amitai Etzioni, another sociologist who has written extensively on issues relating to community and a proponent of community policing, attempts to define community according to only two dimensions:

> [F]irst, a web of affect-laden relationships among a group of individuals, relationships that often crisscross and reinforce one another (rather than merely one-on-one or chainlike individual relationships), and second, a measure of commitment to a shared set of values, norms, and meanings, and a shared history and identity—in short, to a particular culture.[5]

What is unique about Etzioni's definition is that he excludes place as a necessary feature of community, a point that will be returned to later in this chapter.

Clearly, policing by its very nature assumes a community setting, or a place in which community activities occur.[6] Policing involves the best efforts of personnel to preserve and promote public safety among a group of people living within a specific jurisdiction. In a nutshell, policing requires someone and somewhere to police. Nevertheless, policing does not necessarily take the same form in every place or from one period of time to another, as the next chapters will show. Inasmuch as communities differ from one another, public forces must adapt to the public they serve if they want to be fully effective.

## College Cop
### (First published in December, 1938)

#### Karl Detzer

*A young O. W. Wilson shortly after his arrival in Wichita, Kansas, in 1929 to take over as the chief of the Wichita police force.*

Wichita, Kansas, is the town where the cop on the beat goes to college. It's also the town which many cops tell you has the best police force in America. It's the town where you're rarely arrested for a traffic violation, and never bawled out, and where traffic accidents are few. It's the town where life and property are safer than in the vast majority of American cities; where fewer policemen cover more miles of beat; where police costs are at the lowest level, and percentage of crime solved is the highest.

The man who has built this model department is Orlando Winfield Wilson, chief of police since 1928. He doesn't look like a chief in the movies, and probably less like the chief in your hometown. A tall, lean, sober man with a mop of brown hair, quiet gray eyes and a quiet voice, he might be a law school professor.

It is Chief Wilson's theory that courtesy and human understanding are as important a part of police equipment as jujitsu and marksmanship; further, that policing is a profession, like law or medicine, and requires trained, educated men.

You meet police courtesy the day you move to Wichita. The morning you arrive as a stranger, a policeman knocks at your door, and greets you with a snappy salute and a welcoming smile. He's usually an enthusiastic young man with a university degree, a marksman's medal, and an air of knowing his business.

"I'm the man on the beat," he explains cordially. "I'm here to serve you." He offers you such information as newcomers need, about schools and churches and hospitals, how to report a fire, traffic and sanitary requirements, then adds: "For your ☞

❖ ❖ ❖ ❖     ☞   own protection, will you fill out this card."

You do, gladly. For on it the Wichita police list against theft. Whatever you own, typewriter, bicycle, car, washing machine, vacuum cleaner or watch, the police file its description and serial number. Files and records, Chief Wilson believes, are more important than nightsticks and guns.

Wichita was a cow town at the turn of the century. Today, with 120,000 people and diversified industries, is has, like all cities, its share of crime.

Last year, however, Wilson's scientific department cleared 51 out of each hundred burglaries, against a national average of 34. Only three of its 239 missing persons remained missing. It convicted five of its murderers, and two from the previous year. In Wilson's town, 45 percent of all larcenies lead straight to jail, rather than 26 percent, the national rate. Fewer than one fifth of American automobile thieves are caught; Wichita catches more than half, and last year recovered all 125 cars stolen in the city, 21 taken elsewhere.

How does Wichita do it? By spending lots of money? In 1936, latest year for which figures are computed, police cost the 42 cities in Wichita's population class an average of $3.30 per capita. Wichita paid $1.81. By hiring lots of men? Again, no. The ratio of police to population is smaller than in most middle-sized towns. Nor was Wichita always a policeman's paradise. In Chief Wilson's second year, there were five robberies to one now; there were three times as many burglaries, four times the stolen cars.

Wilson was twenty-eight years old when he came to Wichita in 1928. He had worked his way through the University of California by pounding a beat on August Vollmer's scientific Berkeley police department. With diploma in pocket, he continued to tramp the beat, continued to absorb Vollmer's revolutionary ideas, chief of which was that police work is a profession. Then, in 1925, he was made chief of police of Fullerton, a small city in southern California.

When Wichita called, he brought along Vollmer's theories. But he didn't have smooth sailing. Politicians raised patriotic objection to an "outsider" getting the job. They dubbed him "the boy scout cop," laughed at his ideas, and predicted that like many another Wichita chief, he wouldn't last a year.

They stopped laughing at him several years ago. Young Chief Wilson tossed out the chairwarmers at headquarters, retired men unfit for duty, sent others to beats. He bought enough cars to mount his entire department, and started each man out *alone*, not riding in pairs as is customary.

"Two men in two cars cover twice as much ground as two men in the same car," he points out logically. "And they can get all the help they need, merely by picking up a microphone from the dashboard."

When Wilson started America's "police cadet corps," several states followed his example and now have courses for men who wish to become police executives. But only in Wichita is every cop on the beat required to come up through the university route.

Each fall, at Wichita's Municipal University, Wilson selects a dozen able third-year students, and sells them the idea of police work as a career. The next two years, while finishing college, they work four hours daily in the Wichita department as rookies, earning $51 a month. On the campus, meantime, they study police science and related courses—traffic regulation, police jurisdiction, criminal law, practical psychology, and ethics. Graduating, they get B.S. or B.A. degrees, certificates of police science, plus jobs at $125 a month on the Wichita force.

When skeptical educators asked, "Why would any smart lad spend four years learning to walk a beat?" Wilson had a practical answer. "Hundreds of city managers are hunting well-trained police executives," he said. "We will furnish them."

He's doing just that. The new chief in Flint, Michigan, is one of Wilson's college cops. Another now heads the Honolulu detective force. One captains the Kansas state highway patrol. One is in the Secret Service, five hold key jobs in the U.S. Border Patrol, others are teaching police science in universities.

Being of an exploring mind, Wilson has made his department a testing ground for theories which in most cities haven't passed discussion stage. Many large city detective bureaus now use the Keeler "lie detector" on murder suspects. Only in   ☞

☞ Wichita must every person brought to the booking desk face the machine.

Last year, out of 710 vagrants tested, 61 admitted crimes elsewhere; 60 of 190 burglary suspects showed such positive results that 59 burglaries were cleared. Further, every recruit, seeking a place in the cadet corps, is tested by the machine for honesty and emotional stability.

At police headquarters in Wichita there is a scientific laboratory equipped with microscopes, test tubes, chemists' scales, cameras, ultraviolet ray machines. In addition, Wilson has mounted small laboratories in cruising cars.

Last summer a patrolman discovered a broken window in an alley. He snatched up his microphone; in 50 seconds three other patrol cars and the nearest cruising laboratory arrived. The laboratory investigator made plaster casts of tire tracks that the thief had left, and of chisel marks gouged in the window frame. He photographed the scene, hunted fingerprints, collected dust from the window sill. In it the microscope showed fragments of blue lint.

Twenty minutes later every policeman in town was hunting a burglar with a certain make of tire, a chisel with a broken point in his tool box, and wearing a blue sweater. An hour later they found him. Chisel and tire fitted the plaster casts. He was allowed to peer through a microscope and compare lint from his sweater and that from the window sill. He looked, and confessed; and next day, facing the lie detector, he admitted that he was wanted for burglaries elsewhere.

Of Wilson's innovations, he considers his new crime prevention bureau most important. Its captain, a trained sociologist, has every clergyman in town, and many doctors and teachers, as volunteer assistants.

Last year an eleven-year-old boy, a petty larceny "repeater," took physical, emotional and psychological tests in this bureau. They revealed, among other things, that he converted all loot into candy. Doctors arranged for a heavier sugar content in his diet, a preacher took him to Sunday school, his teacher wormed him into the school baseball team—and he doesn't steal anymore.

Wilson's police maintain a Boy Scout troop that carries off many honors, and this, too, is a fine job of crime prevention, Wilson says. The police run a model farm, where short-term prisoners work at creative tasks, grow their own vegetables, and at the same time gain self-respect and a new outlook on life.

But not only in handling crime does Wilson lead. The U.S. Chamber of Commerce in the past five years has placed Wichita at the top of its population class in traffic safety. And, strangely, arrests have had little to do with this record.

If you pass a red light in Wichita, a policeman politely hands you a "request card," which asks you not to break the law again. If you repeat, or if your violation is flagrant, you attend a traffic clinic, where alone and unembarrassed you take tests in driving, vision, reaction speed, and vehicle laws. Your weakness discovered, the police try to help you conquer it.

Should this fail, there's always traffic court. Last year, as against 5672 warnings and requests, only 149 violators were arrested. *Every one* of these was found guilty. *Every one* went to jail or paid a fine. There's no "ticket fix" in Wichita.

Ask this model chief whether other towns can have the same protection, and he replies, "Why not? Any town that wants it need only take politics out of the police business and put intelligence in."

A clerk steps into the office, interrupting him.

"That city manager from Wisconsin is on the phone again," the clerk says. "He wants to know whether you're ready, yet, to send him a new chief."

"I'll have a man go and look the job over," he answers, and turns back to you. "Any town can have good protection," he repeats. "And a lot of towns seem to be wanting it."

Karl Detzer. 1938. "College Cop," *The Kiwanis Magazine* (December 38). Reprinted with permission from *The Kiwanis Magazine*.

One community will differ from another in terms of social, economic, and political dimensions. For example, some communities will be as fairly well organized, while others might be described as relatively disorganized. Such differences generate beliefs, opinions, and expectations about how best

❖ ❖ ❖ ❖    to keep the public safe that cause police forces to differ from one place and time to another.

Some police departments may see their role in protecting the public from crime limited mainly to the task of law enforcement, as was common in the professional era of policing. Other police departments may view themselves as having a wider mission that includes maintaining order, preventing crime, and providing social services. For example, police departments during the community policing era believe that effective policing involves doing all that can be done to solve crime-related problems. The extent to which one police department remains reactive or tries to be proactive largely depends upon its leadership and what the community expects from the police.

## Social Evolution and the Need for Community

Most people probably see community generally as the people who live in a given area, but some study it more specifically in a sociological context.

For example, sociologist Robert Nisbet views community as one of the central themes that distinguishes a sociological approach to understanding human behavior from any other social science approach. For Nisbet, community is the most important of five "unit-ideas" that sociologists use when they study groups of people (the other four unit-ideas being authority, status, the sacred, and alienation). "Community includes but goes beyond local community to encompass religion, work, family, and culture; it refers to social bonds characterized by emotional cohesion, depth, continuity, and fullness."[7]

Considering what early social philosophers have written about community might help with an understanding of why a sense of community is important in the first place. What do we know about human existence that has made community seem like a good idea? What does community do for human beings and how does policing support it?

Nisbet credits German sociologist Ferdinand Tonnies as a key figure in the development of a sociological definition of community. Tonnies uses the term *Gemeinschaft* ("community") to distinguish a close-knit group of people who live together and depend upon one another over time. He contrasts *Gemeinschaft* with *Gesellschaft* ("society"), which refers to a looser association of people who tend to live near one another but who do not necessarily experience kinship or friendship.[8]

*'Community' is hard to define. (Photo: Mark C. Ide)*

❖ ❖ ❖ ❖

When Tonnies developed the ideas of *Gemeinschaft* and *Gesellschaft*, he had in mind medieval European towns and modern European cities, respectively. For Tonnies, *Gemeinschaft* was a positive concept that characterized people who thought and behaved in similar ways for the good of the group. The byproducts of *Gemeinschaft* were a concern for the welfare of others, a sense of belonging, and feelings of attachment to a shared way of life. Tonnies recognized family and friendships based upon common experiences, beliefs, or causes, as the building blocks of community.

In sharp contrast to *Gemeinschaft*, *Gesellschaft* refers to unions and associations based upon rationality and the need to live close together for protection and convenience. Tonnies believed that unlike *Gemeinschaft*, which was entirely positive, *Gesellschaft* could be either positive or negative based upon the individual needs of people who interacted. Stated another way, for those relationships characterized by *Gesellschaft*, whether or not the consequences proved good or bad depended upon the individual interests of the parties involved. *Gesellschaft* meant impersonal, businesslike transactions where, although the parties depended on one another for survival, one party might benefit at the expense of the other and each had to constantly watch out for its own interests.

Tonnies also recognized that urbanization and the growth of *Gesellschaft* comes at the expense of *Gemeinschaft*: "[T]he city is the home of *Gesellschaft*."[9] Similarly, Auguste Comte, who is credited as being the father of sociology, saw the industrialization and modernization of Europe as responsible for the demise of community. Comte, like Tonnies, identified the family unit as the foundation of social organization. For Comte, a society was composed of communities, which in turn, was made up of many smaller familial units, or families.

*Comte saw the family as the basic unit through which communities are built. (Photo: Mark C. Ide)*

❖ ❖ ❖ ❖     Another famous sociologist, Emilé Durkheim, like Comte, saw modern society as a larger but diluted form of community. Durkheim used the phrase *mechanical solidarity* to refer to a simpler form of society that most people might recognize as descriptive of small American towns based on agriculture. In such a setting, people tend to get along much as they have for many generations, that is, without much serious conflict or controversy. In contrast, *organic solidarity* tends to be found in more urbanized areas where there is a greater emphasis on individualism, freedom of ideas, and the division of labor.

Although Durkheim welcomed these positive features of organic solidarity, he also saw in them the potential for many negative side effects. For example, individualism might also produce greater anonymity, social isolation, alienation, and crime. As people know less about their neighbors' lives, they forfeit many of the benefits that familiarity offers in a tightly knit community. Neither the residents nor their property will be protected by watchful neighbors in a loosely knit community. Instead, the tendency to keep to one's self, to mind one's own business, means that the presence of strangers in a neighborhood is less likely to be questioned, if indeed the residents know enough about people in the neighborhood to know who belongs there and who does not. Lack of such knowledge leaves residents more vulnerable to the prospect of being both a victim and an offender.

## Communitarianism as a Response to Individualism and the Problem of Careless Neighbors

Quentin Tarantino's film *Pulp Fiction* offers a glimpse of the highly evolved modern city where business associations form the basis for personal relationships. In this film there is little evidence of neighbors, neighborhoods, or neighborly behavior. Instead, the characters convey an absence of concern for other people whom they know casually and a complete lack of empathy for strangers. For example, when one of the two key gangsters in the film accidentally kills a helpful informant whom they had promised to drive from one location to another, their main concern is not remorse but how best to clean blood off the back seat of the car to avoid detection of their crime.

Although Tarantino's film is only a fictionalized account of life in Los Angeles in the not-so-distant future, it suggests an eerie side to Durkheim's idea of organic solidarity. That is, society can become too impersonal and too loosely connected. As the nineteenth-century British prime minister Benjamin Disraeli predicted, urban life built entirely upon the individualism that gives rise to it ceases to be the kind of civilized society where most of us might want to live:

> In great cities men are brought together by the desire of gain. They are not in a state of cooperation, but of isolation, as to the making of fortunes; and for all the rest they are careless of neighbors. Christianity teaches us to love your neighbor as yourself; modern society acknowledges no neighbor.[10]

The tendency of modern society to advance without much concern for the way improvements in technology have tended to isolate individuals has led to the recognition of the importance of community and even perhaps a yearning for a return to it. A social movement mostly invoked by scholars and

intellectuals called *communitarianism* serves to illustrate how valuable the
concept of community becomes when people's attachment to the places they
live and the people who live there weakens.

❖ ❖ ❖ ❖

## The 'Moral Voice' and 'Shared Values' of Communities

Etzioni begins his discussion of community by describing the way most
people start trying to define the term:

> Communities are often viewed as social webs, in which people are attached
> to one another by crisscrossing relationships rather than by one-to-one rela-
> tionships. This is the reason communities are often depicted as 'warm and
> fuzzy' places. In a more popular vein, communities are defined as places in
> which the postmaster knows your first name or someone wants to hear the
> answer when they ask you how you are.[11]

But there is more to the idea of a community than just interactions with
people and a high degree of familiarity with them. In addition to the idea of
"social bonds," there is also the willingness of community members to speak
up about behavior they believe is right or wrong. Here Etzioni refers to a community's *moral voice*, which represents people's commitment to their community concerning the values they all share. He defines *shared values* as those
beliefs that people hold in common to guide good behavior and identify bad
behavior.

> The moral voice is the main way that individuals and groups in a good socie-
> ty encourage one another to adhere to behavior that reflects shared values
> and to avoid behavior that offends or violates them. The moral voice is often
> ignored by casual observers (and, to some extent, by social scientists) be-
> cause it is informal, subtle, and highly incorporated into daily life. It often
> works through frowns, gentle snide comments (and some that are not so gen-
> tle), praise, censure, and approbation.[12]

Etzioni believes that the strength of a community is based on the strength
of its moral voice and shared values. If community members would take it
upon themselves to speak to others in the following situations, then, he reasons, there is a basis for believing that a strong community exists:

> Would you speak up if: (a) you see a family walking away from a pristine lake,
> leaving behind soda cans and paper wrappers; (b) you see a pair of lovers
> carving their initials into the bark of a tree; (c) you see a mother spanking the
> living daylights out of her child in the supermarket; (d) someone pushes into
> a line of four people ahead of you; (e) you see a couple necking heavily in a
> public park in broad daylight right next to a group of small children; (f) you
> see someone you know driving too fast in a low speed zone in your neighbor-
> hood (later, you run into the driver in the store); (g) you witness a teenager of-
> fering to carry a senior citizen's groceries to the latter's car; (h) you see
> someone you know is not handicapped pull into a handicapped-only parking
> space; (i) someone makes a sizable donation (by the standards of their in-
> come) to a cause.[13]

Etzioni suggests that a community demonstrates a strong moral voice
when people speak their concerns at important moments that reflect a community's values. This moral voice is even more effective when such people
share concern for the welfare of those persons with whom they are speaking.

❖ ❖ ❖ ❖       Once again it is a matter of the *social bonds* that develop among people who know one another. Criticism or praise from someone whose opinion you value is more important for reinforcing your behavior than any notice that you might receive from an acquaintance or a passing stranger.

Establishing social bonds and using a moral voice in situations where shared values are being challenged are key indicators of a strong community. Social bonds also are an important link to law-abiding behavior. As Travis Hirschi and other criminologists have pointed out, social bonds create attachments to conventional rules and norms, thereby strengthening social control and consequently keeping people from violating laws and rules that they might otherwise break. When a system of shared social values or informal social control is weak, society must rely on formal social control and its agents (criminal statutes and law enforcement officers) to regulate criminal behavior.[14]

## 'Community' Defined From a Communitarian Perspective

Etzioni defines community as "a shared set of social bonds or a social web, as distinct from one-to-one bonds."[15] For him, community is not just the place that a group of people live or the people who live there. Community is about values and relationships that bind people together for the sake of common goals. These common goals can have as much to do with survival as with promoting a high quality of life in a neighborhood, town, or small city. Etzioni sees communities as

> . . . webs of social relations that encompass shared meanings and above all shared values. Families may qualify as minicommunities. Villages often are, although not necessarily so. Some neighborhoods in cities (such as Little Havana in Miami, Chinatown in New York City) constitute communities. Well-integrated national societies may be said to be communities. Communities need not be geographically concentrated. One may speak of, say, a Jewish community in a city even if its members are dispersed among the population and maintain their social-normative web around core institutions such as a synagogue and private schools.[16]

Ultimately, however, Etzioni acknowledges that there is no single definition of community upon which communitarians can agree; rather, there are three different ways in which this term might be better understood:

> (1) communities of ideas: for example, the participatory democratic and republican models, (2) communities of crisis: for example, the earth community born of the environmental crisis, and (3) communities of memory: for example, religious and traditional ideas of community.[17]

For students of community policing, it is the community of ideas that is central to the use of the term throughout the remainder of this book. Community policing, and its origins in the idea of democratic policing, suggests a way of best serving the public-safety needs of all citizens equally and fairly. Consequently, the authors tend to agree with Etzioni that "There is no single version of participatory community as community, but its advocates emphasize the importance of people deciding together, face to face, conversing with, and respecting each other in a setting which is as equal as possible."[18]

# Individual Versus Group Needs in a Community Setting

❖ ❖ ❖ ❖

Etzioni discusses the importance of the "I and We" in distinguishing individual needs and interests from those of the community to which individuals belong:

> The uncommunitized parts of personhood are sources of creativity and change for the community and personal expression for the person. The communitized part of a person is a source of effective psychological stability and one source of personal and social virtue.[19]

## Everybody Needs Somebody Sometime

### *Steve Dickie*

Not long ago, a *Chicago Tribune* columnist wrote a very honest reflection about her desire for meaningful friendships: "The loneliness saddens me," she shared. "How did it happen that I could be forty-two years old and not have enough friends? But, no matter how much I enjoy my job and love my husband, I still need friends."

The reaction to her column was astonishing. Letters from hundreds of people poured into the newspaper expressing similar feelings of frustration. "I've often felt," one woman wrote, "that I'm standing outside looking through the window of a party to which I was not invited." Another wrote, "I have this fear of becoming a very lonely, old widow sitting around and listening to the clock tick."

The columnist concluded with these words: "Sometimes it seems easier to just give up and accept disconnectedness as a dark and unshakable companion; but, that's not the companion I want. So, I will persevere."[1]

If we were honest, most of us would probably confess the same longing for connection. Disconnection and the corresponding feeling of loneliness have become defining points in a society marked by individualism and isolation. The problem shouldn't really surprise us when we examine several changes that are becoming apparent in modern culture.

### Changes in Family Structure

Trends indicate that of all the children born in 1990, six out of 10 will live in a single-parent household for some period before they reach 18.[2]

- As parents struggle to get by, energy needed to cultivate relationships and meet family needs is spent on the mere act of earning income.

- Children are being left alone to care for themselves while parents work. As a consequence, close parent-child relationships are less likely to develop.

- The traditional foundation of building family relationship, dinner time, is disappearing. The TV has replaced family conversation. Most homes now have several TVs, thus allowing family members to watch separate programs in different parts of the house.[3]

### Changes in Neighborhood

- Neighborhoods and friends are seen as transitory. About one in five Americans move every year, thus leading to the logic expressed by the wife of an executive who had moved three times in seven years: "To decrease the pain of saying 'good-bye' to our neighbors, we no longer say 'hello.' "[4]

- Our relationships often become based on our own functional need rather than on personal need. We have little, if any, relationship with the mailman, grocery store clerk, or gas station attendant. If we don't know people, then we really can't care.[5]

- The neighborhood fence has become a symbol of community anonymity. ☞

❖ ❖ ❖ ❖    ☞

## Changes in the Workplace

- The workplace used to be a place where one could belong. It was a place where you would be cared for and others would care for you. Today, as a result of competition of workers in the corporate structure, personal relationships with coworkers can become a hindrance to advancement.[6]

- As mergers and downsizing increase, employees can become disposable.

- Automation, computers, the internet, and other technological advancements leave workers interacting more with machines and less with people.

While these changing patterns have changed the way we interact with others, they have also created an inner longing for community. One of the ways we are seeing this desire is in the reviewed emphasis on the values of home and family. The evidence is everywhere. Hospitals are changing their delivery floors to look home-like, and many retailers are designing their stores to make you feel as if you're walking into a well-decorated home. Magazines and newspapers are featuring regular family-life sections on everything from parenting tips to home improvement; a national television network has declared the phrase "Welcome Home" as its motto. In the workplace, "family ties" has replaced "cost of living" as the top reason for workers refusing to relocate, and a large percentage of major companies are now allowing their employees to work at home and share a job. We are even seeing this trend lived out in the way advertisers are targeting their audience. In one fast-food commercial, a salesman tries to intrude on the family dinner but is chased away by a lion while the mother warns, "Don't mess with dinner!" In another advertisement, a mattress company that once used photos of models in nightgowns is now showing scenes of families lounging on the bed.[7] Isn't it amazing that while society tends to isolate itself, it still finds itself returning to places of connection?

The great social paradox of the new century is that our quest for independence runs up against our desire for interaction. We want to be alone, but our aloneness leaves us with a longing for real and authentic relationships. One area that provides an excellent if not sobering reference point is our children. According to social worker Judy Frank, "What we hear over and over from kids is 'I want someone to play with me.'" We see kids who are hungry for personal interaction, somebody to really sit and play with them. Playing with a machine, no matter how brilliant the responses, still leaves a child basically alone. Richard Louv in his book *Childhood's Future* echoes this concern: "I came to believe that much of the reason so many of us today spend so much time in the company of machines is because the true company of people is becoming harder to come by."[8]

We have found ourselves alone, and I strongly believe that most of us don't want it that way. Our sense of loss sounds like the anguished cry of Robinson Crusoe: "I am cast upon a horrible, desolate island, void of all hope of recovery. I am singled out and separated, as it were, a solitary; one banished from human society. I have no soul to speak to or to relieve me."

What are we to do? The answer needs to begin in the understanding of two very simple yet extraordinary truths: We need others and others need us.

## We Need Others

Each of us has a universal need that can only be met in the community of others. As a matter of fact, I believe that we will really never feel completely whole until we experience community. No matter how far some may go to remove themselves from the impact and influence of others, they will fall short of what they were meant to be.

This truth was beautifully illustrated in the movie *The Mighty*, based on the book by Rodman Philbrick.[9] In the story, two young misfits discover personal significance when they join forces. Kevin has a disease that has stunted his growth and left him crippled and confined to leg braces. He is also brilliant and extremely imaginative. Max is not very intelligent and sticks to himself. He is also big and exceptionally strong. In a profound discovery, they learn that they can hurdle their limitations by becoming one. Everywhere they go, Max carries Kevin on his shoulders, providing him with mobility that he could never attain on his own. In the same way, Kevin empowers Max with insight and articulation that gives him a new    ☞

☞ sense of confidence. As Max becomes Kevin's legs and Kevin becomes Max's mouth, they both are able to go above and beyond what they might ever hope to be by themselves. It's true. We need others because others make us better people.

## Others Need Us

I find that despite the benefit that others bring us, some people would rather stand alone. We see it in many ways. The angry teenager who keeps to himself the elderly woman who isolates herself in the neighborhood the family that moves into the country to avoid contact with everyone the apartment dweller who hides behind locked doors in distrust of anyone who comes near the business executive who crawls over everyone for personal achievement—their isolation is unfortunate, because they are not only denying themselves of the rich impact of others but they are also denying others the gifts, talents, and abilities that they might offer.

At the beginning of our church service, we provide a time where we invite everyone to stand and greet one another. When we first started doing this, a few people complained that it seemed contrived and a little phony. I'll never forget the response of one leader: "It may feel phony to you, but I bet it doesn't feel phony to the person who needs it." When we remove ourselves from the community of others, we are denying them what we have to give. Believe it or not, somebody really does need us. Each of us has been gifted in some way and if we choose not to exercise it, we all lose out.

There's a great story of a community whose teenagers had a somewhat negative view of senior citizens. A group of the seniors got together to devise an action plan. They came up with the idea of going to the school bus stops every morning simply to smile and greet kids as they arrived. The plan was a great success, and the community experienced a major shift in teen attitudes toward the elderly. This is a great example of what people can do for community when they put their minds to it.

## A Christian Perspective

I would be remiss if I did not point out my personal perspective on community. While it might not agree with your worldview, it will help you understand my frame of reference. As a Christian minister, I see community at the very core of my faith. Throughout the Bible the importance of community is consistently stressed. In the New Testament the phrase "one another" is used more than 50 times. It is often connected with a commandment and taken together with it gives a guideline for the kind of community we need to be for one another. We are told to "Honor one another," "Accept one another," "Serve one another," "Forgive one another," "Encourage one another," and "Love one another," to name a few. We Christians don't always do a good job at this, but we all could learn something from these directives.

When you think about it, we all were meant for something more. Charles Du Bois writes: "The important thing is this: to be willing at any moment to sacrifice who we are for what we can become." I believe, through the dynamic of interconnection of community, we can achieve that goal. The results can change us forever.

---

Steve Dickie graduated from California State University at Fullerton and attended Fuller Theological Seminary in Pasadena, California. He is a 20-year veteran of youth ministries, about which he has authored several articles and books. For the past five years he has served as the director of family ministries for the Eastminster Presbyterian Church in Wichita, Kansas.

---

## Endnotes

1. Lee Strobel, *The Outrageous Claims of God* (Grand Rapids, MI: Zondervan, 1988).
2. George Barna, *The Frog in the Kettle* (Ventura, CA: Regal, 1990).
3. *Ibid.*, p. 70.
4. Charles Swindoll, *Dropping Your Guard* (Waco, TX: Word, 1983).
5. Julie Gorman, *Community That Is Christian* (Wheaton, IL: Victor, 1993).
6. Ibid.
7. Ben Freudenburg, *The Family-Friendly Church* (Loveland, CO: Group, 1998).
8. Richard Louv, *Childhood's Future* (Boston: Houghton Mifflin, 1990).
9. Rodman Philbrick, *The Mighty* (New York: Scholastic, 1993).

❖ ❖ ❖ ❖    Similarly, Anthony Bouza, a recently retired Minneapolis police chief, has written that

> A nation full of zest and vigor, growing under values that emphasize 'us' rather than 'me,' altruism over hedonism, sacrifice over pleasure, and service over self, will provide for a much safer society than the one we have today.[20]

Reorienting policing to the needs of all citizens invites the public to help in the identification of problems, to recommend solutions, and to participate in problem solving itself.

## Communitarianism as a Social Movement

Etzioni describes the communitarian movement as "an environmental movement dedicated to the betterment of our moral, social, and political environments."[21] He goes on to give some features of communitarians:

> Communitarians are dedicated to working with our fellow citizens to bring about the changes in values, habits, and public policies that will allow us to do for society what the environmental movement seeks to do for nature: to safeguard and enhance our future.[22]

Etzioni, when trying to figure out how the need for community developed, points to anecdotal evidence and explains it this way:

> A study has shown that young Americans expect to be tried before a jury of their peers but are rather reluctant to serve on one. This paradox highlights a major aspect of contemporary American civic culture: a strong sense of entitlement—that is, a demand that the community provide more services and strongly uphold rights—coupled with a rather weak sense of obligation to the local and national community. Thus, most Americans applauded the show of force in Grenada, Panama, and in the Persian Gulf, but many were reluctant to serve in the armed forces or see their sons or daughters called up.
>
> First prize for capturing this anticommunitarian outlook should be awarded to a member of a television audience who exclaimed during a show on the savings and loan mess, 'The taxpayers should not have to pay for this; the government should,' as if there really were an Uncle Sam who could pick up the tab for us all.[23]

In order to correct this mistaken view that Americans are not bound by principles to uphold the common good, Etzioni suggests that there is a need to understand the difference between rights and responsibilities:

> Correcting the current imbalance between rights and responsibilities requires a four-point agenda: a moratorium on the minting of most, if not all, new rights; reestablishing the link between rights and responsibilities; recognizing that some responsibilities do not entail rights; and, most carefully, adjusting some rights to the changed circumstances.[24]

## Great Expectations

If people can agree that a strong community sounds like a good idea, they might begin to wonder about the common features that strong communities share. What are the attributes or characteristics of a strong community? What cities or towns come to mind as an example of a strong community?

---

## A Good Community                    ❖ ❖ ❖ ❖

### *Quint Thurman*

What is a good community to me? From my experience, it is a place like Moscow, Idaho, where a farmer with a busted alternator on his combine during the hectic pace of harvest season can still count on Jim Robinson at Electrical Specialists to get him back in the field in short order, or where Jim's dad, Ron, might deliver a Christmas tree, freshly cut from his own land, to a new family in town that he barely knew.

In Moscow, a city of 23,000, we might see a full range of seasons, although winter weather can still make a showing at the fourth of July fireworks display. And in spite of the University of Idaho being located there, the campus doesn't tend to dominate the city's landscape, its politics, or its economy the way it might in Moscow's neighbor to the west, Pullman, Washington, home to another state university. While both places are similar in size, Moscow has a feel to it and a pace that the first-time visitor can quickly discern. Simply put, Moscow has a community sense about it and its people come out to support local needs and causes, not because they're activists by nature (although some may have been activists at another time in their lives) but because it's the right thing to do when you care about the place you live and the people who live there with you.

Living in Moscow reminds me of that story about the old fellow rocking on his porch when a stranger looking for a new place to live approaches him and asks what it is like to live there. The old-timer answers with a question of his own: "What's it like where you come from?" "People there are ill-tempered, rude, and generally untrustworthy," said the stranger, to which the old man replied, "then you probably won't like it much here either!" A few days later, another passerby appeared on the old man's porch, wondering aloud about what kind of town it was. This time when the old man asked him first to tell him about the place he had just left, the passerby described the people there as kind, considerate, and willing to help a neighbor in need. To this the old man responded, "Friend, you'll like living here too!"

I know Moscow is like the place the second stranger left and rediscovered. I suspect that even the first passerby would have eventually come to see it that same way if given the chance. I know I did, and he and I weren't all that different when I first came to live there.

---

Although it might seem that less formal towns in rural areas are places where shared values are the most likely to be found, Etzioni notes that some American authors might argue with that idea. In fact, American writers such as Sinclair Lewis and John O'Hara satirized small towns as insular, claustrophobic places, inhabited by petty, mean-spirited people. They were depicted as the opposite of 'big cities,' whose atmosphere was said to set people free. Anonymity would allow each person to pursue what he or she wished rather than what the community dictated.[25]

Etzioni is quick to point out that the even the most popular urban centers in the country are not without their drawbacks.

Throughout twentieth-century America, as the transition to *gesellschaft* evolved, even its champions realized that it was not the unmitigated blessing they had expected. Although it was true that those who moved from villages and small towns into urban centers often shed tight social relations and strong community bonds, the result for many was isolation, lack of caring for one another, and exposure to rowdiness and crime.[26]

❖ ❖ ❖ ❖        It seems that the recognition of the need for recreating close social bonds among people who choose to live in urban environments has not gone unnoticed by American social scientists.

> Criminologists report that young farmhands in rural America in the early nineteenth century did not always work on their parents' land. However, when they were sent to work outside their home they usually lived with other farmers and were integrated into their family life. In this way they were placed in a community context that sustained the moral voice, reinforced the values of their upbringing, and promoted socially constructive behavior. It was only when these farmhands went to work in factories in cities—and were housed on their own in barracks without established social networks, elders, and values—that rowdy and criminal behavior, alcoholism, and prostitution became common. Even in those early days attempts to correct these proclivities were made not by returning these young people to their families and villages, but by trying to generate Communitarian elements in the cities. Among the best analysts of these developments is James Q. Wilson, a leading political scientist. He notes that associations such as the Young Men's Christian Association (YMCA), temperance societies, and the Children's Aid Society sought to provide a socially appropriate, morality-sustaining context for young people.[27]

Etzioni goes on to pose some key questions:

> Does this mean that we all have to move back to live in small towns and villages in order to ensure the social foundations of morality, to rebuild and shore up we-ness? Can one not bring up decent young people in the city?[28]

He then answers these same questions accordingly:

> Even in large metropolises, such as New York City, there are neighborhoods in which many people know their neighbors, their shopkeepers, and their local leaders. They are likely to meet one another in neighborhood bars, bowling alleys, and places of worship. They watch out for each other's safety and children. They act in concert to protect their parks and bus stops. They form political clubs and are a force in local politics.[29]

The reader may well be asking at this point, where might we find community if the positive aspects of either towns or cities are not sufficient in themselves to guarantee that their inhabitants will want to join together to form a strong community? Similarly, Etzioni asks,

> How does one reconcile the two sociological pictures—the James Q. Wilson concept of the city as *gesellschaft*, with little community or moral base, and the Herbert Gans image of *gemeinschaft*, of urban villages? The answer, first of all, is that both exist side by side. Between the urban villages, in row houses and high rises, you find large pockets of people who do not know their next-door neighbors, with whom they may have shared a floor, corridors, and elevators for a generation. Elderly people especially, who have no social bonds at work and are largely abandoned by their families, often lead rather isolated lives.[30]

Etzioni writes about what he thinks we as citizens need to do to ensure strong communities:

> To strengthen the Communitarian nexus requires four measures, each of which deserves some discussion: changing orientation; changing the 'habits of the heart'; working out conflicts between career needs and community bonds; redesigning our physical environment to render it more community-

friendly; and fostering volunteer endeavors that do not trivialize and squander our commitments to the commons.[31]

❖ ❖ ❖ ❖

Etzioni suggests: (1) that we should rededicate ourselves less to our own greedy self-interests (for wealth does not lead to happiness) and instead devote more time to activities that bring us closer to those who share our neighborhoods and towns. We should join a church, form an association, get involved in positive social functions! He argues (2) that we need to consider careers that are socially productive such as "nursing, teaching, and social work"[32] or take advantage of social-service opportunities that are presented to us in normal occupations (e.g., mediation and conflict resolution for attorneys; family practices for physicians; Habitat for Humanity projects for retired presidents!) He recommends (3) that we create or redesign community-friendly places that promote positive interactions (for example, on a "small scale," add park benches where people might congregate; design playgrounds that encourage parents to interact and courtyards in apartment complexes that bring people together). He also suggests (4) that we make communitarian action count by recognizing volunteer efforts that benefit communities and promoting significant responses such as learning cardiopulmonary resuscitation (CPR) and engaging in worthwhile community-service projects.[33]

Etzioni's own story is compelling:

> Some time ago I was driving home in snow that had snarled Washington, D.C., and was forced to abandon my car and hitch a ride with someone whose car had four-wheel drive. When I finally arrived at my home in Bethesda, Maryland, neighbors were standing in my kitchen—crying. I found out that my wife had been in a serious car accident. My young son had been taken to an emergency room with her. Two of my neighbors offered to drive me to the emergency room, despite the icy roads (we did spin out of control on the way), and others simply stated that they were going to stay on at my place to wait for my other sons to arrive. My wife did not survive the accident, and in the weeks that followed, my neighbors took care of me. They brought over food; one couple spent the entire evening with me, although it was one of two evenings their son was home from college. Another dedicated his only day off from work to go to the car wreck and retrieve some documents, a task I could not face. They called on me frequently for weeks on end.
>
> I know, as clearly as one can ever tell about human motivations, that they did not calculate how much I had done for them in the past or would do for them in a future moment of need. It was quite evident that they did what they could to help out of a sense of compassion. True, there is, quite properly, in any relationship or community some *vague* sense of appropriate reciprocity, of the need to contribute to a climate of mutuality. But basically people help one another and sustain the spirit of community because they sense it is the right thing to do.[34]

Lyon suggests that there really may be no one definition that captures all the qualities that might come to mind when trying to come up with a single description of a good community. That is, it is unlikely that there exists any one good community to serve as a measuring stick for all communities. Instead, he suggests it is better to think in terms of how one good community differs from another that might also be identified as a good one.[35]

Lyon identifies six components that he considers are the bare necessities for a good community. A good community must provide its citizens with "(1) public safety, (2) a strong economy, (3) health care, (4) educational opportu-

❖  ❖  ❖  ❖

*Police officers attending a community gathering. Getting out among the public helps build trust among citizens and provides important opportunities for the police to identify problems and resources. (Photo: Courtesy of the Omaha Police Department)*

nities, (5) a clean, healthy natural environment, (6) and an optimum population size."[36] In addition to these common "objective" features, which form the basis for a high quality of life in all communities, Lyon suggests a minimum of seven "more subjective, more debatable components": (1) individual liberty, (2) categorical equality, (3) communal fraternity, (4) representative, responsive government, (5) community viability, (6) local identification, and (7) resident heterogeneity."[37] Communities differ according to the priorities that they place on each of these seven subjective components.

Although Lyon's six objective bare necessities are self-explanatory, his seven subjective components need some explanation.

For example, consider his first subjective component, individual liberty. Communities that place a high value on freedom and anonymity may be great places to visit for the entertainment and other recreational activities they provide, but they may not be ideally suitable places to live for people who value low heterogeneity, that is, who prefer to associate mostly with people who think the way they do. Similarly, people who place a high value on categorical equality may prefer to live in cities and towns where housing is not segregated by race and women are paid the same wages as men for similar kinds of work. From the authors' experiences, medium-size cities that have to state universities are examples of good communities that subscribe to the ideal of categorical equality.

Communities made up of people who for generations have chosen to live their whole lives in that place might qualify as admirable because of their high degree of communal fraternity. Here, Lyon identifies a basic quality that defines *Gemeinschaft* itself, that is, "relationships that are based on a natural will."[38] This natural will, termed *Wesenwille* by Tonnies, consists of "sentiment, tradition, and common bonds as governing forces."[39]

For the police, community may be those people who live in a certain area or jurisdiction who wish to belong there or who are actively engaged in belonging. As such, the residents might fit best what Etzioni has referred to as a community of ideas. Community policing may mean a form of policing that appeals to the greatest assortment of families who live in an area. Whatever the form of community policing in a given time and place, one thing is certain. It has to be jointly produced by those charged with protecting public safety and those residents or groups of residents who wish the area to be a safer place to live and work. Working together, the police and the residents can identify goals, strategies, and resources well suited to the local environment.

David Weisburd and Jerome McElroy have suggested that when community policing is faced with severely disorganized social settings and asked to make a difference, the result will be less than the community expects.[40] It is in just such an environment, however, that positive change is most crucial. As Thurman has argued,

> Co-producing solutions to crime and social problems seems the best means at hand for bringing together human resources and the police for mutual benefit, while at the same time respecting the ability of residents to make important contributions to solving their community's problems.[41]

## Conclusion

It seems that the term *community* refers to a place where a shared set of ideas exists such that people are willing to join together to work toward a high quality of life. Although public safety alone might not be a necessary and sufficient feature of a good community, it is difficult to imagine a good community where it is not safe to live. Indeed, what other alternatives are there to building stronger communities and safer places to work and raise children? To paraphrase Lyon, maybe we cannot save the world, but together we can improve our communities![42]

## Study Questions

1. What is Rothenbuhler's definition of community? How does it differ from Park's and Etzioni's definitions?

2. From a communitarian viewpoint, what definition of community fits best the idea of community policing and why? (Hint: What does a "community of ideas" mean for community policing?)

3. From your own experiences, write a descriptive paragraph or two about the "best" community that you have ever lived in? What features cause you to consider it the best?

4. What difference can community policing make in severely disorganized communities?

❖ ❖ ❖ ❖       **Endnotes**

1. Larry Lyon, *The Community in Urban Society* (Philadelphia: Temple University Press, 1987), p. 4.
2. Jayne Seagrave, "Defining Community Policing," *American Journal of Policing* 15 (1996): 1–22 [pp. 4–5].
3. Eric W. Rothenbuhler, "Understanding and Constructing Community: A Communication Approach," in *Reinventing Human Services: Community and Family-Centered Practice*, ed. Paul Adams and Kristine Nelson (New York: Aldine de Gruyter, 1995), pp. 207–221 [pp. 207–208].
4. Robert E. Park, "Human Ecology," *American Journal of Sociology* 42 (1936): 1–15.
5. Amitai Etzioni, *The New Golden Rule: Community and Morality in a Democratic Society* (New York: Basic Books, 1996), p. 127.
6. Actually, another more modern dimension of community that poses a challenge to policing is "virtual communities" produced by the Internet and cable TV. These communities too must contend with problems associated with vice, fraud, harassment, and other crimes.
7. Robert A. Nisbet, *The Sociological Tradition* (New York: Basic Books, 1966), p. 47.
8. Ibid, p. 48.
9. Ibid, p. 77.
10. *Ibid.*, p. 52.
11. Etzioni, *New Golden Rule*, p. 127.
12. *Ibid.*, p. 124.
13. *Ibid.*, p. 124.
14. Travis Hirschi, *Causes of Delinquency* (Berkeley: University of California Press, 1969); Quint C. Thurman, "Estimating Social-Psychological Effects in Decisions to Drink and Drive: A Factorial Survey Approach," *Journal of Studies on Alcohol* 47 (1986): 447–454.
15. Amitai Etzioni, *New Communitarian Thinking: Persons, Virtues, Institutions, and Communities* (Charlottesville: University Press of Virginia, 1995), p. 17.
16. *Ibid.*, p. 24.
17. *Ibid.*, p. 88.
18. *Ibid.*, p. 89.
19. *Ibid.*, p. 19.
20. Anthony V. Bouza, *The Police Mystique: An Insider's Look at Cops, Crime, and the Criminal Justice System* (New York: Plenum, 1990), p. 273.
21. Amitai Etzioni, *The Spirit of Community: Rights, Responsibilities, and the Communitarian Agenda* (New York: Crown, 1993), p. 2.
22. *Ibid.*, p. 3.
23. *Ibid.*, p. 3.
24. *Ibid.*, p. 4.
25. *Ibid.*, pp. 116–117.
26. *Ibid.*, p. 117.
27. *Ibid.*, p. 117–118.
28. *Ibid.*, p. 119.
29. *Ibid.*, p. 120.
30. *Ibid.*, p. 120.
31. *Ibid.*, p. 123.
32. *Ibid.*, p. 126.
33. *Ibid.*
34. *Ibid.*, p. 145.
35. Lyon, *The Community in Urban Society*.
36. *Ibid.*, p. 243.
37. *Ibid.*, p. 245.
38. *Ibid.*, p. 7.
39. *Ibid.*, p. 7.

40. David Weisburd and Jerome McElroy, "Enacting the CPO Role: Findings From the New York City Pilot Program in Community Policing," in *Community Policing: Rhetoric or Reality?* eds. Jack R. Greene and Stephen D. Mastrofski (New York: Praeger, 1988), pp. 89–101.

41. Quint C. Thurman, "Community Policing: The Police as a Community Resource," in *Reinventing Human Services: Community and Family-Centered Practice*, eds. Paul Adams and Kristine Nelson (New York: Aldine de Gruyter, 1995), p. 185.

42. Lyon, *The Community in Urban Society.* ✦

# Chapter Four

❖ ❖ ❖ ❖

# Policing in a Time of Change

❖ ❖ ❖ ❖

*It is not the strongest of the species that survive, nor the most intelligent, but the one most responsive to change.*

—Charles Darwin

Organizations change over time in a variety of ways. Police departments are similar to other organizations in many respects in how they change; and in other respects, they differ. All organizations have an internal dimension that consists of employees, job assignments, lines of authority, resource allocation, and overarching goals that tell what the organization is trying to do and how it will do it. All organizations also have to contend with an external dimension that affects what they do. Community policing represents change in police departments across the country. It is new and innovative. This chapter will discuss economic, social, and legal factors that help provide boundaries for how a police department operates internally.

## Setting the Stage for Change

To look back from the end of the twentieth century, it seems fair to characterize this period as a time of substantial change for police departments.[1] One notable sign of such change was improvement in the technology the police used to control crime.[2] For example, the introduction of motorized patrol and two-way radios made police departments more efficient in patrolling a geographic area and supervising patrol officers. Today, more than 85 percent of the patrolling in U.S. cities employing more than 100 officers is carried out by motorized patrols.[3]

Despite many highly visible technological advances, however, there are many areas of policing that have been very slow to change if they changed at all. For example, the rank system that was borrowed from the British military for the London Metropolitan Patrol has remained virtually unchanged in American policing. Every police department the authors know uses some form of military ranking system to distinguish who gives orders and who must follow them.[4] Similarly, the ratio of first-line supervisors to officers under their control remains remarkably consistent over time and from one department to another since the beginning of modern policing—one sergeant usually supervises eight officers on the street. Such consistency suggests that certain aspects of a police department are very resistant to change.[5]

Scholars who study organizational change and the police in particular offer a number of explanations for explaining such change.[6] The following section will explore the definition of organizational change and how to measure it. The next sections will introduce the major theories that might explain different types of organizational change. Finally, the chapter examines three eras of organizational change in policing in greater detail.

# The Concept of Organizational Change    ❖ ❖ ❖ ❖

Organizations change in a number of ways and for many reasons. A university, for example, can set new policies for student recruitment in order to attract nontraditional students, or it can adopt guidelines for faculty that suggest better ways for integrating computers into the classroom. Similarly, a police department can experiment with new ways to reduce crime by working with urban planners to design new buildings that incorporate crime-prevention features.

Aspen Police Department patrol supervisor bicycling in Aspen, Colorado. Bike patrols have become popular with citizens and police officers in the community era and have proven themselves to be effective in increasing officer visibility and accessibility and criminal deterrence. They also are an effective way to detect crime on the streets. (Photo: Courtesy of the Aspen Police Department)

Organizational change usually means making new policies or adding something new to an existing practice.[7] Changes of these kinds can be aimed at modifying employees' attitudes, behaviors, interaction patterns, or organizational practices.[8] Generally, organizational change is defined as the introduction of a new program, process, policy, or service in order to change the current practice of some element or elements of an organization.[9]

On many occasions, there is little difference between organizational change and innovation. Both represent the idea of doing something new and presumably better. In fact, many organizational theorists use the terms *change* and *innovation* interchangeably.[10] The authors, however, define organizational change as the kind of change that modifies the practice of police departments in a significant way.[11] In our view, organizational change is an event that reflects a permanent break from that which preceded it or it represents a new direction or trend that police professionals are attempting to follow.[12] Consequently, isolated new programs or other innovations in a police department that do not contribute to some general trend of change in the police profession are not included in our definition.

❖ ❖ ❖ ❖     ## Levels of Organizational Change

According to Paul Goodman and Lance Kurke, change can happen on three levels of an organization.[13] The first level concerns individual employees. They are the essential building blocks of any organization and can serve as a focus for change in several areas. For example, an employee's values are often a target for change. Similarly, another target of change might be improvement in a person's skills that are directly related to job performance, usually through training in new technology, methods, and equipment. Both values and job skills are seen as important areas for change in the implementation of community policing. Indeed, both values and job skills are often linked in the organizational change process. For example, police departments often offer employees new skills and methods in problem solving as an important first step in the change to community policing.

The second level of organizational change involves groups and group processes. The cohesiveness of a group is a crucial element for predicting the outcome of change. The degree of cohesion and the potential for successful change depend on good intercommunication skills, conflict resolution, and interpersonal trust.

Finally, the third level of change is the organization itself. Many changes in policing began at the organizational level. Police departments all across the country were targeted for change during the professional era as noted in O. W. Wilson's textbook on police administration. More recently, the implementation of community policing in the Houston Police Department in the mid-1980s was primarily targeted at the organizational level with the strong support from the police chief at the time, Lee Brown.

It is important to keep in mind that the three levels of change are not entirely independent—change can take place at the same time at all three levels. For example, consider the Omaha Police Department. In the fall of 1995, the department decided to implement total quality management (TQM), an approach that assumes involvement at every level in the department. At the individual level, training was provided to the employees who were expected to be most involved in TQM. Between December 1995 and May 1997, over 30 percent of employees (over 200 people) received at least eight hours of TQM training, and of this group, a large percentage received over 40 hours. At the group level, six specific problem-solving teams were organized to work on problems identified by employees as key concerns. Finally, at the organizational level, a quality council was established to supervise the implementation of TQM throughout the department. Members of the quality council were chosen from all ranks and bureaus.

## Understanding Organizational Change as a Process

Another important issue regarding organizational change is that change should be understood as a process that involves movement from a beginning point to some endpoint where the transition is considered complete.[14] Once completed, any changes then become part of the routine of the daily operation of an organization and are no longer considered new. For example, the introduction of motorized patrol in the Berkeley Police Department during the 1920s was a dramatic departure from the traditional method of foot or

## Is Community Policing a Fad?

❖ ❖ ❖ ❖

### *Captain Randal B. Landen*

I think it's fair to say that most of us became police officers because we wanted to serve our community. Certainly, that was my ideal when I joined the department over 18 years ago. When community policing came to Wichita, Kansas, I was assigned as the supervisor for the narcotics unit, where I was just completing my fifth year of working undercover. I was also one of two supervisors for the department's strategic weapons and tactics (SWAT) team. We were vaguely aware of that thing called community policing, but it really didn't have much relevance to our assignments. Besides, we didn't have time to attend picnics, hug little kids, and hand out teddy bears. After all, we were crime fighters, not social workers.

As officers who've worked on undercover investigations can attest, such an assignment tends to isolate you from uniformed patrol and routine contact with the community. As a result, we were only vaguely aware of what was happening outside the confines of our section. The traditional reactionary approach to policing had become ineffective, the overall morale of our officers was at rock bottom, and regrettably, the community had lost its trust in the department and its officers.

Just about that time, through the grace of God and the charity of the new chief, I was promoted to the rank of captain. I liked that part. They also made me forego the earrings and ponytail and sent me back to the real world, a world in which the community policing craze had taken over. I wasn't so enamored with that. To say that I was one of the last people on board with the community policing philosophy would be a vast understatement. Like many of my peers, I was confident that community policing was a fad that wouldn't last, just another name for what we'd been doing all along.

Four years have passed, and during that time our department has evolved rapidly. Through a philosophical change and an intense educational process, we've successfully integrated a problem-solving philosophy with fundamental policing concepts, and developed crucial relationships with the community. I've had the opportunity to work closely with the community through the volume of special events coordinated by Special Operation, and more recently through assignment to one of the department's four patrol bureaus. I've seen firsthand the change in community attitudes toward the police, and, more important, I've seen the officers' attitudes toward the community change. Officers are once again focused on serving the community, not as one lone cop fighting crime but as a partner with the community, solving problems.

All right, so I might have been wrong. Community policing isn't a fad, and it's certainly not a new name for the same old stuff we'd always done. Community policing affords the police an opportunity to form partnerships with the community, through which we are able to solve problems, reduce fear, and prevent crime. Community policing has given the police additional resources. I'm not talking about grants or added tax dollars but rather the additional resources realized through community support. And it has given officers on the street the authority to make use of those resources in solving community problems. Most important, community policing has restored the public's confidence in the police.

I believe that what Peter F. Drucker said about organizations holds true for community policing: it allows ordinary people to accomplish extraordinary things.

---

Captain Randal B. Landen is an 18-year veteran of the Wichita Police Department in Wichita, Kansas. His career includes assignments in patrol, investigations, internal affairs, vice, narcotics, SWAT, and Special Operations. He is currently assigned as the commander of Patrol West, one of the department's four patrol bureaus. He is a FLETC-certified community policing trainer and a 1998 graduate of the Midwest Criminal Justice Institute's Law Enforcement Executive Leadership Institute. He received his bachelor's degree in administration of justice from Wichita State University in 1991 and his master's degree in 1999.

❖ ❖ ❖ ❖   bicycle patrol. It attracted the attention of police departments across the country at that time.[15] Today, however, motorized patrols are commonplace and something the layperson might believe that the police have always used since the invention of the automobile. Motorized patrol is no longer viewed as innovative.

Some scholars attempt to think of the organizational change process in terms of several interconnected stages. For example, Robert Yin likes to view change as a three-stage process.[16] In his case study of organizational change in 19 public agencies (including four police departments), he identified three stages of organizational change. The first is the improvisation stage. During this period one or more innovations are proposed and then adopted. This is the most crucial stage because it is here that the innovation stands to be rejected if it does not fit the expectations of the organization.

The second stage is marked by the expansion of the innovation to other areas within the organization or to other organizations. The extent of expansion usually depends on how successful the innovation is during the first stage. Yin suggests that the expansion stage is closely watched by administrators and employees because it is at this stage that the organization's investment is greater and that it considers making more resources available to the innovation.

For Yin, the final phase of an organizational change is institutionalization. For example, when the four police departments decided to computerize their entire operations, they moved from the expansion to the institutionalization stage. Police departments from Indianapolis, Nashville, Miami, and Boston between late 1976 and early 1977 all adopted the use of computers, which were incorporated into all the major areas of police work. It was at this point that organizational change became part of the routine.

Although all organizational change is a process, it does not always happen in the same way.[17] Some changes can be described as occurring in a linear fashion, where each change sets the stage for a higher-level change, as in the development of the computer industry. It would be difficult for most computer users today even to imagine using a computer with a 286 processing chip despite the fact that we were glad to have that chip less than a decade ago. In contrast, other changes can be understood as occurring cyclically. That is, after a long process of change, an organization returns to its beginning point and starts all over again. For example, many large companies that diversify their product lines by acquiring other smaller companies may in hard economic times return to their original product. Similarly, some police historians have suggested that community policing may represent the desire of American policing to return to its pattern at the beginning of the twentieth century before officers carried guns or wore uniforms.

## Four Models of Change

Based upon their study of more than 200 studies, Andrew Van de Ven and Marshall Poole concluded that there are four models or schools of thought on the way change occurs.[18] Evolutionary change represents the first model or school. Here change is viewed as a slow process that results from a purposeful action. Innovations are selected and implemented when they are believed to make an organization more competitive in the marketplace or serve cus-

❖ ❖ ❖ ❖

tomers better. According to this model, change is not a dramatic but a gradual, cumulative process. Organizations that fail to respond to change in a competitive world might be expected to suffer economic hardship to the point of elimination.

The second model of change is dialectical, an idea that is deeply rooted in German philosophy. According to this view, organizations exist in a complex world of colliding forces or contradictory values that compete with each other for control. Organizational change occurs when competing values inside the organization or contrary forces outside it results in conflict that is resolved through compromise or synthesis. However, although a balance of power between values or between force and organization may result in compromise, there is no guarantee that each conflict will result in a positive synthesis. Sometimes an opposition mobilizes sufficient power to completely change the current practice of an organization, resulting in an organizational change that is drastic and quick.

The third model of change, the life cycle, is based on the growth of plants and animals but has its origins in the field of management science. Organizations may start out weak and small; then, if they survive, they may grow over time into more mature units able to perform at optimal levels. Eventually, like plants and animals, organizations die to complete a cycle.

The final model of change is teleological. This view assumes that an organization has a goal that it is destined to fulfill. Proponents of this view believe that the goal or destiny of an organization is preset and follows a course that is impossible to alter, although constraints from both inside the organization or outside might slow or temporarily interrupt the process of change.

## Seven Indicators of Change

A study of the history of American policing might reveal which model of change best explains organizational change in policing in the United States. Once that model is determined, scholars may be in position to see where policing is headed next.

Most police scholars would agree that tremendous changes have taken place in American policing during the past 160 years. They have occurred at all three levels—individual, group, and the organization itself. To understand these changes better, they can be studied in three corresponding time periods.

George Kelling and Mark Moore have proposed that much of the change witnessed in American policing corresponds to the three eras of policing—the political era, the professional era, and the community era—described in Chapter 2.[19] In order to better understand changes that mark the end of one era and the beginning of another, Kelling and Moore developed seven indicators, categories, or areas of policing that they believe are closely associated with organizational change in law enforcement agencies. Six of the seven indicators they identify are presented below, plus a seventh called the theoretical framework. These seven indicators will be used to illustrate how policing has changed in each era.

❖ ❖ ❖ ❖     **1. Authorization**

There are many sources of authority that "authorize" a law enforcement agency to deliver public services. The usual sources are laws, legislative bills, politics, and tradition. For example, the office of the U.S. Marshal and Deputy Marshal was established by the Judiciary Act of 1789, which also created the U.S. Supreme Court. The U.S. Marshal Service performs a number of functions such as escorting and transporting federal prisoners and protecting the safety of federal judges.[20] Similarly, the expansion of the jurisdiction of the Federal Bureau of Investigation in the 1930s mainly was the result of the economic recession of the time and President Roosevelt's New Deal. In 1934 the 73rd Congress added provisions to the federal criminal code to place bank robbery, kidnapping, and racketeering under federal jurisdiction, where they remain today.[21]

Authority not only provides the legitimacy for the police to exist but also establishes boundaries within which they must operate. Because they have relatively great authority to maintain public safety, they have wide operational boundaries. For example, police scholars have recognized the legal authority of law enforcement agencies to use force or the threat of force to bring people into compliance with criminal codes.[22] In particular, Egon Bittner has argued that the authority to use force is the most distinguishable feature of police departments.[23]

## 2. Function

Like any organization, a police department's function depends upon what the department views as its goals and mission. In turn, functions also shape the methods that the police use to achieve their goals.[24] Herbert Simon has pointed out that an organization usually is multifunctional or has more than one purpose that it is attempting to achieve at any one time.[25] It is important to understand that each function is not necessarily given equal attention. The police, like most organizations, must prioritize their functions as much as possible and try to maintain minimal support for lesser functions.[26] For example, historically American policing has identified three main functions—crime control, order maintenance, and the provision of social services.[27] Most modern police forces, however, view crime control as their main function.

## 3. Theoretical Framework

A larger, theoretical framework helps explain why police departments behave in a certain way at a certain time. For example, Wilson's ideas about police administration are a direct application of Max Weber's sociological explanation for the existence of bureaucracies.[28] American policing has had a bureaucratic style for more than 50 years.[29]

## 4. Organizational Design

The organizational design of a police department includes (1) its structure, (2) its style of management, (3) the way it allocates human resources,

*Organizations must prioritize resources to implement community policing effectively. (Photo: Mark C. Ide)*

and (4) the technology it uses to conduct its business.[30] Its structure will differ from that of a hospital, for example, in many ways. A police department has a rigid hierarchy of who gives orders and who follows them. A hospital is less hierarchical and gives doctors considerable individual authority in making decisions about treating patients. Police officers in the field are closely monitored by a field sergeant; doctors have very little scrutiny from supervisors.

An organization's design attempts to organize resources in such a way as to achieve effectiveness in accomplishing the organization's goals. There is no exception for police departments.[31] Similarly, management issues having to do with planning, leadership, supervision, and rewarding performance reflect the approach that managers take in mobilizing employees to work for a common goal.

## 5. Environment

The environment, or external conditions, within which the police must operate cannot be ignored when the police carry out their duties. The environment influences the goals the department sets, daily operations, and even the technology that the employees use in the field, from weapons (semiautomatic versus single-fire) to motor vehicles (from bicycles to armored assault vehicles). Kelling and Moore suggest that the environment includes technological, economic, social, and political components.[32] The political component tends to be the most influential and complicated, ranging from distinctive styles of the local political culture to court decisions that place legal limits on law enforcement procedures.[33]

❖ ❖ ❖ ❖  ## 6. Operational Strategies

Operational strategies are the methods and procedures the police adopt to achieve specific goals that fit within their larger mission.[34] The strategies are largely determined by the goals. In policing, a wide variety of operational strategies is available to fulfill the functions of crime control, order maintenance, and the provision of social services. For example, "weed and seed" operations to eliminate drug houses involve intensive surveillance and sweeps in an area followed by civil abatement procedures to recapture space used for illegal drug activity and then redevelop it into space for conventional, noncriminal use.

## 7. Outcomes

Outcomes are the results of the department's operations and serve as the yardstick for measuring its effectiveness. Outcomes can be either positive or negative. When positive outcomes are achieved, departments tend to view them as a sign that their operational strategies are working, and such success in turn tends to reflect favorably upon the department's organizational design and even its authority to deliver services. In contrast, negative outcomes may signal the need for rethinking operational strategies, organizational goals, and ultimately, the department's main mission.

The seven indicators mentioned above help explain police departments as they change over time. Comparisons of departments, however, are made even more complex in view of the large number of departments. One recent survey revealed that there are more than 17,000 law enforcement agencies in the United States.[35] Furthermore, they represent an extremely diverse group that includes municipal police departments, county sheriff's departments, and state police departments, even though this book refers to them all as police.

This book looks primarily at organizational change and community policing from the perspective of local police departments since they make up 72.2 percent of the entire law enforcement population. In particular, most historical accounts of organizational change in policing are based upon the experiences of large police departments. In 1993, there were 162 municipal police departments that employed more than 250 police officers (1.3 percent of total number of municipal police departments).[36]

Organizational change in policing is more often noticed when it occurs in the largest police departments. The total number of police officers working in the largest 162 local departments is nearly half (46.9 percent) of the 393,554 sworn employees in the United States. Because large departments are so highly visible, they tend to be viewed as barometers for tracking changes in American policing and predicting future trends for smaller police departments.[37]

# The Political Era

This section will consider the situation during the political era according to each of the seven indicators. In general, the political era began in the second half of the nineteenth century when many cities established full-time police services. A primary feature of this era is that police departments were subject to the influence of local politics. Police officers were selected from the ward so they were closely related to the local politicians at the neighborhood level. At the same time, there was no tenure for a police chief. He served at the pleasure of the mayor. Local politics penetrated every level of police departments.

In a certain sense, this control of local politics reflects an idea that government agencies should be accountable at the local level. Even today, we find evidence of local control because American police departments are highly decentralized. There is no centralized police force in the United States such as we find in most European countries.

There is a consensus that police departments were moving out of the political era at the beginning of the twentieth century when social disorder called for a more professional force.

## 1. Authorization

Many police historians have noted that American police organizations in their early years were controlled primarily by local politicians. This local source of police control differed sharply from the British police experience that was discussed in chapter 2. Fogelson noted that "From the start, most Americans had only vague ideas about what the police should do except it should be local, controlled by municipal government, not like Italian or German police."[38]

Since the birth of this nation, Americans have tended to be suspicious of any form of centralized government at the state or federal level.[39] For example, no states had organized state police forces until the beginning of the twentieth century.

In the United States, law enforcement has always been subject to local control. However, the influence of local control during the political era far exceeded that which existed during the following two eras in several respects. First, local control during the political era affected police employees at every level. At the top, the chief of police typically had to carry out his duties under the tight control of office holders in city government. At the bottom, patrolmen had to answer to politically powerful ward bosses. Because ward bosses could control hiring and firing practices, they typically had more power over the lives of patrol officers than did the chief of police.[40]

A second distinct feature of local control during the political era was that a police officer's career was closely tied to the particular political party that ran the city government. After an opposing political party won a city election, all current police employees were replaced by supporters of the winning party.[41] And finally, a third distinguishing characteristic of police during the political era was that law enforcement was not their top priority. Instead, policing meant emphasis on different functions.

## 2. Function

Urban police during the political era had a wide range of responsibilities, many of which were tied to the provision of services.[42] For example, in New York the police department was responsible for sweeping city streets until the

❖ ❖ ❖ ❖          1870s. Similarly, very few government agencies in the 1900s offered special services such as welfare for the unemployed and orphans. These and other services typically fell to the responsibility of the police. Roger Lane observed that "Newer functions with obvious place elsewhere also gravitated to the police."[43] Annual reports documenting police activity in the twin cities of Minneapolis and St. Paul in 1898 included record keeping on oil lamps that were not lit, defective walks, and meals served to prisoners.[44]

Police work during the political era also included a preoccupation with keeping order. Police devoted considerable time to handling people who were intoxicated in public places, mediating fights among neighbors, and keeping an eye on local children who might bring trouble to other families. As Gary Sykes has argued, the "street justice" used by patrol officers played an important role in maintaining order.[45]

Local police also were charged with enforcing laws against such "vices" as prostitution and gambling. In those days, however, it was a question of how much enforcement they actually did. The function of crime control was thought to be one of the least important because of the low crime rates throughout most of the nineteenth century in American cities. For example, robbery was considered a rare event compared to today's cities.[46]

## 3. Theoretical Framework

A theoretical framework for police departments during the political era can be derived from traditional political theory concerning not only the police but also the broader role of government in American society at the time.[47] The principles of rule by democracy and the natural right of individuals to pursue happiness are the foundation of American political heritage according to Alexis de Tocqueville in 1835. He observed that "The striking characteristic of the social condition of the Anglo-Americans is its essential democracy."[48]

The New England township, as a natural consequence of the sovereignty of the people, was a good example of municipal independence during the political era. It was expected that government should serve the will of the people, particularly at the local level, and decentralization of political power was considered a cornerstone for government during the first 150 years of American history.[49] The goals of police forces created during the second half of the nineteenth century reflected these democratic principles.

Overall, the theoretical framework at that time was not to provide a specific type of organizational design for police forces but instead to serve as a general guide for shaping the role of the police in a democratic society. Even today American police are locally based. Slightly more than half (51.6 percent) of the nation's local police departments employ fewer than 10 officers, and 851 of them have only one officer.[50] With few exceptions, local police departments hire people locally ensuring that local standards of behavior will be known and upheld.

## 4. Organizational Design

Compared to police departments today, police during the political era were highly decentralized. The reason was in part that the British military model had not been fully adopted by most police departments until the late 1800s. Structurally, there were few layers of rank separating patrolmen and the police chief and little division of labor from one police officer to another. Nevertheless, the more powerful, parallel system of control by city government, consisting of elected officials at the top and ward bosses at the bottom, meant that the short chain of police command was not particularly influential.

One feature of decentralization is limited supervision of patrol officers working their beats. Without modern technology, the primary form of communication between patrolmen and police stations was the call box. Requiring patrol officers to call in every hour was the most direct method for keeping track of patrol activities in the field. Call boxes persisted into the 1900s; they remained the sole source of field communications until 1911, when the chief of police in Camden, New Jersey, announced in a speech to the International Association of Chiefs of Police that his department had installed lights on city streets for signaling to patrol officers when they needed to check in with the station.[51]

## 5. Environment

City politics played a central role in police work during the political era. In fact, local police typically were treated as an extension of the party that ran the city government. For example, on January 18, 1895, a report on the New York Police Department released by the Lexow Committee drew the following two conclusions. First, police behavior at public polling places gave the appearance that the police were less oriented toward guarding the public peace than acting as agents of the local ruling party, Tammany Hall, to harass voters sympathetic to the opposition party. Second, rather than doing their best to wipe out gambling and prostitution, police officers routinely licensed vice in return for a share of the illegal proceeds.[52]

The social environment at the time also placed great demands upon police departments. In addition to performing specific functions at election time, police officers were expected to respond to the social needs of the wards, particularly maintaining order in the neighborhood. For example, the recent discovery of a diary written by a Boston patrolman in 1895 presents a vivid account of his daily activities involving neighbors' disputes and fighting among couples.

## 6. Operational Strategies

Foot patrol was the main operational strategy of the police throughout the nineteenth century. Ironically, proponents of community policing have called for the redeployment of foot patrol. Its primary advantage—placing officers in close proximity to the residents of the neighborhood they patrol—makes good sense today just as it did then.

Jonathon Rubinstein has suggested that during the political era, interactions between the police and local residents typically occurred in public places. By the second half of the century riots were taking place with some regularity in most large cities. Until then riot control required no equipment other than a sufficient number of police officers who could be summoned to

❖ ❖ ❖ ❖      the scene.[53] Key changes during this time included the use of the patrol wagon to transport suspects to the station and the introduction of the phone box and the light-signal system. Before the 1860s, as a former chief of police in Baltimore during the 1800s recalled, there was no patrol wagon service.[54] A patrolman who arrested a suspect literally had to drag his prisoner to the station, often requiring the help of bystanders.

## 7. Outcomes

There was no single, systematic measure of the outcome of police performance during the political era. Instead, the police were judged by the quality of service they provided to their neighborhoods as evaluated by ward bosses and by their efforts to maintain order when dealing with riotous crowds as judged by factory owners. Thus, the satisfaction of local residents was an important indicator of officer effectiveness, along with satisfaction of ward bosses and other politically powerful people.[55] It should be noted, however, that measures of outcome were more likely to be approached from an unsystematic and qualitative viewpoint than by any particular systematic, quantitative form of evaluation such as might be used today. The systematic collection of data to measure police efficiency taken for granted today is less than a century old.

In sum, the following are the seven indicators or areas of policing during the political era:

1. Authorization: local municipalities and law.

2. Function: social services and order maintenance.

3. Theoretical framework: grass-roots democracy.

4. Organizational design: decentralized and lacking supervision.

5. Environment: politically and socially motivated.

6. Operational strategies: foot patrol and police stations.

7. Outcomes: lack of systematic measures of police effectiveness.

Generally, by the 1870s full-time police departments had appeared in almost every city in the Northeast, South, and Midwest,[56] marking the end of the initiation phase of organizational change. The expansion phase of the political era was in the end of the nineteenth century, when most cities established their police departments in response to the need to keep peace and order. They shared similar organizational characteristics of decentralization and local political control. Police departments offering 24-hour service were nothing new but a must for municipal areas. The main functions of the police were to provide services and maintain order. Patrol wagons and phone boxes were widely adopted and used in the police agencies. Police officers worked full time and wore identified uniforms. At the turn of the century, the weakness of the political era began to reveal itself. Corruption was a major problem for most municipal police departments. The change to a professional model had begun.

# The Professional Era     ❖ ❖ ❖ ❖

There is some disagreement among police scholars about when the initiation phase of change in the professional era began. Fogelson suggested that the police began to change in the 1890s when a few big-city police departments attempted to narrow their functions and improve the quality of personnel. For example, Theodore Roosevelt made his mark as a reformer when he served as chair of the New York City Police Commission. Roosevelt's achievements in this post later led to his successful bid for President of the United States.

By contrast, Walker has argued that the real signs of change did not occur until the late 1910s when the Progressive Movement to change the political landscape of this country was fully underway.[57] The Progressive Movement involved mostly upper-class and upper-middle-class people who sought large-scale social reform in city politics, the court system, schools, and urban institutions. One particular aim was to destroy the system of machine politics that had controlled the police from the beginning. The Progressive Movement ultimately proved more successful in the Western states, where local political machines were relatively weak. The result was professional police departments in cities governed by the council-manager system.[58]

Professionalizing the police was seen as the key to upgrading the police. An essential element of professionalism, which includes improvement in both personnel and organizational design, is to specialize in, or "monopolize," an area, or "turf," making it difficult for other professions to compete. For example, the medical profession "owns" the right to treat people who have physical ailments. No other profession is eager to challenge medical doctors directly on the privilege of diagnosing or treating illness.

Five signs reveal the extent to which an occupation has become a profession: (1) an awareness of a common mission, (2) a body of theory and knowledge, (3) ethical standards, (4) a formal organization to promote the interests of the group, and (5) a list of recognized persons in the history of the profession who are its significant leaders.[59]

Policing in the professional era, can be examined according to the same seven indicators used to study the political era. All of them show an awareness on the part of reformers that policing needed to transform itself into a profession.

## I. Authorization

Inspired by the Progressive Movement, police during the professional era rejected local politics as the major source of their authorization. Although the police will never be entirely shielded from the influence of local politics, in the professional era that influence was significantly reduced, particularly in daily operations. This reduction was achieved by shifting the primary source of police authorization to law, particularly criminal law, as the justification for the existence and role of the police. In the first quarter of the twentieth century, separation of politics from the daily operation of public-service agencies became a social mandate.[60]

❖ ❖ ❖ ❖        ## 2. Function

With a focus on criminal law as a primary source of legitimacy, the police narrowed their focus to concentrate on crime control and catching criminals.[61] Making crime control their unique mission did not, however, occur overnight. The shift of emphasis from services and order to crime control was a slow process. By some estimates, it took the police about 40 years to complete it, beginning in the 1890s and ending in the 1930s.[62] Many police officers deeply embraced this change, eager to rid themselves of many services that police had traditionally provided.

Most scholars agree that the police had firmly established their reputation as crime fighters at the local level by the late 1930s.[63] No single department on the local level was as successful at achieving this feat as the FBI at the national level. The remarkable success of the FBI in creating an image of its field employees as professional crime fighters is largely attributable to the young director at the time, J. Edgar Hoover. By publicly recognizing and then hunting down a few notorious criminals in the 1930s, Hoover caused the public to see G-men as relentless heroes in the pursuit of dangerous "public enemies."

The highly publicized and heroic efforts of these trained FBI agents to track down and catch known criminals made the agents a popular ideal among local police, an ideal to which they still subscribe. Bittner points out that the police's means of crime control support them in this professional mission. He observed that by the late 1960s there was wide recognition that the police, and the police alone, have the exclusive right to use deadly force to enforce criminal laws.[64] The legitimate use of force is an important aspect of the "turf" that the police have claimed a monopoly on during the professional era and still hold today, although constitutional constraints and department policies place necessary limits on when, what kind, and how much force can be applied in circumstances that arise.

## 3. Theoretical Framework

Two primary theoretical perspectives have influenced organizational change in policing during the professional era. The first was the Progressive Movement (as noted earlier), which marked the beginning of change in police departments by seeking to end the influence of local political patronage on the police and other public-service organizations. In a well-known essay on public administration in 1887, Woodrow Wilson, who later became President of the United States, made it clear that "The field of administration is a field of business. It is removed from the hurry and strife of politics. . . ."[65] In place of patronage the Progressive Movement strongly supported a merit system in the public sector to ensure that the most qualified people who applied for government jobs were hired rather than choosing candidates based on their loyalty to a particular political party. An important contribution of the Progressive Movement was that it made a clear distinction between politics and administration, or management. For policing, it meant that the daily operation of a police department had to be recognized as a managerial issue, which should not be subverted or controlled by local politics.

A second theoretical development that produced lasting effects on policing during the professional era came from educators who studied how organizations operated. Inspired by Max Weber's organizational theory about bureaucracy and Frederick Taylor's scientific management, police departments, like other organizations during the 1930s, began to reexamine how they were organized.

Weber, a German sociologist, was interested in the development of a highly rational form of organization, which, he believed, was bureaucratic. He suggested that a bureaucracy had such positive features as a hierarchical structure with a clear delineation of authority at each level, a division of labor in specialized areas, and impersonal rules and regulations to control the behavior of employees.[66] Implicit in Weber's theory was that a formal bureaucracy controls employees in order to produce uniformity and efficiency. A central aim of bureaucracy is to promote predictability by ridding the organization of human factors that might negatively influence the daily operation of an organization.

*August Vollmer.*

During the 1930s, Luther Gulick's work on the managerial function in the delivery of public services gained recognition. The managerial function according to Gulick was made up of seven crucial components: planning, organizing, staffing, directing, coordinating, reporting, and budgeting (**POSDCORB**).[67] Gulick considered efficiency the most obvious sign of organizational performance.

Specific organizations began taking note of the body of knowledge about organizations in general. One professional organization, the International Association of Chiefs of Police (IACP), founded in the late 1890s, sought to provide a forum for police chiefs to exchange information about ways to improve policing. Prompted by progressive leaders such as Berkeley Chief of Police August Vollmer, policing in the United States developed an appetite for transforming itself from a political to a professional form of organization. O. W. Wilson's book *Police Administration* (1950), strongly influenced by Weber's principles of bureaucracy, underscored efficiency as a primary organizational goal that professional police departments should pursue. The book signalled the arrival of the professional era and was widely adopted as the authoritative manual for police administrators through the 1950s.[68]

## 4. Organizational Design

Centralization and the professional development of personnel were central themes of change during the professional era. Centralization means the development of a top-down chain of command. The department recognizes that its most qualified personnel are those highest in rank, at the top of the chain, and therefore in the best position to make decisions, set policies, and make rules. Professional development requires division of labor within a department. As a department becomes more complex, employees working in different areas are assigned specific responsibilities and given the necessary authority to carry out job-related tasks.

Civil service reform, which made government jobs dependent on the merit system rather than political patronage, greatly affected policing during the professional era. The merit system, created by the Pendleton Act in 1883, applied originally only to federal employees. The Progressive Movement, as

❖ ❖ ❖ ❖    noted, succeeded in extending it to government employees at the local level during the first three decades of the twentieth century. The merit system granted tenure to employees at all levels of a police department, from the chief of police to the officer on patrol. Officers were assured that if they adequately performed their jobs for a probationary period, they did not have to worry about losing them as a result of shifts in local politics or the whims of a disgruntled superior. As a further protection from political interference, many cities created public-safety commissions to reduce the direct involvement of the city's top administrator in the daily operation of municipal employees such as the police.

The merit system also affected the hiring and training of new police officers. Now people were hired on the basis of what they could do rather than whom they might know. Qualifications such as physical fitness, psychological conditions, and educational attainment became important criteria in hiring police officers. Also, training in criminal law and the daily skills used in police work was developed for new recruits. Civil service, organizational centralization, and professional development conformed to the formal bureaucratic design proposed by Max Weber. The new professional model of policing brought with it expectations for efficiency and rationality that had never before existed in U.S. police work.[69]

## 5. Environment

Police emphasis on crime control rather than order and service meant they had less informal contact with the public. Since the police were no longer responsible for running soup kitchens, finding jobs for new immigrants, or constantly being seen in the neighborhood, police-citizen interactions mainly resulted from calls to the police made by local residents who had problems they could not solve by themselves.[70] The reduced role of the police in society meant that the police became less public servants and more formal agents of social control. They became primarily devoted to law enforcement and the public was relegated to the role of either victim, witness, or criminal.

## 6. Operational Strategies

Two operational strategies that gained importance during the professional era were preventive patrol and criminal investigation. Professional police departments tend to view these strategies as two pillars supporting crime control as the most crucial function of the police.[71] Typically, about 85 percent of a department's officers are assigned to work in these two areas.

Professional police departments rely on two assumptions to justify their heavy emphasis on preventive patrol. First, patrolling is thought to provide an efficient response to calls for police services. Officers assigned to drive around specific city streets at random are free to respond quickly to emergency calls, thus increasing their chances of apprehending criminal suspects. Second, patrolling is believed to deter crime because potential criminals are likely to think twice before committing a crime if they know that patrol officers may happen by at any time.[72]

A number of technological developments since the 1930s have improved the ability of patrol officers to communicate with centrally located police dispatchers and consequently have improved the efficiency of the police to respond to calls for service. One was the introduction of two-way radio, which improved communication both vertically and horizontally. That is, two-way radio made it possible for patrol officers to remain in the field while speaking with superiors at police headquarters. At the same time, two-way radios also allowed patrol officers to talk with other officers in the field. It was the first time that both patrol coverage and managerial supervision were able to increase together. Later, quick appearance on the crime scene became a primary focus of patrol work.

Another technological innovation aimed at patrol and improvement in communication was the use of the telephone number 911. The 911 system was installed in many cities during the 1950s and 1960s in order to enable citizens to reach the police more quickly during emergencies and also to shorten the time between priority calls and an emergency police response. Since police administrators saw preventive patrol as the "backbone" of police operations, they welcomed such improvements in the efficiency of patrol.

Besides patrol, police departments also sought to improve the efficiency of criminal investigation. Detective units were created in many cities at the start of the twentieth century. Since that time, detectives have developed a public image as the major weapon in a police department's arsenal to control crime. Detectives have become known as experts in solving serious criminal cases; like their FBI counterparts, they use scientific methods and hard work to discover the identities of criminal offenders. Police departments did little to dispel the myth that detective work was very efficient for catching criminals. In fact, criminal investigation is generally boring and moreover is highly unproductive.[73]

## 7. Outcomes

An accurate measure of crime control is an essential feature of policing in the professional era. Recorded levels of crime are at the center of measuring the outcomes of police performance. At the beginning of the twentieth century several police departments in large cities began to collect crime data. In the 1930s, the FBI began to take the responsibility for compiling crime data from local police. Police departments across the nation were (and still are) asked to send crime statistics to the state police and FBI for tabulation. The annual publication of the *Uniform Crime Report* (*UCR*) provides information on the eight most serious types of crimes (Part I offenses), namely murder, rape, robbery, aggravated assault, burglary, larceny theft, motor vehicle theft, and arson. Part II offenses are less serious. These data underscore the concept of police efficiency that was emphasized during the professional era. Increases and decreases in local crime rates were thought to indicate how well the police were doing in a specific area to control crime. Furthermore, since the *UCR* data can be broken down into eight different categories, local departments could draw conclusions about which types of crime needed better control measures and which ones were being efficiently policed.

When the FBI began to collect *UCR* data, only a small number of police departments originally agreed to submit information on local crime. Today, more than 16,000 city, county, and state police departments (95 percent of all eligible agencies) regularly report local crime incidents to the FBI. These data

❖ ❖ ❖ ❖    are still considered one of the most important indicators of crime levels in this country. In addition to *UCR* statistics, a department's clearance rate (the number of crimes reported to the police that are "cleared" by an arrest) is a second important measure of police efficiency at the departmental level. Similarly, the productivity of individual officers can be assessed based on the traffic citations issued and the number of arrests they make within a given period of time.

In sum, the following are seven indicators of change in policing during the professional era:

1. Authorization: criminal law and local government.

2. Function: crime control, order maintenance, and services.

3. Theoretical framework: the Progressive Movement and Weberian bureaucracy.

4. Organizational design: centralized and hierarchical in structure.

5. Environment: limited formal interaction with the public; formal control.

6. Operational strategies: preventive patrolling and criminal investigation.

7. Outcomes: crime rates as a central measure of efficiency.

As a result of organizational change, policing in the professional era was distinguished from policing in the political era in several respects. First, police in the professional era specialized in crime control and had a monopoly on the use of deadly force. Second, they relied on the merit system to select officers. Third, they recorded crime statistics as a way to measure the efficiency of local police. Fourth, reliance on a bureaucratic organizational design, preventive patrol, and criminal investigation gave police confidence in their ability to control crime.

These organizational changes in policing evolved slowly. Although they began at the start of the century with the agenda proposed by the Progressive Movement, the police were not fully professionalized until the publication of O. W. Wilson's book, *Police Administration*. By this time, the change process could be observed at all three levels of a police department. At the individual level, police officers were professionals who specialized in law enforcement. At the group level, improvement in communication technology made policing more dynamic. At the organizational level, bureaucratic structure made policing more efficient.

## The Mission Matters Project

### Ben A. Menke

On April 20, 1999, Captain Bob Armstrong, the duty commander at the Arapahoe County Sheriff's Office (ACSO), left a staff meeting at 11:30 A.M. On entering his car he heard the radio traffic requesting that all available officers in the Denver metro area respond to reports of gunfire and explosions at Columbine High School. Cap- ☞

☞ tain Armstrong, a Columbine parent, drove the three miles to the school and arrived with the first wave of officers from the Jefferson County Sheriff's Office. So began law enforcement's massive response to the terrible tragedy at Columbine High School.

These events, the victims, the effects on lives forever changed, the motivations of those responsible, and the massive mutual aid response by public-safety and other agencies have been well publicized. Less well known, however, are the numerous efforts made prior to this tragedy by these public-safety agencies to engage the community in proactive problem solving efforts and partnerships such as the ACSO's Mission Matters Project.

The ACSO, headquartered in Littleton, Colorado, is responsible for an area of 864 square miles. The ACSO's 560 employees manage a jail with an average inmate count of 800 and engage in a variety of cooperative activities within the community. In 1998, as the first step in the Mission Matters Project, Arapahoe County Sheriff Patrick J. Sullivan Jr. and Undersheriff Grayson Robinson arranged for the Colorado Regional Community Policing Institute to deliver a two-day course on middle management and organizational change to all supervisors and managers at ACSO. Subsequently, ACSO contracted with me to deliver a variety of short courses on strategic planning, organizational and community assessments and development, evaluation, and related training.

The project had three goals: the creation of an employee-driven strategic plan, the enhancement of quality through participation, and the further development of a community-driven public-safety model. The project was based on three principles: (1) involvement—from all levels of the ACSO as well as community members in planning, problem identification, and proposing and implementing solutions; (2) capacity building—developing new skills, directions, and behaviors for the future; and (3) follow through—"walking the talk" and evaluating the change process and outcomes.

As part of the change process, an organizational assessment was conducted. On mandatory training days 454 employees were asked to complete a voluntary and anonymous survey. Ninety-nine percent of the questionnaires were returned. With the help of trained ACSO employees as facilitators, a number of focus-group interviews were completed. In addition, a community-wide survey was mailed to 1,300 citizens.

The data showed that the employees are committed to the ACSO and the community, see their work as modestly enriched, are satisfied with most aspects of their jobs, take personal pride in their work, perceive departmental goals as reasonably clear cut, and perceive the ACSO as highly centralized yet very innovative. The employees also revealed some areas where improvement was needed. They noted some unevenness in supervisory practices, the need for more teamwork, an unevenness in knowledge of community-oriented policing (COP) or problem oriented principles (POP), dissatisfaction with a number of personnel practices, and general agreement about a number of obstacles in the workplace.

In the initial phases of the Mission Matters Project there was significant skepticism among employees about whether or not there would be any tangible outcomes or organizational change. Although it is too early to point to hard data to argue the success or failure of this project the ongoing enthusiasm of employees and the initiatives that have emerged promise positive outcomes for the future. We attribute the successes to date to the following factors:

## 1. Send a Message From the Top

- At the initial training (the course on management and change), held off-site and announced by formal invitations mailed to all supervisors and managers (sworn and nonsworn), both the sheriff and the undersheriff made forceful presentations about community policing, new initiatives, and the importance of training.

- The undersheriff got involved as a regular, participating team member. He has used his position only to reinforce the ACSO's values and to provide direction about format and ideas for the group to consider. ☞

❖ ❖ ❖ ❖     ☞

## 2. Make Participation Special, Powerful, Action-Oriented

- Membership in the strategic planning committee, open to all employees, was based on an application submitted to the undersheriff.

- Selection criteria included past performance but, most important, a demonstrated ability to be both solution and team oriented. A number of applications were rejected. The undersheriff met personally with each rejected applicant to explain the decision.

## 3. Response Time Matters—Create Momentum

- The success of the project depended on a rapid response to identified problems.

- Rapid response demonstrated that issues raised by the employees, the community, or members of the strategic planning committee were taken seriously.

- The ACSO acknowledged input by placing these issues on the agenda and communicating that agenda as widely as possible, thus giving employees immediate concrete evidence that someone was listening.

## 4. 'Walk the Talk'

While this phrase has been overused, it describes clearly the emerging style of the ACSO. For example:

- When the research data (both survey and focus group) showed that civilian employees believed they were not a respected part of the ACSO organization, the undersheriff and Kat Skrien, senior secretary of Administrative Services, immediately organized meetings with a civilian team to search for solutions and scheduled regular monthly meetings with them where they were located (the undersheriff did the driving). Civilians were immediately included in the community-oriented police training program. Arrangements were made for civilians to be exposed to the activities of other parts of the ACSO. Plans were made for a civilian panel to present material and issues during training of sworn officers.

- The assessment data showed that participatory and team-building supervisory skills were unevenly distributed across the ACSO. Lt. Joe Ferro, director of the training division, immediately revised and standardized the four-day promotional academy for sergeants and lieutenants, emphasizing these skills.

- When the preliminary analysis of the citizens' survey showed that the residents of the most rural part of Arapahoe County felt that they were out of touch (they reported not knowing the officers in their district anymore), Lieutenant Vern Werner of the Community Oriented Policing Subcommittee of the Strategic Planning Team, immediately began to spend the better part of his time, along with the deputies in the district, stopping at service stations and knocking on doors, reacquainting themselves with the citizens.

- The assessment data showed that dispatchers believed that there was a communication problem with the deputies who serve most rural areas. Deputy Larry La Flam immediately extended the urban ride-along program for dispatchers to include most rural areas. This program serves to acquaint them with the geography of Arapahoe County and opens dialogue between dispatchers and rural deputies.

## 5. Employee Empowerment

- People matter! Simply put, ACSO's leaders have demonstrated a commitment to creating an environment where people (both employees and citizens) are thought bright enough, are taken seriously, and are trusted enough to be part of teams that identify issues, propose solutions, and take action. This commitment is not just consultative but is characterized by its depth, range, and breadth. It pays dividends for ACSO and the community.     ☞

☞ | The Columbine High School massacre has intensified the ongoing efforts of police departments such as the Arapahoe County Sheriff's Office to create more effective organizations and to engage in proactive problem-solving partnerships with the community. Has the ACSO reached its goals? In part. Is the ACSO the "perfect" organization? No, but it is devoting time and effort toward continuous improvement by focusing on involvement, quality, and community engagement. Is this process without critics? No. In the attempt to embrace the critics by offering them a role as active problem solvers, a maxim seems to have emerged in the department's culture, "Dogs bark but the parade goes on."

Ben A. Menke is a community policing consultant living in Littleton, Colorado. He is a former professor of criminal justice and a past president of the Academy of Criminal Justice Sciences. He also founded one of the nation's first community policing institutes, the Washington State Institute for Community Oriented Policing. Menke occasionally teaches at the University of Massachusetts, Boston and Colorado State University, Colorado Springs.

# The Community Era

The community era marks the most recent organizational change in policing.[74] As for changes during the professional era, most conclusions drawn from the community era are based on observations of a few large police departments that have taken the lead in the initiation phase of change. Again as in the professional era, external influences have played an important role in this latest round of change. Finally, as in the professional era, changes in the community era are a significant departure from the preceding style of policing.

Generally, the late 1960s to the mid-1980s saw the decline of the professional era. Civil unrest and rioting during the 1960s posed challenges that the police appeared to be ill-equipped to deal with and prompted a few thoughtful scholars and administrators to question the fundamental role of policing in American society. For example, A. C. Germann published an article in 1969 questioning the effectiveness of a bureaucratic design for the delivery of police services.[75] In 1977, Herman Goldstein published a book in which he tried to redefine the role of police in a democratic society.[76] By the mid-1980s, a few police departments led by reform-minded chiefs had begun to implement a number of community policing programs, marking the beginning of the community era.

## I. Authorization

The local community becomes an important source for problem identification, resources, and evaluating police services during the community era.[77] No longer are the police the sole experts on crime. Instead, they actively seek community input to help determine how to allocate scarce resources. Although criminal law still is seen as an important source of authority for policing, people realize that not all laws can be fully enforced. The community becomes an important ally for the police in deciding what issues should receive the greatest police attention. In other words, a police-public partnership is developed that helps define a focus for scarce police services and also helps to increase the resources available by calling on volunteers and sharing and processing information more effectively.[78]

❖ ❖ ❖ ❖          ## 2. Function

The priorities of police functions are rearranged in the community era. Dealing with social disorder becomes a top priority because it is believed that social disorder and community disorganization lead to crime. Similarly, the service function takes on greater importance. Finally, crime control is de-emphasized compared to its importance during the professional era. Although police departments continue to patrol, take reports, answer calls, and investigate crimes, proactive policing that focuses on preventing crimes before they occur takes on greater significance than before. Furthermore, coactive policing appears, that is, the formation of police-citizen partnerships aimed at solving crime and related community problems.

Some scholars argue that this reprioritizing of police functions makes the police of the community era similar to their predecessors in the political era.[79] Others disagree. In either view, it seems reasonable to conclude that policing during the community era sets a high priority on both containing social disorder and providing service.

## 3. Theoretical Framework

Two broad perspectives have played important roles in the development of a theoretical framework for understanding organizational change in policing since the late 1960s. The first is the idea of coproduction of order, which was developed by scholars from the disciplines of public administration and political science. Jeffrey Brudney offers the following definition of coproduction of order:

> Coproduction can be understood as the cooperative relationship between government, on the one hand, and citizens, neighborhood associations, community organizations, or client groups, on the other, for the delivery of public services.[80]

Central to the coproduction of order is an understanding of the limited capability of government agencies to deliver public services. Effective public services require the help of citizens. Coproducing order by citizens and government provides mutual benefits for government agencies and the local community, as a rich body of knowledge accumulated over the last 20 years in public administration has shown.[81] The police in particular are one of the most important service providers in the public sector. Therefore, the concept of coproduction of order is at the heart of this latest change in police organization, namely redefining the role of police in a democratic society.

The second perspective is the behavioral school which focuses on the role of employees in an organization. These behavioral theories include (1) the importance of the informal work group at a workplace as described by Chester Barnard,[82] (2) the needs theory proposed by Abraham Maslow,[83] (3) theory X and theory Y outlined by Douglas McGregor,[84] and (4) the job enrichment theory developed by J. Richard Hackman and Greg Oldham.[85] Each of these theories emphasizes the importance of employees either acting as individuals or in a group to influence organizational change.

Weber's bureaucratic model, prominent during the professional era, assumed that individual employees should be controlled. Therefore, impersonal rules such as departmental structure and control mechanisms are

needed to keep them. From this point of view, group working processes were          ❖ ❖ ❖ ❖
not considered a very fruitful area for research.

The behavioral perspective emphasizes that individual employees are the primary contributors to organizational success.[86] Individuals like to contribute when they are properly motivated. A primary means of motivating them is to redesign the work environment to give them more freedom in creative or problem-solving activities. Too much control will destroy their motivation.

In particular, several decades of articles in scientific journals on the police subculture, the misuse of discretion, and officer stress confirm that Weber's bureaucratic model was dominant during the professional era. More recent articles that emphasize the importance of individual employees in achieving organizational goals fit nicely with articles on the coproduction of order because both perspectives place employees at the forefront of public service and both encourage public employees to work with local residents.

## 4. Organizational Design

An important feature of police departments in the community era is decentralized decision making. Rank-and-file officers are empowered to work with local residents in order to more effectively address local needs.[87] Similarly, communication with a cross section of local residents is essential to collect information about the community and create a participative, employee-oriented department.

## 5. Environment

Police departments in the community era are expected to listen and respond to the citizens who make up the local environment. More impor-

*Police executives must seek out and solicit responses from residents representing different groups who make up the community. (Photo: Mark C. Ide)*

❖ ❖ ❖ ❖     tantly, interactions between police and the community they serve must be frequent and consistent. More than just reading newspapers and keeping abreast of local news, police executives must go to extra lengths to ensure that the flow of information about community needs is constant and representative. One way to do this is to seek out residents who can represent the various social, ethnic, and economic groups who make up the community, especially groups who may feel that they have been left out of making decisions about criminal justice in the past.

## 6. Operational Strategies

Police departments that can mobilize the local community in a positive way are especially valued in the community era. Such department initiatives can occur at three stages—identifying the problem, developing an appropriate response, and carrying out some strategy or program to effect change. Although some police might use a departmentwide approach that places all sworn personnel in closer proximity to local residents and thus ensures citizen input about community problems, the most common form of community mobilization is community policing programs. Such programs often rely on citizen volunteers to staff storefronts, to patrol neighborhoods as neighborhood watches, to make phone calls, or to help with other tasks of benefit to the community.

## 7. Outcomes

There is no single measure by which police in the community era judge police performance. In fact, efficiency is less of a concern than effectiveness. Effectiveness is making a difference in some problem or quality of life issues. The central attention of effectiveness in police departments is given to make a change in a community life, which has more profound influence on local residents.

Police effectiveness can be measured in a variety of ways depending on what outcomes police want. Since one significant organizational change is a shift toward emphasis on the contribution that employees might make, the level of satisfaction among police officers is one important measure of effectiveness. Similarly, levels of social disorder in a neighborhood or the level of satisfaction among residents concerning their fear about crime are other important measures of outcome. (Measures of effectiveness in the community era are discussed in some detail in chapter 11.)

In sum, the following are seven indicators of change in policing during the community era:

1. Authorization: community, criminal law, and local politics.

2. Function: reducing social disorder, providing services, and controlling crime.

3. Theoretical framework: coproduction of order and behavioral perspectives.

4. Organizational design: decentralized and employee oriented.

5. Environment: close and continual interaction between police and citizens.

6. Operational strategies: programs that promote close interactions between police and community.

7. Outcomes: satisfaction of police and citizens and a low level of social disorder.

## Conclusion

From this survey of three eras of American policing, several important characteristics of organizational change can be observed. The first observation is the length of the change process. It took several decades to complete the change from the political to the professional era (the change to the community era by this timetable is probably in the latter part of the initiation stage). For example, during the professional era, the initiation stage of change occurred between the 1890s and the 1920s, when many large police departments began organizational change. From the 1930s to the 1940s, the change process gained full momentum with the implementation of many innovations in police departments across the country. The final phase occurred during the 1950s when motorized patrol and two-way radios became the standard for police operations. Today, few police administrators would even consider these practices innovative.

A second observation concerns the pace of change in American policing. For the most part, the changes are evolutionary. Change in policing has been slow, but each element has moved the police toward a new form of organization, especially in the shift from the political era to the professional era. The other three types of organizational change discussed earlier—life cycle, dialectic, and teleological—do not fit the development of American policing. Few police departments have begun and then finished their life cycle by closing their doors.

A third observation is that the changes in American policing have been fairly extensive, affecting all three levels of a department. At the individual level, professionalism and the civil service system in the professional era sought to improve both the quality and ability of police officers. At the group level, the managerial philosophy (based on Weber's model of bureaucracy emphasizing a hierarchical chain of command) brought about changes in the communication and interaction patterns among police employees and played a significant role in how groups within the department interact. At the organizational level, the shift in function from providing service to crime control during the professional era has had far-reaching consequences for the daily operations of the police. Another round of fundamental changes for policing at these three levels has begun during the community era.

A final observation is that the three eras outlined above depict typical police departments. In reality, organizational change in policing varies by regions, sizes, time, and extent. For example, the early development of police departments was heavily concentrated in the Northeast and the Midwest. New York, Boston, Philadelphia, and Cincinnati were the first few cities to establish police departments. In the professional era, a few police departments in the West took the lead in reform, notably the Berkeley Police Depart-

❖ ❖ ❖ ❖      ment. Furthermore, change usually takes place in large police departments and then spreads to smaller ones, and urban police departments are more active in changing their ways than their rural counterparts.

## Study Questions

1. What are the three eras in the history of American policing?

2. Discuss the seven major indicators as they relate to each of the eras of American policing.

3. What organizational changes took place during the professional era?

## Endnotes

1. Albert Reiss, "Police Organizations in the Twentieth Century," in *Criminal Justice: A Review of Research*, vol. 15, eds. Michael Tonry and Norval Morris (Chicago: University of Chicago Press, 1992), pp. 51–97; Erick Monkkonen, "History of Urban Police," in *Criminal Justice: A Review of Research*, vol.15, eds. Michael Tonry and Norval Morris (Chicago: University of Chicago Press, 1992), pp. 547–580.

2. Peter Manning, "Information Technologies and the Police," in *Criminal Justice: A Review of Research*, vol. 15, eds. Michael Tonry and Norval Morris (Chicago: University of Chicago Press, 1992), pp. 349–398.

3. Brian Reaves and Pheny Smith, *Law Enforcement Management and Administrative Statistics, 1993: Data for Individual State and Local Agencies with 100 or More Officers* (Washington, DC: U.S. Department of Statistics, 1995).

4. Roger Lane, *Policing the City: Boston, 1822–1885* (Cambridge, MA: Harvard University Press, 1977).

5. Egon Bittner, *The Functions of Police in Modern Society* (Washington, DC: National Institute of Mental Health, 1970); Carl Kockars, "The Rhetoric of Community Policing," in *Community Policing: Rhetoric or Reality?* eds. Jack Greene and Stephen Mastrofski (New York: Praeger, 1988), pp. 239–258.

6. George Kelling and Mark Moore, "From Political to Reform to Community: The Evolving Strategy of Police," in *Community Policing: Rhetoric or Reality?* eds. Jack Greene and Stephen Mastrofski (New York: Praeger, 1988), pp. 1–26; John Eck and Dennis Rosenbaum, "The New Police Order: Effectiveness, Equity, and Efficiency in Community Policing," in *The Challenges of Community Policing: Testing Promises*, ed. Dennis Rosenbaum (Thousand Oaks, CA: Sage, 1994), pp. 3–23.

7. Paul Goodman and Lance Kurke, "Studies of Change in Organizations: A Status Report," in *Change in Organizations: New Perspectives on Theory, Research, and Practice*, eds. Paul Goodman and associates (San Francisco: Jossey-Bass, 1982), pp. 1–46.

8. Chris Argyris, "Some Limits of Rational Man Organization Theory," *Public Administration Review* 33(1973): 253–267; Lawrence James and Allan Jones, "Organizational Structure: A Review of Structural Dimensions and Their Conceptual Relationships With Individual Attitudes and Behaviors," *Organizational Behavior and Human Performance* 16 (1976): 74–113.

9. Fariborz Damanpour, "Organizational Innovation: A Meta-Analysis of Effects of Determinants and Moderators," *Academy of Management Journal* 34 (1991): 555–590.

10. Robert Yin, *Changing Urban Bureaucracies* (Lexington, MA: Lexington Books, 1979); Damanpour, "Organizational Innovation."

11. Many scholars of community policing argue that the recent change in policing is represented by a reprioritizing of major functions of police departments. For a discussion of this topic, see John Angell, "Toward an Alternative to the Classic Policing Organizational Arrangement: A Democratic Model," *Criminology* 8(1971): 185–206; Herman Goldstein, *Problem-Oriented Policing* (New York: McGraw Hill, 1990).

12. In this regard, community policing represents the most organizational change in American policing because it is assumed to reprioritize the functions of police departments across the country. Currently, community policing certainly represents the trend to reform among law enforcement agencies.

13. Goodman and Kurke, "Studies of Change in Organizations."

14. *Ibid.*

15. Donald E. MacNamara, "August Vollmer: The Vision of Police Professionalism," in *Pioneers in Policing*, ed. Phillip J. Stead (Montclair, NJ: Patterson Smith, 1977), pp. 207–223.

16. Yin, *Changing Urban Bureaucracies*, pp. 73–161.

17. For example, organizational change includes strategic planning and goal setting research in which the goal of an organization is strategically set; a change that occurs in the organization is in a linear fashion. See Balaji Chakravarthy and Peter Lorange, *Managing the Strategy Process* (Englewood, NJ: Prentice Hall, 1991). Similarly, the natural selection theory also holds the view that organizational change is a slow process of evolution moving forward. See Michael Hannan and John Freeman, "The Population Ecology of Organizations," *American Journal of Sociology* 82 (1977): 929–964.

18. Andrew Van de Ven and Marshall Poole, "Explaining Development and Change in Organizations," *Academy of Management Review* (1995): 510–540.

19. Kelling and Moore, "From Political to Reform to Community," in *Community Policing: Rhetoric or Reality?* eds. Jack Greene and Stephen Mastrofski (New York: Praeger, 1988), pp. 1–26.

20. *Ibid.*, p. 4.

21. Tony Poveda, *Lawlessness and Reform: The FBI in Transition* (Pacific Grove, CA: Brooks/Cole, 1990), pp. 18–20.

22. Herman Goldstein, *Policing a Free Society* (Cambridge, MA: Ballinger, 1977).

23. Bittner, *Functions of Police*.

24. James Thompson, *Organization in Action* (New York: McGraw-Hill, 1967).

25. Herbert Simon, "On the Concept of Organizational Goal," *Administrative Science Quarterly* 9 (1964): 1–22.

26. Jihong Zhao and Quint Thurman, "Community Policing: Where Are We Now?" *Crime and Delinquency* 43 (1997): 345–357.

27. *Ibid.*

28. There are several different names to describe police during that period including the bureaucratic model, which tends to focus on the organizational design of policing and the professional model, which emphasizes the impact of professionalism and the civil service system on police departments. Relevant literature is listed as follows. Samuel Walker, *A Critical History of Police Reform* (Lexington, MA: D.C. Health, 1977); Robert Fogelson, *Big-City Police* (Cambridge, MA: Harvard University Press, 1977).

29. Reiss, "Police Organization in the Twentieth Century,"

30. Kelling and Moore, "From Political to Reform to Community."

31. Orlando W. Wilson, *Police Administration* (New York: McGraw-Hill, 1950).

32. Kelling and Moore, "From Political to Reform to Community."

33. For a discussion on the influence of local political culture on police departments, please see James Q. Wilson, *Varieties of Police Behavior: The Management of Law and Order in Eight Communities* (Cambridge, MA: Harvard University Press, 1968).

34. *Ibid.*

❖ ❖ ❖ ❖

❖ ❖ ❖ ❖

35. Please see U.S. Department of Justice, "LEMAS Reports—1993" in *Critical Issues in Policing: Contemporary Readings*, 3rd. ed., eds. Roger Dunham and Geoffrey Alpert (Prospect Heights, IL: Waveland, 1996), pp. 36–73.

36. *Ibid.*, pp. 38–39.

37. Several studies on community policing might help to make a point concerning the early programs implemented in large police departments. Michael Farrell, "The Development of the Community Patrol Officer Program: Community-Oriented Policing in the New York City Police Department," in *Community Policing: Rhetoric or Reality?*, eds. Jack Greene and Stephen Mastrofski (New York: Praeger, 1988), pp. 73–88; David Weisburd and Jerome McElroy, "Enacting the CPO Role: Findings from the New York City Pilot Program in Community Policing," in *Community Policing: Rhetoric or Reality?* eds. Jack Greene and Stephen Mastrofski (New York: Praeger, 1988), pp. 89–101; Mary Ann Wycoff, "The Benefits of Community Policing: Evidence and Conjecture," in *Community Policing: Rhetoric or Reality?*, eds. Jack Greene and Stephen Mastrofski (New York: Praeger, 1988), pp. 103–120.

38. Robert Fogelson, *Big-City Police* (Cambridge, MA: Harvard University Press, 1977), p. 6.

39. *Ibid.*

40. The authors made this distinction concerning two levels of parallel control of police at both chief and rank-and-file level during the political era of policing.

41. Fogelson, *Big-City Police*.

42. Erick Monkkonen, "History of Urban Police," in *Criminal Justice: A Review of Research*, vol. 15, eds. Michael Tonry and Norval Morris (Chicago: University of Chicago Press, 1992), pp. 547–580.

43. Roger Lane, "Urban Police and Crime in Nineteenth-Century America," in *Modern Policing*, ed. Michael Tonry and Norval Morris (Chicago: University of Chicago Press, 1992), pp. 1–50.

44. Alex Muller and Frank Head, "History of the Police and Fire Departments of the Twin Cities," American Land and Title Register Association cited in Donald Dilworth, *The Blue and the Brass: American Policing—1890–1910* (Gaithersburg, MD: International Association of Chiefs of Police, 1976), pp. 497–46.

45. Gary Sykes, "Street Justice: A Moral Defense of Order Maintenance Policing," *Justice Quarterly* 3 (1986): 497–512.

46. Monkkonen, "History of Urban Police."

47. Ralph Gabriel, *The Course of American Democratic Thought* (New York: Ronald Press, 1956).

48. Alexis de Tocqueville, *Democracy in America* (Cambridge, MA: Sever and Francis, 1864).

49. *Ibid.*, p. 81.

50. Please see Table 2 on page 39 from U.S. Department of Justice, "LEMAS Reports 1993."

51. The speech was made by Chief Gravenor, Camden, NJ, at the International Association of Chiefs of Police—18th annual convention, June 13–17, 1911 cited in Donald Dilworth, *The Blue and The Brass: American Policing 1890–1910* (Gaithersburg, MD: International Association of Chiefs of Police, 1976), pp. 162–165.

52. Fogelson, *Big-City Police*.

53. Jonathon Rubinstein, *City Police* (New York: Farrar, Straus and Giroux, 1973).

54. Fogelson, *Big-City Police*.

55. *Ibid.*

56. *Ibid.*

57. Walker, *Critical History*.

58. James Q. Wilson, *Varieties of Police Behavior: The Management of Law and Order in Eight Communities* (Cambridge, MA: Harvard University Press, 1968).

59. Darrel Pugh, "Professionalism in Public Administration: Problems, Perspectives, and the Role of ASPA," *Public Administration Review* 49 (1989): 1–8.

60. Fogelson, *Big-City Police*.

61. Kelling and Moore, "From Political to Reform to Community."

62. Most scholars of police history have a discussion concerning the change of police function during this time. See Walker, *Critical History*; Fogelson, *Big-City Police*; Rubinstein, *City Police*.

63. *National Commission on Law Observance and Enforcement: The Police*, No. 14 (Washington, DC: U.S. Government Printing Office, 1931).

64. Bittner, *Functions of Police*.

65. Woodrow Wilson, "The Study of Administration," in *Political Science Quarterly* 2 (1887) cited in *Classics of Public Administration*, eds. Jay Shafritz and Albert Hyde (Chicago: Dorsey Press, 1987), pp. 10–25.

66. Max Weber, in *From Max Weber: Essays in Sociology*, trans. and 3rd ed., eds. Hans Heinrich Gerth and Charles Mills (New York: Oxford University Press, 1977); Frederick Taylor, "Scientific Management," in *Classics of Public Administration*, eds. Jay Shafritz and Albert Hyde (Chicago: Dorsey Press, 1987), pp. 29–33. The original version of this paper was a testimony before the U.S. House of Representatives on January 25, 1912.

67. POSDCORB represents eight crucial functions of management including planning, organizing, staffing, directing, coordinating, reporting, and budgeting. For more details, see Luther Gulick, "Notes on the Theory of Organization," in *Classics of Public Administration*, eds. Jay Shafritz and Albert Hyde (Chicago: Dorsey Press, 1987), pp. 79–89. The original version of this paper was published in 1937.

68. For a discussion on the development of police science, please see Fogelson, Chapter 7: "The Second Wave of Reform," in *Big City Police*; Wilson, *Police Administration*.

69. *Ibid.*

70. *Ibid.*

71. Joan Petersilia, "The Influence of Research on Policing," in *Critical Issues in Policing*, 3rd ed., ed. Roger Dunham and Geoffrey Alpert (Prospect Heights, IL: Waveland, 1996).

72. *Ibid.*

73. *Ibid.*

74. Robert Trojanowicz and Bonnie Bucqueroux, *Community Policing: A Contemporary Perspective* (Cincinnati: Anderson, 1989); George Kelling, "Police and Communities: The Quiet Revolution," *Perspectives on Policing*, No. 1 (Washington, DC: U.S. Department of Justice and Harvard University, 1988); Herman Goldstein, "Toward Community-Oriented Policing: Potential, Basic Requirements and Threshold Questions," *Crime and Delinquency* 33(1987): 6–30.

75. A. C. Germann, "Community Policing: An Assessment," *Journal of Criminal Law, Criminology and Police Science* 60 (1969): 89–96.

76. Goldstein, *Policing Free Society*.

77. Kelling and Moore, "From Political to Reform to Community"; John Eck and Dennis Rosenbaum, "The New Police Order: Effectiveness, Equity, and Efficiency in Community Policing," in *The Challenges of Community Policing: Testing Promises*, ed. Dennis Rosenbaum (Thousand Oaks, CA: Sage, 1994), pp. 3–23.

78. Many police programs are developed to respond to special needs of local neighborhoods in community policing. In fact, early literature on problem-solving activities focus closely on problems at the neighborhood level. Please see John Eck and William Spelman, "Who Ya Gonna Call? The Police as Problem-Busters," *Crime and Delinquency* 33(1987): 31–52; Herman Goldstein, *Problem-Oriented Policing* (New York: McGraw-Hill, 1990).

79. Zhao and Thurman, "Community Policing."

80. Please see Jeffrey Brudney, "Using Coproduction to Deliver Services," in *Handbook of Public Administration*, ed. James Perry (San Francisco: Jossey-Bass,

❖ ❖ ❖ ❖          1989), pp. 513–526; Jeffrey Brudney and Robert England, "Toward a Definition of the Coproduction Concept," *Public Administration Review* 43 (1983): 59–64.

81. Research on this topic includes Robert Warren, Mark Rosentraub, and Louis Weschler, "Building Urban Governance: An Agenda for the 1990s," *Journal of Urban Affairs* 14 (1992): 399–422; Gordon Whitaker, "Coproduction: Citizen Participation in Service Delivery," *Public Administration Review* 40 (1980): 240–246; Jihong Zhao, *Why Police Organizational Change: A Study of Community-Oriented Policing* (Washington, DC: Police Executive Research Forum, 1996).

82. Chester Barnard, *The Functions of Executive* (Cambridge, MA: Harvard University Press, 1938).

83. Abraham Maslow, "A Theory of Human Motivation," *Psychological Review* 50 (1943): 370–396

84. Douglas McGregor, *Human Side of Enterprise* (New York: McGraw-Hill, 1960).

85. J. Richard Hackman and Greg Oldham, *Work Redesign* (Reading, MA: Addison-Wesley, 1980).

86. Many police programs are developed to respond to special needs of local neighborhoods in community policing. In fact, early literature on problem solving activities focus closely on problems at the neighborhood level. Please see Eck and Spelman, "Who Ya Gonna Call?"; Goldstein, *Problem-Oriented Policing*.

87. Kelling and Moore, "From Political to Reform to Community." ✦

# Chapter Five

# Why Police
# Departments
# Change

❖ ❖ ❖ ❖

*When you're finished changing, you're finished.*

—Benjamin Franklin

In the previous chapter, the focus was on *how* police departments have changed throughout the history of American policing. That change was characterized as an evolutionary, rather than a revolutionary, process, for reasons that will become apparent later in this chapter. The focus of this chapter is to understand *why* police departments change. To a large extent, why they change is more important than how. As Paul Lawrence, a renowned organizational theorist, has observed,

> To advance our understanding and practice in regard to major organizational change, I believe we need to develop a fresh perspective on the basic question of *why* organizations change. It seems to me that change professionals are focusing too much on the questions of how and what to change. Only by digging into the *why* question can we make progress on the how and what.[1] (italics in original)

There are many "why" questions that can be asked regarding organizational change and community policing. For example, Why did interest in changing police departments begin in the 1970s? Did police departments at that time actively seek to change in response to something well defined and concrete? Was the need to adopt community policing more subtle, perhaps due to broader social change that left police executives and the departments they ran feeling out of touch, left out, or less effective? Furthermore, why did police departments across the nation choose to begin moving toward a community-oriented approach, with its distinctively different philosophy of policing and operational strategies? For example, why have foot patrol, storefront stations, and crime prevention through education programs become so popular over the past 20 years?

---

### Call Type: Attempted Suicide

#### *Deputy Chief Terri Moses*

When asked the reason behind crime statistics for the first half of 1999 that showed Wichita having its lowest crime rates in two decades, I credit community policing and increased citizen participation. "Simply put, we're doing things different, better."

As I prepared to write this essay, I thought about several ways to describe the impact of community policing on the Wichita Police Department (WPD). I could have mentioned decreasing crime statistics or employee surveys that show a huge improvement in departmental morale. Instead, I decided to write about how community policing has changed our response to one type of call for service and to describe the impact of that change on the department and the people who work here.

I joined the WPD in 1981 at a time when the department was moving toward team policing. Team policing centered on the idea of improved police responsiveness based upon the assignment of the same group of officers to handle most types of calls for service in a specified geographic area. I was both formally and informally graded on my team-policing performance, and in both situations, statistics were ☞

☞

❖ ❖ ❖ ❖

examined to judge my performance. Numbers were recorded on how many cases, arrests, and tickets I wrote each month. In order to remain competitive with other officers, I had to move quickly from call to call.

At the time, WPD also was operating primarily from a professional model. This called for strict adherence to policies. The administration wanted all situations to be handled in a similar manner. One consequence of this approach was that patrol officers limited themselves to situations that needed law enforcement or immediate action; less clear situations were to be avoided, passed along to someone else, or otherwise refused ownership as not being "police problems."

As the crime rates in Wichita rose, so it seemed did public distrust of the police and local government. The city's self-image was poor, and morale within the ranks of the WPD suffered. Running from call to call with no relief in sight also was taking a toll on WPD patrol officers. Something needed to change. Like so many other law enforcement agencies across the country at the time, the WPD began experimenting with community policing in targeted areas. That was in 1993 and in 1996 the department took community policing citywide.

One kind of service call that illustrates to me the value of community policing is attempted suicide. Eighteen years ago a call about a suicide attempt would have meant an immediate police response. The person attempting the suicide would have been disarmed, taken to a hospital, and admitted by officers or family members. The officer handling the case would have no follow-up contact with the individual and most likely no knowledge as to the help eventually provided. Any additional knowledge about the outcome of the situation would probably have come from reading daily activity reports or learning secondhand of the individual's next suicide attempt, perhaps successful this time.

Community policing stresses a much different approach to the same kind of call for service. It stresses connecting the person in crisis with resources that are available through community involvement and creative problem solving. Fundamentally, it is proactive rather than reactive. Instead of waiting to see (or hear of) the other shoe drop, community policing tries to avert the next serious call for service.

In January 1998, for example, a WPD officer who answered an attempted suicide call addressed it as if it were a critical incident. After stabilizing the caller, rather than simply leaving the situation in the hands of unknown others, the officer further investigated the problem. That is, he talked with the suicidal individual and learned why he was depressed.

The officer then treated the event as a problem-oriented project (POP). He learned that alcohol abuse led to job loss and that job loss led to financial difficulty, which in turn led to poor living conditions (such as a clothes dryer that did not work and infestations by insects). Also affected were two young children in the home who dropped out of school because of poor self-esteem linked to poor living conditions. Consequently, the father saw himself as the root of the family's problems and felt suicide was the best way he could help his family out of this situation.

Over a three-month period following the initial call the responding officer arranged counseling for the father with a pastor and assisted in finding him employment. The officer also contacted a local social-service agency and helped the family to receive a low-interest loan. The loan enabled the family to provide themselves with new furniture, working appliances, and insect extermination. Donations of clothing and personal items also were made available to the family.

Community policing encourages and allows officers to work with communities, families, and individuals to solve problems. Eighteen years ago an attempted suicide call would have been treated merely as another statistic. With community policing, the officer is encouraged to investigate further to solve the problem and prevent future calls of a similar and tragic nature. The city ends up a winner, as does the officer and the family. The city benefits from having another productive member of its community at work and two children who have a chance to become productive members in the future rather than immediate victims. At the same time, the police department benefits from lower crime rates, and officers benefit from the knowledge that they have indeed made a difference in the lives of the citizens that they are sworn to protect.          ☞

❖ ❖ ❖ ❖

☞     A lot can be said about statistics and lower crime rates. The true success of community policing, however, is reflected by lives changed and crimes prevented.

---

Terri Moses is a Kansas native and a graduate of Wichita State University. She began her career with the Wichita Police Department and worked her way through the ranks to become its first female deputy chief in 1995. She currently supervises personnel assigned to the city's four police substations made up of 450 officers and civilians who comprise the Field Services Division. Deputy Chief Moses received her master's degree in criminal justice from Wichita State University in 1990. She also is a graduate of the FBI National Academy and has received numerous awards, including the Kansas Chiefs of Police Silver award. In addition to her police duties, she teaches criminal justice at Wichita State University.

This chapter first discusses the important role of theory in answering the question of why organizations change. Second, it develops an argument based on contingency theories to explain why police departments changed from a professional model to a community-oriented one. Assumptions and factors associated with the existing conditions will be identified and applied to the analysis of the emergence of community policing.

## The Role of Theory

People often say that something may be fine in theory but not very useful in practice. Such a viewpoint undervalues the role of theories in the social sciences. Theories are used to organize existing facts or observations and explain relationships between them.[2] Once people understand why something works the way it does, then they can begin to think about ways to improve it. For example, Why has social disorder become a priority of police work since the 1970s?

For example, according to the broken-windows theory made popular by James Q. Wilson and George Kelling (a theory discussed in more detail in later chapters), if social disorder is not controlled, crime will follow. Wilson and Kelling theorize that social disorder and crime are related because if the conditions that give rise to disorder are left unchecked, then often the result is criminal activity.[3] When a house, apartment building, street, or neighborhood gives the appearance that no one person or group has much interest in protecting the area's people and property, street criminals get the idea that they can commit crimes there without much risk of detection or apprehension. According to the broken-windows theory, fixing broken windows and making other repairs in an area is the first step to creating order and reducing crime.

In the example above, the theory predicts a relationship between social disorder and incidents of crime. Carried a step further, the theory suggests that a policing style that directly responds to social disorder in a community can have an immediate impact on crime. Accordingly, the theory explains why police departments might want to change; that is, in order to be more effective in reducing criminal activity, they might want to consider expanding beyond their usual law enforcement role and devote attention to crime prevention and other proactive policing strategies.

*The Boise Police Department opens its newest police substation inside a local supermarket in July, 1999. Why have substations increased in popularity over the last 20 years? (Photo: Courtesy of the Boise Police Department)*

The validity of any theory depends upon empirical evidence that can tell us about its accuracy in predicting relationships between facts or observations (variables) and real-life events. The following section introduces the contingency school of theories to explain why organizations change.

## The Contingency Theories

The contingency school of theories was developed during the early 1950s when a number of scholars recognized the importance of an environment in explaining and predicting organizational behavior.[4] Organizational actions, it was observed, are contingent upon its unique environment. Contingency theorists offer four propositions.

The first proposition identifies three factors that serve as a starting point for discussion: strategy, structure, and environment.[5] Strategy concerns the decision making and operational procedures employed by an organization to accomplish its goals. Structure is defined as the organizational arrangements used to coordinate operations such as reporting and supervision. Finally, environment generally refers to all the factors outside the organization that affect its operation.

The second proposition is that an organization's external environment shapes the strategies and structures of the organization.[6] For example, the average income of citizens in a city (the external environment) largely determines the level of consumer spending within the city. In a small city with a lower than average household income, it would be unlikely that a local auto dealer could profit from selling luxury cars.

An organization must, therefore, adapt itself to the environment. Social scientists refer to the environment as an independent variable that functions to influence organizational structure, which is referred to as a dependent variable.

❖ ❖ ❖ ❖     The third proposition is that the environment itself is not static but dynamic and constantly changing. As the environment changes, the organization must adapt to the new environment by making adjustments, such as implementing innovative strategies and redesigning its structures. For example, the manner in which college classes are taught has changed substantially in the last 25 years. Particularly, new technology has made the world much smaller than it was in the 1970s—students learn by using the Internet, interactive multimedia CD-Rom computers, and other high-tech information systems. Many professors post their syllabi, assignments, or lecture notes on the Internet, affording students access to them at any time. Further, more students are using electronic mail to keep in touch with their professors and some professors, now teach using "power-point" presentations that are more visually stimulating. Technological change is a continuous process that has resulted in many changes in higher education.

The fourth proposition is that during the process of change an organization strives for a close fit between itself and the external environment. Successful companies seek a tight fit between their products and the demands of the market. For example, computer software giant Microsoft has been able to respond successfully (and profitably) to the demands of the market during the past decade, making it one of the most profitable corporations in the world and making its owner one of the world's richest people. The Windows operating system, produced by Microsoft in the early 1990s, has prompted other software companies to modify their products. In contrast, a misfit between an organization and the external environment results in low performance and ineffectiveness.

In sum, the following is the theoretical framework for contingency theories:

1. An initial fit exists between an organization and its environment.

2. Environmental change (e.g., due to technological change) results in a misfit.

3. Such a misfit affects performance and forces the organization to make corresponding changes or adaptations, both in structure and operational strategies, or risk becoming irrelevant or obsolete.

4. A new fit is found between an organization and its external environment.

## Types of Organizations: Mechanistic Versus Organic

A widely cited study of organizational response to the external environment was conducted by Tom Burns and G. M. Stalker in the late 1950s. They examined more than 20 industrial firms in the United Kingdom with the purpose of finding "how the management systems change in accordance with changes in the technical and commercial tasks of the firm. . . ."[7] They were particularly interested in how managerial practices responded to certain facets of the external environment. For example, did organizational structure and managerial styles differ among firms according to variations in the envi-

ronment? How did the organizations change in order to find a better fit
between themselves and the external environment? Through field observations and extensive interviews with key managers in these firms, Burns and
Stalker discovered two different systems of management. Each system
seemed to correspond to a particular external environment.

❖ ❖ ❖ ❖

## Mechanistic Type

The first management system, which they called *mechanistic*, has the following characteristics:

1. Task specialization is applied to routine work (that is, work is
   specialized so that each employee takes care of only his or her
   narrow assignment).

2. The means of accomplishing a task are emphasized over the
   ends resulting from the task (that is, what workers do is more important than why they do it).

3. There is a hierarchical structure of control and supervision with
   many levels.

4. Knowledge and planning are centralized at the higher end of the
   organizational structure (that is, knowledge and power are
   found at the top).

5. Communication patterns are vertical (from supervisors to subordinates), and cross-sectional communications are discour-
   aged (that is, there is a top-down structure of authority).

6. Employee behavior and operations tend to be governed by the
   instructions and decisions issued by supervisors (without any or
   much input from subordinates).

Burns and Stalker suggested that the mechanistic system of management
is likely to be found in situations where the environment is relatively stable. A
stable environment places consistent demands on an organization over time.
If the demand for a product stays the same or rarely changes, there is little
need for a manufacturer to undertake research for improvement or develop a
new product. For example, in a study of organizational response to the external environment in the United States, Paul Lawrence and Jay Lorsch found
that there was almost no research and development (R & D) in the container
industry in 25 years. The industry used the same technology to produce the
same big iron boxes it had always made.[8] Not surprisingly, managers focused
primarily on quantity (how many they could make at any one time) and quality (how cheaply could they make an adequate container for a set amount of
money). Therefore, mechanical precision and the tight control of employee
behavior were their main concerns in order to continue producing the same
product for the same cost.

## Organic Type

Burns and Stalker called the second type of management *organic*.
Organic management practices share the following characteristics:

❖ ❖ ❖ ❖

1. Employees are encouraged to join in a common goal of the organization, instead of specializing in only one area (that is, workers are viewed as generalists, rather than specialists in their approach to nonroutine work).

2. Employee work assignments change depending on the needs of the organization.

3. Change is accomplished through interaction between coworkers and supervisors (there is open communication and employee input).

4. Employee originality and creativity are valued and encouraged at all levels of the organization.

5. Organizational structure is relatively flat, emphasizing individual contributions and responsibility for one's own work (that is, distance from the top to the bottom of the organization is reduced, with a team spirit driving workers to make individual contributions to the work).

6. Rules and regulations are based on mutual interests, not on the needs of production alone (that is, rules provide reasonable standards for job-related performance rather than long lists of specific infractions that are to be avoided).

Organic management systems can be found in organizations that are in changing environments. A dynamic external environment requires new responses from the organization for the sake of its survival. Because of the need for adaptation, employee creativity can play an important role in improving organizational performance (e.g., market share, products, or services). In changing environments, opportunities are lost when the organization strictly follows the formal chain of command to make a decision. For example, in a study of the history of the Nike corporation, David Hurst found that

> The unstructured and nonroutine [nature] of the work in a new organization requires that people work with the minimum of structure. Typically this requirement is met by the use of innovative and motivated teams. Like hunting bands, such teams can form and dissolve at a short notice. . . . In emergencies (and almost everything is an emergency in a young organization), there is no time for hierarchy or formality. Whoever has the skills should do the job. People seem to come from nowhere to address the problems and then disappear as fast as they came.[9]

In sum, the findings of Burns and Stalker and other researchers suggest that distinctive managerial systems and organizational designs depend upon the unique external environment of an organization. Static environments create very little need for organizational change. In contrast, dynamic environments require an organization to change to a more flexible managerial style, accept a less formal organizational structure, and rely more on the creativity of its employees.

Why an organization changes can be answered by looking at the degree of change in the organization's environment. For policing, failure to adapt to environmental change may mean that local residents will look elsewhere for answers to their needs for better public safety, even if that answer means moving to gated communities policed by private security firms.

# Primary Factors in the External Environment        ❖ ❖ ❖ ❖

This section examines a few of the primary factors in the external environment that help explain the organizational change process in policing. It seems likely that broad social changes over the past 30 years have been behind the need for changes in policing goals, structure, and strategies. Traditional police departments simply no longer fit well with the environment, as they did during the professional era, and a new fit is needed. Before considering the need for change, a brief review of the bureaucratic model can be helpful.

A basic assumption of the bureaucratic model of policing is that the police can control and enforce their will on the external environment. The police control crime, not the other way around. The external environment is assumed to be stable, and law enforcement is thought to be concerned with catching criminals. This function does not change because the environment does not change all that much; there is a more or less constant supply of criminals to be arrested and locked up and a relatively stable amount of resources available to do the job, which are distributed among the police, the courts, and prisons.

The bureaucratic model of policing clearly has a mechanistic system of management. The structure found in professional police departments is typically hierarchical, with directives that flow down the chain of command. Police officers are trained as specialists who catch criminals, not as generalists who work on a wide variety of tasks. Rules are designed to bring about conformity and ensure predictability in times of crisis or emergency. A participative style of management or the empowerment of individual officers is unheard of.

*A mechanistic, unidirectional flow of information from the top down is characteristic of a bureaucratic model which would be slow to adapt to environmental change. (Photo: Mark C. Ide)*

❖ ❖ ❖ ❖     Under the bureaucratic model, two quantifiable measures—crime rates and clearance rates—are viewed as the primary indicators of police effectiveness. Because these statistics show how effectively a police department is doing its job over time, quantification becomes very important in assessing police work. Police departments are very "number driven."

From the 1960s through the 1980s, symptoms of a changing environment begin to emerge.

## 1. Increase in Crime

One change was that in the mid-1960s, police departments across the nation seemed to run out of luck with respect to the conditions that had previously helped them achieve success. The proportion of the U.S. population in the "crime-prone" ages (14 to 24) rose sharply, as did crime rates. In particular, as Figure 5.1 shows, violent crime began to increase in 1965 and continued to climb, thereby increasing public fear of crime. In the span of just 25 years, the rate for violent crime—murder, rape, robbery, and aggravated assault—rose approximately 240 percent, from about 200 incidents per 100,000 citizens in 1965, to almost 700 per 100,000 in 1991!

Similarly, the rate of property crime larceny, burglary, and auto theft— climbed sharply between 1965 and 1981 before eventually leveling off (Figure 5.2). In addition, population growth during the same period was approximately 25 percent! Police departments, which had uniformly built their reputations on the basis of crime-control and crime-fighting expertise, were being

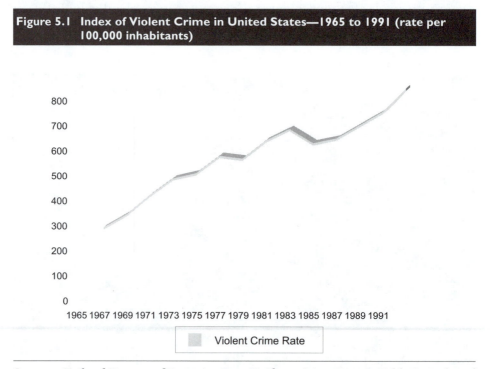

**Figure 5.1   Index of Violent Crime in United States—1965 to 1991 (rate per 100,000 inhabitants)**

Violent Crime Rate

Sources: Federal Bureau of Investigation, *Uniform Crime Report*, Table 2: Index of Crime, United States, 1960–1975, p. 49; FBI, 1975, *Uniform Crime Report*, Table 1: Index of Crime, United States, 1972–1991, p. 58, 1991.

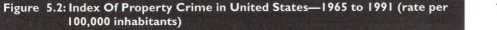

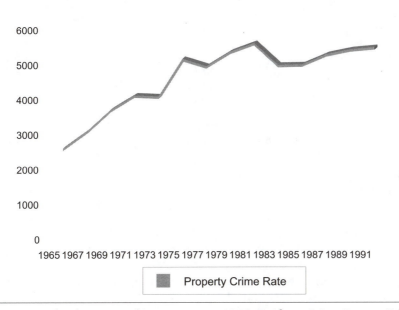

Sources: Federal Bureau of Investigation, 1975. *Uniform Crime Report*, Table 2: Index of Crime, United States, 1960–1975, p. 49; FBI, 1975. *Uniformed Crime Report*. Table 1: Index of Crime, United States, 1972–1991, p. 58.

challenged to defend their effectiveness in the face of rising crime rates and increasing fear. These conditions placed the police in an awkward position: If they were responsible for crime control, then why had they not done a better job to keep the streets safe?

How well did police departments respond to the rising crime rates of the 1970s and 1980s? Table 5.1 shows the total number of arrests in 1960, 1970, and 1980. The frequency distributions show that the total number of police arrests increased significantly for almost all offenses during this 20-year period. For example, the arrest rate for robbery and aggravated assault rose by approximately 200 percent. In fact, arrest rates increased substantially for all crime categories except vagrancy. This trend is particularly significant in that the number of police officers did not increase as quickly as the increase in their productivity (as measured by the total number of arrests). In a study of police expenditures and personnel in 88 cities with populations over 100,000, the increase in the number of police officers per 1,000 residents was only marginal, as shown in Figure 5.3. Further, the adjusted spending per resident, in 1967 dollars, increased by about 77 percent; however, police productivity in these same 88 cities increased even more, suggesting that departments at that time were operating more efficiently and more cost effectively than before.

❖ ❖ ❖ ❖

| Table 5.1   Total Arrest Trends, 1960–1980 | | | | |
|---|---|---|---|---|
| Offense Charged | 1960 | 1970 | 1980 | % change (1960–80) |
| Population* | 180,671 | 205,052 | 227,757 | +26.1 |
| **Part 1 Offenses** | | | | |
| Violent Crimes | | | | |
| Murder and non-negligent manslaughter | 5,008 | 10,109 | 12,310 | +145.0 |
| Rape | 7,149 | 11,094 | 19,612 | +174.3 |
| Robbery | 33,794 | 74,401 | 107,428 | +217.9 |
| Aggvted. assault | 57,006 | 93,012 | 169,438 | +197.2 |
| Property Crimes | | | | |
| Burglary | 123,891 | 200,261 | 317,313 | +156.1 |
| Larceny | 207,584 | 432,272 | 763,505 | +267.8 |
| Auto theft | 57,931 | 97,124 | 89,213 | + 54.0 |
| **Part 2 Offenses** | | | | |
| Prostitution and commercialized vice | 29,060 | 45,803 | 67,920 | +133.7 |
| DWI laws | 147,819 | 281,450 | 614,620 | +315.8 |
| Disorderly conduct | 424,843 | 436,862 | 509,121 | + 19.8 |
| Vagrancy | 140,602 | 82,311 | 22,500 | –84.0 |

*Population in thousands, cited in U.S. Department of Commerce, *Statistical Abstract of the United States—1991*, Table 13, p. 13.

Sources: The 1960 and 1970 data were obtained from the Federal Bureau of Investigation, *Uniform Crime Reports, 1970*, Table 24, p. 122. The 1980 data was obtained from *Uniform Crime Report, 1980*, Table 26, p. 194.

How do these findings compare with clearance rates, the second key measure of police effectiveness? Unfortunately, not well. The clearance rates for the four types of Part I offenses in cities over 250,000 between 1966 and 1986 appear in Figure 5.4. Police departments in large cities traditionally have had more difficulty controlling crime than their counterparts in smaller cities or rural areas; therefore, data from the largest cities provide the most conservative estimate of police effectiveness. The clearance rates for murder, forcible rape, robbery, and burglary show that police effectiveness in solving crimes decreased considerably in all four areas. For example, the clearance rate for murder was 67 percent in 1986, compared to 88 percent in 1966. Similarly, the clearance rate for burglary dropped by about half during the same period.

Data for cities with populations of 50,000 to 100,000 yield clearance rates for four offenses that show a similar pattern of decline (Figure 5.5). For example, the clearance rate for murder declined by almost 20 percent. Indeed, the decrease in clearance rates for murder and rape was found to be quite similar in both large and medium departments. Once again, the data suggest that the effectiveness measures endorsed by the bureaucratic model of policing indicate that the police had failed to accomplish what they set out to do, that is, they had failed to control crime.

According to the contingency theories introduced earlier, the external environment influences the police, not the other way around. Police have few effective means of controlling the fluctuation of crime trends. For example, it

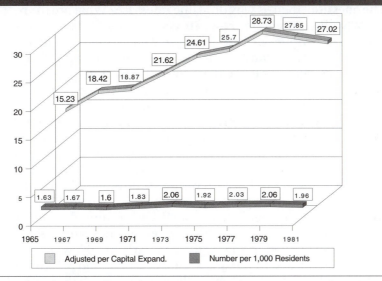

**Figure 5.3  Police Expenditures per Resident and the Number of Sworn Officers per 1,000 Residents in 88 U.S. cities—1965 to 1981***

\*The expenditure was in 1967 dollars.
Sources: Bureau of Justice Statistics, *Police Employment and Expenditure Trends* (Washington, DC: U.S. Department of Justice, 1986), Table 1 and Table 2, p. 2.

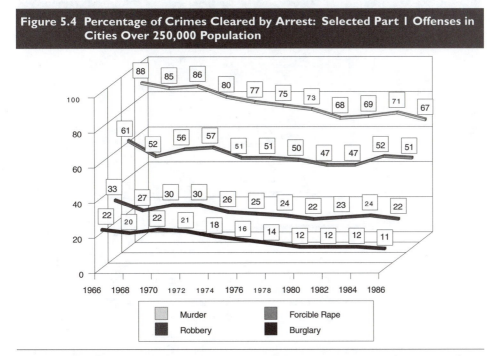

**Figure 5.4  Percentage of Crimes Cleared by Arrest: Selected Part 1 Offenses in Cities Over 250,000 Population**

Sources: Federal Bureau of Investigation, *Uniform Crime Report*. Information above was obtained from the following reports: *UCR* 1966, Table 12, p. 100; *UCR* 1968, Table 12, p. 100; *UCR* 1970, Table 12, p. 108; *UCR* 1972, Table 14, p. 107; *UCR* 1974, Table 18, p. 166; *UCR* 1976, Table 20, p. 162; *UCR* 1980, Table 20, p. 182; *UCR* 1982, Table 19, p. 158; *UCR* 1984, Table 20, p. 154; and *UCR* 1986, Table 20, p. 156. The figure was compiled by the authors. Decimal points are rounded to the next integer.

❖ ❖ ❖ ❖     would be very difficult for the police to explain in terms of their efforts why property crimes leveled off after 1981, only to rebound after 1985.

The question, then, is why do crime rates rise? What are the root causes of crime? Why did crime rates rise between the late 1960s and the 1980s?

***Increased number of young people.*** One cause of an increase in crime during a given period is an increasing number of young people in that period. Criminologists agree that incidents of criminal activity become more frequent as a child grows older and then decline after the person reaches a certain age. Delinquent behavior usually begins around the age of thirteen and reaches its peak about age eighteen. After the age of twenty-four, a person has passed the crime-prone years. Therefore, the presence of a large cohort of young people in a population will drive crime rates up simply because they are in the age group most likely to commit criminal offenses. Conversely, it is unlikely that a 60-year old person would commit a robbery. Table 5.2 shows the percentage of Americans between the ages of 10 and 24. This is the age group that is most generally associated with criminal incidents, either as offender or victim. Interestingly, the percentage of young people in the general population peaked in the 1970s and early 1980s, which corresponded with the general crime trends shown in Figure 5.1 and 5.2. By 1988, this age group had declined to 22 percent of the population, similar to statistics from 1960. Ironically, both violent crime and property crime have declined since

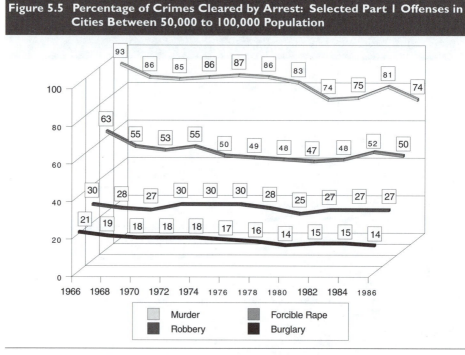

**Figure 5.5   Percentage of Crimes Cleared by Arrest: Selected Part I Offenses in Cities Between 50,000 to 100,000 Population**

Sources: Federal Bureau of Investigation, *Uniform Crime Report*. Information above was obtained from the following report: *UCR* 1966, Table 12, p. 100; *UCR* 1968, Table 12, p. 100; *UCR* 1970, Table 12, p. 108; *UCR* 1972, Table 14, p. 107; *UCR* 1974, Table 18, p. 166; *UCR* 1976, Table 20, p. 162; *UCR* 1980, Table 20, p. 182; *UCR* 1982, Table 19, p. 158; *UCR* 1984, Table 20, p. 154; and *UCR* 1986, Table 20, p. 156. The figure was compiled by the authors. Decimal points are rounded to the next integer.

the early 1990s, including in cities such as New York, Chicago, and Los Angeles.

| Table 5.2 | Percentage of Population From 10 to 24 Years Old | |
|---|---|---|
| Year | 10 to 24 years | 65 years and over |
| 1960 | 23.0 | 9.2 |
| 1970 | 28.0 | 9.8 |
| 1980 | 26.8 | 11.3 |
| 1988 | 22.0 | 12.3 |

Source: U.S. Department of Commerce, *Statistical Abstract of the United States—1991*, Table 13, p. 13.

*Social disorganization.* Another root cause of crime is social disorganization. For example, more people work outside the home now than 40 years ago. Empty homes afford potential offenders with more opportunities to commit property crimes. Furthermore, as American society has become more affluent— as evidenced by the 847.1 percent increase in GNP in 1982 constant dollars—more things are available to steal. [10] Based on the routine-activities theory, the amount of durable goods available is a good measure of national crime rates.[11] Also, there are more households headed by single mothers than in the past. It is estimated that more than half of all children today will experience living in a single-parent home before reaching adulthood. The lack of supervision and the absence of appropriate role models are assumed to be factors correlated with an increase in juvenile delinquency.[12]

## 2. Increase in Public Fear of Crime

Another change in the environment was an increase in the public's fear of crime. Furthermore, the nature of crime in America has changed. There are more violent crimes. Arrest rates for weapons offenses more than doubled between 1965 and 1993.[13] Figure 5.6 shows that a substantial number of Americans felt that crime rates in their own areas were up. These numbers have risen from over 45 percent in 1967 to about 70 percent in 1977. Similarly, for the 12-year period between 1966 and 1978, over 40 percent of Americans reported feeling more personally uneasy on the street than they felt during the previous year (Figure 5.7). Fear of crime has become a constant companion to most Americans, often occupying the front page of local newspapers or capturing the prime-time news spots on local TV. In response, a considerable number of citizens have changed their lifestyles. Some avoid going out at night, many add safety devices to their homes, and still others join together to keep a watchful eye on the street for suspicious persons

Over the past 30 years, crime also has become a major political issue. The war on crime and the war on poverty waged by the Johnson administration and the war on drugs mounted by the Reagan and Bush administrations have put crime in the national spotlight. Most often, street crime has been at the center of this political focus, capturing the attention of Americans nationwide.[14]

This increase in the public's fear of street crime has raised questions that wrongly or rightly have landed at the doorsteps of police departments and

❖ ❖ ❖ ❖

**Figure 5.6  Attitude Toward Changes in the Level of Crime in Own Area, United States, Selected Years 1967–1978 (In percentage)**

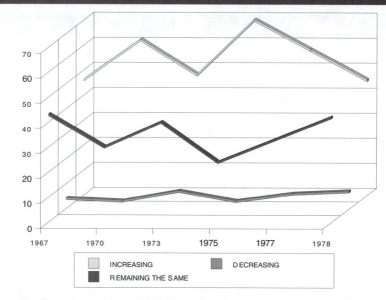

Question: "In the past year, do you feel the crime rate in your own area has been increasing, decreasing, or has remained the same as it was before?"

Sources: Louis Harris, *The Harris Survey*, May 9, 1977, p. 1; The ABC News-Harris Survey, May 17, 1978, p. 3. Cited in Hindelang et al. 1981. *Sourcebook of Criminal Justice Statistics—1980* (Washington, DC: U.S. Department of Justice, 1980), Figure 2.1, p. 166.  Figure constructed by *Sourcebook* staff.

sheriff's offices around the country. Are police responsible for reducing the level of fear among citizens? If so, why has the world's most advanced nation, and presumably the country with the best capacity to detect and control crime, not been more effective at keeping American streets safe? And, what should police departments be doing to bring crime under control?

A primary explanation might be that the fear of crime may not be rational. In fact, there is little correlation between the actual chances of being victimized and the level of fear of being victimized among most Americans. For example, elderly people have a higher level of fear than do teenagers, yet teens and young adults are much more likely to be victimized than retirees. Similarly, females fear crime more than males, although their rates of criminal victimization are considerably lower than those for males.

The association between criminal victimization and the perception of crime across the nation is shown in Figure 5.6. The fluctuation in the public's perceptions of crime in the figure do not closely follow a pattern of actual increases or decreases in crime rates as displayed in Figures 5.1 and 5.2. Between 1972 and 1975, there was a 15 percent decrease in the number of respondents who believed that the crime rate in their own area was up, although the violent crime rate had increased sharply during this same period. This discrepancy illustrates an important point. If the fear of crime and the rate of victimization are not linked, what chance has a police chief or

**Figure 5.7  Attitudes Toward Personal Safety on the Streets Compared to a Year Ago, United States 1966 to 1978 (In percentage)**

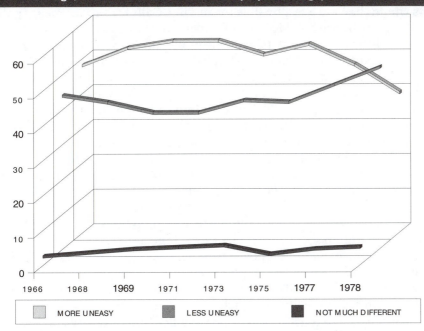

Question: "Compared to a year ago, do you personally feel more uneasy on the streets, less uneasy, or not much different?"

Sources: Louis Harris, *The Harris Survey*, May 9, 1977, p. 2; The ABC News-Harris Survey, May 17, 1978, p. 3. Cited in Hindelang et al. 1981. *Sourcebook of Criminal Justice Statistics—1980* (Washington, DC: U.S. Department of Justice, 1980),  Figure 2.3 p. 173. Figure constructed by Sourcebook staff.

sheriff to control the fear of crime by relying directly on their usual approach to law enforcement? The answer probably is that very little can be done to control the fear of crime by law enforcement alone. The fear of crime is a part of the external environment that the police simply cannot control through traditional means!

## 3. The Challenge of Police-Community Relations

A third change in the external environment concerned police-community relations, particularly in minority communities. A bureaucratic model of policing assumes a high level of technical expertise in controlling crime that places very little reliance on interaction between the police and the law-abiding public. Accepted policing practice during the professional era was to put police officers into roaming patrol cars to be dispatched from a central location to specific spots as calls for service came in. This reactive style of policing meant virtual isolation from the large majority of residents who did not bother to call the police when victimized or from those not yet in immediate need of police services.

❖ ❖ ❖ ❖     Isolation from the majority of the public had several serious consequences. First, the police themselves had limited exposure to the kinds of residents whom they were responsible for serving. Calls for service meant police met citizens primarily as victims, offenders, or witnesses, thereby robbing the police of the opportunity to view the public under more positive circumstances. Second, reactive policing tended to deal with symptoms of larger problems, rather than with solutions that might more effectively address the root causes. And third, reactive policing meant that the majority of good citizens who supported the police never interacted with them in meaningful ways in noncriminal or nonemergency situations. As a result, positive police-community relations that might have built public confidence in the police, reduced the fear of crime, and built a network of volunteer labor for problem solving, never materialized. At the same time, police officers themselves had little opportunity to learn about the public's high level of support and the important work that they do to keep the community safe.

A fourth consequence of isolation was failure to be kept informed about how best to maintain social order. The 1960s, for example, were a tumultuous time for the police, when the peacekeeping capacity of the "thin blue line" was put to the test. Because the police had the legitimate use of force and their primary responsibility was to enforce laws, they were the first to be called by government leaders to quell urban riots.

In particular, the tension between the police and minority communities during the 1960s reached an all-time high. For example, the 1968 Presidential Commission pointed out that police and minority relations had become a serious social problem that needed to be addressed. Three decades later, this same issue remained the subject of debate, with police brutality and racially discriminatory enforcement of the law leading to many incidents of civil unrest. More recently, the beating of Rodney King in 1991 captured the attention of the national media as one of many such incidents that put the Los Angeles Police Department on trial and eventually erupted into violence that set parts of the city ablaze.

The deterioration of police relations with minority groups stems from broad social changes during the late 1960s and 1970s. Since the 1970s, middle-class white families began to migrate to the suburbs to escape high crime rates and avoid paying high city taxes. As a result of this "white flight," the proportion of minority populations, particularly African Americans, in the inner city increased, but the people remained poor and underrepresented in the best-paying jobs in the labor force.[15] For example, in 1960, 54.8 percent of Washington, D.C., residents were nonwhite compared to 70.3 percent in 1980.[16] From the 1960s to the 1980s, the realignment of the economic infrastructure in big cities, particularly in the Northeast, made African Americans the primary victims. Well-paying blue-collar jobs had disappeared. According to William Julius Wilson, the 1970s saw more than 700,000 jobs disappear from large northeastern cities.[17]

Unemployment rates among African Americans remained disproportionately high throughout the 1970s and 1980s. For example, in 1975, 39.5 percent of African Americans between the ages of 16 and 19 and 24.5 percent between the ages of 20 and 24 were unemployed, compared with 17.9 percent and 12.3 percent of whites in the same age groups.[18] In addition, more than half of the African-American children were growing up in families headed by single mothers, placing many children in higher-risk categories for juvenile delinquency.

The fact that these social and demographic changes are beyond the control of the police does not make them any less relevant. Not only do the police represent a highly visible form of local government that is not well appreciated by some members of economically disadvantaged communities, they also must play an active public-safety role in these same areas. Typically, the proportion of both criminal offenders and victims is higher in poorer neighborhoods than in wealthier neighborhoods. Crime occurs in these poor communities more frequently, and persons most often arrested for criminal behavior (e.g., African-American males) also reside there. For example, based on the 1991 incarceration data of Thomas Bonczar and Allen Beck from the Bureau of Justice Statistics, 28.5 percent of African-American males are likely be incarcerated in a state or federal prison in their lifetime. This figure is almost 550 percent higher than the 4.4 percent incarceration rate for whites, and considerably higher than the 16 percent incarceration rate for Hispanic males.[19]

In addition to there being a higher rate of offenders in minority communities, there are more minority victims. A Bureau of Justice Statistics report found that the victimization rate of African Americans is substantially higher than for whites for the crimes of murder, rape, and robbery. There is a considerable amount of research confirming the consequences of high victimization rates in minority communities.[20]

These facts mean that police have more contact with minority and poor neighborhoods in their efforts at law enforcement and maintaining order. The problem is that both the victims and offenders in these communities may not welcome the presence of the police. It is easy to understand why offenders are averse to police presence; victims of crimes are also antagonistic because of incidents of police brutality and the misuse of discretion.

The findings from the 1968 Report of the National Advisory Commission served as a catalyst for change in police departments. For example, the commission found that social turmoil in the 1960s was caused by a number of factors including pervasive discrimination, African-American in-migration and white exodus, and the presence of African-American ghettos. The report stated that

> [S]egregation and poverty converge on the young to destroy opportunity and enforce failure. Crime, drug addiction, dependency on welfare, and bitterness and resentment against society in general and white society in particular are the results. To some Negroes police have come to symbolize white power, white racism and white repression. And the fact is that many police do reflect and express these white attitudes. The atmosphere of hostility and cynicism is reinforced by a widespread belief among Negroes in the existence of police brutality and in the 'double standard' of justice and protection—one for Negroes and one for whites.[21]

This was the first time that police and minority relations had become an important area of concern. Consequently, changes in the external environment have forced police departments to improve relations with local communities, particularly minority communities. When enforcing the law in individual communities, police officers need the support of local residents who can provide information, offer assistance, and organize themselves.

*Youths ranging from 13 to 24 years of age make up the group criminologists refer to as 'crime-prone.' (Photo: Mark C. Ide)*

## Contingency Theories and Community Policing: Why Change?

In the light of the three external environmental factors associated with police change—increase in crime, increase in fear of crime, and poor community relations—it should be apparent that the bureaucratic style of policing is no longer appropriate. The assumption that the police control crime is refuted by a rising crime rate, which shows that it is the environment that affects the police. The bureaucratic style is poorly prepared to respond to the public fear of crime because reduction of such fear is not the goal of the bureaucratic style. Demographic changes such as a larger proportion of young people and larger proportions of minorities in the cities portray a dynamic society that the bureaucratic style, better suited to a static society, is ill-equipped to deal with.

According to contingency theories, if there is a misfit with the environment, police departments need to change in order to form a better fit. This change should focus on the demands created by the environment, and police strategies and structure should be redesigned accordingly.

## Community Policing as a Police Response to the Demands of the External Environment

The demands of the external environment mean that the police response must be multidimensional rather than unidimensional. Police departments must expand their operations to cover more tasks in order to meet the demands of the external environment. There are several ways police agencies might respond in order to find a better fit with a changing environment.

❖ ❖ ❖ ❖

## Reprioritize Police Functions

The primary focus of the police in the bureaucratic style was law enforcement. From the 1960s to the late 1980s, the police tried to make more arrests but still failed to keep up with rising crime rates. Their effectiveness in solving crimes also declined during this period. At this point, it appeared that the police needed to reassess their functions and strategies for reducing crime.

Accordingly, they made order maintenance just as important a function as law enforcement. The rationale for this reprioritization was quite straightforward. The broken-windows theory suggests that social disorder is responsible for the deterioration of law and order in local neighborhoods. Therefore, the police need to control social disorder before they can win the fight against crime. New programs are needed to combat social disorder. For example, foot patrol and assignment to specific beats are supposed to have a direct effect on reducing social disorder. Police officers assigned to foot patrol are able to work on problems of social disorder. Further, special task units can be created to respond to specific problems experienced by local residents in a neighborhood.

## Reduce Fear of Crime

Recent studies suggest that there is a close relationship between social disorder and fear of crime. As street criminals move into a neighborhood, honest citizens are forced to relocate. Foot patrol programs, storefront police stations, victim-contact programs, and public education aimed at crime prevention are innovative programs aimed at reducing fear of crime and social disorder. In the early 1980s, an evaluation of a foot patrol program in Newark, New Jersey, found that foot patrol may not reduce crimes *per se*, but it nonetheless reduces the fear of crime among the public. Residents felt safer after the implementation of the foot patrol program.

## Improve Police-Community Relations

Police-community relations, particularly in regards to minority communities, was a problem during much of the late 1960s. Since then, police departments have continued to implement new programs to reduce strained relations. For example, many departments using community policing started programs to form partnerships between police and local residents based on mutual trust. Such cooperation allows all parties to be engaged in crime prevention. A few examples include local community meetings sponsored by the police department, the establishment of a public police academy to train citizens, the installation of neighborhood watch programs, and other programs such as Drug Awareness and Resistance Education (DARE). In Chicago, police officers regularly hold neighborhood meetings to share information with residents and to listen to public concerns.

❖ ❖ ❖ ❖   ## Conclusion

Using contingency theories to analyze police change reveals that community policing is a reasonable response to changing society. The analysis suggests that the misfit between the police and the external environment became obvious in the late 1960s and early 1970s. The effectiveness of police departments nationwide gradually decreased—crime rates rose and clearance rates dropped. Therefore, the police were forced to find a new fit.

This attempt was primarily focused on three areas—rising crime rates, high public fear of crime, and poor police-community relations. In the 1980s, police departments gradually began to address these problems, starting in a few larger cities. Taking cues from previous experiences, police designed community policing programs to be multipurpose instead of single purpose. For example, foot patrol was introduced almost as a cure-all for problems of social disorder. Foot-patrol programs make local residents and business owners feel safer because of greater police officer visibility. Further, such programs can improve police-community relations by enabling police officers to talk with local residents, collect information for the department, and organize crime prevention.

## Study Questions

1. Discuss strategy, structure, and environment as they relate to the contingency school of theories.

2. Compare and contrast organic and mechanistic management styles.

3. Explain how crime rates, public fear of crime, and community relations inspired a change in policing.

## Endnotes

1. Paul Lawrence, "Why Organizations Change," in *Large-Scale Organizational Change*, eds. Allen Mobrman, Susan Mobrman, Gerald Ledfor, Thomas Cummings, Edward Lawler, and associates (San Francisco: Jossey-Bass, 1990), pp. 48–61.

2. Alan Isaak, *Scope and Methods of Political Science*, 4th ed. (Homewood, IL: Dorsey Press, 1985).

3. James Q. Wilson and George Kelling, "The Police and Neighborhood Safety: Broken Windows," *Atlantic Monthly*, (March, 1982): 29–38.

4. Charles Perrow, "A Framework for the Comparative Analysis of Organizations," *American Sociological Review* 32 (1967): 194–208.

5. Andrew Van de Ven and Robert Drain, "The Concept of Fit in Contingency Theory," *Research in Organizational Behavior* 7 (1985): 333–365.

6. For example, see Peter Blau and R. Schoenherr, *The Structure of Organizations* (New York: Basic Books, 1971).

7. Tom Burns and G. M. Stalker, *The Management of Innovation*, 3rd ed. (Oxford: Oxford University Press, 1995), p. 4.

8. Paul Lawrence and Jay Lorsch, *Organization and Environment: Managing Differentiation and Integration* (Homewood, IL: Richard D. Irwin, 1969).

9. David Hurst, *Crisis and Renewal: Meeting the Challenge of Organizational Change* (Boston: Harvard Business School Press, 1995), pp. 36–37.

10. GNP data are based on U.S. Department of Commerce, *Statistical Abstract of the United States*, (1991) Table 690, p. 425.

11. For a discussion of the theory, see Lawrence Cohen and Marcus Felson, "Social Change and Crime Rate: A Routine Activity Approach," *American Sociological Review* 44 (1979): 588–608.

12. For a discussion of the relationship between parental supervision and juvenile delinquency, see Joseph Rankin and Roger Kern, "Parental Attachments and Delinquency," *Criminology* 32 (1994): 495–516; Robert Sampson and John Laub, *Crime in the Making: Pathways and Turning Points Through Life* (Cambridge, MA: Harvard University Press, 1993); Travis Hirschi, *Causes of Delinquency* (Berkeley: University of California Press, 1969).

13. Bureau of Justice Statistics, *Weapons Offenses and Offenders*, (Washington, DC: National Institute of Justice, 1995).

14. James Q. Wilson, *Thinking About Crime*, rev. ed. (New York: Vintage Books, 1985).

15. Please see Charles Juret, "Structural Change and U.S. Urban Ethnic Minorities," *Journal of Urban Affairs* 13 (1991): 307–336; and Nan Maxwell, "Demographic and Economic Determinants of United States Income Inequality" *Social Science Quarterly* 70 (1989): 245–264.

16. U.S. Department of Commerce, *Statistical Abstract of the United States* (1969), Table No. 21, p. 22; and *Statistical Abstract of the United (1991)*, Table No. 40, p. 36.

17. William Julius Wilson, *The Truly Disadvantaged* (Chicago: University of Chicago Press, 1987); William Julius Wilson, "The Black Community in the 1980s: Questions of Race, Class, and Public Policy," *Annals of the American Academy of Political and Social Science* 454 (1981):26–41.

18. U.S. Department of Commerce, *Statistical Abstract of the United States* (1991), Table No. 652, p. 396.

19. Thomas Bonczar and Allen Beck, *Lifetime Likelihood of Going to State or Federal Prison* (Washington, DC: Bureau of Justice Statistics, 1997).

20. Herbert Koppel, *Lifetime Likelihood of Victimization* (Washington, DC: Bureau of Justice Statistics, 1987), Table 1, p. 2.

21. "The 1968 Report of the National Advisory Commission on Civil Disorders—Summary," cited in Steven Brandl and David Barlow, *Classics in Policing* (Cincinnati: Anderson, 1996), p. 48–49. ✦

❖ ❖ ❖ ❖

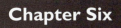

**Chapter Six**

# Community Policing in Action

❖ ❖ ❖ ❖

*People may doubt what you say, but they will believe what you do.*

—Lewis Cass

*Even if you are on the right track, you will get run over
if you just sit there.*

—Will Rogers

Community policing, discussed in the preceding chapters, is a fairly complex style that is unprecedented in the history of American policing. Community policing alters almost every aspect of professional-style police work, including organizational culture, managerial style, and the role of police officers and sheriff's deputies. This new and more comprehensive approach to policing has been difficult for scholars and police to describe with much precision. To some, it simply means doing traditional things better; to others it may mean adding programs for the benefit of good community relations. The following pages help clarify what community policing might look like wherever it is fully implemented.

Two general perspectives can be found in the historical development of community policing. According to the first perspective, there is a clear movement by police across the country to adopt community policing and it is expected that community policing eventually will replace the professional style of policing by redefining the fundamental goals and operations of law enforcement.[1] Furthermore, proponents of this view admit that the evolutionary process of police change is slow in many respects but is, nonetheless, concrete and moving forward. In short, community policing represents the future of American policing.[2]

In contrast, according to the second perspective, almost any new program or change implemented by a police department can be held up as an example of community policing because so very little is known about the real intentions of community policing or its effectiveness.[3] The popularity of the concept of community policing combined with so little real knowledge about it allows many police departments to claim that they are doing community policing without having to produce any systematic proof.

This chapter tries to answer the question, Does community policing really exist? Are innovative programs implemented in police departments across the country a signal that real organizational change has occurred in American policing? To what extent are such innovative programs being implemented?

Over the last 10 years, there have been several books and other studies about the implementation of specific local programs.[4] The cases reported in these studies provide detailed accounts of community policing programs, including their initiation, implementation, and impact. In addition, they identify some common programs that have been introduced under the banner of community policing, such as foot patrols and storefront stations. In order to determine if community policing has succeeded nationwide, however, we need to use national data.

## Is Community Policing Real?

Whether or not community policing is real depends partly on the observable changes it effects. These changes occur in many areas, including how a police department works with the public, what programs it creates or considers high priority, and how it organizes its employees to meet its goals.

This third area, organizational change, is a very important feature of community policing. Two essential components of such change are a theoretical model and actual programs. A theoretical model provides reasons why a police department (or other organization) needs to change, or move, in a certain direction and suggests how that is to be done. Programs or activities are the implementation of the change. For example, if the police want to reduce the fear of crime in a neighborhood, one theory suggests that an increase in personal communication between police officers and local residents is an effective means of achieving that goal. That theory is put into practice by initiating such activities as reestablishing citizen contacts with foot patrols, making use of police-citizen academies, or creating a police athletic league for youths.

Determining whether change is real cannot be done by examining a theoretical model in itself, because a theory is composed of assumptions and propositions, that is, of ideas. It is possible, however, to discover change by looking at it on the philosophical level, that is, how widely it is accepted by

*Neighborhood recreational centers allow youths opportunities for self-improvement. In addition, such centers provide opportunities for police and youth to become better acquainted and as a result serve to benefit the community in terms of better crime prevention and crime control. (Photo: Courtesy of the Mountlake Terrace (WA) Police Department)*

❖ ❖ ❖ ❖    key figures in a department, and on the practical level, by measuring the number of programs in operation. For example, Robert Trojanowicz and Bonnie Bucqueroux have noted that the most important element of community policing is its philosophical perspective. "Community policing is a new philosophy of policing, based on the concept that police officers and private citizens working together in creative ways can help solve contemporary community problems related to crime." Similarly, other scholars identify police-citizen partnerships and community mobilization as the hallmarks of the community policing.[5]

The next two sections will examine community policing at both the philosophical and practical levels. The first will look at the results of a national sur-

---

## Community House

### *Chief Norman Williams*

*Wichita Police Department Chief Norman Williams.*

A flood of crack cocaine washed through the streets of Wichita, Kansas, in 1988; with it came a treacherous, rising tide of gang violence that engulfed several neighborhoods in the city's northeast region. By 1993, the gangs had a strong grasp of those neighborhoods, and the residents felt they were losing control. Sustained gunfire night and day was common; few children ventured outside to play; senior citizens barricaded themselves in their homes; and families slept crowded on the floor in back rooms, as far from the street as possible.

The neighborhood that suffered the worst devastation was an area 13 blocks long and 10 blocks wide. According to data from the 1990 census, this area was 92 percent African American, 5 percent other minorities, and 3 percent Caucasian. Housing was predominately single-family units with a median value of $35,000. There were 547 single-family dwellings and three multiple-family dwellings consisting of 52 apartments. Nonresidential structures included three churches and 10 businesses. In June 1996, 63 single-family dwellings were vacant and abandoned, resulting in an occupancy rate of 88.5 percent. This neighborhood also was suffering from outward migration as a growing number of homeowners chose to move out of the area and turn their houses into rental properties.

Initially, a survey was conducted by community policing officers from the Wichita Police Department in order to learn about concerns of the residents. Due to apathy and quite possibly outright fear, only 6 percent of those sent surveys responded. In May 1996, the police department sponsored a community meeting in the neighborhood at a local church. Over 100 residents attended to discuss their concerns and ways they might resolve neighborhood problems. This meeting was an important first step, laying the groundwork for these residents to take back their community.

Officers continued to work with neighborhood residents and local community leaders to identify and discuss issues affecting their neighborhood and quality of life. The community agreed upon three main goals. Improving public safety by the removal of the gangs and their associated violent criminal activities was deemed first priority. Improvement of police-community relations and cooperation, which ☞

☞ would lead to the reclamation of their neighborhood, was recognized as next most important. Finally, neighbors wanted overall improvement in the appearance of the physical environment as a sign of their commitment.

In the initial phase of the strategic community policing plan, during the May 1996 meeting, the community house concept was presented to the attending residents and news people. The concept involved transforming a vacant city-owned house in the neighborhood into a functional facility that could provide safe meeting space for classes, health services, counseling, meetings, and access to legal services, including law enforcement. The community house would have a community policing officer and various patrol officers present during hours of operation. Officers also would use the house after hours for completion of paperwork and to show a continued presence in the area.

*Some houses in the neighborhood looked like this prior to a community policing intervention. (Photo: Courtesy of the Wichita Police Department)*

*The results suggests that effectively 'weeding' and 'seeding' a 'broken-windows' site sends a message of ownership and hope to law-abiding citizens and a message to lawbreakers that unwelcome behavior will not be tolerated. (Photo: Courtesy of the Wichita Police Department)* ☞

❖ ❖ ❖ ❖     ☞

The local housing authority representative sought and received authorization from the Department of Housing Urban Development (HUD) to use a HUD unit for conversion into a community house. A HUD representative stated that this project was "the first of its kind where a HUD house was donated to any city for use by the community." The community house was renovated and opened to the neighborhood residents in October 1996. Since then it has been the site of more than 300 meetings, multiple neighborhood events, and many hours of health-related, legal, and counseling services.

Local residents also wanted a public telephone in their neighborhood since many of their households lacked phone service. This request, which was previously unrecognized as a community need, resulted in a combined effort between the local phone company and the community policing officer to install a public pay phone, which was located outside the community house. In addition, the phone company agreed to donate, on a sliding scale, a percentage of revenue generated from the pay phone to the neighborhood association.

The community house also provided office space for the Wichita Metropolitan Family Preservation Agency. This agency is the steering committee for the federal "Weed & Seed" money that was awarded to the city of Wichita. The "Weed & Seed" money made a significant contribution to neighborhood law enforcement efforts and to the success of the neighborhood. The Family Preservation Agency also provided classes on parenting skills, teenage peer resistance, and alternatives to gang lifestyles. In addition, the community house hosted a monthly food program that provided low-cost, high-quality food to the community; it was packaged and distributed by volunteers and police officers.

---

Chief of Police Norman D. Williams is a 24-year veteran of the Wichita Police Department. He has commanded the Support Services, Field Services, and Investigations Division, as well as Patrol, Special Operations, and Public Affairs Bureaus during his career. He has a B.S. degree in the administration of justice from Wichita State University and recently finished his M.A. in public administration at WSU. A graduate of the FBI Academy, Williams holds certificates from the U.S. Secret Service Dignitary Protection Seminar and the 1998 and 1999 Midwest Criminal Justice Institute's Law Enforcement Leadership Seminars. His numerous awards include the Gold Wreath of Honor and several Bronze Wreaths. He also has been recognized several times as Police Officer of the Year and is a recipient of the NAACP Image Award.

---

vey of chiefs of police to find out the level of their acceptance. The second will examine implementation based on data from 201 police departments nationwide. The findings in these two sections will provide an answer to the central question of this chapter: Does community policing really exist? The last section will consider four successful community-policing programs.

## Acceptance of the Philosophy of Community Policing Among Police Chiefs

The findings reported in this section are derived from a national survey of police chiefs and sheriffs conducted in 1993. The purpose of this survey was to evaluate the degree of organizational change toward community policing from a philosophical standpoint. Based on the 1990 Justice Agency List developed by the Bureau of Census, the original sampling frame contained a listing of 17,542 police and sheriff's departments. Because most community policing took place in medium or large departments, a stratified random sample of 2,337 departments was selected. This sample included (1) all

municipal and county enforcement agencies with 100 or more sworn personnel, (2) 50 percent from departments with 50 to 99 sworn officers, (3) 10 percent from departments with 10 to 49 sworn officers, and (4) 5 percent from
small departments with fewer than 10 law enforcement sworn officers. The
final data set included 1,606 departments.

The survey consisted of the personal responses of police executives. A
number of questions concerning community policing were asked, including
the amount of support for the community policing philosophy, the degree of
change required, and the outcomes.

## Community Policing Buy-in

Because the surveyors believed the chiefs' views of community policing
were crucial to its adoption, the first question was, Did the chiefs surveyed
buy into the community policing philosophy? The answer is reported in Figures 6.1 and 6.2. An overwhelming majority (95.1 percent) of police executives agreed with the following statement: "The concept of community policing is something that police departments should pursue." The high level of
consensus certainly indicates that the community-policing philosophy was
almost universally accepted by top policing executives. The survey also examined the attitudes of the chiefs toward specific aspects of community policing
such as overall utility, extent of departmental change, and anticipated outcomes. The ratings on each aspect are consistent with the theoretical model.
Clearly, a majority of police executives believe in the concept of community
policing.

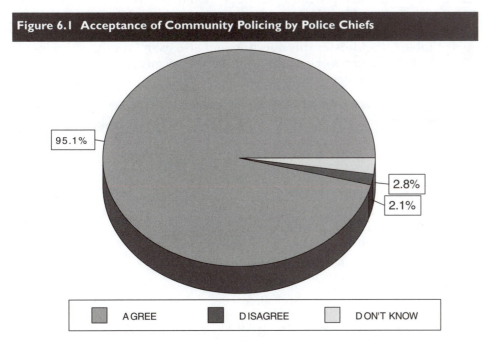

**Figure 6.1  Acceptance of Community Policing by Police Chiefs**

95.1%

2.8%

2.1%

AGREE          DISAGREE          DON'T KNOW

Statement: The concept of community policing is something that police departments
should pursue.

❖ ❖ ❖ ❖

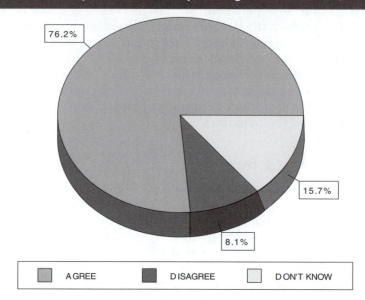

**Figure 6.2  Overall Impact of Community Policing**

76.2%

15.7%

8.1%

AGREE            DISAGREE            DON'T KNOW

Statement: Community policing is a highly effective means of providing police service.

## Structural and Managerial Change Required

Historically, the three primary goals of American policing have been crime control, maintaining order, and providing services. Since crime control was the top priority in the professional era, as discussed in chapter 4, maintaining order and providing services should receive most emphasis in the community era. Therefore, the second question was, How much change is necessary to modify the goals of police departments as estimated by police chiefs? Table 6.1 addresses this question and also examines the attitudes of police chiefs in the areas of evaluating employee performance, participatory management, and police officer training.

**Table 6.1    The Extent of Structural and Managerial Changes in Law Enforcement Agencies According to Police Chiefs**

| Statement | Agree | Disagree | Don't Know |
|---|---|---|---|
| 1.  Community policing requires major changes of organizational policies, goals, or mission statements. | 52.2% | 46.0% | 1.8% |
| 2.  Performance evaluation should be revised to support community policing. | 79.4 | 15.5 | 5.0 |
| 3.  Some form of participatory management is necessary for the successful implementation of community policing. | 95.4 | 2.5 | 2.1 |
| 4.  Community policing requires a major change in the approach to law enforcement training. | 63.2 | 33.6 | 3.2 |

N = 1,171

Overall, police chiefs were split on the statement, "Community policing requires major changes of organizational policies, goals, and mission statement." More than half (52.2 percent) believed that community policing requires a fundamental change in departmental goals and policies. The executives surveyed were more likely to agree with statements concerning the changes that should be made in specific areas. For example, almost all (95.4 percent) agreed that the bureaucratic style of policing, which emphasizes tight control, should be replaced by a participatory management style, in which supervisors try to help patrol officers do their job. The relationship is more akin to coaching than to direct supervision.

Similarly, a majority of the executives surveyed held the view that corresponding changes in performance evaluation and training are needed if community policing is to be fully implemented. Performance evaluation is particularly important because the productivity of police officers is redefined. During the professional era, the primary criterion used to evaluate performance was number of arrests or calls for service. Community policing encourages officers to develop problem-solving skills. Other criteria, such as working with local residents and controlling social disorder in a neighborhood, become important measures of the productivity of officers.

## Outcomes of Community Policing

The third question was, What do police administrators anticipate are the outcomes of community policing programs and strategies? Will they, for example, (1) improve police-community relations, (2) increase the level of trust, and (3) reduce social disorder in the community? In addition, will the improved working environment increase the level of job satisfaction among officers?

| Table 6.2 | Possible Impacts of Community Policing Implementation According to Police Chiefs | | | |
|---|---|---|---|---|
| Statement | Not Likely | Somewhat Likely | Likely | Don't Know |
| 1. The problems that citizens care about would be reduced. | 3.7% | 41.6% | 49.8% | 5.0% |
| 2. The physical environment of neighborhoods would improve. | 4.6 | 33.7 | 53.5 | 8.1 |
| 3. Citizens would feel more positive about their police departments. | 0.6 | 16.4 | 81.0 | 2.0 |
| 4. The potential for physical conflict between citizens and police would decrease. | 7.4 | 40.9 | 43.2 | 8.5 |
| 5. Officer and deputy job satisfaction would increase. | 3.0 | 33.8 | 53.5 | 9.6 |
| 6. Crime rates would decrease. | 6.7 | 47.7 | 25.6 | 19.9 |

Table 6.2 shows the opinions of police executives in each of these areas. Their perceptions are consistent with the predictions proposed by the com-

❖ ❖ ❖ ❖     munity policing model. For example, over 90 percent thought that community policing could lead to a more positive attitude among citizens toward the police. Similarly, they also anticipated that an improved working environment could lead to a higher level of job satisfaction for police officers.

An interesting observation concerns the relationship between community policing and local crime rates. A primary principle of community policing is the promotion of partnerships between the police and local communities, in order to address the root causes of crime, namely social disorder. This suggests that the relationship between community policing programs and crime rates is not direct, and indeed there is very little evidence to suggest that community policing directly reduces crime rates. This view is reflected in the survey. Only a quarter of the chiefs thought that community policing would cause a decline in crime rates, and another 20 percent did not know the effect of community policing on crime.

## Crime-Free Multifamily Housing—Eliminating Drug and Crime Problems in Multifamily Housing in Tacoma, Washington

### Jack Bodnar and Lucy Edwards Hochstein

Over the last few years Blockwatch, Crimestoppers, Community Alert, and a host of other programs have been implemented across the United States to improve public safety. A highly successful program that partners the police with other public-service agencies and the public has been observed in Tacoma, Washington. Referred to as Crime-Free Multifamily Housing, (CFMFH), this innovative project involves collaboration between the Tacoma Police Department and the Tacoma Human Rights Department to empower tenants, managers, and landlords of low-rent public housing to promote safer neighborhoods and improve the quality of life in poor urban areas.

CFMFH strives to create a useful and replicable program that might be applied in any community under similar circumstances to achieve any of several goals related to education, inspection, and certification of the area's apartment communities. These goals include the reduction of calls for police services involving juvenile crimes in particular; increases in social activities for youth; provision of landlord information regarding eviction and intervention; the facilitation of voluntary registration of rental units; and the creation of city ordinances that would help the project continue beyond its initial funding.

As an important part of the program, participating property owners and managers are provided Crime Prevention Through Environmental Design (CPTED) training and then an evaluation of their property. They are next offered the opportunity to certify their rental units as Crime-Free Multifamily Housing compliant. With certification come signs that make prospective tenants aware of property management's participation in the program and forewarn applicants of an in-depth background check that precludes accepting tenants with criminal records.

The authors of this essay evaluated the program to determine its impact on crime reduction, perceptions of quality of life and police services, and objective measures of physical and social disorder. We based our conclusions on data collected from three primary sources. First, we conducted focus group interviews with individuals involved with the project, such as tenants, landlords and managers, residents, and other stakeholders. Second, we took guided tours of the housing units to observe residential conditions in participating apartment buildings and in those who were considering joining. Finally, we examined official statistics from the Tacoma Police Department involving calls for police services made by landlords, managers, and tenants. These data compared calls for services for a variety of misdemeanor and felony crimes recorded by the police over several months both prior to and after ☞

☞  CPTED training.

We presented our findings at the 1999 Academy of Criminal Justice Sciences Conference in Orlando, Florida. We noted that most respondents had noticed positive changes in their neighborhoods since the implementation of the program and felt safer, more secure, and less fearful of criminal attacks in their residences and around their neighborhoods. Improved public safety was attributed to the CPTED training and the applicant-screening process mandated by those dwellings participating in the program.

Data comparing neighborhood crimes for the six-month period from January to June 1998 with the same period in 1997 indicated the following: homicides dropped from 2 to 0; rapes decreased from 14 to 4; robberies fell from 98 to 15; commercial burglaries from 37 to 23; residential burglaries from 197 to 40; aggravated assaults from 93 to 49; nonaggravated assaults from 157 to 106; auto theft from 98 to 45; and other thefts from 439 to 124.

We also reported that 76 active block groups shut down 60 drug houses. Forty-seven multihousing units showed reductions in calls for police service, and the average calls for service among certified units fell from 12.76 to 10.56 calls per month—a reduction of 17.2 percent.

Overall, the acknowledgment of positive physical and social improvements in the neighborhood was attributed to CFMFH activities, such as improved lighting, better security measures, more efficient grounds maintenance, the increase in local businesses, structural and aesthetic improvements, expanded rapport with police officers, and a better feeling about the neighborhood itself. As a consequence of CFMFH, residents noted a marked decrease in drug-related activity, solicitation for prostitution, loitering, traffic, and roaming gangs. People became friendlier, got more involved in their community, and felt safer in their neighborhoods—one more example where an effective partnership between the police, other public officials, and the public can make a meaningful difference in promoting public safety!

---

Jack Bodnar is the coordinator of justice studies and an instructor in social sciences and criminal justice at Lewis-Clark State College in Coeur d' Alène, Idaho. He is also a retired police officer and a doctoral candidate in criminal justice. Lucy Edwards Hochstein formerly worked for the Spokane (Washington) Police Department as program evaluator for the Spokane regional domestic violence team. She is currently an assistant professor at Radford University with research interests in the way law enforcement, government, and nonprofit agencies collaborate to respond effectively to crime.

In sum, the survey shows that most police chiefs have accepted the community-policing philosophy, agree that there should be changes in management style and goals, and anticipate positive outcomes from community-policing programs. In short, they accept the concept of community policing at least on the theoretical level.

## Programs That Implement Community Policing

On the practical level of programs in operation, they fall into two areas—externally focused change and internally focused change. Externally focused change typically includes the reorientation of patrol operations and crime-prevention activities. Internally focused change involves reorganization within the department.

Perhaps the most obvious indicator of a shift to community policing is the implementation of community policing programs in the public realm, that is, externally focused change. Systematic evaluations of departments

❖ ❖ ❖ ❖     indicate that a wide variety of innovative programs and strategies have been developed by police across the nation. A rich body of literature has accumulated over the last 10 years that describe the actual programs.

Innovations in police management, or internally focused change, are not nearly so visible to the public. Nevertheless, internal change is important if community policing is to survive. Because the programs and strategies of community policing are different from those of the professional era, it follows that participatory management style of community policing will have to replace the impersonal bureaucratic style of the professional era.

*Police officers walking beats, riding bicycles, or on horseback are highly visible to the public and would-be criminal offenders. They are also readily accessible to the public for sharing information, asking questions, and building trust. (Photo: Courtesy of the Omaha Police Department)*

## Externally Focused Change

Two cornerstones of external change may be distinguished: patrol and crime prevention.

***Reorientation of patrol operations.*** An early cornerstone of community policing programs was the reorientation of patrol operations. A first characteristic of such operations was the effort to increase and improve interactions between the police and local residents. For example, bike patrol and foot patrol allow police officers to interact with citizens and gain first-hand information about who belongs in a neighborhood and who does not.

Early research on the effectiveness of foot patrols focused on the neighborhood foot-patrol program in Flint, Michigan, during the early 1980s. Researchers found that foot-patrol programs reduced crime and improved the public's perceptions of the police in neighborhoods where the program was implemented.[6] Another foot-patrol experiment was in response to public concern over an increase in street crimes in downtown Newark, New Jersey. Researchers found that the public was more aware of the presence of police officers patrolling on foot than in cars. Although actual crime rates remained unchanged during the experiment, foot patrol reduced the fear of crime among local residents.[7]

A second characteristic of reoriented patrol operations was that police officers were given some measure of ownership of the areas that they were responsible for policing. Police officers are assigned to patrol a particular neighborhood for a fixed period of time instead of being on call. Such fixed

❖ ❖ ❖ ❖

assignments enable them to get to know local residents, the dynamics of the neighborhood, and community problems and resources. Such knowledge promotes the use of problem-solving skills, allowing patrol personnel to work closely with local residents or groups to develop solutions to community problems.

A third characteristic of reoriented patrol operations is that police departments are actively involved with collecting information and providing services as part of their formal mission. Conducting community surveys (discussed in a later chapter) is one of the commonly used methods for actively seeking information.

The data referred to below were derived from a national survey of 281 municipal police departments in 1993 and 1996 and illustrate typical community policing practices.[8] The cities were selected from cities with populations above 25,000. Of 281 police departments surveyed, 201 (71.5 percent) responded to both the 1993 and the 1996 surveys. The surveys address two important questions: (1) Has community policing become more popular over time? and (2) To what extent are U.S. cities implementing community policing?

Classrooms can be effective forums for police to create a positive impression on the next generation. (Photo: Courtesy of the Omaha Police Department)

Answers to these two questions may be found in Table 6.3. First, the survey shows that community-policing programs to reorient operations are very popular. The most popular such program was the use of special task forces for solving specific problems in a neighborhood, for example in Newport News, Virginia, during the mid-1980s.[9] The findings of the Newport News evaluation strongly indicate that systematic approaches to specific problems in targeted areas through the use of special units are highly effective. Special units working with local residents can address the underlying causes of the problems, not merely incidents relating to the problem. The SARA method of problem solving (discussed in some detail in chapter 10) was introduced during the late 1980s. Not surprisingly, 90.0 percent of the police departments surveyed in 1993 reported having used special task forces to solve local problems.

❖ ❖ ❖ ❖

| Table 6.3     Externally Focused Change: Reorientation of Police Operations | | |
| --- | --- | --- |
| Programs | 1993 Yes | 1996 Yes |
| 1.  Additional officers on foot, bike, or horse patrol. | 51.0% | 59.6% |
| 2.  The use of storefront stations. | 41.3 | 57.7 |
| 3.  Fixed assignment of officers to neighborhood or schools. | 86.2 | 94.0 |
| 4.  The use of special task force for solving problems in targeted area. | 90.0 | 92.5 |
| 5.  The use of community newsletter. | 51.0 | 59.6 |
| 6.  The use of citizen surveys to keep informed. | 63.8 | 77.1 |

The next most popular program was fixed assignment of officers to neighborhoods or schools. In the 1993 survey 86.2 percent of police departments adopted this practice. Also well received were the use of community newsletters and citizen surveys. These two programs are important ways for police to collect and disseminate information.

Second, in terms of the extent of change between 1993 and 1996, the survey shows that the number of programs increased substantially. For example, the use of storefront stations rose 16.4 percent (from 41.3 percent in 1993 to 57.7 percent in 1996). The average increase of programs in general was nearly 10.0 percent, from 63.9 percent in 1993 to 73.4 percent in 1996. These findings allow us to conclude that the majority of police departments surveyed were adopting (implementing) community policing programs and strategies.

***Crime prevention.*** The second cornerstone of externally focused change is crime prevention. Whereas policing in the professional era emphasized law enforcement, community policing attempts to prevent crime from happening in the first place. An important way to achieve this goal is to gain the cooperation of the community. Local residents need to be mobilized to participate in crime prevention activities because community policing explicitly acknowledges the limited ability of police to control social disorder and reduce crime all by themselves. Neighborhood and business watch programs mobilize citizens and form joint partnerships as ways to prevent crime.

| Table 6.4     Externally Focused Change: Crime Prevention Efforts | | |
| --- | --- | --- |
| Programs | 1993 Yes | 1996 Yes |
| 1.  Neighborhood watch program. | 97.0% | 97.0% |
| 2.  Business watch program. | 65.0 | 72.6 |
| 3.  Block meetings between police and community residents. | 85.8 | 90.5 |
| 4.  Victim-contact programs. | 64.4 | 69.0 |
| 5.  The use of unpaid civilian volunteers. | 68.4 | 73.6 |

The percentage of crime-prevention programs adopted in the 201 police departments surveyed is shown in Table 6.4. Five programs and strategies were selected. Besides the two watch programs, block meetings, victim-contact programs, and the use of civilian volunteers are other core elements of crime prevention.

Overall, a comparison of Table 6.4 with Table 6.3 shows that police departments adopted more programs and strategies in crime prevention than in reorienting operations. Particularly, almost every department (97 percent) in the survey had a neighborhood watch program. Similarly, business watch programs were found to be popular in the municipalities surveyed. The percentage of change in these five prevention programs shows that there was a noticeable increase in such programs between 1993 and 1996.

## Internally Focused Change

There has been very limited research on the extent of internally focused change in police departments in the past. Most attention has been given to the reorientation of police operations and crime prevention because they are more visible and are relatively easy to implement and measure. Research in management science, however, reveals that there is a close association between externally focused and internally focused change. External changes are essential, but they require corresponding internal changes in management to put them on a more permanent, institutional basis. Research suggests several notable innovations in the area of internal change that fit with the community policing style. For example, in their book *The New Blue Line: Police Innovation in Six American Cities*, Jerome Skolnick and David Bayley noted that one obvious indicator of community policing is an increase in hiring civilian employees for positions formerly held by sworn officers.[10]

The use of quality circles to improve problem-solving capabilities among police officers is another important area of recent managerial change. Police officers are encouraged to work together with middle managers and citizens to identify and solve local problems. This participatory style requires a substantial change from the bureaucratic style of policing where communication tends to travel just down the chain of command. This new style means a shift in the primary role of middle-level managers toward a role of facilitation. Related changes include the implementation of total quality management (TQM) and the use of the SARA model of problem solving at the individual and group levels. Other forms of internal change are shown in Table 6.5.

The percentages in Table 6.5 indicate that police departments are more active in adopting the first three programs and strategies than the other three. A majority reported hiring civilians, reassessing rank structure and assignments, and giving authority to rank-and-file officers in both the 1993 and the 1996 surveys. Also, nearly half (46.2 percent) of the police departments reported implementing quality circle programs. Only 22.6 percent had a "master police officer" designation to reward line officers. The reported changes among these programs between 1993 and 1996 were generally in the direction of more community policing. An increase in adaptation was noticeable in five out of the six new programs, as shown in Table 6.5.

This section, on the practical level of community policing, has attempted to answer the question: To what extent is community policing being implemented? Such implementation can be observed in terms of externally focused change and internally focused change. Surveys from 201 police

❖ ❖ ❖ ❖   departments revealed that an overwhelming number of departments implemented such externally focused changes as the reorientation of patrol operations and crime prevention activities. At this point, it seems reasonable to suggest that police departments across the nation are actively engaged in such activities that respond to the external environment. The surveys showed a noticeable and sometimes substantial increase in the number of departments that implemented five of six key kinds of internally focused changes. Of a total of 17 externally and internally focused changes, 15 were found to be more frequently adopted. This increase in implementation at the practical level, combined with consistency in surveys of positive views of police chiefs at the theoretical level, leads to the following conclusion. At both these levels it seems reasonable to say that community policing is a reality today, although it is not yet universal in American police departments.

| Table 6.5   Internally Focused Change: Managerial Changes | | |
|---|---|---|
| Programs | 1993 Yes | 1996 Yes |
| 1. Increased hiring of civilians for non-law enforcement tasks. | 68.0% | 70.6% |
| 2. Re-assessment of ranks and assignments. | 67.1 | 75.1 |
| 3. Authorizing crime scene control to first officers at the scene. | 74.4 | 82.0 |
| 4. Reassigning some management positions from sworn to civilian personnel. | 36.0 | 42.8 |
| 5. Adding the position of 'Master Police Officer' to increase rewards for line officers. | 22.6 | 18.9 |
| 6. Quality circles (problem solving among small groups of line personnel) | 46.2 | 52.5 |
| N=201 | | |

## The Role of the Federal Government in Implementing Community Policing

During the 1990s, the federal government played an important role in implementing community policing. Particularly significant was the passage of the Violent Crime Control and Law Enforcement Act in 1994. This statute represents "an investment of more than $30 billion over 6 years . . . [it] is the largest Federal anti-crime legislation in the Nation's history."[11] Furthermore, community policing received a strong endorsement from the White House during the Clinton administration. As a direct result of this legislation and administration support, the federal government is actively involved in the national implementation of community policing. This act subsidizes the hiring of an additional 100,000 officers, who must promote community policing goals in departments that use these funds. It also established the Office of Community Oriented Policing Services (the COPS Office), which coordinates and supervises federal community policing programs, and created 35 regional community policing institutes (RCPIs) across the nation.[12]

## Community Policing in Action: Lessons From an Observational Study

❖ ❖ ❖ ❖

### *Stephen D. Mastrofski, Roger B. Parks, Albert J. Reiss, Jr., and Robert E. Worden*

Community policing, a relatively recent addition to law enforcement, aims to increase interaction and cooperation between local police and the people and neighborhoods they serve. Its goals are to reduce and prevent crime and to increase feelings of safety among residents. Passage of the Violent Crime Control and Law Enforcement Act of 1994 brought federal support for implementing and evaluating many community policing programs.

One study conducted in Indianapolis in 1996, sponsored by the National Institute of Justice and the Office of Community Oriented Policing Services, focused on police-community interactions in jurisdictions that have implemented some form of community policing. The research project had the following objectives:

- To compare past and present policing methods, particularly in light of the emerging popularity of community policing.

- To reveal more about the nature of police discretion and which features of police organizations influence it.

- To study the effects of factors outside the police department on officer and citizen behavior relevant to policing.

- To determine the consequences of policing on the general public.

This preview of research in progress is an initial report of a large study. Other analyses of data are expected. One striking finding was that as cooperation between police and citizens in solving neighborhood problems increased, the residents felt more secure in their neighborhoods. The study also revealed several factors affecting police responses to citizen requests for assistance, as well as information about the attitudes of police supervisors toward their roles and their relations with subordinates.

### Methodology

In 1996 researchers observed police in 12 neighborhoods (police beats) in Indianapolis about three years after the city had begun to move toward community policing. These police beats experienced various degrees of socioeconomic distress but were not selected to be representative of the city as a whole. Data were gathered through systematic observations of officers on patrol, observations of supervisors, private interviews with patrol officers and their supervisors, and telephone interviews with residents (supplemented by interviews of residents of the city's other 38 police beats).

### Neighborhood Context

Researchers characterized the neighborhoods, using an index of socioeconomic distress that was the sum of the following percentages: labor force that was unemployed, population that was very poor, and families that were headed by single women. Based on this index, the neighborhoods were clustered in groups of low, medium, and high distress.

The study revealed strong positive correlations between the level of socioeconomic distress and several measures of involvement with the police, including the number of calls for service received at the police dispatch center, the number of officers responding to the scenes of reported problems, and police and citizen perceptions of the severity of problems in the neighborhood. Moreover, as socioeconomic distress increased, residents felt less safe walking in their neighborhoods at night, an indication of the perceived level of safety.

Researchers developed scales representing citizens' perceptions of neighborhoods, residents' cooperation with police, and of police cooperation with residents. ☞

❖ ❖ ❖ ❖    ☞

As police-citizen cooperation increased, residents considered the neighborhood to be safer.

## Requests for Assistance and Police Responses

Researchers also looked at requests by one person for officers to control another person. Requests for such assistance were ranked according to the degree of restriction they placed on the freedom of the targeted party, from advice and persuasion, through warnings and threats, to making someone leave the scene, to arrest. On the basis of their observations, researchers gleaned data about the people requesting assistance, police responses, and factors affecting whether police fulfilled such requests.

Compared to other citizens with whom police had contact, citizens requesting the control of other citizens were disproportionately people of low income and women dealing with a male officer. The situations were generally less serious than other police calls: no emergency existed and evidence did not indicate violence or theft. About half the cases were domestic disputes that had not yet become violent. Two-thirds of the requesters asked for only one form of control of another citizen.

Researchers found that police were least likely to arrest the target (33 percent of requests for arrest were fulfilled) but most likely to send the target away (75 percent of such requests were fulfilled). When citizens requested more than one form of control, police nearly always granted either all or none of these requests. Nearly 60 percent of the citizens requesting control had their most restrictive request carried out.

A number of factors proved to be statistically significant predictors of police responsiveness to calls for control. The following increased the probability of assistance: strong evidence against the target, a middle-income (as opposed to low-income) requester, and an officer with more training in community policing principles. Decreasing the chance that the request would be fulfilled were a requester who asked for an arrest, a requester who behaved disrespectfully to police, a requester who was a crime suspect, and a responding officer with more years of police experience.

Variables that were not statistically significant included the age of the requester, whether the requester or the target was intoxicated, whether the requester was injured, the race and gender of the requester and target, whether the target was disrespectful, and the severity of the problem. Also not significant were several characteristics of the responding officer: whether the officer had a specialized community policing assignment, the officer's attitude toward maintaining order, and whether the officer had a college degree.

Future data analysis will compare situations when the target of control was present with those when the target was not.

## The Role of Police Supervisors

The adoption of community policing principles affects the role prescribed for supervisors. Previously, supervisors' predominant concern was control, achieved mainly through manipulating limited punishments and offering even more limited incentives. Today, police supervision is expected to place more emphasis on supporting subordinates.

Data gathered in the Indianapolis study showed that supervisors considered supportive activities (helping officers develop sound judgment, providing feedback on their performance, and helping them work on problems in the neighborhoods they serve) more important than constraining ones (enforcing rules, disseminating information on departmental directives, and monitoring officers' completion of reports).

Researchers suggested that the emphasis on support is due in part to the supervisory structure in Indianapolis. Supervisors are not individually responsible for a squad of officers, and on any given shift, two or three supervisors may share responsibilities. Researchers believe this deemphasis on control affects how the supervisors perceive their role.    ☞

☞ | **Issues for Further Study**

The Indianapolis research demonstrated that community policing efforts may make a difference. Perceived safety in a neighborhood was higher when police and residents cooperated in problem solving; officers with more community policing training were more willing to grant a citizen's request to control another citizen; and the police supervisors interviewed emphasized their support of, rather than their control of, subordinates.

The study's findings raised a number of topics for further consideration by researchers and policymakers. One avenue for further consideration is even stronger encouragement of police-citizen cooperation. Another is modifying training programs to address the challenges of dealing with the circumstances under which these requests are most likely to arise: low-income female requesters who are not suspects but who may be disrespectful to a male officer. Researchers also need to learn more about the long-term consequences of fulfilling these requests. Finally, researchers noted the need for more refined measures of supervisors' styles and to what extent they affect subordinates' performance patterns.

This document is based on a discussion of research conducted by Stephen Mastrofski, professor, Michigan State University; Albert J. Reiss, Jr., Professor Emeritus, Yale University; Roger B. Parks, professor, Indiana University; and Robert E. Worden, associate professor, State University of New York-Albany. Co-sponsored by National Institute of Justice and the Office of Community Oriented Policing Services, the research was conducted under NIJ grant number 95-IJ-CX-0071. Points of view in this document do not necessarily reflect the official position of the U.S. Department of Justice.

With the financial and technical support of the federal government, the progress of community policing has been significant since 1994. For example, as of May 29, 1998, more than 75,000 additional community policing officers were funded under the 1994 act.[13] Numerous programs were created across the nation.

Government support is particularly crucial given the nature of American politics. Americans tend to be highly suspicious of centralized government. Consequently, unlike Britain and France, there is no centralized police force in the United States. Instead, individual police departments are administered by local governments. The total number of U.S. police departments is more than 12,000. In order to promote community policing, it is important to have central organization that can facilitate the collection and dissemination of information and provide financial and technical assistance.

## Successful Community Policing Programs

This section discusses four successful case studies of community policing.[14] The contents of these four programs vary significantly, but they all represent a new way of doing police work, emphasizing community partnerships and problem-solving skills.

### Case Study 1: Collaborative Effort Between Teenagers and Police Reduced Graffiti in Redmond, Washington

In early 1993, Redmond, a Seattle suburb, faced a citywide graffiti problem. The 42,000 residents of the city were filing more than 60 graffiti com-

❖ ❖ ❖ ❖        plaints each month. At first, police officers tried traditional approaches to the problem by establishing organized cleanup procedures and stepping up enforcement patrols in areas that had graffiti. These measures had no significant effect.

Looking for different approaches, the officers interviewed a number of youths believed to be associated with the graffiti. From these discussions, officers learned that most of the youths considered the vandalism to be a form of hip-hop art. Initially, officers questioned the assertion that the graffiti was a form of self-expression, believing it to be gang related. After an officer analyzed the department's case reports and researched the problem of graffiti in general (by reading popular literature and consulting other sources), it became clear that the Redmond problem did not involve gangs. One reason for this conclusion was that the content of the graffiti in Redmond was not generally violent, whereas graffiti perpetrated by gangs in other cities sometimes included coded references to murder and other violent acts.

Consequently, officers met with teenage "taggers" (youth slang for graffiti artists) with the hope of developing a solution to the problem. Rather than being subjected to increased enforcement efforts, the teenagers suggested the city establish a legal place for them paint in return for an end to illegal tagging. The officers helped the taggers obtain permission from the city council to erect a graffiti wall and solicit donations from local businesses for materials needed to construct it. Since the wall was constructed, citizen complaints about graffiti have decreased from more than 60 per month to an average of four per month. The decline in graffiti complaints has been maintained to this day. As of 1997, only 11 citizen complaints for graffiti had been filed for the entire year—an average of 0.6 per month.

## Case Study 2: Minnesota Police Reclaimed Park for Law-abiding Citizens

A park in Mankato, Minnesota, had become a popular gathering, drinking, and socializing spot for a group of car devotees who called themselves Motorheads. Motorhead parties in the park began each day about noon and would draw 300 to 400 people by 10 P.M. Participants were unruly and tormented other park users—typically citizens who gathered for reunions or games at the park's baseball diamond. The Motorhead parties were linked to a number of problems, including assaults, public and juvenile drinking, public urination, suspected drug dealing, and $15,000 worth of criminal property damage to the park over several years. In response to the problem, police tried a number of approaches, including the installation of flood lights in the party area, and the scheduling of a large number of nonparty events at the park. None were particularly successful.

The police then decided to take a more analytical approach to the problem. Officers spent several weeks watching and then interacting with people attending the party. Once the partygoers were comfortable with the officers, the officers interviewed them to learn why they gathered in the park and in one particular area. The officers learned that the party goers liked the spot because it was out of sight, had two exits, contained a large parking lot in which they could drive around, and allowed them to see the police coming from a distance. Officers then interviewed other park users to find out why

they no longer used the area. Officers discovered that other park users were
intimidated by the party group. An analysis of park usage figures confirmed
that no one but the partygoers used the area. The officers then hosted a community meeting to elicit additional information about the problem.

The officers worked with the city parks director to develop a long-term
solution to the problem. Sensing that the partygoers would not use the park
for rowdy socializing if the area was less appealing, the police and parks officials decided to reduce the size of the massive parking lot and restrict the flow
of traffic to one way so that traffic safety in the lot would improve. The officers then worked with city engineers to draw up the proposed changes and
obtain the necessary authorizations. At the same time, the officers located an
empty downtown parking lot near the police department for the party group.
The lot was highly visible and could easily be monitored by the police.

The Motorheads stopped gathering in the park when the environmental
changes were made to the parking lot. Once they moved downtown, young
families began using all areas of the park again. The new downtown lot was
fairly isolated, so the Motorheads did not generally bother others in the area.
However, there was some displacement of Motorhead-related juvenile drinking, narcotics sales, and reckless driving problems to the area of the downtown lot. To address these problems, the police conducted several targeted
enforcement efforts. The Motorheads realized they would not be able to keep
the downtown lot unless the problem behavior stopped. At that point, the
group agreed to self-police its activities, and their behavior became more
socially acceptable.

## Case Study 3: Police Reduce Street Drinking and Related Crimes in Portland, Oregon

Due to public consumption of alcohol by problem street drinkers, Portland's residents and businesses in the Old Town and Chinatown areas were
experiencing a high level of disturbances, assaults, drug dealing, loitering,
panhandling, disorderly conduct, and other criminal activity. Officers typically arrested the drinkers, issued citations, or referred the problem drinkers
to social service programs. Since these responses did not significantly reduce
the problems, the police decided to take a different approach.

Officers coordinated the formation of a task force of citizens, police officers, and city government workers to develop a survey to assess the impact of
the street drinkers on the community. From information gathered through
the survey and other sources, the task force learned that the beverage of
choice of the street drinkers was 32-ounce and 40-ounce containers of malt
liquor, each of which had the alcoholic equivalent of a six-pack of regular
beer. When two stores that sold the 40-ounce malt liquors came up for
renewal of their liquor license, the police and license bureaus asked the stores
to stop selling these large containers. Those stores refused, but six other
major retailers agreed to a voluntary ban. Because the ban helped reduce
complaints about the drinkers, police persuaded another 40 downtown businesses to participate in the ban.

Since the ban was expanded in late 1992, the problem street drinking and
associated criminal activity has diminished and citizens and merchants have
reported a better quality of life in the downtown area. By 1994, detoxification

❖ ❖ ❖ ❖    holds in the Old Town and Chinatown areas decreased by 20 percent, drug arrests declined by 51 percent, and other related problems, such as assault, robbery, theft from auto, drinking in public, and disorderly conduct, decreased by 38 percent.

Initially, there were fears that the street drinkers would be displaced to other Portland communities still selling the 40-ounce malt liquor containers. However, while total serious crime declined in the Old Town and Chinatown areas by 15 percent from 1992 to 1993, the downtown area also experienced a very small decline (3 percent), and all Portland neighborhoods experienced a 1 percent decline over the same period, indicating that the problem-solving effort did not result in displacement to other areas of the city. Also, some community-based partners in the effort felt that displacement of the problem drinkers would actually be a favorable outcome. A representative of the Salvation Army said that dispersing the drinkers into other areas would reduce concentrated street drinking by groups, which often leads to more problems than individual street drinkers.[15]

## Case Study 4: The Police Reduce Public Underage Drinking Problem in South Boston

During the summer of 1995, police were concerned about the problem of underage drinking in South Boston, an area consisting of several square miles. Although standard crime reports did not clearly identify the scope of the problem, community resident complaints and officer observations pointed to the development of a potentially serious problem.

To affirm officers' anecdotal evidence and verify the extent of the problem, the area commander reached out to neighborhood groups such as South Boston Against Drugs (SoBAD) and the local housing authority tenant associations to assess their knowledge and concerns about the problem. This community assessment confirmed what most beat officers already knew—youths were spending summer evenings drinking in parks and other public spaces in South Boston.

To learn more about the specific nature, causes, and scope of the problem, the police conducted interviews with offending and nonoffending youth, consulted parents, and initiated a dialogue with the courts, probation officers and judges, SoBAD, and the Boys and Girls Clubs. Based on these inquiries, police determined that the penalties for underage public drinking were too light and infrequent to be a deterrent. Also parents were not well informed about the problem or involved in solving it.

Police, probation, community, and tenant groups then designed several interventions aimed at addressing the specific elements of the problem. First, area police conducted intensified surveillance of common sites for public drinking. When youths were arrested, the police offered them a deal, the terms of which had been worked out during a meeting between community groups, police, and the courts. Arrested youths would not be prosecuted if they agreed to an eight-session program on substance abuse to be held on summer evenings at six locations. Parents had to agree to attend one session with their children.

This approach was coupled with traditional means of reducing public underage drinking. The district police commander and community-service officers called a public meeting and invited all liquor store owners and managers, parents, community youth, and members of the general public. At the meeting, it was announced that the police department would begin implementing stings to catch underage buyers and sellers who failed to check identification.

During the summer of 1995, 32 youths were arrested for public drinking and all accepted the terms of the deal. Twenty-eight of the 32 arrestees completed the program and were not rearrested or observed drinking again. Community calls for service about the problem decreased. The courts also benefited because these minor cases, which had clogged the dockets but resulted in little punishment, were eliminated. Perhaps most important, youth reported that the program acted as a deterrent to future public drinking because most were not willing to attend the eight sessions on summer evenings for this minor offense.

The program was not repeated during the summer of 1996 because the problem appeared to have abated. There was not a single arrest of a juvenile for violating liquor laws that summer. There was no obvious evidence of displacement of the problem because South Boston is geographically isolated. The surrounding area is demographically and socially different from South Boston and not as conducive to public drinking. However, according to one probation officer, the problem may have returned somewhat during the summer of 1997, and South Boston police were considering taking additional steps to inform youth of the consequences of public drinking during the summer of 1998.

## Conclusion

To answer the question, Does community policing really exist?, this chapter examined community policing at two levels. At the theoretical level, which cannot be directly observed, it analyzed the opinions of police executives surveyed in 1993. They revealed substantial acceptance of the community-policing philosophy among police chiefs, agreement on required areas of change, the popularity of several community-policing programs, and the widespread adoption of these programs. Such findings lead to the conclusion that community policing is indeed real.

The chapter also discussed the role of the federal government in giving financial and technical support to community policing. Finally, four successful examples of community policing programs provided a clearer picture of community policing at work.

## Study Questions

1. Discuss the findings of the 1993 and 1996 national surveys of police chiefs.

2. Compare externally focused and internally focused change.

3. Describe the successful community policing programs discussed in this chapter.

❖ ❖ ❖ ❖   **Endnotes**

1. Robert Trojanowicz and Bonnie Bucqueroux, *Community Policing: A Contemporary Perspective* (Cincinnati: Anderson, 1990).

2. George Kelling, "Police and Community: The Quite Revolution," in *Perspectives on Policing*, No. 1 (Washington, DC: National Institute of Justice, 1988).

3. Michael Buerger, "The Limits of Community," in *The Challenge of Community Policing*, ed. Dennis Rosenbaum (Thousand Oaks, CA: Sage, 1994), pp. 270–273; Peter Manning, "Community Policing," in *Critical Issues in Policing: Contemporary Readings*, eds. Roger Dunham and Geoffrey Alpert (Prospect Heights, IL: Waveland, 1989), pp. 395–405.

4. For example, Jack Greene and Stephen Mastrofski, *Community Policing: Rhetoric or Reality?* (New York: Praeger, 1998); Dennis Rosenbaum, *The Challenge of Community Policing: Testing the Promises* (Thousand Oaks, CA: Sage, 1994).

5. John Eck and Dennis Rosenbaum, "The New Police Order: Effectiveness, Equity, and Efficiency in Community Policing," in *The Challenge of Community Policing*, ed. Dennis Rosenbaum (Thousand Oaks, CA: Sage, 1994), pp. 3–23.

6. Trojanowicz and Bucqueroux, *Community Policing*.

7. National Institute of Justice, *Foot Patrol* (1985). This is a series of videos moderated by James Q. Wilson.

8. The survey was conducted by the Division of Governmental Studies and Services at Washington State University, which has conducted mail-out/mail-back surveys of the same set of 281 municipal police departments in three intervals since 1978.

9. John Eck and William Spelman, "Problem-solving: Problem-oriented Policing in Newport News," *Research in Brief*, January (Washington, DC: National Institute of Justice, 1987).

10. Jerome Skolnick and David Bayley, *The New Blue Line: Police Innovations in Six American Cities* (New York: Free Press, 1986).

11. National Institute of Justice, *Criminal Justice Research Under the Crime Act—1995 to 1996* (Washington, DC: U.S. Department of Justice, 1997).

12. Office of Community Oriented Policing Services, *Community Policing*, February/March, (Washington, DC: U.S. Department of Justice, 1997).

13. Office of Community Oriented Policing Services, *President's Program to Add 100,00 Community-Policing Officers Three Quarters of the Way There*, May, (Washington, DC: U.S. Department of Justice, 1998).

14. The source for these four case studies was the Office of Community Oriented Policing Services website: www.cops/wsredmond.htm.

15. Case studies 1 through 3 were compiled from *Problem Solving Quarterly*, a publication of the Police Executive Research Forum (PERF) and nominations for PERF's 1994 Herman Goldstein Excellence in Problem Solving Award. ✦

# Chapter Seven

# The Effect of Organizational Environment on the Implementation of Community Policing

❖ ❖ ❖ ❖

*The truth of the matter is that you always know the right thing to do.*
*The hard part is doing it.*

—Norman Schwarzkopf

More and more police departments are beginning to implement community policing. For example, the 1996 survey of 281 U.S. police departments in 47 states (discussed in chapter 6) showed that over 90 percent of respondents placed a greater emphasis on community policing in 1996 than they had during the previous three years. Several specific programs such as neighborhood watch, foot patrol, and storefront police stations were identified as proof of a department's commitment to community policing.

In addition to implementing a wide variety of community policing programs, many departments also indicated that their employees actively engaged in innovative policing practices. Other departments, however, admitted that their personnel were engaged in very few "real" community policing activities and did most police work in more traditional ways. The difference in the responses of these two groups of departments raises an important question: What accounts for the differences? Why do some police departments implement community policing programs when others do not?

To a large extent, the answer lies in the influence of the organizational environment. The purpose of this chapter is to take a closer look at the influence of the organizational environment—top executives, middle managers, and line officers—on innovations leading to community policing.

This chapter identifies five organizational factors that are crucial to organizational change in policing. They are the role of chief, the role of middle management, the influence of organizational structure, the role of rank-and-file officers, and the influence of organizational culture. Each of these factors is discussed in the following sections.

## The Role of the Chief

The implementation of community policing occurs over an extended period of time, anywhere from three to five years, or even longer. It is during this period of change that the chief executive (chief of police, sheriff, or public-safety director) plays an essential part in organizational change. In fact, it is his or her leadership that is crucial for the success or failure of new and innovative practices.

In their studies of the literature on leadership, House and Podsakoff note the importance of effective leaders. "Common to all of these definitions is the notion that leaders are individuals that, by their actions, facilitate the movement of a group of people toward a common or shared goal or objectives."[1]

Sixty years ago, Chester Barnard identified three essential functions of a leader in his well-known book, *The Functions of the Executive*. According to Barnard, the first function of leadership is to provide a good system of communication in an organization. Barnard argued that a smooth flow of information is essential in any successful organization. The chief executive is the person who is able to supervise and keep the information network running efficiently. Generally, a top administrator has the most access to information concerning the organization and everyone else who reports to him or her.[2]

Next, Barnard noted that a leader is someone who is responsible for creating an environment that is friendly for the growth of an organization. In this sense, an important responsibility of a leader is to secure necessary funding and generate external, community support for the organization and its mission.

Finally, Barnard recognized that a leader is expected to develop and define a sense of purpose for an organization. An effective chief executive serves as the primary designer of an organizational structure that will help the organization achieve its goals. Given the important role of leadership in an organization, it is clear that organizational change needs the full commitment and support of the leader.

It is well documented in the literature that police chiefs have considerable independence to act as they see fit in a number of areas. James Skolnick and David Bayley, for example, argue persuasively that the success of innovations in six police departments they studied depended heavily on the commitment and support from the six chiefs of police. In particular, a visionary leader who can see the future of policing is crucial for change to succeed. In this regard, police chiefs act as the primary architects of departmental policies and procedures.

Major changes in policing during the professional era largely depended on the contribution of a few notable and progressive chiefs. For example, August Vollmer led reforms in four areas by advocating: (1) the introduction of scientific policing, (2) an emphasis on education for police officers, (3) the establishment of police professionalism, and (4) the acknowledgment of formal organizational structures and policies to supervise patrol officers. Recognizing Vollmer'contributions, Donal MacNamara noted several specific innovations.

> During these 15 years of emerging police leadership, Vollmer accelerated his pattern of innovation. In 1913 he instituted motorcycle patrols and followed in 1914 with the first automobile patrol service in American policing. In 1914 he set up the Berkeley Junior Police and shortly thereafter reorganized the Berkeley Police School curriculum, a training program which over the next several decades was copied in whole or in large part by police agencies not only in many American states but also by a number of police departments abroad."[3]

Similarly, O. W. Wilson, who began as a police chief in Wichita, Kansas, and later became chief of the Chicago Police Department, crystallized the science of police administration in his 1950 book, *Police Administration*. The book provides detailed information about the "ideal" organizational structure of a police department and the criteria for measuring policing efficiency and effectiveness. Wilson's book was considered the "bible of modern policing" by the police administrators of his time and even for decades later.[4]

Police chiefs since the beginning of the professional era have been perceived to play a more critical role in the direction of a police department than any other single person either inside or outside of it. For example, a survey sponsored by the International Association of Chiefs of Police (IACP) that included 493 county and municipal police departments, found that 84 percent of the participants identified the chief of police as the person "having

❖ ❖ ❖ ❖ major responsibilities for establishing personnel policies for sworn personnel."[5]

G. W. Greisinger and his colleagues also have reported on the importance of police chiefs in developing personnel policies and the fact that their influence has been rated higher than that of city administrators. Although such findings may seem unremarkable, given the high status of chief executives in present-day police departments, readers are reminded that persons other than the chief executive often played a key role in directing police operations during the political era.[6]

Police chiefs continue to play the pivotal role in organizational change during the community era. During the early phase of the community policing movement in the 1980s, each of the few police departments that were singled out as innovators was led by a police chief known for progressive leadership. For example, former Houston police chief Lee Brown played a significant role in the implementation of community policing in that city, which was not previously known for innovation. In a 1985 article, Chief Brown argued that changes in society required a new form of police leadership. He suggested that the new type of chief executive should be both an "educator and motivator," encouraging changes in employee behavior and the community at large.

> If police chiefs' efforts in fostering community crime prevention are to be effective, there must be specific processes and structures that clearly indicate to both the public and police officers that the community has input in the operation of the police agency.[7]

In this sense, a chief of police is the primary engineer of organizational innovation.

Mark Moore and Darrel Stephens have asserted that police executives should not be limited to the orthodoxy of management, a limitation that is deeply rooted in the concept of scientific management and O. W. Wilson's doctrine of police administration:

*Professional development through training and the open exchange of ideas is an essential feature of good leadership and increasingly important as employees rise in rank.*

In this orthodoxy, the mission and goals of police departments are established externally—by law, by formal policy or simply by tradition. The role of police executives is to find efficient means—administrative, programmatic and technological—for achieving those goals. They do so through the traditional managerial functions: planning, organizing, coordinating and controlling.[8]

Moore and Stephens argue that this traditional model of management leaves no room for police executives to reconsider the basic mission of police and to be engaged in organizational change in order to meet society's changing demands. In their view, the demand for change is a result of several forces. First, as discussed in the early chapters, there is a need to reconsider the role of American police in society. Reliance solely on crime control does not meet society's demand for change. Second, the professional approach to police work has been found inadequate or ineffective to the tasks now facing the police. Finally, the development in management theories has highlighted the important role of key employees in an organization.

## The Role of Middle Management

Middle management in an organization always plays an important part in the process of organizational innovations. This chapter defines the middle management of a police department as those employees with the rank of sergeant or lieutenant. Though not as noticeable as a police chief or rank-and-file officers who actually work the streets, middle-level managers serve as front-line supervisors in the process of change and maintain the crucial communication link between the top administrators and of subordinate employees.

---

**A Preview of** *Managing Innovation in Policing: The Untapped Potential of the Middle Manager*

### *William A. Geller and Guy Swanger*

Although conventional management thinking assumes that middle managers will subvert organizational change, their power and responsibility to convert leaders' words to organizational deeds place great challenges in middle managers' bailiwick. Whether they are part of the problem of bringing about innovation or part of the solution is being tested by police departments that have recently embraced community policing and problem solving as operating strategies. At issue is whether a critical mass of police middle managers can contribute productively so that strategic changes called for by chiefs to implement community policing deeply and enduringly permeate in the department.

A new book, prepared under a National Institute of Justice grant, concludes that middle management's power to affect change can be harnessed to advance community policing objectives by including those managers in planning, acknowledging their legitimate self-interests, and motivating their investment in long-range solutions that enhance community safety and security.

### Tapping Middle Managers' Time-Tested Strengths

Community policing reorients police philosophy and strategy away from primary reliance on reactive tactics toward the view that crime, disorder, fear, and other community problems can be better redressed and prevented proactively—through multifaceted, consultative, and collaborative relationships among police, ☞

❖ ❖ ❖ ❖    ☞ diverse community groups, and public and private institutions.

When the book's authors looked for examples of middle managers—lieutenants, captains, and their civilian employee counterparts—who had led their departments toward strategic innovation, they identified those with several personal qualities likely to enhance success. These qualities included comfort with unpredictability, clarity of direction, a desire to make a difference for "customers," thoroughness, participative management style, persuasiveness, persistence, and discretion. The book notes that, under the right leadership and conditions, many in middle-ranking police positions today would be comfortable with, and make a significant contribution to, change.

Architects of the strategic transformation from professional to community policing must build on such time-tested strengths of middle management as these: close relationships with beat officers, breadth of organizational vision (vis-à-vis first-line officers and sergeants), knowledge of departmental culture (including strengths, weaknesses, and receptivity to innovation), the know-how to get things done without undermining resource commitments to preexisting programs, and attention to detail.

## Empowerment: Delegating Authority for Implementing Community Policing

Respecting middle managers, recognizing their demonstrated abilities, and committing the departments to progress through building on strengths are the starting points for enlisting support. Even those middle managers unwilling or unable to lead innovation can bolster the department's changeover by ensuring that traditional essential capacities (e.g., rapid response to citizens' genuine emergency problems) are improved or at least not weakened by the shift to community policing.

Community policing's emphasis on problem solving necessitates that middle managers draw on their familiarity with the bureaucracy to secure, maintain, and use authority to empower their subordinates. The goal is to help officers to actively and creatively confront and resolve issues, sometimes using unconventional approaches on a trial-and-error basis. Recognizing the occasional need for strict top-down operational control, middle managers must generally shift the emphasis of their responsibilities from controlling others to coaching them and from ruling by rules to leading by reason.

Without abdicating responsibility, they must delegate authority to well-trained and motivated officers who can make and share responsibility for decisions and actions. Middle managers, in turn, need support and authorization from chiefs to devise strategies and modify systems and procedures to support multishift, team problem-solving approaches. Such delegation of authority entails these elements:

- Visibly involving middle managers in planning for change to increase their credibility with subordinates.

- Maintaining consultative relationships with middle managers to motivate ongoing thinking about effectively meeting goals.

- Developing a clear linkage of rewards to performance in implementing desired changes.

- Making a serious commitment to training middle managers well in the skills they need in their adjusted roles.

To lead and guide these changes, police chiefs, senior managers, local government officials, and other stakeholders should take the following steps:

- Articulate and adhere to an unambiguous, powerful, and consistent vision for the department.

- Provide a clear mandate to all department employees for the changes they must help achieve.

- Help secure resources needed for adequate planning, any needed pilot testing, subsequent redesign, and assessment of impact.                                    ☞

☞    ❖ ❖ ❖ ❖

- Allow middle managers and others to make honest, constructive mistakes—to "fail forward" and provide ample room for them to turn mistakes into opportunities for significant innovation.

- Develop powerful external constituencies through considered openness to the news media, the community at large, and community leaders regarding needs and opportunities to reduce fear of crime.

- Ensure that long-term police-community strategies are sheltered from the short-term timetables and vicissitudes of electoral politics.

The book's research underscores the potential power of middle managers to devise, implement, and monitor police innovation. Much more needs to be learned about what does and does not work in community policing, but it is evident that middle managers will continue to play a key role in implementing this strategy.

---

This preview is based on the book *Managing Innovation in Policing: The Untapped Potential of the Middle Manager* by William A. Geller, associate director of the Police Executive Research Forum (PERF) and Guy Swanger of the San Diego Police Department. It is part of a project supported by the National Institute of Justice (grant number 92-IJ-CX-K004) to the Kennedy School of Government at Harvard University. Points of view in this preview do not necessarily reflect the official position of the U.S. Department of Justice.

A cursory review of the literature reveals very limited knowledge about the actual role of middle managers in the process of organizational change toward community policing. Such lack of information leaves many unanswered questions. For example, how much power should be delegated from middle management to rank-and-file officers in problem-solving activities? How difficult would it be for a sergeant or lieutenant to play a dual role as both supervisor and advisor?

Most of the research on community policing concerns the actual implementation of programs and, in particular, the outcomes. Studies typically report whether or not a foot patrol program actually reduces the fear of crime or how much a special drug unit has reduced drug sales in a targeted area. The authors believe that there is a primary reason for the lack of research on the role of middle management. First, since they do not work in uniform out on the streets, like foot-patrol officers, the part they play is not all that visible to either the public or to researchers. Second, because most evaluations of community policing focus on programs and their outcomes, they do not observe many middle managers, whose work is usually behind the scenes.

The authors have found only two studies of community policing that involved middle management. After briefly contrasting the traditional role of middle management during the professional era with the management style of community policing, we present the two studies.

According to the traditional, bureaucratic style of management, sergeants and lieutenants are seen as front-line regulators. Influenced by Frederick Taylor's principles of scientific management, set forth at the start of the twentieth century, police departments seek the most efficient way to achieve their primary goal, to control crime. Consequently, it is the productivity of employees, not their needs, that receives most attention. It follows that a key role of the middle management is to keep an officer's behavior under control. A sergeant needs to ensure that his or her officers meet their productivity requirement, usually to make a certain number of arrests or respond effi-

❖ ❖ ❖ ❖

ciently to a certain share of service calls in a shift. At the same time, supervisors keep an eye on officers to ensure that they follow the rules of the department.

In contrast, the behavioral school of management, which characterizes community policing, emphasizes the role of ordinary employees in the process of organizational change. Based on behavioral theories developed by Mary Parker Follett in the 1920s, the behavioral school focuses on meeting the needs of individual employees. It attempts to explain and then improve employee satisfaction and productivity by emphasizing human potential and self-motivated outcomes attributable to participative management. Therefore, the role of middle management should be to support employee efforts to do their best work, not to simply control them.

## Study of the Madison Police Department

The first study of policing that examined the role of middle management was made by Mary Ann Wycoff and Wesley Skogan, who investigated the Madison (Wisconsin) Police Department (MPD). Between 1987 and 1990, the MPD implemented an innovative program called *quality policing*. It attempted to improve the quality of the delivery of police services and raise public satisfaction with the department through frequent interactions between the police and local residents.[9]

Madison's quality-policing program was implemented across an area of 10 square miles, that is, about one-sixth of the city, and all the police officers in the area were involved. Specific principles of management were established, and police administrators were encouraged to follow them. These were the principles:

1. Believe in, foster, and support teamwork.

2. Seek employees' input before you make key decisions.

3. Believe that the best way to improve the quality of work or service is to ask and listen to employees who are doing the work.

4. Manage on the behavior of 95 percent of employees, not on the 5 percent who cause problems.

5. Be a facilitator and coach. Develop an open atmosphere that encourages providing and accepting feedback.

6. With teamwork, develop with employees agreed-upon goals and a plan to achieve them.

These principles reflect a behavioral management significantly different from the more traditional bureaucratic style. Middle-level managers operating in the behavioral style are expected to be facilitators and organizers rather than agents of control.

Wycoff and Skogan found that the new roles played by the sergeants working in the target area included setting work schedules that would maintain necessary staffing levels and helping officers succeed in solving problems. Further, the managers held meetings to provide officers with needed training and deal with other personnel matters. Similarly, the lieutenants' role in the project was to keep open communication channels and secure necessary resources for the team members. In addition, they acted as liaisons with neighborhood groups and other agencies. The researchers found that there was a significant increase in employee satisfaction with the sergeants and lieutenants who were involved with the project.

❖ ❖ ❖ ❖

## Study of the Brooklyn Police Department

The second study of middle management in policing was directed at the 72nd Precinct of Brooklyn, New York, where the New York Police Department implemented the Community Patrol Officer Program (CPOP) to promote police-community partnerships for preventing and controlling crime. This comprehensive project included (1) the fixed assignment of police units to specific neighborhoods, (2) identification of neighborhood problems, (3) use of formal and informal mechanisms to mobilize local residents in crime prevention, and (4) delegation of responsibility to the community-police unit for addressing both crime and disorder.

Police sergeants in the 72nd Precinct, like those in Madison, played a pivotal role in the implementation of the project. Researchers summarized three essential roles of CPOP sergeants. The first role was to represent the unit within the department by relaying valuable information up the chain of command about the effectiveness of the project and about specific strategies used to deal with local problems. In this way, the sergeants acted as "sellers" and "promoters" of the project in the department.

The second role of CPOP sergeants was to support activities aimed at helping the rank-and-file officers, including meeting regularly with individual officers, sharing information with the rest of the team, and securing the resources for solving problems. In this role the sergeants were "coaches" who had the responsibility of pulling officers together to work as a team.

The role of mid-management is vital to establishing community policing in a department. (Photo: Mark C. Ide)

❖ ❖ ❖ ❖     The third role of CPOP sergeants was to represent the department to the community. Because they were at the center of field operations, sergeants were better prepared to inform the community about the purpose of a program or its effectiveness to control or prevent crime.

The study highlights the important role of middle management in the change process to the behavioral school of management. When middle managers act as facilitators and organizers in the delivery of community policing, line officers can rely on their help when they encounter problems, need additional resources, have to disseminate information, or work with other units.

## The Influence of Organizational Structure

Because the structure of an organization affects its performance, organizational structure has received considerable attention throughout the history of management science. During the 1960s and 1970s, a number of management scientists examined the relationship between structure and organizational change in order to profile a general typology of structural characteristics that tend to promote innovations in an organization.

According to William Stevenson, organizational structure can be examined in three dimensions.[10] The first dimension is *structural differentiation*, which can be both vertical and horizontal. The vertical direction, or hierarchy of an organization, is measured by the number of layers or ranks in the organization. The horizontal direction, or range of functions performed by an organization, is usually measured by the number of units, the degree of specialization, and the amount of geographic space.

The second dimension is *formalization*. Formalization is the amount of regulation found in an organization to control employee behavior, such as the number of officially recognized rules and regulations. Generally, the more rules, the more formal the organizational structure.

The third dimension is the level of *centralization*. Centralization is the concentration of authority, in particular, decision making. If every decision made in an organization comes from the top of the administration, the organization is highly centralized.

Research by Burns and Stalker, as discussed in chapter 5, suggests that two types of structure arrangements are directly related to change, the mechanistic and the organic.[11] According to these researchers, the location of any individual firm varies on a continuum from mechanistic to organic, usually depending on the particular form of the environment. During the professional era, police departments seem most closely matched to the structural design of mechanistic organizations, with tall vertical structure and a fairly narrow horizontal one. They emphasized highly centralized authority and formal rules to control employees. These bureaucratic, mechanistic departments were influenced by three theoretical perspectives: (1) scientific management, which focuses on efficiency and one best way of achieving the goal of crime control; (2) the Weberian model of bureaucracy, which emphasizes impersonality and rules; and (3) Arthur Gulick's science of administration approach based on the use of chain of command and span of control. All the three perspectives are reflected in O. W. Wilson's *Police Administration* (1950).[12]

A primary weakness of the bureaucratic model of policing is that it assumes a stable external environment. Unfortunately, the external environment of police departments tends not to be stable and, to a large extent, is very dynamic. Community policing, in contrast to mechanistic-style policing, assumes an unstable environment and seeks to regain control of it through collaborative partnerships. True collaboration requires an "organic" organization. Police departments moving from a mechanistic structure to an organic one will find it necessary to flatten their vertical direction by reducing the total number of ranks and to increase their horizontal direction. In addition, they will have to deemphasize rules and policies and decentralize the control of authority and decision making.[13]

Such an organic structure enables police administrators to respond more quickly to the demands of a changing environment because fewer layers of rank enable them to process information more quickly. A wider horizon enables more personnel with general levels of skill to be spread out in direct contact with people in the external environment, thus providing them greater opportunity to respond and engage in problem-solving activities. At the same time, the deemphasis on rules and decentralization of authority place more trust on individual officers, so they can make their own choices in problem solving and community outreach.

## The Role of the Rank and File

Herman Goldstein has observed that ultimately, "community policing will work only if rank-and-file police officers buy into the concept."[14] In order for them to buy into the concept, however, police officers must have values that are consistent with those of community policing. How, then, to sell community policing to the troops? This section examines two areas that are deemed to be crucial if police officers are to buy into the community policing concept. One is the values of individual employees; the other is evaluation of their performance.

---

### Is There Really Enough Time to Do Community Policing?

*Michael L. Birzer*

Over the past several years, I have had the opportunity to provide community policing training to a host of police and sheriff's departments. These departments have varied in size from four officers to over 400. During these training sessions I have heard a fair share of criticisms (or "whining" as it's referred to in police work) leveled at community policing and myriad excuses why it won't work. Among the most frequently heard are the following: (1) my job is not to hug criminals, (2) this stuff is soft on crime, (3) my boss will never let me do community policing, (4) my responsibility is to arrest criminals and not solve problems, and (5) we don't have enough time to do community policing because we are running from call to call.

Community policing is designed to take a strong stance against crime and disorder in neighborhoods, so it is really not "hugging criminals" or being "soft on crime." Maybe the name "community policing" itself implies something softer to most police (maybe it should have been labeled some macho title such as "tactical neighborhood recovery team").

❖ ❖ ❖ ❖    ☞

If a police department has gone to the trouble of spending valuable time and effort to provide community policing training, then obviously there is some commitment present and the argument that "my boss won't let me do community policing" becomes a leadership concern within the department. The argument that "it is my job to arrest criminals and not solve problems" is one that truly amazes me. No matter how you look at it, police work is about problem solving. If the problem being investigated requires the traditional use of the criminal law, then that is exactly what is expected. The suspect in this case is arrested and booked into the local jail. Community policing revolves around the idea that if the police and citizens work together to solve small problems before they have a chance to become large crime-related problems, then everyone wins when the police become more proactive.

The criticism of not having enough time to do community policing is perhaps the most amazing excuse. To my bewilderment, I have heard this complaint not only from patrol deputies but also from supervisors. As a result, I began to examine activity logs at the end of each watch. I reviewed a number of activity logs from second watch (3:00 P.M. to 11:00 P.M. shift) whose calls contribute to the majority of the complaints about the lack of time, expecting them to be exhaustively filled with calls and activity. What a surprise I had! The first log, as I vividly recall, had six entries. The first entry was recorded as in-service and subject to call (basically the officer was coming on duty). Approximately 50 minutes later was a burglary report. Further analysis revealed that it had taken about five minutes to drive to the burglary scene (in this case a residence had been broken into) and another 35 minutes to investigate and take the report. The officer was logged back in-service and subject to a call 40 minutes later (inclusive of driving time). In all, it took 40 minutes to complete this call. About one hour later the third entry was logged, lunch break. It was reported as 35 minutes but in reality was probably a little longer. Some 40 minutes later came the fourth entry, a vehicle stop. A citation was written and the stop was logged as taking 12 minutes. About 90 minutes later the fifth entry was recorded, a suspicious character call. The activity log revealed that it took the officer four minutes to drive to the call and 10 minutes to investigate it (although nothing unusual was observed and no contact was made). There was no report completed on this call, and the officer was logged back in-service after a total of 14 minutes.

The point to be made here is the fact that this officer logged 101 minutes on call for the entire shift, including lunch! Even if time to complete the burglary report was included (about an hour), the total time out of service amounts to two hours and 41 minutes (161 minutes). An eight-hour tour of duty consists of 480 minutes. Doing the math in this case meant that there was a total of 319 minutes (five hours and 19 minutes) not answering calls. So the question is, what was the officer doing for the remaining five hours and 19 minutes when he or she supposedly was too busy to do community policing?

I asked a few officers informally about what they did with the three, four, or five hours that they are not on call during their tour of duty. The overwhelming and most common reply (usually in a defensive manner) is, "I'm patrolling my beat and checking buildings." The next question I asked an officer who had about 18 years of service was what he looked for when he checked buildings. The answer I received, "I'm looking for doors left open and businesses that have been broken into."

I do not think the complaints and criticisms revolving around the issue that there is not enough time to do community policing have much merit. Clearly these accounts, my own experiences, and the data I collected on this issue indicate that police officers even in a large metropolitan area have a considerable amount of uncommitted patrol time, reminding me of an internal study that was conducted in the late 1980s in my own department. Basically, the study looked at what deputies were doing during their tours of duty and how much time they were spending on specific activities. Unsurprisingly, that study showed that different deputies used their spare time in different ways. The study concluded that deputies spent an average of about three hours on call per tour of duty. It also revealed that deputies were not being very effective or efficient with their use of time when on call. ☞

☞    It has been my experience that most law enforcement officers do not use their time wisely, and they usually get pretty defensive when asked about it. For the most part, officers do have a lot of free time that goes unaccounted for (checking buildings and patrolling the beat) every tour of duty. It seems to me that a better, more effective use of their uncommitted time would be to apply it to community policing. Taking all of the mostly unproductive time not spent on a call (time spent checking buildings and patrolling the beat) and refocusing it on more proactive activities could have a real impact on crime. Parking the patrol car and walking around talking with citizens, making appearances at neighborhood watch meetings or neighborhood association meetings, conducting a survey of residents in an effort to determine what is important to them and maybe even learning something new about the neighborhood, studying crime reports of the area looking for patterns and causes, working at solving problems with citizens and spending as much time as possible talking with juveniles in the area are a few of the more productive alternatives that come to mind. If sheriff's deputies and police officers could refocus uncommitted time and effort in these ways, the rewards and benefits would be overwhelming and would assuredly be more effective in the prevention of crime and the improvement of the quality of life in the community. Now that would be effective crime fighting and smart policing!

---

Michael L. Birzer is an assistant professor of criminal justice at Washburn University in Topeka, Kansas. Previously, during 18 years with the Sedgwick County Sheriff's Department in Wichita, Kansas, where he became a lieutenant, he held assignments in detention, judicial services, patrol, detectives, training, community policing, and the gang unit. He has a B.S. and M.A. in the administration of justice and currently is a doctoral candidate at Oklahoma State University.

## The Values of Employees

Values can be defined as a person's beliefs about what is important in life and what an individual should do. A value has three essential characteristics: (1) it is a conviction about what is desirable, (2) it is affective, that is, associated with emotions that suggest appropriate courses of action, and (3) it has a behavioral component that can lead to action. Therefore, individual attitudes can be considered to be an expression of values in most cases.[15]

The values of traditional police officers probably are most consistent with a bureaucratic style of policing. The officer on the street views his or her role primarily as that of a crime fighter, although, as is discussed in the next chapter, that is somewhat of an overstated image, if not even a mythical portrayal, of the people who do police work.

Community policing requires a change in the values of police officers. The relationship between the values of employees and those of the prevailing culture in a department can be thought of as being reciprocal, that is, a two-way street. The values of individuals strongly influence their behavior in the police department. They bring their own personal beliefs, preferences, and ingrained attitudes to bear on the department in important ways. In fact, the strength of the departmental culture depends directly on the range and depth of shared values held by its employees.[16]

In a recent evaluation of community policing innovations in eight cities, Susan Sadd and Randolph Grinc found that the value orientations of police officers might explain why community policing innovations are more difficult to implement in some departments than others. For example, they found that the traditional values of law enforcement remain fairly popular among most police officers,

❖ ❖ ❖ ❖

> Because most officers had little knowledge of community policing beyond its 'social work' aspects, those bent on pursuing traditional policing had few qualms about rejecting community policing in its entirety. Indeed, many police officers believed that community policing did not involve 'real' police work (i.e., tasks involving the apprehension of criminals). Therefore, officers who were actually involved with community policing projects in those cities were often viewed as 'empty suits.'. . .[17]

who do little to reduce crime. Sadd and Grinc argue that distinctive value orientations among those police officers made them less likely to accept anything innovative, and as a result, they clung to the status quo, preferring to do things the way that they had always done them even if it meant being ineffective.

Clearly, it is important to discover how to change the value orientations among police officers from professional values that focus mainly on law enforcement to a new set of values that emphasize problem solving and collaborative partnerships between the police and the community. The successful implementation of community policing depends on a parallel shift of a department culture at the organizational level and employee values at the individual level.

## Evaluating Employees' Performance

The professional evaluation of police performance typically focuses on measures of traditional outcome, such as the numbers of tickets written or arrests made, because a close link has been established between the organizational goal of crime control and the effect of individual performance related to this goal. Police officers typically like this type of evaluation because an individual officer is able to know exactly what he or she needs to do to succeed.

Community policing is a new way of doing police work. Logically, there should be a new type of performance evaluation based on the new criteria rather than on citations issued or arrests made. However, Robert Reiner's research has determined that the development of a new performance evaluation lags far behind the implementation of community policing.

> What is good police performance, and how can it be assessed? Throughout the now voluminous academic research literature on the police that has burgeoned in Britain, North America, and elsewhere in the past 30 years, this has seldom been raised as an issue, let alone resolved.[18]

Consequently, lack of clear measures of performance causes many officers to be suspicious that community policing activities are primarily involved with "shaking hands" and "making a smile."

The authors identify two factors that might explain why performance measures have remained largely unchanged 20 years after community policing was introduced. The first factor concerns the relationship between departmental goals and performance measures. Generally, performance measures are developed based upon the goals and objectives of a department. Scholars and police, however, have a hard time defining what community policing is. A review of the literature suggests that the definition of community policing varies substantially at the theoretical level. There is no single ideal type of community with which all might agree. Rather, existing defini-

❖ ❖ ❖ ❖

Rank-and-file officers must accept organizational and subcultural changes if community policing is to be successfully implemented. (Photo: Mark C. Ide)

tions show varying degrees of abstraction. For example, community policing may be considered a single concept, a "plastic" concept, or a complex concept containing a number of challenging, general ideas. Police departments generally like to use the "plastic" (or loosely defined) concept because almost any program they implement can be labeled community policing. The side effect of this plasticity definition, however, is that it is difficult to develop performance measures because the goals are not clear.

The second factor concerns the scope of performance evaluation. Measures of community policing performance need to consider both the old measure of outcome (productivity) and the new measure of process (the implementation of new programs). Evaluating performance in community policing thus expands the scope of individual performance from a single dimension (productivity) to two dimensions (productivity and process). In addition, the role of police officer expands from that of a professional-style law enforcer to a multirole player doing community policing. For example, Jerome McElroy found that in the New York Police Department, police officers involved with community policing are expected to be planners, community organizers, information collectors, and problem solvers.[19] Activities such as planning and collecting information clearly are process oriented.

Three studies explore the topic of performance evaluation under conditions of organizational change. In his book *Problem Oriented Policing*, Herman Goldstein proposed a new kind of performance evaluation that considers the problem-solving capabilities of individual police officers based on two primary criteria. The first is job performance, which deals with an officer's understanding of a problem and the proper methods that are needed to solve it. The second area is the effectiveness of problem-solving activities,

❖ ❖ ❖ ❖ measured on a scale ranging from total elimination of the problem to reducing its seriousness.[20]

Based on their research in the Houston Police Department, Timothy Oettmeier and Mary Ann Wycoff suggested that evaluation criteria can be derived from an officer's three primary functions. The reactive function is usually related to the professional-style responsibilities of police work, such as responses to service calls. The proactive function deals with the efforts initiated by police officers attempting to address a localized problem, such as collecting information, developing strategies, and actually implementing these strategies. Finally, the coactive function involves the cooperation between police officers and community residents in problem solving, establishing contact with local residents, soliciting their input, and mobilizing them. Oettmeier and Wycoff believe that the development of performance criteria based on these three essential functions can provide a better measure of police officers' job performance in an era of community policing.[21]

More recently, Geoffrey Alpert and Mark Moore argue that, in addition to traditional measures of crime rates, total arrests, and clearance rates, police performance should be measured by the following elements:

1. Police-related activities that improve the social fabric of the community.

2. Projects with the help of private industry that improve informal and formal social control in the community.

3. Efforts to reduce fear of crime in a neighborhood.

4. Other support programs to help victims and promote community spirit.[22]

The focus of performance measures proposed by Alpert and Moore is more concerned with the improvement of quality of life in a community at the organizational level. That is, activities attempting to improve the quality of life become a top priority for a police agency to evaluate their performance. The development of performance measures at the individual level should follow this general principle of community orientation. The issue of performance appraisal in a community policing era is also reviewed in chapter 11.

## The Influence of Organizational Culture as a Determinant of Change

During the last 10 years, organizational culture has received considerable attention in research on organizational change. Steven Ott defines organizational culture in the following way: "Culture is to the organization what personality is to the individual—a hidden, yet unifying theme that provides meaning, direction, and mobilization."[23]

❖ ❖ ❖ ❖

### Charting a Course for Change: The Use of Citizen and Employee Survey Data to Assess Policing Progress Over Time

*Lee Parker and Randal Landen*

By the late 1980s, crime and the fear of crime had ascended to the top of the list of public concerns in the United States. Further, the fear of crime was not a hazard confined to the most heavily populated cities but an affliction that spread nationwide. By the early 1990s, even Midwestern states that had long been viewed as the heartland, where family values reigned supreme, churches were filled on Sundays, and streets were relatively free of violence, found themselves increasingly concerned about crime.

That was true of the largest city in Kansas, where increases in the magnitude and visibility of crime left residents fearful of violence and skeptical of solutions. Citizen responses to a 1993 community survey administered in Wichita, a city of 300,000 people and a police force of 525 sworn personnel, revealed a community extremely dissatisfied with the level of public safety. Approximately three-quarters of the respondents felt that the Wichita Police Department's response to gang and drug-related activity and proactive approach to crime was substandard; just over 58 percent reported that they only sometimes, rarely, or never felt safe on the streets of their city. According to survey results, the community wanted additional police services that focused on crime prevention.

In the face of growing public dissatisfaction with police services, in May 1995 the Wichita Police Department implemented its Strategic Plan for Community Policing and Resource Allocation. The plan established limited "community policing" activities in four target areas. The goal of the "target-area" approach was the delivery of police services tailored to meet the needs of a specific geographic area. Even though this approach was fragmented, it signaled the department's intent to move toward a new philosophy of public safety. Unfortunately, not all of those involved openly welcomed the changes in store for the department; at least initially, community policing was viewed as an add-on service, and community policing officers were largely looked down upon by traditionally assigned patrol units.

A survey of all sworn personnel some two months later revealed the monumental task that lay ahead for a police department in transition. The results from this survey indicated the critical importance of communication, particularly in an organization undergoing significant changes.[1] More than 93 percent of the respondents acknowledged that input from the community was essential to crime prevention, and 97 percent believed that communication with citizens was critical to solving crime. Although more than 80 percent reported that the key to effectively reducing crime was improved communication and cooperation between citizens and the police, nearly 93 percent believed that citizens were reluctant to work with the police because they lacked confidence in the department. Low morale and a perceived lack of departmental direction were also evident from the survey results.

Within months, a new police chief was appointed from within the department. The new chief immediately began to make strategic shifts in organizational philosophy and structure designed to improve performance and provide quality customer service tailored to the community through its public safety initiative (PSI). The initiative supported the adoption of citywide community policing and proposed the addition of 126 personnel (112 commissioned and 14 civilian employees) over a two-year period to address four stated goals.[2]

***1.1. Make Wichita a safer community through a reduction in crime:*** By developing partnerships through the community, the root of crime problems will be determined and solutions to those problems will be designed and implemented in conjunction with the community. By addressing the community's public safety problems through partnerships, existing crime and the prospects for future crime will be reduced.

***1.2. Provide high quality customer service:*** By providing the community with a better staffed and equipped police force that is specially trained in the community

❖ ❖ ❖ ❖    ☞

policing philosophy, the Police Department will improve its ability to deliver police services in a more timely, customer-oriented way.

*1.3 Ensure timely, effective follow-up on investigations:* One of the major improvements provided by the public safety initiative is the addition of personnel and equipment assigned to investigate crimes. These improvements allow the Police Department to both investigate more crimes in a more efficient manner and to improve communications with the community regarding the status of investigations.

*1.4 Institute accountability at all levels within the department:* By assigning officers to work with citizens throughout the community, officers will be more accountable to citizens through the development of partnerships. In addition, increased numbers of frontline supervisors are provided to ensure that the beat teams remain focused on community goals. The personnel evaluation process will be revised to ensure that personnel are responsible for accomplishing performance goals tailored to the unique needs of the community they serve.

In September 1997, approximately 18 months after the implementation of the public safety initiative (PSI), a second community survey[3] was conducted. As in the 1993 survey, residents' opinion about quality-of-life issues and delivery of police services were of key concern. The results of the 1997 survey showed that 91 percent of the respondents believed that community policing was making their neighborhood safer. In stark contrast to the 1993 findings, more than two-thirds of those surveyed in 1997 gave public safety in Wichita a moderate-to-high rating. Nearly 82 percent of the respondents were now willing to participate in public safety efforts to solve neighborhood problems. Even though it was less than two years old, the citywide community policing plan implemented through the public safety initiative appeared to have gained strong support from the community. More than 58 percent of the respondents called for increased spending for community policing, and more than 37 percent were willing to absorb an increase in taxes to pay for improved community policing programs.

The results of the survey indicated substantial improvement in the community's satisfaction with police services and a willingness to participate in partnerships with police to solve problems within their neighborhoods. Researchers concluded that the public was pleased with the department's transition to community policing. What remained to be seen was the reaction to public support for community policing from sworn employees themselves.

In 1999, a survey of Wichita Police Department personnel was conducted to assess the impact of the transition to community policing. Key issues such as training, autonomy, morale, and each officer's opportunities to interact with the community were studied. Here the results indicated that more than 98 percent of all officers said that they felt citizen assistance was required to prevent crime. Data presented to Table 7.1 compares police officers' perceptions of public trust in policing in 1995 and 1999.

| Table 7.1    Police Perceptions of the Public Trust—Comparing Data From 1995 and 1999 | | |
|---|---|---|
| (Percentages) 1995 N=311 1999 N=437 | | |
| Statement: Citizens have confidence and trust in the Wichita Police Department. | | |
|  | 1995 | 1999 |
| Definitely false | 8.6 | .05 |
| Probably false | 27.5 | 1.9 |
| Not sure | 34.8 | 15.0 |
| Probably true | 27.5 | 69.2 |
| Definitely true | 1.6 | 13.0 |

Table 7.1 indicates that in 1995, only about 29 percent of Wichita police officers believed citizens in the community had confidence and trust in the Wichita Police    ☞

Department. By 1999, this number had risen to over 82 percent, and only 2.4 percent believed that public trust and confidence had not improved. Also by 1999, over 94 percent of the department's sworn personnel believed they had a good understanding of the department's community policing philosophy and just over 81 percent believed that departmental changes resulting from the community policing initiative were positive. Although changes in department administration also were perceived as positive, more than 85 percent of officers felt that the increase in community support primarily was the result of the department's transition to community policing. Accordingly, the overall morale of department personnel had improved significantly since 1995 as is evident in Table 7.2.

| Table 7.2   Morale Comparison 1995 to 1999 | | |
|---|---|---|
| (Percentages) 1995 N=307 1999 N=439 | | |
| | 1995 | 1999 |
| Very low morale with substantial negative impact on performance | 22.8 | 1.8 |
| Low morale with moderate impact on performance | 54.4 | 13.4 |
| Medium morale level with a balance between positive and negative impact on performance | 20.8 | 50.6 |
| High morale with more positive than negative impact on performance | 2.0 | 30.5 |
| Very high morale with a mostly positive impact on performance | 0.0 | 3.6 |

Officers who believed the morale of the department was low or very low decreased from just over 78 percent in 1995 to over 15 percent in 1999, representing an improvement of over 63 percentage points since the implementation of community policing.

The results of the 1999 survey indicated that Wichita police officers supported the department's community policing philosophy and believed that the transition to community policing was, to a great extent, responsible for the increase in public support for the department. Just as important, rank-and-file officers appeared to be comfortable with their newly acquired community policing knowledge and their active involvement in policing in partnership with the community.

Lee Parker is an assistant professor of criminal justice in the School of Community Affairs at Wichita State University and coauthor of *A Guide to Resources for Conducting Criminal Justice Research*. Randal Landen is an 18-year veteran of the Wichita Police Department and commander of the Patrol West Bureau.

### Endnotes

1. Les Poole, "Organizational Change," a lecture presented to the Law Enforcement Executive Leadership Institute, June 8, 1998. Wichita State University, Midwest Criminal Justice Institute: Wichita, KS.
2. Wichita Police Department Public Safety Initiative (1996).
3. Mark Glaser, Lee Parker, Robin Clements, and Allison Ohlman, *Honoring Citizen Values in Strategic Decision Making: Citizen-Demand Assessment, Quality of Life, and Taxation* (Wichita: Wichita State University, Hugo Wall School for Urban and Public Affairs, Institute for Communities and Government, 1997).

Ott's definition has several important implications. First, each organization or group of organizations has a distinctive culture. For example, research from other countries suggests that organizations in a single country

❖ ❖ ❖ ❖       may share many distinctive features that set them apart from similar organizations in other countries. Research by William Ouchi determined that Japanese companies tend to demonstrate certain cultural traits that differentiate them from their American counterparts in key ways. The successful experience of total quality management (discussed in chapter 9) in Japan highlights the relationship between cultural difference and adoption to innovation.

The second implication is that organizational culture tends to support an organizational rationale that explains why an organization behaves in certain ways. For example, James Thompson has observed that public agencies have to respond (or appear responsive) to public demand no matter how badly they are treated by their constituents.[24] In contrast, private companies do not have similar constraints and can reallocate resources elsewhere to produce a different kind of product if they choose to do so.

The third implication is that organizational culture is heavily influenced by employees, who bring to an organization their own values. At the same time, organizational culture influences the ways that employees do their daily work. Overall, organizational culture gives an organization its identity within in a social setting.

Many researchers have concluded that the culture of professional police departments does not readily lend itself to organizational change. For example, Gary Cordner argued that a primary feature of a professional police culture is to embrace crime control as the police's primary mission. He suggested that this police culture is a closed system, isolated from the general public.[25]

Organizational culture also helps explain why individual organizations behave in predictable ways. In his analysis of the Rodney King incident in Los Angeles in March 1991, Jack Greene made the following summary of the organizational culture of the Los Angeles Police Department LAPD):

1. The department took a rather tough stance on police corruption, but not on issues of police use of force.

2. The department saw itself as outgunned and outmanned, which in turn justified an aggressive, "in-your-face" police style.

3. The department had adopted policies that alienated it from the community.

4. The department had created an internal system based on loyalty and to a certain extent "fear of reprisal."[26]

For many years in the LAPD, this distinctive organizational culture had translated into an aggressive way of policing shared by many officers at the street level. Particularly disturbing was the scene captured by video camera of a dozen patrol officers watching their colleagues brutally beat Rodney King. Not even a single officer in the group bothered to intervene. Given the LAPD culture at that time, it seems fair to say that the Rodney King incident was not a bizarre or isolated event.[27]

It is important to discuss what kind of organizational culture might support organizational change in policing. The U.S. Department of Justice identified a set of values that are necessary for a department to be successful in adopting community policing:

The 'culture' of a police department reflects what that department believes in as an organization. These beliefs are reflected in the department's recruiting and selection practices, policies and procedures, training and development, and ultimately, in the actions of its officers in delivering services. Clearly all police departments have a culture. The key question is whether that culture has been carefully developed or simply allowed to develop without benefit of thought or guidance.[28]

The Department of Justice also has identified five specific principles that should be incorporated into the culture of a police department:

*1. The police department must preserve and advance the principles of democracy.* All societies must have a system for maintaining order and providing services. Police officers in the United States must accomplish their tasks based on the democratic form of government. In doing so, they must protect the rights of individual citizens.

*2. The police department places its highest value on the preservation of human life.* Police departments should hold the view that human life is our most precious resource. Consequently, human services should be given the top priority in police work. The use of force should be minimized in order to protect the lives of citizens.

*3. The police department believes that the prevention of crime is its number one operational priority.* This statement is a substantial departure from the professional style of policing in which crime control is considered as the top priority. Community policing reprioritizes the functions of police by highlighting crime prevention.

*4. The police department will involve the community in the delivery of its services.* This statement reflects an important principle of community policing—police need the help and assistance from local communities. As discussed in the previous chapters, research in the 1970s found that police alone cannot control crime because crime is a social problem. Furthermore, many strategies used by the police are actually ineffective in controlling crimes. Consequently, the partnership between the police and local residents is crucial for crime control.

*5. The police department believes it must be accountable to the community it serves.* This statement acknowledges that police departments do not simply provide services. They are also held accountable for the services provided. The priorities of service are crime prevention and community mobilization. It is believed that success in these priority areas will result in long-term reductions in crime.[29]

The five principles stated above clearly advocate a totally different police culture than was prominent during the professional era. Police departments that attempt to promote these five principles are likely to create a more favorable environment for innovation and change.

## Conclusion

This chapter has identified five important factors of an organizational environment that are directly associated with change.

Although it is not clear if any one factor is more important than another, it is important to note that five factors make up an environment that, to a large extent, determines (1) why a police department wants to change, (2)

❖ ❖ ❖ ❖    how it is going to change, and (3) the outcome of organizational change. Furthermore, these five factors appear to be closely associated. Officers' values have strong influence on the culture of the organization and vice versa. At the same time, a chief's commitment to change certainly has consequences for the behavior of both the middle managers and rank-and-file officers.

These five factors cannot be judged as simply as they have been presented. For example, police departments do not neatly fit into categories of being centralized or decentralized. Instead, any individual department will fall somewhere on a continuum of this dimension. Similarly, it will fall on a continuum in terms of other dimensions. The prospects for a department to implement community policing improve as its scores on these five organizational factors move toward the "ideal type"end of the spectrum for each of these dimensions. (For example, if a department can move toward a decentralized organizational structure, then there is a better chance for the successful innovation required by community policing.) Since organizational change is a long, drawn out process, taking stock of where a department stands on each of the five organizational factors can help the department understand how far it has come and how much further it has to go in order to succeed.

## Study Questions

1. In what ways did August Vollmer lead the reform movement during the professional era?

2. Discuss the three dimensions of organizational structure as described by Stevenson.

3. What are the primary theoretical perspectives that serve as blueprints for the design of police departments?

4. Identify the principles that should be incorporated into the culture of a police department as described by the U.S. Department of Justice.

## Endnotes

1. Robert House and Philip Podsakoff, "Leadership Effectiveness: Past Perspectives and Future Directions For Research," in *Organizational Behavior: The State of the Science*, ed. Jerald Greenberg (Hillsdale, NJ: L. Erlbaum Associates, 1994), pp. 45–82.

2. Chester Barnard, *The Function of the Executive* (Cambridge, MA: Harvard University Press, 1938).

3. Donal E. MacNamara, "August Vollmer: The Vision of Police Professionalism," in *Pioneers in Policing*, ed. P. J. Stead (Montclair, NJ: Patterson Smith, 1977), pp. 178–190.

4. Gene Carte and Elaine Carte, "O. W. Wilson: Police Theory in Action," in *Pioneers in Policing*, ed. P. J. Stead (Montclair, NJ: Patterson Smith, 1977), pp. 207–223.

5. Terry E. Eisenberg, Deborah A. Kent, and Charles C. Wall, *Police Personnel Practices in State and Local Governments* (Washington, DC: International Association of Chiefs of Police and the Police Foundation, 1977).

6. G. W. Greisinger, J. S. Slovak, and J. J. Molkup, *Civil Service Systems: Their Input on Police Administration* (Washington, DC: U.S. Department of Justice, 1979).

7. Lee Brown, "Police-Community Power Sharing," in *Police Leadership in America: Crisis and Opportunity*, ed. William A. Geller (New York: Praeger, 1985), pp. 70–83.

8. Mark Moore and Darrel Stephens, *Beyond Command and Control: The Strategic Management of Police Departments* (Washington, DC: Police Executive Research Forum, 1991).

9. Mary Ann Wycoff and Wesley Skogan, *Community Policing in Madison: Quality from the Inside Out* (Washington, DC: Police Executive Research Forum, 1993).

10. William Stevenson, "Organization Design," in *Handbook of Organization Behavior*, ed. Robert Golembiewski (New York: M. Dekker, 1993), pp. 141–168.

11. Tom Burns and G. M. Stalker, *The Management of Innovation* (London: Travistock, 1961).

12. Orlando W. Wilson, *Police Administration* (New York: McGraw-Hill, 1950).

13. Please also see: Gary Cordner, "Community Policing: Elements and Effects," in *Community Policing: Contemporary Readings*, eds. Geoffrey Alpert and Alex Piquero (Prospect Heights, IL: Waveland, 1998), pp. 45–62.

14. Herman Goldstein, "Toward Community-Oriented Policing: Potential, Basic Requirements, and Threshold Questions," *Crime and Delinquency* 33 (1987): 6–30.

15. Milton Rokeach, *The Nature of Human Values* (New York: Free Press, 1973).

16. For a discussion about the influence of individual police officer values on the department, see: Michael Lipsky, *Street-Level Bureaucracy: Dilemmas of the Individual in Public Service* (New York: Russell Sage Foundation, 1980); William Muir, *Police: The Streetcorner Politicians* (Chicago: University of Chicago Press, 1977).

17. Susan Sadd and Randolph Grinc, "Innovative Neighborhood Oriented Policing," in *The Challenge of Community Policing: Testing the Promises*, ed. Dennis Rosenbaum (Thousand Oaks, CA: Sage, 1994), pp. 27–52.

18. Robert Reiner, "Process or Product? Problems of Assessing Individual Police Performance," in *How to Recognize Good Policing Problems and Issues*, ed. Jean-Paul Brodeur (Washington, DC: Police Executive Research Forum, 1998), pp. 55–72.

19. Jerome McElroy, "Evaluating Service Delivery of Police Agencies: Suggestions for Focus and Strategy," in *How to Recognize Good Policing: Problems and Issues*, ed. Jean-Paul Brodeur (Washington, DC: Police Executive Research Forum, 1998), pp. 73–87.

20. Herman Goldstein, *Problem Oriented Policing* (New York: McGraw-Hill, 1990).

21. Timothy Oettmeier and Mary Ann Wycoff, "Police Performance in the Nineties: Practitioner Perspectives," *American Journal of Police* 13 (1994): 21–49.

22. Geoffrey Alpert and Mark Moore, "Measuring Police Performance in the New Paradigm of Policing," in *Community Policing and Contemporary Readings*, eds. Geoffrey Alpert and Alex Piquero (Prospect Heights, IL: Waveland Press, 1997), pp. 215–232.

23. Steven Ott, *The Organizational Culture Perspective* (Pacific Grove, CA: Brooks/Cole, 1989).

24. Gary Cordner, "Open and Closed Models in Police Organizations: Traditions, Dilemmas, and Practical Considerations," *Journal of Police Science and Administration*, 1978, 6:22–34.

25. James Thompson, *Organization in Action* (New York: McGraw-Hill, 1967).

26. Jack R. Greene, "The Road to Community Policing in Los Angeles: A Case Study," in *Community Policing: Contemporary Readings*, eds. Geoffrey Alpert and Alex Piquero (Prospect Heights, IL: Waveland Press, 1998), pp. 123–158.

27. Jerome Skolnick and James Fyfe, *Above the Law* (New York: Free Press, 1993).

28. U. S. Department of Justice, "Principles of Good Policing," in *Critical Issues in Policing*, 2nd ed., eds. Roger Dunham and Geoffrey Alpert (Prospect Heights, IL: Waveland, 1993), pp. 182–207.

29. *Ibid.* ✦

# Chapter Eight

# Selecting and Training Employees to Do Community Policing

❖ ❖ ❖ ❖

*Every calling is great when greatly pursued.*

—Oliver Wendell Holmes

The organizational changes that a police department must accomplish in order to prepare itself to implement community policing were discussed in the last chapter. The administration must set the tone for change and then support the middle-level and rank-and-file personnel who carry out the policy. This chapter will look at the people in the department who have the greatest contact with the general public on a daily basis. These are patrol officers. It is at this level that the community will actually see and learn about community policing and begin to understand its benefits.

## Hiring for Success: What Kind of Officer Do We Really Want Anyway?

Gerald Heuett, Jr., a Phoenix police officer and a technical advisor to the Arizona Regional Community Policing Institute, when training police about what citizens expect of them, uses an exercise that helps distinguish a professional police perspective from one that views community policing as its primary goal. He begins the exercise by asking a class of 30 or so to identify the characteristics of the ideal patrol officer. Typically they describe a person who has courage, is brave under fire, and who can be counted on to come to the aid of a fellow officer in trouble. Heuett next asks them to describe the officer they might want on the scene of a hypothetical situation involving their own son or daughter in a serious automobile crash. Here the group describes an officer in terms such as compassionate, sensitive, fair, and calm under pressure. This exercise puts police in the same position as the citizens they serve. Heuett believes that the striking difference in the responses to the first and second questions is that in the second the participants have unknowingly answered the same way that citizens do when they are asked to describe their image of the ideal police officer. Although police admire colleagues who exhibit bravery and know how to take charge in dangerous situations, when the people they care most about are the recipients of police services, they prefer them to be treated with compassion and fairness just as ordinary citizens do.

This exercise raises an interesting question. What accounts for differences in the way in which officers and the public view the role of police in the world?

### Explaining the Law Enforcement Perspective Among Uniformed Personnel

Police scholars have noted differences in the orientation of the police and the public. For example, Victor Kappeler, Richard Sluder, and Geoffrey Alpert suggest that key among public-police differences is their "worldview."[1]

The way the police view the world can be described as a 'we/they' or 'us/them' orientation. Police tend to see the world as being composed of insiders and outsiders—police and citizens. Persons who are not police officers are considered outsiders and are viewed with suspicion.[2]

❖ ❖ ❖ ❖

People who are police officers develop their own particular *ethos*, involving three specific traits that are central to the police profession. It has been suggested that the high value placed on bravery, autonomy, and secrecy distinguish the police as an occupational group.[3]

As part of their occupation, police are expected to be brave in the face of danger, braver than any other group because they are the people who have the legitimate right to use force, and they are the ones whom the public calls when such force may be needed to maintain or restore order. Similarly, they value autonomy, that is, considerable discretion in deciding how to handle situations because no rulebook can cover every situation that an officer might encounter, nor does the administration necessarily want to control their every action. Finally, the police value secrecy in the way they obtain information and in their procedures, because they tend to view civilians as outsiders who might not understand or fully appreciate the way the police control crime.

Three major reasons explain why police and citizens have different views about how policing should be done and what skills are needed.

One reason they differ might be the kind of people society selects to do this job. Owing to the kinds of people drawn to careers in policing in the first place, and to the kinds of people that police departments prefer to hire, the policing profession tends to consist of people who share certain traits that make them very similar to one another and different from citizens in general.

From the authors' experience, college students interested in careers in law enforcement (mostly criminal justice majors) usually choose policing for the opportunity it might present for working outdoors and because it gives them the chance to do work that helps people. Research on this topic reveals that applicants for jobs in policing come from backgrounds not all that different from the backgrounds of citizens in general. For example, scholar Lawrence Sherman writes,

> The limited evidence suggests police work attracts the sons and daughters of successful tradespeople, foremen, and civil servants—especially police. For many of them, the good salary (relative to the educational requirements), job security, and prestige of police work represent a good step up in the world, an improvement on their parents' position in life.[4]

Sherman goes on to point out that police recruits typically are drawn to policing for understandable reasons, rather than based upon personality quirks or dysfunctions.

> The motivation to become a police officer flows naturally from the social position of the people who choose policing. People do not seem to choose policing out of an irrational lust for power or because they have an 'authoritarian personality.'. . . Police applicants tend to see police work as an adventure, as a chance to do work out of doors without being cooped up in an office, as a chance to do work that is important for the good of society, and not as a chance to be the 'toughest guy on the block.'[5]

At the same time, police hiring practices in the professional style have favored applicants who appreciate rules and regulations, demonstrate a need

*A sergeant instructs new recruits during training. New recruits must master a wide variety of skills before they may pass from the academy classroom to the streets. (Photo: Courtesy of the Wichita Police Department)*

for order, believe strongly in the legal system as a legitimate source of author-ity, and tend to support the idea of a chain of command as an appropriate way to manage personnel. Kappeler and his colleagues suggest that the prefer-ences of police departments for certain traits in job applicants seem to indi-cate that the police favor "conformity to a middle-class life style" as one key indicator of the acceptability of prospective candidates. They even suggest that

> Police selection practices, such as the use of physical agility tests, back-ground investigations, polygraph examinations, psychological tests and oral interviews, are all tools to screen-out applicants who have not demonstrated their conformity to middle-class norms and values. Many of the selection techniques that are used to determine the 'adequacy' of police applicants have little to do with their ability to perform the real duties associated with police work. . . .[6]

Furthermore, Kappeler and his colleagues conclude that, "A consequence of the traditional police personnel system is that it selects officers who are un-able to identify with many of the marginal groups in society."[7]

A second explanation for differences between the worldviews of citizens and police officers is that the training received by new recruits introduces them to, and then helps them accept, a perspective that they may not have previously subscribed to when they were civilians. In the terminology used by sociologists, academy training serves to "resocialize" the new recruits, help-ing them to devalue their old way of looking at the world and replace it with a new view that fits the job and the labor force that is responsible for providing police services.

Despite the fact that official statistics refute the highly risky nature of police work, academy training tends to place a heavy emphasis on the dangerousness of police work. This focus is accomplished primarily through the "war stories" that police trainers use to depict the kinds of dangers that lie in wait for the unsuspecting new recruit.

> Police vicariously experience, learn and relearn the potential for danger through 'war stories' and field training after graduation from the police academy. In fact, an inordinate amount of attention and misinformation concerning the dangers of police work is provided to police recruits at police academies.[8]

## 'You Better Be Careful Out There'

### *Jason Jolicoeur*

When I began my law enforcement career I was determined to succeed and eager to prove myself. I entered my police training, as most officers do, with a zealous desire to learn everything I would need to know so that I might eventually become a good officer. Even now, seven years after I finished my initial law enforcement training, I can still remember the other officers in my academy class and many of the instructors who taught us.

One of the main reasons that I decided to enter the law enforcement profession was that I wanted to make a difference in my community. I was determined to arrest all of the bad guys, clean up the city in which I lived, and generally make the world a safe place for old people, children, and small fuzzy animals. Given my enthusiasm for the profession and tremendous determination to succeed, I entered the academy with all the attributes of an ideal student. I wanted to be there, was intent on learning, and was willing to accept what I was taught without question.

My entrance to the academy also served as a point of transition in my life from being a civilian to becoming a police officer. Unfortunately, I realize now that during this time I, and the recruits around me, also began developing a "we vs. them" type of mentality that is often mentioned by police researchers. We went from being people who were part of, and attached to, the community to being part of a group that was, in many ways, its own community.

There are probably a number of reasons why all of us began to view the world in terms of us (the police) against them (everyone else). For starters, many of the classes in the academy, such as defensive tactics or firearms training, focused directly on officer safety. These classes burned a graphic image into our minds of the dangers the public posed to all of us. In turn, these classes were later reinforced by the "war stories" told to us by seasoned police veterans.

These stories vividly illustrated the dangers people in uniform faced, and they also served to underscore the importance of what we had previously learned in the classroom. These war stories eventually wound up being a part of almost all training that we received, whether it was related to officer survival or not. Even in classes with no apparent relation to officer survival, such as report writing, war stories would somehow surface. They would serve to remind us that even in the most mundane circumstances, like writing a simple report, there was a potential for a deranged person to be waiting for us to drop our guard so that he might be able to harm or even kill us.

The result of the academy's continual focus on officer survival was that we began to see the public as a potential threat and to view them with great suspicion. The training also introduced, and continually reinforced, our notion that cops could only really rely on the other cops because they were the only people who cared about, understood, or would come to the aid of a fellow officer. This realization was most clearly illustrated in one war story in particular. It was about an officer who was being assaulted after making a traffic stop, along a well-traveled roadway, during rush hour. None of the passing motorists would stop to offer any assistance to the officer, and in the end, he had to be rescued by his fellow officers, who were the only ones with any apparent concern for his safety.

❖ ❖ ❖ ❖   ☞

Coincidentally, actual events sometimes supported the war stories that we were told in class. These real-life events had a significant impact on our view of the world because they were a tangible representation of what had been told to us. They provided proof that the stories we had heard were an accurate depiction of what we would eventually face on the streets. Whenever one of these real-world events occurred, our instructors would always make sure that we knew about it.

An excellent example comes from a defensive tactics class. The instructor informed us that everyone could be a potential threat to us. The age, sex, size, race, or demeanor of the individuals we would soon be encountering had no bearing on their ability to harm us. A few days after, the instructor called all of us together in order to tell us about an incident that had just occurred out on the streets. An officer on a routine shoplifting call had arrested a suspect, who turned out to be an elderly female in her eighties. As the officer was finishing his paperwork, the suspect asked if he would allow her to get her medicine from her car that was parked in the lot. The officer agreed and walked her to her vehicle. After the suspect opened the car door she quickly reached under the front seat. The officer was able to grab her hand and when he looked under the seat he found a loaded handgun. The story confirmed in our minds the idea that the public cannot be trusted and that even an 80-year-old grandmother could be dangerous if we weren't careful.

I have no doubt that the training we received in relation to officer survival, and the war stories that supported the training, were well intentioned. Obviously, law enforcement can be a dangerous profession, and every year officers are tragically killed on our nation's streets. It is very likely that there will always be a need for police to provide officer-survival training to new recruits. Unfortunately, the training that I received, which appears to still be present in many police departments today, failed to take into account that the way an officer relates to and interacts with the public may be just as important to his or her safety as is familiarity with defensive tactics, impact weapons, or firearms.

Although policing can be dangerous, my on-the-job experiences taught me that police training often overemphasizes these dangers. In addition, the overemphasis on survival training tended to make me suspicious of anyone from the community who didn't carry a badge. I think our officers and our communities both deserve better than this. In the end, one of the simplest solutions to these types of problems may be to simply make police academy training more representative of the types of activities officers will actually engage in on a regular basis when they hit the streets, so that they are able to develop the skills they will need to be successful in the current environment of rapidly changing public expectations.

Jason Jolicoeur is a doctoral candidate in criminal justice at the University of Nebraska at Omaha. He holds B.S. and M.A. degrees in criminal justice from Wichita State University.

The emphasis on the potential for danger that is supposed to alert new recruits to the need to be prepared for nearly any situation typically leads to two negative consequences. Although raising officer awareness about the unpredictability of human behavior may benefit officer safety and forewarn new recruits about the peculiarities of the career path they have chosen, the traditional academy curriculum and the war stories told by police veterans help to build a chasm between those people who are sworn to uphold the law and those other people—civilians—who are seen as potential victims, witnesses, and offenders. In so doing, the traditional curriculum reinforces and elevates the subculture of policing as the thin blue line (or as retired Minneapolis police chief Anthony Bouza calls it, the "brotherhood in blue")[9] that keeps ordered society from becoming chaotic. At the same time, the curriculum encourages police officers to be suspicious of the public as the group that will produce both unworthy victims and offensive criminals.

Traditional training practices underscore the need to maintain social distance between those in uniform ("us") versus the public ("them"), thereby justifying a gap between police officers as professionals and citizens as mere consumers of police services. Observations of academy training and data collected from academy cadets support the view that traditional training reinforces police insularity and negative stereotypes of civilians. For example, John Stratton's interviews with new police recruits colorfully illustrate the impact that training has on individual officers and their families. He quotes the wife of one police cadet undergoing training:

> Those cadets sure change a lot when they go through the academy. He's only been there six weeks and I'm trying to find a way to let him know that the kids and I are not 'assholes' or 'pieces of shit.'[10]

A third explanation for differences in the perspectives of police and citizens is that experiences on the job ultimately shape the way police officers view their world. Bouza suggests that the nature of police work and the police subculture itself can ruin the altruism of well-intentioned new recruits:

> A wrong assumption made about the police is that they're not very adept at weeding out the palpably unfit at the entrance level. On the contrary, the thoroughness of the background investigation nearly guarantees that new recruits will be qualified for the job.[11]

Speaking from his experiences, Bouza instead suggests that it is the policing experience itself that determines what kind of officer the department will produce:

> The background investigators (other cops trained for that purpose) find out an enormous amount of information about a candidate's life. Those later found to be unfit are usually exposed because of a predilection for brutality. They tend to be veterans, shaped by the agency rather than by their genes or preentrance proclivities. Most of the brutes I encountered, in three police agencies, were probably formed and subtly encouraged by the agency's culture. The background check tends to exclude the feckless, the irresponsible, and those with poor or unstable school, work, or military records.[12]

Research by James Q. Wilson is in agreement with Bouza: It is the policing experience within an organizational setting that ultimately molds the officer and helps to shape his or her worldview.[13]

What a police department expects from (and ultimately, how it treats) its police officers depends to a large extent upon the perspective from which the department predicts human behavior. McGregor's Theory X and Theory Y offer a good illustration. McGregor suggests that management's beliefs about the basic orientation of workers toward their job assignments determine what managers think motivates employee performance and how best to manage them. For example, managers who subscribe to Theory X tend to believe that most employees have little enthusiasm for their assigned duties and that close supervision, combined with negative reinforcement for misbehavior, are necessary to ensure that employees do what they are told. Low expectations for employee performance based upon employees' negative attitudes toward their organization and the work in general then lead to low morale and cynicism. In contrast, proponents of Theory Y have a more optimistic image of employees. They believe that employees will perform their duties to the best of their abilities when they have input into the work they do, see great

❖ ❖ ❖ ❖     value in their work, and believe that the work they do makes a positive contribution to their organization, another group, or the greater society.[14]

Although neither perspective may fully capture all workers in a police department, researchers who write about professional-style policing tend to portray the cadre of uniformed personnel as a subculture of people who are cynical, secretive, and resistant to change. Researchers who are proponents of community policing, however, tend to be more optimistic about the capacity of the police subculture to change and adapt to community policing. Which group more accurately describes the police profession? In part, the answer probably has to do with the amount of time a department has invested in professional-style police work. For example, Theodore Ferdinand suggests that police officer "solidarity" is greatest among experienced line officers and least well developed among academy cadets.[15] In part the answer may be that it depends on which era of policing is being discussed. Theory X seems well suited to explaining employee attitudes and behavior that result from bureaucratic styles of policing developed during the professional era, while Theory Y appears to better fit more promising expectations for police officers during the community era. McGregor's Theory X and Theory Y will be discussed further in chapter 9.

*The use of simulators and virtual reality can increase training effectiveness. (Photo: Mark C. Ide)*

New police recruits, before they have become socialized into the subculture of policing, may approach the job with enthusiasm and energy, only to find out from more experienced employees that peer expectations for performance that are less ambitious or different from what recruits anticipated. For example, John Van Maanen, a noted scholar, writes that

> The novice patrolman soon learns that there are few incentives to work hard. He also discovers that the most satisfactory solution to the labyrinth of hierarchy, the red tape, and unpleasantness which characterizes the occupation is to adopt the group standard, stressing a 'lay-low-and-don't-make-waves'

work ethic. And the best way in which he can stay out of trouble is to mini-mize the amount of work he pursues.[16]

Available research tends to support the idea of a subculture of policing that is created out of the shared experiences of the people in uniform. In fact, it is easy to imagine even the most optimistic officers being let down by con-stantly dealing with the kinds of circumstances that police face when doing traditional, reactive policing. Former police officer and popular novelist Jo-seph Wambaugh writes that the most disheartening aspect of policing has lit-tle to do with having to deal with the least desirable segment of society oper-ating at its worst behavior, for this is to be expected, but rather, having to answer calls where the best members of society are caught at their worst mo-ments.[17] Human behavior that falls under the category of "something-that-ought-not-to-be-happening-and-about-which-someone-had-better-do-something-now," as the scholar Egon Bittner has referred to it, taxes the po-lice officer's ability to view the general public in a positive light.[18]

In addition to the kinds of situations that new patrol officers encounter in the field with civilians, the negative attitudes of their colleagues also fuel their cynicism toward the public and the department they work for. Van Maanen's interview with one veteran patrol officer illustrates how the tradi-tional police subculture views itself with respect to the administration and the people they are sworn to protect:

> . . . You gotta learn to take it easy. The department don't care about you and the public sure as hell ain't gonna cry over the fact that the patrolman always gets the shit end of the stick. The only people who do care are your brother of-ficers. So just lay back and take it easy out here. Makes things a lot smoother for us as well as yourself.[19]

Similarly, police cynicism can be fueled by poor management, as Bittner has noted:

> Because police superiors do not direct the activity of officers in any impor-tant sense they are perceived as mere disciplinarians. Not only are they not actually available to give help, advice, and direction in the handling of diffi-cult problems, but such a role cannot even be projected for them. Contrary to the army officer who is expected to lead his men into battle—even though he many never have a chance to do it—the analogously ranked police official is someone who can only do a great deal *to* his subordinates and very little *for* them. For this reason supervisory personnel are often viewed by the line per-sonnel with distrust and even contempt.[20]

Nevertheless, with all the negatives that have been written about the po-licing subculture, it is not necessarily true that the subculture as a whole is uniformly bad in itself or bad for community policing. John Crank argues that seasoned police officers have a great deal to offer in the implementation of community policing if only the administration will trust them to use their street skills and experience for the sake of organizational change.

Crank eloquently describes the positive features of the police subculture:

> Seasoned officers are culture carriers, the department's living traditions acted out daily. They have acquired a practical understanding about people on their beat. They know how to deal with them. They have 'toolkits' of solu-tions to the everyday, garden-variety problems to which they are long accus-tomed. They have a sense of when to speak softly, when to use command voice, when to ignore, or when to look closer. They know the saturnine alleys,

❖ ❖ ❖ ❖        the quiet roads where lovers sneak away, the fields where teenagers go to drink on Saturday night, the safe havens, and the areas that need pressure. They chafe at the limits of their ability to respond to problems—to arrest bad guys, to provide activities for young people.[21]

For Crank, and for community policing, the police subculture holds a great deal of promise for policing reform.

> The key to successful community policing lies in the way that administrators engage a street cop's heart. The rank and file need to be involved in some capacity in all planning sessions, in the development of training programs, and in the ongoing evaluation of their work. They must be given self-accountability.[22]

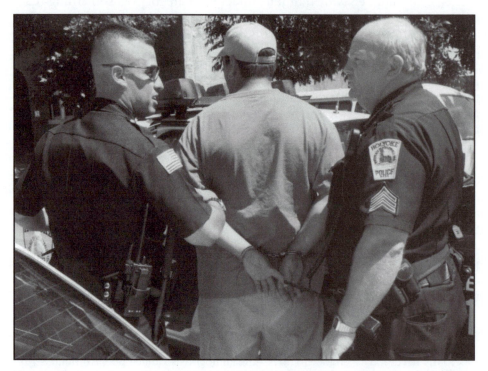

*Veteran officers can impart both positive and negative habits and outlooks to new patrol officers. (Photo: Mark C. Ide)*

In addition to making full use of an officer's innate abilities and skill, community policing attempts to expose police personnel to a wider assortment of people and positive experiences than was customary in professional policing. Rather than meeting only victims, witnesses, and offenders, in community policing officers are broadly exposed to contacts with citizens interested in and supportive of public safety. Community policing encourages favorable interactions with the public that tend to reaffirm the high value of the police to the community. In short, community policing invites the police to initiate contact with business people, local residents, civic group leaders, and religious leaders, among others, rather than simply reacting to calls from dispatch or patrolling the streets simply to deter and detect lawbreakers. That is, community policing means the police are coactive, as well as reactive and proactive.

## Hiring Practices ❖ ❖ ❖ ❖

Policing in any era requires officers who are fully functional and well trained to deliver the appropriate services at the right time. In a nutshell, it requires good training, knowledge of the law, an awareness of departmental policies and procedures, and most important, discretion. As Keith Haley has noted, however, there is much more to good policing than training by itself. An important first step is selection. "Communities must select recruits who have both the potential for learning the requisites of police work and the motivation to serve citizens and visitors in their localities."[23] After all, he adds, "Police officers are community leaders with broad discretion."[24]

In order to appreciate good policing, it is useful to understand how police departments choose the people whom they entrust to do such an important job. Indeed, if community policing represents a new and different way to deliver police services, it might be asked whether we need to hire different people from those hired in the past to do this different job.

In the professional era, police officers were selected on the basis of objective measures of their ability to do the job. Applicants were screened for acceptability based upon their clean criminal record, a background check, a favorable psychological profile, high scores on a standardized test, physical qualifications, and a personal interview. Such a process was far better than the procedure during the political era when selection often was based on who was voted into a local political office or depended on an influential person whom an applicant or a family member might know. The professional era's more objective measures allowed for a fairer appraisal of an applicant's abilities and helped to ensure that the people who were hired were adequately qualified for the job.

The selection process used in most departments today continues the practices of the professional era. Although the current practices are noticeably more equitable, additional improvement is needed to make them better suited to choosing personnel during the community era.

## Recruitment

Recruitment and assessment are two preliminary steps in the hiring process in any era. It is at these stages that a pool of applicants from which people will eventually be hired and trained is formed.

Recruitment today involves the posting, advertising, and promoting of available positions to the public. Job announcements are placed in accordance with a city or county's policies for posting such notices. They give information about deadlines, how to apply, and the job description itself.

In order to ensure an optimum pool of candidates, job openings may also be advertised in local newspapers and trade journals. Recruiting officers may visit local or regional colleges and universities in order to seek qualified applicants. As Chris Eskridge has noted, the selection of college-educated applicants in particular offers many advantages to police departments. College-educated recruits tend to have a greater awareness of social and ethnic problems, draw fewer citizen complaints, receive higher satisfaction ratings from the public, and tend to be "less authoritarian" in their approach to others. Furthermore, Eskridge notes that college-educated police officers seem to make better workers overall, demonstrating "higher levels of morale and

❖ ❖ ❖ ❖   better work attitudes," which probably accounts for the fact that they are more likely to be promoted than those without college experience.[25]

Advertising and promotion are especially crucial in the community era in order to encourage a wide diversity of applicants. Not only should the police adequately represent their communities in terms of racial and ethnic diversity, they should also have a knowledge of community values and needs and show tolerance for the wide variety of the people who live there.

Potential applicants from the community who may not have been attracted to the idea of working in a professionally oriented department might be drawn to the prospect of serving their community in a department that is committed to the broader and more comprehensive role of community policing. It is up to the department for the most part to define for the community what it is looking for in a successful applicant and to encourage a broad cross section of eligible citizens to apply.

## Assessment

Once the job applicant pool has been established, the selection process moves to the assessment or "screening-in" stage.

> Screening-in applicants denotes a process through which only the best of the qualified applicants are considered for employment. Screening-out applicants, by contrast, involves removing all unqualified applicants from the applicant pool and then considering for employment anyone who is at least minimally qualified—those who are not screened out.[26]

Larry Gaines and Victor Kappeler note that job applicants can be assessed according to minimum standards and testing procedures that help to determine which qualified candidates are more highly desirable than others as job prospects:

> Police employment standards vary from department to department, but may include requirements relating to vision, hearing, age, height, weight, biographical characteristics, educational levels, residency, and the absence of a history of drug use.[27]

In comparison to preemployment minimum standards, testing creates a situation in which candidates compete against each other rather than against some preestablished standard. The two most commonly used tests in police selection are the written test and the oral interview.[28]

After reviewing much of the literature on selection and testing, Gaines and Kappeler conclude that the hiring process for police officers poses a difficult challenge for departments: "Selection should be considered a balancing act in which numerous problems and forces are constantly weighed and considered."[29] Although this statement holds true for police departments during the professional era, it is particularly appropriate for those agencies trying to hire well-rounded and qualified applicants during the community era.

Three key improvements are needed at the screening-in, or assessment, stage to make the hiring process more compatible with the need to find personnel well suited to the challenge of community policing. First, as discussed earlier, police departments during must encourage innovation in order to promote change. Departments moving away from a military-style bureaucracy will have to reevaluate their testing procedures. For example, they may want to consider ways to ensure that candidates who display creativity and risk-taking abilities will not necessarily be scored below those who value structure and certainty over all else. Similarly, they may want to examine how well the standardized forms they use test for problem-solving ability.[30]

A second improvement that is needed involves bringing the community into the assessment process itself. Citizen representatives can help with the screening to identify those candidates who might work well with diverse groups and who display strong attachments to the community that will help the police develop strong partnerships with community groups. Citizen advisory boards that exist in many places can be helpful in selecting new employees. Lacking such boards, representatives from civic groups can be recruited at different times to sit during oral board interviews of job applicants or even to spend a few days at a time to help conduct mini-assessment centers similar to the way in which many police chiefs are selected around the country.[31]

Although involving the community in the assessment process is more difficult and time consuming than not doing so, weighing the long-term benefit of hiring the right person for the job against the cost of putting the wrong person in the field makes the additional time spent well worth it. After all, having community input at this stage helps to bond the community to the new recruit immediately when he or she becomes a uniformed officer.

A third improvement that is needed during assessment is to test applicants for important communication skills. Professional-style police work has demanded contact with citizens under adverse conditions that require the use of voice to control situations, console victims, interview witnesses, and interrogate suspects. With community policing, verbal skills become even more important. Officers will meet citizens from a wider variety of economic and social backgrounds, since much of the time the officers will be making contacts on their own rather than simply answering calls. Also, they will be expected to speak at public functions and make public addresses, something earlier patrol officers rarely ever did.

## Training for Success

After the right people to do the right job have been hired, they must be trained. According to 1993 data collected by the Bureau of Justice Statistics (BJS) through the Law Enforcement Management and Administrative Statistics (LEMAS) program, formal police training was a requirement for newly hired police recruits in nine out of 10 police departments. Furthermore, since the departments that did not require training tended to be small, the 90 percent of the departments that required training accounted for 99 percent of all sworn police personnel in the United States.[32]

Although smaller police departments tend to require less training, the typical new recruit is exposed to a minimum of 457 training hours and up to a maximum of 1,176. According to the LEMAS data, an average recruit will undergo 425 hours in an academy setting and another 215 hours in the field, for a combined average of 640 training hours. Furthermore, the numbers are higher for new sheriff's deputies. BJS estimates that new deputies received approximately 750 total training hours on average in 1993.[33]

*Effective policing builds bridges between those in uniform and citizens of all ages. Listening and problem solving are key ingredients to training skilled police officers in the community era. (Photo: Courtesy of the Wichita Police Department)*

Requiring a substantial number of hours of training is not to say that all training is uniformly effective. For example, Vance McLaughlin and Robert Bing write that

> Strangely enough, police training continues to vary throughout the United States. There is considerable disagreement with regard to the rigor of these programs and time allocation for them. The state of Missouri, for example, requires 150 hours of training in smaller departments, while Hawaii requires 790 hours (plus four months of field training). Moreover, the focus on mandatory training has regrettably been on the number of hours at the expense of quality and skill retention. As a result, many P.O.S.T. Councils have less than rigorous standards. In many programs, for example, the curriculum for recruits is written at the sixth grade level.[34]

The goal of academy training is to introduce newly hired applicants to a wide range of subjects over the span of a few short weeks. They are expected to learn about criminal statutes, proper arrest procedures, officer safety, personal defense, firearms, and pursuit driving, among other technical skills. Although much of their training is considered crucial in preparing new recruits for life on the streets as a uniformed officer, the reliance on such skills for officer survival leaves little room for newer subjects that may prove equally, if not more, useful to officers expected to succeed at community policing. After all, research has documented that police officers spend disproportionately little of their time doing "real police work," that is, detecting and apprehending criminals and investigating crimes. For example, Priss Dufford notes that most of a patrol officer's daily activities (75 percent to 90 percent) are spent on noncriminal activities.[35]

## Community Policing: Is There a Role for Detention Operations?

❖ ❖ ❖ ❖

### Michael L. Birzer

There is much literature that discusses the evolving community policing philosophy that currently is being implemented across the United States. Much of it, however, is applicable to metropolitan police departments. What is sorely lacking is discussion about how community policing is implemented and nurtured in sheriff's departments.

Sheriff's departments by their very nature are unique and different from police departments in their roles, duties, and responsibilities. Sheriffs, unlike police chiefs, are legally responsible for detention operations (e.g., securing and housing inmates awaiting trial or those who have been sentenced to jail for no longer than one year). This function raises compelling questions. Does the detention, or jail, division have a role in community policing? And if so, what is that role?

Community policing has been extolled as a philosophy that should permeate every division and section of the organization.[1] Detention operations have an intricate role and should be fully involved in the community policing philosophy of the department. It has been the author's experience that some sheriffs and their command staff mistakenly see those deputies assigned to the patrol function as the sole performers of community policing. The detention division performs an invaluable service to the community and should not be left out when the department implements community policing, which should become the prevailing subculture of the entire organization.

Citizens come into contact with the jail and the deputies assigned to work there for a variety of reasons. Citizens may need assistance or directions to another section of the department or another department within the criminal justice system. They may be trying to contact a relative or friend who has been arrested. The vast majority of citizens who come into contact with the jail are surprisingly not the inmates housed there, but rather attorneys, parole and probation officers, social workers, clergy, and friends and families of the inmates.[2] Thus detention deputies perform a vast amount of service activities for many different kinds of citizens.

Because detention deputies answer questions for citizens and criminal justice professionals on a daily basis, it is paramount that these deputies be trained in many of the same skills as the deputies on patrol. These skills include communication skills, resource identification skills, conflict resolution skills, and a myriad of other customer-service skills. In addition, detention deputies should become familiar with the various resources within the criminal justice and social-service fields so that they may make appropriate referrals.

Not only do detention deputies have a vast amount of contact with the law abiding public, but they are also in daily contact with prisoners incarcerated in the jail. Detention deputies can easily equate the jail cells or pods to a community neighborhood. Like a patrol deputy, the detention deputy's job is to patrol and keep the peace during her or his specific tour of duty. If a problem arises within the jail cell or pod, the deputy should try to solve it. This may involve employing conflict-resolution skills when mediating a dispute between several inmates or referring an inmate to a proper resource. It may involve a long-term problem-solving endeavor in which the detention deputy actually initiates the scan, analyze, respond, and assess (SARA) model of problem solving in response to a jail problem.

Detention deputies assigned to the booking area have a viable opportunity to demonstrate the professionalism of the department. For example, a patrol officer working in the field makes a traffic stop. Upon checking the driver's license of the violator, the officer discovers a traffic warrant. In some cases the arresting officer is anything but professional and is not very helpful in answering the violator's questions. The violator arrives at the jail facility irritated and upset. The detention deputy can use some basic de-escalation skills to change the attitude of the contact from negative to positive. Such skills may involve giving the violator a couple of additional phone calls so that he or she can call a relative or friend in order to ☞

❖ ❖ ❖ ❖    ☞

receive money to pay a fine or bail. It is important to point out that detention deputies may be working with persons who have never come into contact with a deputy or a police officer in the past. Furthermore, it may be the only contact that the violator may have with the department and the criminal justice system. A courteous, friendly, and helpful detention deputy, who demonstrates some empathy, can leave a lasting impression. The community policing strategy stresses that police departments should become user friendly and an ambassador of services to the public they are sworn to protect and serve. This attitude is just as important within the framework of detention operations as in patrol.

Detention operations are an important part of a sheriff's department. It is a grave disservice to leave them out of the department's community policing efforts. Detention deputies should attend sessions on community policing and problem solving along with the rest of the department. It would even be helpful for detention deputies to ride with patrol deputies and the local police department to better understand the role of patrol. Furthermore, it might prove beneficial to patrol deputies to spend some duty time observing the detention deputies in the jail environment. Learning more about the other assignments in the department will ultimately result in more effective cooperation between the two divisions. Likewise, every division and section with the department can benefit from this process of organizational learning. Community policing will be a dim and spurious reality until every entity with the department is practicing the philosophy and strategy, including those deputies protecting us from behind the bars.

Michael L. Birzer is an assistant professor of criminal justice at Washburn University in Topeka, Kansas. Previously he spent 18 years with the Sedgwick County Sheriff's Department in Wichita, Kansas, where he held assignments in detention, judicial services, patrol, detectives, training, community policing, and the gang unit, rising to the rank of lieutenant. He holds a B.S. and M.A. in the administration of justice and is a doctoral candidate at Oklahoma State University.

### Endnotes

1. R. Trojanowicz and B. Bucqueroux, *Community Policing: How to Get Started* (Cincinnati: Anderson, 1994); E. M. Watson, A. R. Stone, and S. M. Deluka, *Strategies for Community Policing* (Upper Saddle, NJ: Prentice-Hall, 1998); D. L. Carter and L. A. Radelet, *The Police and the Community*, 6th ed. (Upper Saddle River, NJ: Prentice-Hall, 1999); R. L. LaGrange, *Policing American Society*, 2nd ed. (Chicago: Nelson-Hall, 1998); G. Alpert and R. Dunham, *Policing Urban America*, 2nd ed. (Prospect Heights, IL: Waveland Press, Inc, 1992).
2. G. W. Etter and M. L. Birzer, "Community Oriented Policing: Why Train the Jail Officer," *American Jails* (May–June, 1997).

Subjects directly related to community policing and other useful topics are not usually taught in police academies or are given only scant attention. One reason for this lack stems from a crowded curriculum that has little room for newer subjects unrelated to officer safety or nonlegal matters. The reliance on a traditional curriculum and the reluctance to incorporate new training subjects, however valuable they might be, is due primarily to the idea that policing is a particularly dangerous occupation. On the one hand, there is the potential for danger in the form of personal injury or even death to the officer or someone being protected. Understandably, then, training devoted to officer safety under adverse conditions commands one of the highest priorities of time and attention at the academy. On the other hand, the potential for danger of a different type also demands training time and attention. That danger is the threat of lawsuits against an individual officer or the department. Accordingly, knowledge of the law is another major area of emphasis in the academy.

❖ ❖ ❖ ❖

Another reason for the lack of new subjects is that police trainers are unfamiliar with them because they themselves were schooled in the old approach.

Also, community-policing related topics are given little attention in academy classrooms because of the challenging nature of the subject matter itself. In contrast to fairly concrete, easily demonstrable technical skills that can be learned through rote exercises (such as pursuit driving, firearms training, CPR, and a host of other, similar activities) and legal procedures that are covered in lectures based on law books, the central themes of community policing are difficult to teach. Information about how best to know your community and how to engage in problem solving involves concepts and principles that are fairly abstract. Because the subject matter of community policing generally requires more listening than hearing and more thinking than memorizing, it poses a considerable challenge to both teachers and recruits.

Other forms of training that might help officers work successfully with their colleagues and the public pose similar kinds of challenges. Consequently, for example, training in public speaking and facilitating small and large meetings are not routinely offered to new recruits. Former police chief Anthony Bouza echoes the need for police to acquire good communication skills and stresses their importance over the course of an officer's career:

> The ability to get up and speak effectively in front of a group; skill in dealing with the press; a grasp of the issues needed to cope with unions, prosecutors, the various publics, and others—all should be provided through arduous preparation and training. Yet, there is little evidence that American policing is even aware of this challenge, much less rising to meet it.[36]

Not only must the curriculum be expanded if community policing is to succeed, there also may be a need to train new recruits to accept a certain amount of risk. Risk taking in the face of professional-style practices that have the endorsement of a strong police subculture will challenge new recruits to be morally courageous. Bouza suggests that

> Training recruits in the importance of moral courage, such as is so piously and consistently included in the widely ignored code of ethics that every police agency adopts as its credo, is as important as teaching the recruit to cope with street dangers, yet police training usually neglects this critical aspect. In fact, it might be held that the opposite message is being transmitted, that the thing to be is a 'stand-up guy.'[37]

Furthermore, Bouza writes that

> If cops are to develop the moral courage it takes to cleanse their agencies of corruption and brutality, they are going to have to learn that courage takes many forms, and that the type needed for such reforms is different from the street heroism they value so dearly.[38]

## Field Training

Field-training officers (FTOs) are responsible for supervising freshly trained recruits (often referred to as rookies) during the initial stages of their probationary period of employment. It is at this point that new recruits actu-

❖ ❖ ❖ ❖    ally are exposed to patrol duties and situations on the street that training cannot fully prepare them for. It is at this point that they begin to develop a sense
of discretion and autonomy that undergird the patrol experience. It is here
that they also are most directly exposed to the subculture of policing. As Van
Maanen writes:

> During a newcomer's first few months on the street he is self-conscious and
> truly in need of guidelines as to his actions. A whole folklore of tales, myths,
> and legends surrounding the department is communicated to the novice by
> his fellow-officers, conspicuously by his FTO. Through these anecdotes—
> dealing largely with 'mistakes' or 'flubs' made by policemen—the recruit be-
> gins to adopt the perspectives of his more experienced colleagues.[39]

One particular challenge for departments committed to community policing is the traditional practice of assigning the less experienced officers to
the most undesirable work schedules. In most departments, rookie officers
are first assigned to patrol during third, or graveyard, shift (11 P.M. to 7 A.M.).
As day shift (7 A.M. to 3 P.M.) and swing shift (3 P.M. to 11 P.M.) slots become
available, more senior personnel assigned to third shift bid for them, leaving
graveyard slots to those with less seniority, including rookies.

Rookie officers trained in community policing are in great need of practicing what they have learned with the community groups that may have had
a hand in selecting them. Unfortunately, assigning them directly to the third
shift means that most officers will have greatly reduced chances of interacting with civic and volunteer groups, who normally do not have meeting times
that fit the 11 P.M. to 7 A.M. work schedule. Even if there are few such opportunities during the graveyard shift, officers assigned that time need even
greater innovation and dedication in order to do community policing with
much success.

## In-Service Training

Once new recruits have settled into their roles and advanced beyond the
probationary period of employment, the amount of supervision given to their
work in the field drops off dramatically, as is shown in Van Maanen's research
on one department:

> In Union City, as in all large city departments, the work of patrolmen is diffi-
> cult, if not impossible, to evaluate. There are the required annual patrolman
> performance ratings submitted by the sergeants, but these are essentially
> hollow paper exercises in which few men receive low marks.[40]

Officers who seem to keep as busy as others doing similar work are
mostly left alone to work through their shifts. Although daily reports that officers prepare for sergeants are routinely monitored, most departments fail to
scrutinize individual officers closely except under unusual circumstances
(e.g., cases involving deadly force or a citizen complaint) or during regularly
scheduled evaluations (usually annual) of officer performance that typically
are not all that telling, as Van Maanen's words suggest.

With very little personalized assessment of officer performance by the
department, officers must look to other sources for feedback about how well
they are doing their jobs. The usual sources include their colleagues and the
wide assortment of citizens with whom they might come in contact on any
given day. However, in-service training sessions sometimes provide officers

with opportunities to examine specific police practices and assess how well they may be performing certain duties.

In-service training is meant to help officers achieve one or more of four goals. First, it may help them maintain seldom used skills such as pursuit driving, self-defense tactics, or firearms training. Second, it may help them sharpen skills that are used more frequently but may have fallen off, such as those having to do with proper arrest procedures, investigating traffic accidents, and preserving evidence. Third, in-service training may provide officers with information about changes in procedures and practices that result

---

## Advanced Problem Solving: Making SARA Work

### Pete Gazlay and Rick Holman

By now you already have learned about SARA (scan, analyze, respond, assess) in a criminal justice class, in-service training, or a special conference on community policing. SARA sounds great in theory, but does it work on the street? The answer is an emphatic *YES!* The challenge is to hold back the natural desire to respond instantly and fix the problem without sufficient problem analysis. Rushing in to fix a problem before its roots are fully understood is the way traditional policing worked. It still has its place, but it's not problem solving.

How do you get out of the reactive mode that deals only with the symptoms of problems rather than its roots? Two tools used by the Colorado Regional Community Policing Institute (CRPI) have been found to be extremely effective in helping police officers make SARA work. The first is the Why? Why? diagram and the second is force field analysis.

### Why? Why? Diagram

The Why? Why? diagram (Figure 8.1) is an easy tool to use.[1] On the left hand side of a flip chart or sheet of paper state your problem. For example, it could be an increase in calls for service at a fast-food restaurant between 1:30 and 3:30 A.M.

Next you ask why at least five times. You will want to ask why there is a problem. When you record several answers, you will ask why each of these is occurring. When you get to the last one, you should be at or near the root cause. It's that simple.

**Figure 8.1  Why? Why? Diagram**

|  | Traffic congestion into and out of lot | Not enough parking for all customers | Loitering in parking lot | Slow service at drive-through window | Poor traffic flow and design |
|---|---|---|---|---|---|
|  | Six bars near fast-food restaurant | "Last call"—close 0130–0200 | Bar customers want food | Fast food only place open | Many fast-food customers intoxicated |
| Increased calls 0130–0330 at fast-food restaurant | People hanging in parking lot | Some customers, some are not | Pedestrian/car accidents | Fights and assaults | Public urination and lewd acts |
|  | Assaults in parking lot and restaurant | Customers intoxicated | Staff doesn't know how to handle drunks | Not enough staff to watch customers | Officers spend more time on serious cases |
|  | Adjacent neighbors complain | Vandalism and property damaged | Traffic and crowd noise | Fast-food trash | Drunks in neighborhood |

❖ ❖ ❖ ❖    ☞

An officer could complete a Why? Why? diagram on his or her own, but it would be more effective if others affected by the problem also were included in the process. For example, in the fast-food scenario depicted above, if the officer included the night manager and general manager of the restaurant then he or she would have a more complete picture of the problem.

In real life the officers working to solve a problem such as the one described could dramatically reduce the calls for service by having the restaurant close its lobby and serve customers only through the drive-through window, erecting and enforcing no loitering signs in the parking lot, redesigning the traffic flow to handle this peak period, and hiring a private security guard to provide a presence. These measures would provide an example of a true problem-solving partnership with the police and restaurant management each contributing to the solution.

### Force Field Analysis

Force field analysis is a second useful tool for advanced problem solving. Although the name may sound intimidating, the concept is fairly simple. First state the problem in clear objective terms. Do not get fancy here or use a lot of jargon. Make the sentence something you might say to a friend over a bagel and cup of coffee. This seems simple, but it is one of the most challenging tasks. A clear statement here will pave the way for quality solutions down the line. Write down your problem statement at the top of a flip chart or piece of paper (Figure 8.2).

*Worst Case Scenario.* Under your problem statement draw a line down the middle of the page. On the left side write down the worst-case scenario. How bad could it get if nothing is done about the stated problem? Let your imagination run wild.

*Best Case Scenario.* On the right side of the page write down the best possible scenario. What could this situation evolve into if it were completely solved? Think paradise, utopia, or the ideal. Again, let your imagination run.

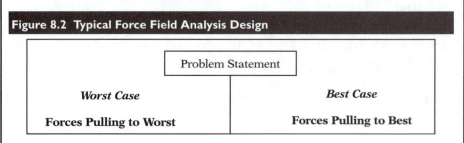

**Figure 8.2  Typical Force Field Analysis Design**

Problem Statement

*Worst Case*

**Forces Pulling to Worst**

*Best Case*

**Forces Pulling to Best**

*Tug of War.* Brainstorm the forces that are creating the problem, both good and bad. Place all the forces that are pulling the situation toward the worst-case scenario on the left side of the page. Put all the forces that are pulling the situation toward the best-case scenario on the right side of the page. Keep brainstorming on forces that would create both scenarios. This is the work. Do not get lazy during the brainstorm, or worse, skip it altogether. Research has found that of all the ideas produced in an extended brainstorming session of, say, 40 minutes, 73 percent of the best ideas are produced in the second half of the session.[2]

*The Key.* Use one or more of the items in the force field to solve your problem. How do you do that? On the positive side strengthen an already existing strong best-case force. For the negative side weaken an already existing worst-case force. You may find the golden key and want to create a new best-case force or a new worst-case force that will push the situation closer to ideal.

### Digging at the Roots

Tools like the Why? Why? diagram and force field analysis help you get to the root of your problems. The time you spend on the analysis is time you will save on the implementation of a response that really works. Maybe you've given a response you thought was perfect, but that created new spin-off problems. In reviewing similar cases, the authors have often found that sufficient analysis was missing. The Why? Why? diagram and force field analysis are simple tools, that, like a rototiller, will    ☞

☞ | dig up your solution and take your problem solving to the next level.

❖ ❖ ❖ ❖

Pete Gazlay is president of Quantum Performance. As an expert on community-oriented policing and problem solving, he speaks around the country to police and community groups. Rick Holman is director of the Colorado Regional Community Policing Institute. He has over 20 years of law enforcement experience and is currently with the Northglenn (Colorado) Police Department assigned to the State of Colorado Division of Criminal Justice.

**Endnotes**

1. Pete Gazlay and Rick Holman, *Advanced Problem Solving for Community Policing* (Denver, CO: Colorado Regional Community Policing Institute, 1999).
2. James M. Higgins, *101 Creative Problem-Solving Techniques* (Winter Park, FL: The New Management Publishing, 1994).

from new legal statutes or changes in previous laws. Finally, it may introduce them to advancements in the field or innovative ways to think about criminal detection, crime prevention, problem solving, and community mobilization.

Most departments require sworn personnel to acquire 40 or so hours of in-service training annually. Although such training could be used to teach community policing, few departments have required such training or even made it available to those who might wish it.

Officers working in many departments are guaranteed access to the amount of training that will meet their annual in-service training requirement, usually at little, if any, cost to them. The academies that train new recruits often supply in-service training as well, using many of the same instructors teaching many of the same subjects. Although there may be a need in the field for different kinds of training, many officers prefer to select courses on subjects with which they are familiar; similarly, many trainers seem to prefer teaching popular topics that they are experienced in teaching.

Such popular in-service courses typically revolve around officer safety. Another popular subject involves criminal investigation because many officers are interested in promotion to the rank of detective. Furthermore, changes in legal statutes and procedures occasionally necessitate in-service training that all officers must acquire.

Training that meets annual in-service requirements that is not offered free of charge or required by the department or that is too conceptual, not seemingly applicable, or difficult to teach is difficult to sell to the rank and file. To the extent that community policing training to date remains undeveloped or is largely unavailable, many of the nation's police have had only limited exposure to it through in-service training. In addition, few academies offer advanced community policing or devote much time to related topics such as strategic planning, organizational change, and community mobilization. A challenge for academies in the future is to make such topics more accessible to active and veteran patrol officers.

Unfortunately, the limitations noted above do not pertain only to the men and women who patrol our streets and highways, but also seem to apply to the personnel who supervise or command them. Bouza writes that

> The education and training of police managers, nationally, has been not only
> appallingly deficient, but wrongheaded. In common with most American ed-

❖ ❖ ❖ ❖   ucation, the system, such as it is, is vocationally centered, with lots of courses on what can only be called the oxymoron of 'police science.' Law, procedures, regulations, and technical requirements are heavily weighed. The emphasis, a not-altogether-mistaken one, is on developing an effective technician. These skills are essential, but they must be accompanied by an understanding of the broader context within which events take place.[41]

## Conclusion

Similar to the question that Heuett asks his trainees, quoted early in this chapter, the authors ask police officers in training to describe the difference between someone who is rewarded for being a "good" police officer and someone whom they might recognize as a "great" police officer. The replies typically identify a good patrol officer as someone who writes a lot of tickets, gets good "numbers" (meaning numbers of arrests, citations, or whatever else their supervisor is looking for), or maybe has made a big bust. In contrast, the great ones are always the ones everybody looks up to or the ones everyone wanted to be like when first starting out as a rookie. The great ones seem to know how to handle every situation. They are viewed as problem solvers and respected as leaders. Where the good numbers cop might be viewed as efficient, it is the truly great cop who goes beyond efficiency and is seen as effective.

The authors then ask a follow-up question about which kind of officer might be ideally suited to do community policing. The answers from uniformed officers are not all that surprising. They still admire the qualities that made great cops two dozen years ago. Those same qualities are still needed for patrolling the streets today in an era of community policing. We still need people in uniform who can do a comprehensive job as a police officer under the variety of circumstances they encounter today.

It is to be expected that the people who have always done well as police officers will naturally excel at community policing. But today police departments have to be more deliberate in attracting, selecting, and training applicants who will do well at community policing. These applicants will not only have to excel in the demands of professional-style policing, but also be able to show their peers, supervisors, and the public that they are up to new challenges.

## Study Questions

1. What are three possible reasons why the worldview of the police differs from that of the public?

2. How could the assessment of police applicants be improved to ensure that the people chosen are well suited to engage in community policing?

3. From the material presented, discuss whether police departments today should seek applicants to do the job of community policing with different qualifications from those they have sought to perform police duties in the past.

4. How might the role of the police subculture affect the implementation of community policing?

❖ ❖ ❖ ❖

## Endnotes

1. Victor E. Kappeler, Richard D. Sluder, and Geoffrey P. Alpert, "Breeding Deviant Conformity: Police Ideology and Culture," in *The Police and Society: Touchstone Readings*, ed. Victor E. Kappeler (Prospect Heights, IL: Waveland Press, 1995), pp. 243–262 [p. 243].
2. *Ibid.*, pp. 243–244.
3. *Ibid.*
4. Lawrence Sherman, "Learning Police Ethics," in *Policing Perspectives: An Anthology*, eds. Larry K. Gaines and Gary P. Cordner (Los Angeles: Roxbury, 1999), pp. 301–310.
5. *Ibid.*, p. 304.
6. Kappeler, Sluder, and Alpert, "Breeding Deviant Conformity."
7. *Ibid.*, p. 246.
8. *Ibid.*
9. Anthony V. Bouza, *The Police Mystique: An Insider's Look at Cops, Crime, and the Criminal Justice System* (New York: Plenum Press, 1990).
10. John G. Stratton, *Police Passages* (Manhattan Beach, CA: Glennon, 1984).
11. Bouza, *The Police Mystique*, p. 69.
12. *Ibid.*, p. 69.
13. James Q. Wilson, *Varieties of Police Behavior* (Cambridge, MA: Harvard University Press, 1968).
14. Douglas McGregor, "The Human Side of Enterprise," in *Classics of Organizational Behavior*, ed. W. E. Natemeyer (Oak Park, IL: Moore, 1978), pp. 12–18.
15. Theodore H. Ferdinand, "Police Attitudes and Police Organization: Some Interdepartmental and Cross-Cultural Comparisons," *Police Studies*, 3 (1980): 46–60.
16. John Van Maanen, "Kinsmen in Repose: Occupational Perspectives of Patrolmen," in *The Police and Society: Touchstone Readings*, ed. Victor E. Kappeler (Prospect Heights, IL: Waveland Press, 1995), pp. 225–242 [p. 235].
17. Joseph Wambaugh, *Floaters* (New York: Bantam Books, 1996).
18. Egon Bittner, "Florence Nightingale in Pursuit of Willie Sutton," in *The Potential for Reform in the Criminal Justice System* (Beverly Hills: Sage, 1974), pp. 17–44 [p. 30].
19. Van Maanen, "Kinsmen in Repose," p. 238.
20. Egon Bittner, "The Quasi-Military Organization of the Police," in *The Police and Society: Touchstone Readings*, ed. Victor E. Kappeler (Prospect Heights, IL: Waveland Press, 1995), pp. 173–183 [p. 179].
21. John P. Crank, "Celebrating Agency Culture: Engaging a Traditional Cop's Heart in Organizational Change," in *Community Policing in a Rural Setting*, eds. Quint C. Thurman and Edmund F. McGarrell (Cincinnati: Anderson, 1997), pp. 49–57 [p. 50].
22. *Ibid.*, p. 57.
23. Keith N. Haley, "Training," in *What Works in Policing: Operations and Administration Examined*, eds. Gary W. Cordner and Donna C. Hale (Cincinnati: Anderson, 1992), pp. 143–155 [p. 143].
24. *Ibid.*, p. 143.
25. Chris Eskridge, "College and the Police: A Review of the Issues," in *Police and Policing: Contemporary Issues*, ed. Dennis J. Kenney (New York: Praeger, 1989), pp. 17—25 [p. 20].
26. Larry K. Gaines and Victor E. Kappeler, "Selection and Testing," in *What Works in Policing: Operations and Administration Examined*, eds. Gary W. Cordner and Donna C. Hale (Cincinnati: Anderson, 1992), pp. 107–123 [p. 109].

❖ ❖ ❖ ❖    27. *Ibid.*, p. 112.
28. *Ibid.*, p. 118.
29. *Ibid.*, p. 121.
30. Ricky S. Gutierrez and Quint C. Thurman, "Selecting, Training, and Retaining Officers to Do Community Policing," in *Community Policing in a Rural Setting*, eds. Quint C. Thurman and Edmund F. McGarrell (Cincinnati: Anderson, 1998), pp. 75–83.
31. *Ibid.*
32. Bureau of Justice Statistics, *Law Enforcement Management and Administrative Statistics, 1993: Data for Individual State and Local Agencies with 100 or More Officers* (Washington, DC: U.S. Department of Justice).
33. *Ibid.*
34. Vance McLaughlin and Robert Bing, "Selection, Training, and Discipline of Police Officers," in *Police and Policing: Contemporary Issues*, ed. Dennis Jay Kenney (New York: Praeger, 1989), pp. 26–33 [p. 29].
35. Priss Dufford, *Police Personal Behavior and Human Relations: For Police, Deputy, Jail, Corrections, and Security Personnel* (Springfield, IL: Charles C. Thomas, 1973).
36. Anthony V. Bouza, *The Police Mystique*, p. 129.
37. *Ibid.*, p.72.
38. *Ibid.*, p.72.
39. John Van Maanen, "Kinsmen in Repose," p. 236.
40. *Ibid.*, p. 233.
41. Anthony V. Bouza, *The Police Mystique*, p. 128. ✦

# Chapter Nine

# Motivational Strategies and Management Styles for Community Policing

❖ ❖ ❖ ❖

*It's not the badge, but the heart behind the badge.*

—from *Inspector Gadget, The Movie*

$A$s police departments across the United States plan for and implement change from a professional policing approach to one of community policing, top police executives have to find better ways to facilitate innovation, improve creativity, develop a capacity for problem solving, and encourage citizen participation. This chapter first introduces readers to a relatively recent trend in the provision of government services: viewing citizens as "customers." The chapter then discusses some traditional and newer motivational theories and management strategies in the public and private sector. The authors argue that these theories and strategies must be geared toward increasing employee empowerment, innovation, and problem solving if community policing is to be institutionalized within police departments.

## Viewing Citizens as Customers

In 1990, noted scholars Robert Trojanowicz and Bonnie Bucqueroux heralded community policing as a new and promising idea giving primary importance to the service role of police, including neighborhood problem solving, citizen mobilization, and citizen satisfaction.[1] At about the same time, expectations about public service in general began to shift. A move from an efficiency-oriented government to a more responsive and effective government was in part inspired by David Osborne and Ted Gaebler's ideas on "reinventing government."[2] They maintained that government should be reinvented to put "customers" first. That is, they emphasized such themes as customer-driven government, mission-driven government, and results-oriented government. Shortly after Bill Clinton became president in 1993, he appointed Vice President Al Gore to chair a committee to review the federal government. Gore's report essentially underscored the themes of Osborne and Gaebler's book, including putting customers first. That idea implies significant changes in organizational structure and management styles that formally were viewed as closed systems with a top-down management approach. These new, more open management styles, crucial to the success of community policing, are discussed later in this chapter.

---

### What Happens if Organizations Don't Change

#### *Deputy Chief Steve Coufal*

What happens if organizations don't change? Over the years I have paid close attention to organizations that I have been associated with in terms of their ability to prepare their employees and develop programs for the future. The most successful have had some common characteristics.

First, the leaders of the successful organizations tend to know who their customers are and what their mission is. Second, they possess the ability to identify their customer's current and future needs. Third, they have created positive work envi- ☞

Omaha Police Department Deputy Chief Steve Coufal.

ronments where good communication lines exist between management and employees, and employees have input regarding their responsibilities, and the needs and overall mission of the organization. Last, the senior leader successfully developed a vision for the organization, communicated the need for change, and then developed the employee support needed to effect that change.

In contrast, struggling organizations tend to have management that focuses on what has worked in the past, uses an authoritarian approach, and fails to assess the needs of their employees and customers. Such leaders often operate in a "data vacuum," insulating themselves from the very lifeblood of real-time information needed to effectively adjust to the environmental challenges that exist. These organizations, whether they are from the business, public, or nonprofit sectors, often are faced with a loss of their customer base and most valuable employees.

During my experience managing the challenges of change, I have come to recognize that in today's rapidly changing work environment two choices exist—you can either lead or be led. Managers who embrace change create an environment that allows organizations to flourish and attain the mission for which they exist. These are leaders. Managers who fail to adjust to the changing environment are not leaders. Their organizations are destined for failure.

---

Steve Coufal is a 20-year veteran of the Omaha Police Department. Formerly in command of the department's Uniform Patrol Bureau, he is now commander of the Police Operations Division and deputy chief of police. He has a B.S. in criminal justice and an M.S. in administration.

## Theories of Motivation for Understanding Police Personnel

This section reviews many of the classic and contemporary theories dealing with employee motivation. Recalling the discussion in chapter 8 on selecting and training employees for a community policing model, readers may want to ask, "What motivational theories are most appropriate in the effort to promote community policing?"

Motivating a work force is a particularly challenging task for supervisors and managers, in both private and public organizations. The motivated employee is considered to be happier, more satisfied with his or her work, and more productive. However, unlike the days of Frederick Taylor's principles of scientific management when employees were considered something simply like cogs on a wheel, managers today no longer consider efficiency their sole concern. They also want to improve job satisfaction and, ultimately, motivation. To achieve these objectives they need to make changes in the work environment that consider the following factors: the organizational culture, the reward system, and the nature of an employee's work.

Undergirding these factors are various theories about motivation. After a brief examination of several of them, this chapter will consider the organiza-

❖ ❖ ❖ ❖ tional culture of policing, reward systems, and the nature of employees' work within the context of community policing. A comprehensive change process must occur in all these factors if a department is to shift its focus to customer service and problem solving.

There are two general types of motivational theories: *humanistic* and *behavioristic*. Humanistic theories, also called *content* or *need* theories, focus on the individual and his or her internal drives. Individuals, so the theories go, possess various internal needs and desires that may be satisfied through work. It is up to the administrator to provide ways for employees to fulfill their internal needs.[3] Abraham Maslow, Frederick Herzberg, and David McClelland are humanists.[4] Behavioristic, or *process*, theories of motivation attempt to explain behavior through the process of external reinforcement. Rewards and punishments affect future behavior. "Rewarding behavior increases the probability it [the behavior] will be repeated, and punishing behavior decreases the probability it [the behavior] will be repeated."[5] Behaviorist (process theorists) attempt to explain motivation in terms of learned behavior; they discount the importance of instincts or drives, which the humanists (content theorists) find so important. J. Adams and Victor Vroom are considered behaviorists.

## Maslow's Hierarchy of Needs Theory

In 1943, Maslow formulated what is now known as Maslow's hierarchy of needs theory. According to Maslow, there exists a hierarchy of needs; individuals progress from lower needs to higher needs. These needs affect an individual's behavior. A next higher need is activated when a lower-order need is at least partially fulfilled and therefore no longer serves to motivate the individual. As the individual advances up the need hierarchy it becomes increasingly difficult to satisfy higher needs.[6]

At the bottom of Maslow's hierarchy are "physiological needs," for food, clothing, adequate shelter, and water. Fulfillment of these basic needs usually is associated with income. As long as one's income is high enough to pay for one's basic necessities, these needs can be easily satisfied. Taylor's principles of scientific management tended not to look past these very basic needs.

"Safety and security needs" are the second step in Maslow's hierarchy. These needs are associated with the individual's desire for continuity of life and work. Job security, for example, is considered to be a motivator for many people in the public sector. The nature of police work might preclude an individual from achieving this need, especially if one perceives police work might be dangerous.[7]

Once physiological and security needs have been satisfied, "social or belonging needs" dominate an individual's motivation. These third-step needs include the desire to interact, socialize, and be accepted by others. Although these needs are met among workers in an organization (the police subculture, for example), they are less frequently met in the relationship between an employee and a manager.[8]

The fourth step in Maslow's hierarchy is "self-esteem needs." These center on one's self-image and the way one is viewed by peers. These needs typically are fulfilled by prestige or other forms of recognition.

The pinnacle of Maslow's hierarchy is "self-actualization" needs. These needs concern the potential to grow and to do one's best in all endeavors. They can be met only after self-esteem needs have been realized. Self-actualization needs differ for every individual, making it difficult to develop a motivational strategy that is able to meet the self-actualization needs of all employees.[9]

❖ ❖ ❖ ❖

## Herzberg's Theory of Motivation and Hygiene

Where Maslow's hierarchy can be viewed as a continuum across which any individual might fit, Herzberg identifies two primary factors that lead to greater productivity: motivation and hygiene. According to Herzberg, satisfaction concerns the work itself; dissatisfaction concerns the work environment. Motivators are satisfiers; they include individual achievement, recognition, responsibility and growth.[10] It should be noted that they are much like Maslow's higher-order needs. Hygiene factors in an organization include type of administration, supervision, working conditions, salary, relationships with peers and superiors, status, and security.[11] They are much like Maslow's lower order needs.

The distinction between job satisfaction and motivation becomes clearer in light of Herzberg's theory. People can be motivated yet not satisfied and vice versa. If, for example, an organization uses some form of participative management, allowing employees input in shaping organizational policy (and thereby enhancing their self-esteem), but also has substandard salary

*Police officers often rely on collective bargaining to get the rewards they feel they deserve. (Photo: Mark C. Ide)*

❖ ❖ ❖ ❖     and benefits, the employee may be motivated but at least somewhat dissatisfied with the job.

## McClelland's Achievement-Power Theory

According to McClelland's achievement-power theory, two needs are important to certain individuals within an organization: the need for achievement and the need for power.[12] Not everyone has these needs, though, and it is up to managers to figure out which people have them and to use them in a way that satisfies their needs. The need for achievement includes the need to succeed and excel. Some have an internal force (motivation) that drives them toward achievement.[13] The need for power includes the need to control or influence one's environment. Some people have an internal desire to make decisions and ensure that others abide by them (power). According to McClelland, if these needs are suppressed by meaningless tasks or undesirable working conditions, the individual will not be motivated.[14]

## Adams' Equity Theory

The content, or need (humanistic), theories reviewed above see motivation in terms of instincts or needs. Process (behaviorist) theories explain motivation in terms of learned behavior. Adams explains behavior in terms of perceived inequity. According to Adams, a person's perceptions of equity are based on his or her efforts (productivity) and rewards (salaries, benefits, etc.) in relation to other people's efforts and rewards. If, for example, everything else being equal, two persons assigned to a special project that has been shown to be effective are rewarded unequally by management, this inequity will affect the motivation of each. The one rewarded more will show signs of increased motivation, while the one ignored or less rewarded will show signs of being unmotivated. Perceived inequity, then, directly affects one's level of motivation.

## Vroom's Expectancy Theory

In contrast to Adams' equity theory that individuals examine their work and rewards relative to others, Vroom's expectancy theory proposes that an individual will be motivated when his or her own reward is sufficient, that is, when it is equal to or greater than the effort exerted by the individual.[15] When an employee is deciding whether to attempt a task and how much effort to exert, he or she will evaluate the perceived reinforcement (reward) as a consequence of the action. Vroom uses the term *valences* to refer to the level of satisfaction or dissatisfaction produced by various outcomes.[16] For example, if the effort of an employee to implement a new program does not lead to a satisfactory level of reward from the organization, this activity has a low positive valence; it is not worth the effort to pursue the low level of reward attached to the effort.[17]

## McGregor's Theory X and Theory Y                    ❖ ❖ ❖ ❖

Many of the principles of the content and process theories outlined above are incorporated into three management theories of motivation. As we noted in chapter 8, McGregor postulated Theory X, a task-oriented theory of management. It assumes much of Taylor's scientific management principles, namely, that workers' main need is money. In addition, they are considered extensions of machines who need strict guidance to perform well. Although there is some empirical support of this theory,[18] it has generally been rejected in favor of Theory Y.

Theory Y, also proposed by McGregor, contrasts Theory X by holding that the basic motivating force of an individual comes from within (content theory). "Self-motivation and inherent satisfaction in work will be forthcoming in situations where the individual is committed to organizational goals."[19] Therefore, it is important for managers to develop conceptual goals and operational objectives for their employees to follow. The Theory Y manager encourages growth, provides guidance, creates opportunities, and releases the employee's potential.

## Ouchi's Theory Z

Theory Z, proposed by William G. Ouchi in 1981, is a Japanese approach to management that emphasizes participation by employees. Decision making involving both management and subordinates shows employees that they are needed and trusted. Theory Z emphasizes a strong organizational culture as well. As a part of this organizational culture, employees are motivated because their internal needs of self-esteem and self-actualization can be realized (content component), and because they receive the organizational rewards of praise, trust, and a feeling of being wanted (process component).[20]

# Increasing Employee Motivation

As mentioned earlier, three factors need to be considered in changing the work environment in order to increase the motivation of the work force: (1) the organizational culture, (2) the reward system, and (3) the nature of the employee's job.

Since employees spend an average of 40 hours per week at work, it is important to consider the work environment as a motivational factor. The work environment includes not only the tangible factors that can easily be changed (such as installing a water fountain near the employee restrooms), but also intangible factors such as instilling a feeling of community spirit. A close look at each of the above-mentioned theories reveals that changes in the work environment can lead to increased employee motivation. For Maslow, employees are motivated by their physiological, safety, belonging, self-esteem, and self-actualization needs; changes in the work environment may make it easier to fulfill these needs.[21] For Adams, a change in management toward equity for all employees will keep a worker motivated.[22] For Vroom, adequate rewards based on what one perceives he or she deserves will lead to

❖ ❖ ❖ ❖     greater motivation and job satisfaction.[23] Therefore, changes in the work environment should be of great importance to police managers.

## Organizational Culture

Chapter 7 discussed organizational culture (the shared values of employees) as a main determinant of change toward community policing. This chapter discusses the need to transform the organizational culture as the first factor of the work environment in order to motivate employees to do community policing.

At a time when employees are culturally and ethnically diverse, the task of finding shared values and beliefs becomes even more important (and difficult). Terrence Deal and A. Kennedy describe the elements of a strong organizational culture. First, values form the heart of a corporate culture. Strong organizational cultures have a system of values shared by employees, who constantly keep these values in mind and strive to uphold them at all times. Second, strong organizational cultures will have heroes known to virtually any employee who has worked in the organization for a few months. These heroes provide tangible role models for employees to follow. Lastly, a strong organizational culture will have unwritten rites and rituals that shape expected behavior. Thick books on rules and regulations are unnecessary because expected behavior is indicated informally. A strong organizational culture, then, leads to motivation and success because employees find meaning and purpose in their day-to-day lives.

Deal and Kennedy also speak of the "atomized organization" of the future. The atomized organization is composed of (1) small task-focused work groups, (2) decentralized managerial control, (3) task groups interconnected with larger units, and (4) task groups and larger units bonded through strong organizational culture. These small work groups are the key to motivation. In a small work group, an individual employee is given the opportunity to work toward the group goal, to communicate easily with fellow workers and the supervisor, and to feel as though the effort exerted is recognized. Work groups are discussed again later in this chapter.[24]

Police departments generally have a strong organizational culture. As noted in earlier chapters, many departments have switched from the culture of professional-style policing to a culture that is community oriented. In making this change, successful departments also have instilled a strong feeling of the new culture within the department, one that facilitates the implementation of community policing. A strong department-wide commitment to the goals of community policing is the key to successful implementation. Books on conduct and regulations have been replaced by small pamphlets in some departments because the code of conduct has been internalized by employees. Decentralized command posts have been set up to allow each officer a wider latitude of discretion in handling police-community matters. Commitment to service, maintaining order, honesty, helpfulness, and problem solving have been important precursors to community policing. Empirical evidence in some cities show increased job satisfaction as the important consequence of the implementation of community policing.

A strong organizational culture committed to community policing addresses many of the employee needs, which, if fulfilled, will lead to greater motivation at the work place. It has managers who trust and respect employees (Theory Z), who allow employees to grow and do their best while being committed to the organization's values (Maslow's self-actualization and Herzberg's motivators), and who treat employees fairly and equitably (Adams' equity theory).[25]

## Reward System

The second major factor in the work environment and one of the major components of the process theories of motivation is the system of rewards and punishments in reinforcing behavior. Both Adams' equity theory and Vroom's expectancy theory put value on the process of reinforcement determined by the reward system.[26] Because position classification and compensation systems make it difficult (if not impossible) to offer monetary rewards in most public organizations, alternative methods of reinforcing behavior must be examined. This is not to say that monetary rewards are not important; they are for some people the single most important incentive imaginable. Therefore, every effort should be made to allocate the necessary resources to adequately compensate employees.

Rewards are of three basic types, emphasized by the behaviorist school of management: extrinsic tangible rewards, extrinsic intangible rewards, and intrinsic rewards. Extrinsic tangible rewards ordinarily include monetary compensation. In its absence, however, an organization can offer other tangibles such as medals, ribbons, plaques, and certificates to the deserving employee.[27] Still other tangible rewards may include a larger desk, a larger office, or an office with a window.[28] Richard Ritti and Ray Funkhouser suggest that the concept of "space" has much to do with an individual's perception of himself and ultimately the way he or she acts.[29]

Extrinsic intangible rewards are stressed by the humanistic school of management.[30] Mary Parker-Follett argues that simple praise, kindness, and communication will be sufficient to motivate employees. Treating employees as people rather than simply as "human resources" will build self-esteem and increase motivation.[31] Moving away from a hierarchical command structure into one based upon direct communication and verbal rewards is also the focus of McGregor's Theory Y approach to management.[32]

Intrinsic rewards also are important for the humanistic school. A personal sense of accomplishment may be the result of allowing an employee to work on a project from start to finish. A sense of high self-esteem may be reached and self-actualization may be realized if the job design allows this.[33] These issues will be considered in the section below.

The move toward community policing has helped improve motivation by increasing the three types of reward. Professional-style police departments have placed a high value on arrests made and crimes solved, even though officers are generally trained to place a high priority on crime prevention. But increasing crime rates in some areas have given officers a feeling of little accomplishment and few rewards. The change toward community policing allows the community police officer to experience many rewards; by focusing on problem solving, he or she is able to complete a job from start to finish. Rewards come from recognition, praise, and a sense of accomplishment within the department and from certificates and plaques from the citizens

❖ ❖ ❖ ❖  who have been affected by the rectified problem. Rewards such as these result in greater motivation and increased productivity.

## The Nature of the Employee's Job

The third factor in the work environment that must be changed in order to increase employee motivation is the nature of the employee's job. In the 1930s, Frederick Taylor believed that specialization was of utmost importance for the employee. If, for example, a worker was especially skilled in filing, that person would simply file for eight hours a day and it was assumed that he or she was motivated by compensation. A department that is shifting to community policing moves away from emphasis on specialization to emphasis on strategies for job enrichment.[34]

Richard Hackman and his colleagues argue that the design of a job influences three critical, work-related psychological states: (1) experienced meaningfulness, (2) experienced responsibility, and (3) knowledge of results. They further argue that the presence or absence of these states influences personal and work outcomes such as motivation, satisfaction, productivity, turnover, and absenteeism. Enriched jobs have five characteristics: *skill variety* (the extent to which a job requires a number of different skills and talents), *task identity* (the extent to which a job requires completion of an entire piece of work), *task significance* (the impact of one's work on the lives of others), *autonomy* (the extent of freedom, independence, and discretion in one's work), and *feedback* (the extent to which work activities provide direct and clear information about effective performance). These characteristics tend to produce any one of the three psychological states. When that happens, motivation and job satisfaction increase.[35]

Stuart Schein addresses the issue of the quality of work life as a key to motivation. Participation management in the form of quality circles (small groups of employees who regularly meet to discuss, analyze, and solve problems) allows employees to feel important and have some control over their own destiny.[36]

Compressed work weeks and flextime also add to an increase in motivation and productivity.[37] Compressed work weeks allow for an increase in the number of hours per day to compensate for a four-day or three-day work week. Flextime allows for schedules to vary in order to suit an employee's personal needs. If, for example, an employee needs to pick up a child at day care during his or her lunch break, 90 minutes may be used instead of 30 or 60 minutes. The extra time used is simply the amount of time the employee will work after his or her scheduled time to leave. Studies show that both compressed work weeks and flextime reduce absenteeism and tardiness and increase productivity and motivation.[38]

Police departments that have moved toward a community-oriented, problem-solving approach seem to fulfill Hackman's requirements to achieve the three critical psychological states leading to greater motivation. The community police officer typically works on all problems which his or her community feels is necessary (skill variety); works on a problem from start to finish (task identity); solves a problem that usually has a profound positive impact on the community (task significance); and is often given the discretion to work on a problem without interference from superiors (autonomy);

once a problem has been solved, the officer receives praise from within, from fellow officers and supervisors, and from the community as a whole (feedback). The importance of job enrichment on job satisfaction and motivation continues to be realized as more police departments move toward implementing community policing.

❖ ❖ ❖ ❖

## Policing Neighborhoods: A Report From St. Petersburg

**Stephen D. Mastrofski, Roger B. Parks, Albert J. Reiss, Jr., and Robert E. Worden**

Departments implementing community policing are striving to change the way police do their work and the contributions citizens make to policing. This preview reports research on what policing is like in St. Petersburg, Florida, a city that has implemented community policing. The research was carried out by the Project on Policing Neighborhoods, sponsored by the National Institute of Justice and the Office of Community Oriented Policing Services.

### Methodology

In 1997, field researchers observed police officers for approximately 240 hours in 12 of St. Petersburg's 48 community policing areas (CPAs). These CPAs were selected to represent variation in social distress (determined by the amount of unemployment and poverty and the number of female-headed households), which affects service conditions for police. Researchers observed 911 officers responsible for answering 911 calls for service, community policing officers (CPOs) free to focus on problem solving, and supervisors assigned to the selected CPAs. Researchers also personally interviewed nearly all St. Petersburg's 240 patrol officers and their 37 immediate supervisors. In addition, they surveyed more than 1,900 randomly selected residents of St. Petersburg by telephone.

### Findings

*Police role*. Community policing expands an officer's role beyond just law enforcement. Interviews revealed some ambivalence in officers' perception of their role. Ninety-eight percent of officers agreed that assisting citizens is as important as enforcing the law, but 88 percent also said that enforcing the law is an officer's most important responsibility. Almost all officers agreed that citizen input about neighborhood problems is important, but 25 percent said they have reason to distrust most citizens.

CPOs generally favored views associated with community policing more than did 911 officers. CPOs were much more likely than 911 officers to say that minor disorders were police business. They were far more likely to rank reducing repeat calls for service as an important goal and far less likely to rank handling their call load or making arrests as important goals. Some views were related to officers' length of service. Experienced officers were more likely to expect officers to respond to all minor disorders except family disputes (on which there were no clear differences by length of service). They were less likely to stress the importance of making arrests, issuing citations, and confiscating drugs and guns, and were more likely to consider as important public involvement in neighborhood improvement and reducing fear of crime. Contrary to assumptions common to many researchers and police, newer police officers were not the ones with the most positive outlook on community policing.

*Allocation of officer time*. The researchers found that the St. Petersburg officers they studied spent, on average, between one-fourth and one-third of their time not on specific tasks but on general patrol or personal business. Contrary to widely held beliefs about the reactive nature of police patrol, 911 officers were typically free of dispatcher or supervisor assignments for five to six hours of their eight-hour shift. Because of the nature of CPOs' job assignments, virtually all of their time was available for self-directed activities, including officer-initiated encounters with the ☞

❖ ❖ ❖ ❖     ☞  public, involvement with other government agencies, administrative tasks, general patrol, and personal business.

The proactive nature of patrol work in St. Petersburg is revealed by the rate of officer-initiated encounters with the public. On average, 911 officers initiated approximately 45 percent of their public contacts; CPOS, approximately 66 percent. Dispatch calls, supervisor assignments, and contacts initiated directly by citizens at a scene or by telephone accounted for the balance.

Not surprisingly, CPOs spent substantially more time engaged in problem-solving activities than 911 officers (17 percent and 7 to 10 percent, respectively, depending on the shift). Eighty-three percent of CPOs indicated involvement with a problem-solving project in the past year, as did 57 percent of 911 officers.

*Police-citizen interactions*. Community policing is generally concerned with solving problems, but also with improving the quality of police-citizen interactions. Researchers found that CPOs tended to spend substantially less time in face-to-face contact with citizens than 911 officers. CPOs had a somewhat lower rate of contact with the public in general, but they also had much lower rates of contact with suspects or disputants and those seeking help and much higher rates of strictly social contacts.

Community policing promotes greater police-citizen cooperation. The researchers found a relatively high level of such cooperation in everyday police-citizen contacts. The police made a positive response to at least one request from citizens 85 percent of the time. Citizens responded positively to at least one request or demand from police approximately 82 percent of the time.

*Citizen perceptions*. Under community policing, citizens play two important roles—as consumers of police services and as coproducers of policing itself. Eighty-five percent of the interviewed citizens said they were "very" or "somewhat" satisfied with their neighborhood police services. Black respondents were somewhat less likely to give these responses than whites. Two-thirds of survey respondents rated St. Petersburg police as "excellent" or "good" at working with residents to solve problems. Whites were substantially more likely than blacks to give a strong rating, but blacks were more aware of police-citizen problem-solving efforts and were more likely to report participation in such efforts.

Establishing a visible and familiar police presence is important to most police departments. Approximately one-third of residents surveyed said they had seen the police in the previous 24 hours. Twenty-eight percent of all interviewed residents said they knew police officers who worked in their neighborhoods. The researchers examined the relationship between a resident knowing an officer and offering a favorable rating of the police. Familiarity with neighborhood police was associated with positive ratings of police among blacks and other minorities but did not affect ratings of whites.

## Conclusion

The research showed that community policing clearly made inroads in the outlook of St. Petersburg officers and that the strength of those effects was related to whether an officer had a specialized community policing assignment or served as a general patrol officer. There were a number of distinctions between the behavior of CPOs and that of 911 officers. This difference suggests that departments should take considerable care in constructing officer responsibilities if departments are to promote community policing attitudes and behavior. Regardless of job assignments, St. Petersburg patrol officers have substantial self-directed time available for targeted activities. The challenge is to find ways to coordinate and supervise these activities effectively. Citizens of St. Petersburg are relatively satisfied with police services, as are citizens in other U.S. cities surveyed. Although minority citizens tended to evaluate the police somewhat lower than whites did, they showed a stronger willingness to become involved in problem solving. This finding represents an excellent opportunity for strengthening police-community relations and improving the quality of life in minority neighborhoods. These and other research results have been used by the St. Petersburg Police Department to develop and implement plans for the future. Detailed information on these and other community policing issues will be forthcoming in future project reports.     ☞

☞ This document is based on research conducted by Stephen D. Mastrofski, a professor at Michigan State University; Roger B. Parks, a professor at Indiana University; Albert J. Reiss, Jr., Professor Emeritus, Yale University; and Robert E. Worden, an associate professor at State University of New York, Albany. The research was sponsored under NIJ grant number 95-IJ-CX-0071, with funds from the Office of Community Oriented Policing Services. Findings and conclusions of the research reported here do not necessarily reflect the official position or policies of the U.S. Department of Justice.

# Participatory Management Styles

Thus far, various approaches to motivation in the workplace have been discussed. Many of the more recent approaches suggest a need to involve employees at all levels of the organization in decision-making processes. Over the years, various participatory management styles have reflected these needs and have facilitated the implementation of community policing. Among them are quality circles, management by objectives, and total quality management.

## Quality Circles

One activity stemming from McGregor's Theory Y and Ouchi's Theory Z is known as a *quality circle*. Quality circles are small groups of employees who come together on a regular basis with their first-line supervisor and a facilitator to deal with work problems.[39] Circle members choose a problem and then solve it through a process of information gathering. Their solutions typically come in the form of formal recommendations made to middle- and upper-management, whose decision it is whether or not to implement them.

Although quality circles are very popular in organizations using a participative management style, there are two key stumbling blocks to their effective implementation. First, rank-and-file employees—the backbone of the quality circle concept—must be convinced that their participation in the program and their resulting recommendations will be fairly heard and considered by managers. Second, middle- and upper-managers also must buy into the process, rather than simply using it as a mechanism of co-opting employees.[40] Once these are surmounted, quality circles may lead to a more productive, motivated, and satisfied work force, one with considerable influence in the quality of the work environment.

Quality circles are particularly useful for police departments during their transformation from professional-style policing to community policing. In fact, the very same problem-solving process for neighborhoods intrinsic to community policing can be applied to departmental difficulties during the planning or implementation phase of community policing. For example, rank-and-file police officers can be tremendously useful in providing recommendations for necessary structural changes to facilitate community policing. Their recommendations might address performance appraisal systems, beat coverage, selection and recruitment, and in-service training.

❖ ❖ ❖ ❖     ## Management by Objectives

Management by objectives (MBO) first became popular in government in the late 1960s; it received added endorsement in the early 1970s when President Richard Nixon embraced its concepts and applied them to some federal agencies.[41] According to Ralph Chandler and Jack Plano, MBO is an attempt to set organization-wide goals and objectives and track their progress through evaluation.[42] But perhaps the defining characteristic of MBO is its reliance on all organizational members—top to bottom—in the process of setting objectives.

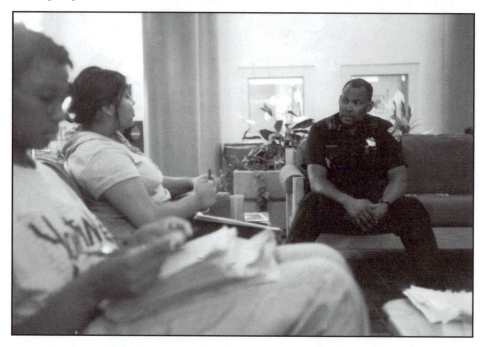

*Seeing the public as customers to satisfy affects the choice of management style for effective community policing. (Photo: Mark C. Ide)*

According to Richard Denhardt, broad goals are articulated at the top of the organizational hierarchy and flow down to all levels of the organization. Specific objectives at the lower levels are negotiated among managers and between managers and other employees. As such, MBO is viewed as a highly participatory and decentralized management style that allows those closest to a problem to determine the way it will be solved. With its emphasis on developing goals, objectives, and specific employee action plans, MBO is related—with some important differences—to its more recent cousin: *strategic planning*. Strategic planning is discussed below within the context of total quality management and in more detail in the next chapter.

## Total Quality Management

One of the more popular and sweeping management reforms in the public sector is known as total quality management. Endorsed by the federal government for its executive branch agencies since the mid-1980s, TQM is now practiced at all levels of the public sector. TQM is a broad management strategy that attempts to improve product and service quality and attend to customer needs. Although the specific techniques used under the rubric of TQM vary from agency to agency, the Office of Management and Budget has stated that the TQM philosophy emphasizes the following seven key dimensions.[43]

*1. Top management leadership and support.* With an emphasis on improving quality throughout their organization, top managers have a pivotal role in the process of TQM. They encourage horizontal communication; exemplify the organization's values, vision, and goals; and remove organizational barriers that discourage innovation, creativity, and organizational problem solving. TQM leaders deregulate work processes and delegate organizational tasks to the lowest possible level of the organization. Managers are encouraged to provide the resources and training necessary to foster positive changes in the organization that will improve the quality of service.

*2. Strategic planning.* Although strategic planning is an activity rather than a management style *per se*, strategic planning embraces a participatory management approach. Essentially, it attempts to involve all organizational employees, as well as other key stakeholders in the organization's activities, in the process of planning goals, objectives, and action plans (strategic planning will be discussed in greater detail in the next chapter). Unlike MBO, strategic planning typically attempts to forecast the changing environmental context within which the organization operates when preparing to plan over a five- to ten-year span. Many police departments across the United States that have embraced the community policing philosophy either have undertaken or are in the process of undertaking the often cumbersome task of strategic planning. Although many of its critics suggest that the task is difficult and inefficient (as compared with a top-down approach), the benefits of the process are being realized both for organizational employees and citizens.

*3. Focus on the customer.* With its increased emphasis on customer needs, expectations, and service, TQM is a logical management style for police departments implementing community policing. Under TQM, employees at all levels of the organization attempt to identify both their internal and external customers and maintain open, two-way communication with them. Customer feedback regarding organizational services often is solicited and then used for strategic planning efforts. In addition, customer satisfaction is one measure used to determine the success or failure of the organization.

*4. Commitment to training and recognition.* Managers of TQM organizations both offer and participate in training modules designed to provide employees with the necessary skills to attain the organization's vision and goals of continuous improvement in quality. Managers reward individuals or teams through recognition or other incentives that reinforce the organization's commitment to its goals.

*5. Employee empowerment and teamwork.* A running theme throughout the TQM philosophy is employee empowerment and teamwork. Managers create an environment that supports employee participation and decision making at the lowest feasible level of the organization. This process typically takes the form of work process teams, which are empowered to find solutions to problems that inhibit quality and productivity. The byproduct of such teamwork is a feeling of ownership, pride, and increased motivation at work.

*6. Measurement and analysis of processes and outputs.* Measurement and analysis are integral components of the TQM philosophy because it

❖ ❖ ❖ ❖

*Good management skills create an atmosphere of teamwork, decision making, and empowerment in both large and small task forces. (Photo: Mark C. Ide)*

strives to *continuously* improve quality. Information is gathered from a variety of sources, including information on similar organizations, work processes, services, and customer satisfaction. This information is then provided to work teams, which engage in a problem-solving process to achieve constant improvement in service.

***7. Quality assurance.*** Here, agency outputs are continually measured against organizational goals and objectives. Police departments using community policing might track changes in citizens' perceptions of quality of life as reported through surveys. If, for example, citizens' fear of crime continues to remain high, work processes and service mechanisms may be modified. Internal goals and objectives also are important in this regard. If, for example, employees' satisfaction at work remains low, work processes may be examined and changed to improve the quality of an employee's worklife.

## TQM and the SARA Problem-Solving Model

In any given police department, patrol operations are considered the backbone of policing. It is with rank-and-file patrol officers that citizens usually encounter a police department. In addition, patrol officers perform many vital functions on a day-to-day basis, including law enforcement, service, and maintaining order. But quite unlike the professional-style departments, those using community policing emphasize the functions of service and maintaining order. This typically is accomplished through TQM, which stresses a problem-solving process known as the SARA model (discussed in greater detail in chapter 10).

Four processes make up the SARA problem-solving strategy: scanning, analysis, response, and assessment. *Scanning* is the identification of potential problems. In the *analysis* phase, information is collected to determine the magnitude and causes of the problem. *Response* is the implementation of potential solutions. *Assessment* is the determination of the effectiveness of responses.[44]

The SARA model is a promising strategy that community police officers can use in collaboration with neighborhood residents to identify and remedy neighborhood problems. John Eck and William Spelman, who conducted an evaluation of the SARA model as designed and implemented in Newport

News, Virginia, found promising evidence that line-level police officers, private citizens, and other agencies not only can implement such a process, but also that the process can reduce the magnitude of the problems. The use of SARA resulted in decreases in burglaries in an apartment complex, reductions in robberies in the central business district, and a reduction in thefts from vehicles in another area of the city.

Some police departments have experimented with SARA as a basis for neighborhood problem solving and for redefining the role of rank-and-file police officers. Others have formed specialized community policing units, which primarily engage in neighborhood problem solving. For example, in the Spokane Police Department, Neighborhood Resource Officers (NROs) are largely relieved of reactive response duties that other patrol officers have and are placed in one of six regions of the city in an effort to mobilize residents for community problem solving and to work with students, teachers, and administrators at neighborhood schools.

In sum, total quality management is a broad management approach that has improved quality in government organizations by putting a renewed emphasis on customer needs. TQM views employees as responsible, competent and motivated, and it provides an organizational culture that supports this approach. Because community policing emphasizes customer service and problem solving, police managers across the country have embraced TQM as the means to reshape the police subculture to achieve that goal.

## Situational Leadership Theory

The management styles discussed above are conducive to the implementation of community policing. But is it possible that under some circumstances a more autocratic management style is necessary or desirable? This question may be discussed in terms of situational leadership theory.

Mary Parker-Follett, a noted administrator and scholar, is credited at the end of the nineteenth century with saying that authority in organizations "is exercised increasingly on the basis of the objective demands of the situation rather than personal and arbitrary mandates."[45] She led the way for other theorists and researchers to refine and test her hypothesis. Situational leadership theory (also referred to as a contingency approach to leadership or normative decision theory) focuses on the interaction between task behavior and relationship behavior.

*Task behavior* is the extent to which leaders organize and define the roles of their subordinates. If a manager is apt to explain what activities each member is to do and when, where, and how the tasks are to be accomplished, he or she would be high on task behavior. *Relationship behavior* is the extent to which leaders maintain personal relationships between themselves and their subordinates.[46] If, for example, a manager is concerned with the emotional well-being of his or her employees, the manager might be considered high on relationship behavior.

What is important to remember with situational leadership theory is that task behavior and relationship behavior can be mutually independent. For example, a manager who scores low on task behavior (i.e., provided little direction for a subordinate for the task at hand) may be high on relationship behavior. The opposite can occur as well. A manager who is high on task

❖ ❖ ❖ ❖  behavior (highly authoritative) can be low on relationship behavior (i.e., not concerned about the emotional well-being of subordinates). These varying combinations of task behavior and relationship behavior provide four distinct management styles that, according to P. Hersey, K. Blanchard, and D. Johnson, are dependent on the situation at hand. These leadership styles are reviewed below.

*Telling leaders.* Telling leaders score high on task behavior, low on relationship behavior. These characteristics are central to the concept of leadership in a highly centralized, bureaucratic police department in which managers are highly authoritative, communication moves from the top down, and managers have little concern about employees beyond their ability to perform specified tasks successfully. Telling leaders have a view of employees similar to that in McGregor's Theory X; that is, subordinates attempt to avoid work, have little ambition, and must be coerced with threats.

*Selling leaders.* Selling leaders, unlike telling leaders, score "high" on both task behavior and relationship behavior. They might discuss both professional and personal issues with employees, but they also feel free to make decisions that may be contrary to the employee's wishes. Because selling leaders score high on task behavior, under some circumstances they can *tell* an employee what to do and how to do it. But they typically try to sell their decisions to employees by facilitating discussions and explaining the rationale for their decisions.

*Participating leaders.* Participating leaders score low on task behavior and high on relationship behavior and can thus be viewed as the opposite of telling leaders. Participating leaders encourage participation in decision-making at all levels of the department. And quite unlike telling leaders, participating leaders tend to give little direction on the means to accomplish a task. The end itself—task accomplishment—is more important than the means to do it. Participating leaders have a view of employees similar to that in McGregor's Theory Y; that is, employees are motivated, responsible, and competent. This approach is similar to Ouchi's Theory Z and total quality management.

*Delegating leaders.* Delegating leaders, like participating leaders, score low on task behavior, believing employees to be responsible, competent, and dedicated. They differ from participating leaders in that delegating leaders score low on relationship behavior. They are less willing than participating or selling leaders to discuss professional or personal unrelated to specific tasks assigned to employees. Delegating leaders rely on employees to exercise their own judgment when it comes to completing an individual task.

This management typology is interesting because it is not static but dependent on context. A manager takes on differing management styles depending on the situation. In fact, there is a long-standing debate among situational leadership theorists. Some believe that leaders easily can move from a more autocratic style to a more participative style and vice versa. Others believe such movement to be more difficult.[47]

Whether the transition from one style of leadership to another is done easily or not, the very nature of situational leadership theory suggests that it is, in fact, done. Which style of leadership is most appropriate is a matter of subordinate readiness. For example, while a new recruit learning the ropes of community policing may have to be told what community policing is and how to engage in neighborhood problem solving, an experienced veteran might provide a middle manager with specific detail on how best to solve a neighborhood problem. In other words, the context of the situation determines the most appropriate leadership style.

## Conclusion

One of the many forces that have led to the change from professional-style policing to community policing is a change in government values so that citizens are viewed as customers. In light of that view, police departments are seen as particularly open organizations that need to be responsive to citizens' requests for service. Such requests might require police officers to use their creative abilities as they work with citizens to solve neighborhood problems. Because more traditional theories of motivation and management tend not to be conducive to innovation, creativity, and employee empowerment, changes in organizational culture, reward systems, job design, and participative management strategies may be necessary to facilitate community policing as an institution.

## Study Questions

1. What factors must be considered in order to increase motivation in the work force?

2. Compare and contrast the types of rewards discussed in the chapter.

3. Identify and discuss the key elements of total quality management.

4. How might SARA and TQM be used together within a police department?

## Endnotes

1. Robert Trojanowicz and Bonnie Bucqueroux, *Community Policing: A Contemporary Perspective* (Cincinnati: Anderson Printing, 1990)
2. David Osborne and Ted Gaebler, *Reinventing Government: How the Entrepreneurial Spirit Is Transforming the Public Sector* (Reading, MA: Addison-Wesley, 1992).
3. Larry Gaines, Mittie Southerland, and John Angell, *Police Administration* (New York: McGraw-Hill, 1991).
4. Abraham Maslow, "A Theory of Human Motivation," *Psychological Review* 50 (1943): 370–396; Frederick Herzberg, "One More Time: How Do You Motivate Employees?" *Harvard Business Review* (January-February, 1968): 27–35; David McClelland, *The Achieving Society* (Princeton, NJ: Van Nostrand Reinhold, 1964).
5. Rensis Likert, *The Human Organization* (New York: McGraw-Hill, 1967).
6. Maslow, "A Theory of Human Motivation."
7. *Ibid.*
8. *Ibid.*
9. *Ibid.*
10. Herzberg, "One More Time."
11. Gaines, Southerland, and Angell, *Police Administration.*
12. McClelland, *The Achieving Society.*

❖ ❖ ❖ ❖     13. John Klofas, Stan Stojkovic, and David Kalinich, *Criminal Justice Organizations: Administration and Management* (Pacific Grove, CA: Brooks-Cole, 1990).

14. McClelland, *The Achieving Society*.

15. Victor Vroom, *Work and Motivation* (New York: Wiley, 1964).

16. *Ibid.*

17. Klofas, Stojkovic, and Kalinich, *Criminal Justice Organizations*.

18. Ralph Chandler and Jack Plano, *The Public Administration Dictionary*, 2nd ed. (Santa Barbara, CA: ABC-CLIO, 1988).

19. Douglas McGregor, "The Human Side of Enterprise," in *Classics of Public Administration*, 3rd ed., eds. Jay Shafritz and Albert Hyde (Belmont, CA: Wadsworth, 1992), pp. 217–223.

20. William Ouchi, *Theory Z* (Reading, MA: Addison Wesley, 1981).

21. Maslow, "A Theory of Human Motivation."

22. J. Adams, "Toward an Understanding of Inequity," *Journal of Abnormal Psychology* 67 (1963): 422–436; Victor Vroom, *Work and Motivation* (New York: Wiley, 1964).

23. Victor Vroom, *Work and Motivation*.

24. Terrence Deal and A. Kennedy, *Corporate Cultures* (New York: McGraw-Hill, 1987).

25. William Ouchi, *Theory Z*; Maslow, "A Theory of Human Motivation"; Herzberg, "One More Time"; Adams, "Toward an Understanding of Inequity."

26. J. Adams, "Toward an Understanding of Inequity."

27. Herman Goldstein, *Problem-Oriented Policing* (New York: McGraw-Hill, 1990).

28. Richard R. Ritti and G. Ray Funkhouser, *The Ropes to Skip and the Ropes to Know* (New York: Wiley, 1987).

29. *Ibid.*

30. Mary Parker-Follett, "The Giving of Orders," in *Classics of Public Administration*, 2nd ed., eds. Jay M. Shafritz and Albert C. Hyde (Chicago: Dorsey, 1992).

31. *Ibid.*

32. McGregor, "The Human Side of Enterprise."

33. Goldstein, *Problem-Oriented Policing*.

34. J. Richard Hackman, Greg Oldham, Robert Jensen, Kenneth Purdy, "A New Strategy for Job Enrichment," in *Public Personnel Management*, ed. Donald Klingneralo (Palo Alto, CA: Mayfield, 1981).

35. *Ibid.*

36. Gaines, Southerland, and Angell, *Police Administration*.

37. Donald Klingner and John Nalbandian, *Public Personnel Management: Contexts and Strategies* (Englewood Cliffs, NJ: Prentice-Hall, 1985).

38. Robert Golembiewski and Carl W. Proehl, Jr., "Public Sector Applications of Flexible Workhours: A Review of Available Experience," *Public Administration Review* 40 (1980): 72–85.

39. Richard Denhardt, *Public Administration: An Action Orientation*, 2nd ed. (Belmont, CA: Wadsworth, 1995).

40. *Ibid.*

41. *Ibid.*

42. Chandler and Plano, *Public Administration Dictionary*, p. 139.

43. Office of Management and Budget, *Draft Circular A-132*, 1990.

44. *Ibid.*

45. Brian Fry, *Mastering Public Administration: From Max Weber to Dwight Waldo* (Chatham, NJ: Chatham House, 1989).

46. *Ibid.*

47. Nicholas Henry, *Public Administration and Public Affairs*, 6th ed. (Englewood Cliffs, NJ: Prentice Hall, 1995). ✦

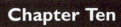

# Chapter Ten

# Ingredients for
# Implementing
# Community Policing

❖ ❖ ❖ ❖

*Thinking is the hardest work there is, which is the*
*probable reason so few engage in it.*

—Henry Ford

A few years ago, one of the authors had the opportunity to participate in the development of curriculum to teach officers what they needed to know in order to go back to their departments and teach their colleagues how best to do community policing. The week-long session was conducted at the Federal Law Enforcement Training Center (FLETC) in Glynco, Georgia. The hosts were FLETC's Steve Kernes, Patsy Andrew, and Adam Harper and Community Policing Fellow Carl Hawkins, a captain and author from the Hillsborough County Sheriff's Office near Tampa, Florida. There were also academic scholars Ralph Weisheit and Mitchell Smith and several well-respected police administrators from around the United States and Canada.

This chapter owes much to the intellect and wisdom of that group and the group that met one year later to test the curriculum that was developed the first year. Since then, FLETC has presented a train-the-trainer seminar on community policing over a dozen times around the United States. One of the group, Steve Rutzebeck, captain of the Training Division for the Maryland State Police, has been instrumental in the development of materials for this training, and his work is featured in this chapter.

In contrast to the last two chapters, which discussed how the composition of a department and the training of personnel affect the readiness of a department to implement community policing, this chapter will introduce some specific ingredients that are required if a department is to make that change. These ingredients are strategic planning, community assessment, collaborative problem-solving partnerships, and community engagement.

Mike Erp, director of the Western Regional Institute for Community Oriented Public Safety in Spokane, Washington, regularly addresses law enforcement personnel concerning their interest in community policing. He routinely begins by recognizing that many departments already are doing community policing, and many claim they have been doing it for a number of years. While he ordinarily does not dispute their claims, he asks them to consider is this question: "Maybe you've been doing community policing for some time, but are you doing it on purpose?"

Erp's tongue-in-cheek questioning of a police department's sincere commitment to community policing implies that more is involved than merely acknowledging its existence or simply claiming an allegiance to its philosophy. Doing community policing on purpose requires the ingredients listed above: making a strategic plan and changing the department to carry it out, studying the community, participating in collaborative problem solving, and involving department personnel in interacting with the community. This chapter will discuss each of these ingredients in greater detail.

❖ ❖ ❖ ❖

# Strategic Planning

Typically, police departments during the political and professional eras spent little time on systematic planning and almost none of it involved bringing average citizens into the process. The limited planning that did occur tended to be a response to some crisis situation that demanded quick action. Sometimes the crisis was financial. Sometimes it was an emergency or criminal event. Planning for organizational change has become a more frequent event in police departments during the community era. Once the leaders of a department see the need to adopt a more community-oriented approach to policing, the next important step in the process is to develop a strategic plan for organizational change.

Strategic planning may start out as an internal process, but in order to realize its full impact it must include an external dimension as well. According to training materials from the Small Town and Rural Community Policing Train-the-Trainer Program (STAR CPTT) developed by FLETC, the strategic plan should have the following five characteristics: (1) it should exist as a "living and breathing document"; (2) it should be adaptable and changeable rather than static and inflexible; (3) it should be viewed as a "road map" or "guide for operational and philosophical growth"; (4) it should provide information about the department; and (5) it should "create a capacity for strategic thinking" about where the department is and where it is headed.[1]

FLETC suggests that the best way to produce a strategic plan involves collaboration with community groups. First, collaboration serves to broaden the organizational perspective of a department by letting leaders know what the community sees as important priorities within the department's mission rather than forcing them to guess what the community wants. Collaboration helps to ensure that the department does not take it upon itself to decide its goals and make the mistake of trying to do a job that the community does not want in the first place or finds irrelevant. Instead, collaboration invites the community into the planning process so that the job citizens expect to see done is actually incorporated into the department's priorities.

One illustration that underscores the importance of needing to know what the community views as important concerns the fear of crime. Typically, when uniformed personnel are asked what the public wants them to focus on to make their community a better or safer place to live, the answer is "to catch criminals," "crack down on violent street offenders," or "arrest drug dealers and gang-bangers." To a large extent, however, the police in most communities do an effective job in these regards and in fact these kinds of issues are not the ones that the public mentions most often when asked. Instead, local residents tend to focus on the signs and symptoms of social disorder that they see on a regular basis. They are concerned much less with serious crimes that occur infrequently than with the relatively mundane, nuisance kinds of behavior that they see every day. Barking dogs, noisy neighbors, speeding cars in residential areas are often mentioned as the things that annoy the public that "someone" needs to do something about.

Second, collaboration with the public ensures that the next phase of strategic planning, the implementation process, will have onlookers who expect organizational change to happen. Department personnel will need to respond to such expectations. Without community input and expectations,

❖ ❖ ❖ ❖

*Input from citizens and community group leaders is essential to community policing strategy. (Photo: Kathy McLaughlin/The Image Works)*

there is a great risk that the strategic planning document will become one more report that sits on a shelf somewhere collecting dust.

Finally, collaboration invites the public to participate in supporting the changes that result from strategic planning. New programs typically require additional resources in terms of personnel who are assigned to a project, volunteer time, and money for materials. Consequently, community "buy-in" is crucial. An energized and motivated community that has been involved in a collaborative process is a natural ally for helping staff a program with volunteers and even for securing funding for supplies and materials.

## The Strategic Plan and Aspects of the Department

The strategic plan addresses questions related to the who, what, why, how, and when aspects of the department. First, *whom* does the agency represent and *who* should have a voice in representing it? Police departments are public-service agencies that are paid for by tax dollars to ensure public safety. As such, they are accountable to the public, local businesses, and other public servants both elected and appointed. Beyond this, departments are regulated by state and local laws and the U.S. Constitution. Individual members of the community and those persons representing larger interests in the community, along with the department's sworn and nonsworn staff, all have a stake in how the agency is administered and its activities.

Second, the *what* is the mission of the department and its work on behalf of the community. During the professional era of policing, as noted earlier, the mission of most police departments was limited to reacting to crime and enforcing the law. During the community era, providing social services and maintaining order became more important, reflecting a greater emphasis on proactive and coactive policing. Proactive efforts to help prevent crime and coactive efforts to identify and solve problems fit well within the broader mission of making communities better places to live.

Identification of problems in the community and setting priorities for their solution is an important part of the *what* aspect of a department. Although officially recorded calls for service may tell part of this story, knowledge about the amount and type of crime that goes unreported also can help provide a fuller understanding of community needs. How such information is gathered is discussed in greater detail later in this chapter.

Third, *why* does the department adopt a particular mission? Traditionally, the rationale for law enforcement is that laws help to protect persons and their property and preserve order. Without laws to regulate human behavior, the government could not ensure public safety or guarantee citizens' freedoms such as the freedom to gather together to exchange ideas and voice opinions. The substantive component of criminal law tells citizens what should or should not be done, while the procedural component tells them of the penalties for noncompliance. But law enforcement by itself, even if every law could be enforced (which probably would not be a good idea), is insufficient to preserve order.

During the professional era, the police were viewed as the crime experts, or as George Kelling and Catherine Coles put it, they were the "front end"of the criminal justice system whose primary responsibilities involved "arresting and processing offenders into this system."[2] "Keeping the peace, solving citizen problems, resolving conflicts, and maintaining order [were] at best seen as distracting peripheral functions and, at worst, as despised 'social work.' "[3] Unfortunately, this approach did not succeed. Kelling and Coles explain why.

> Alas this model has failed dismally in its own terms: serious crime has been at unacceptable levels for three decades. The model has failed because it does not recognize the links between disorder, fear, serious crime, and urban decay. And, the criminal justice system model has also failed because it ignores the role of citizens in crime prevention.[4]

During the community era, the mission of policing shifted away from a heavy emphasis on law enforcement and moved in two new directions. One is that officers on the street have a tremendous amount of discretion in the decisions they make during a work shift. The other is that both police educators and police officers are much more aware of the factors that are linked to crime. For example, preventing the first broken window or fixing broken windows as soon as they are discovered are smarter approaches to making communities safer places than waiting for reports from victims of serious offenses. Kelling and Coles write that

> Those of us who live, work, and play in cities face an amalgam of disorder, fear, serious crime, and urban decay: the crime problem does not begin with serious, or 'index' crime. Conceiving of it and addressing it as such, as has occurred for thirty years in national debates about crime, leads to bad public policy, poor legal thinking and practice, and distorted criminal justice practices and priorities.[5]

❖ ❖ ❖ ❖

# The Cheryl Steele Story

### *Cheryl Steele*

Cheryl Steele.

Our 10th wedding anniversary, (April 14, 1990)—what should we do? We put the kids in the car and drove east! We drove to Spokane, some 270 miles from home (Mill Creek, Washington). We got a room at the Shilo Inn and started exploring. The kids swam in the pool with Dad while I looked at real estate magazines by the poolside. I could not believe that there were houses from $17,000 to $55,000 still left for sale anywhere in America. During our weekend visit we really fell in love with Spokane. We decided that we were living a life in the fast lane and moving to Spokane would slow us down and give us the "quantity" time we needed as a family because the Sunday "quality" time was not working! A few weeks later my husband came back, looked at five pieces of real estate, and bought our house. The real estate agent told him it was a nice, older, quiet, established neighborhood. We moved July 30, 1990, to our new home in the West Central neighborhood of Spokane. It seemed the house of my dreams, Victorian, with a 27-foot-long front porch with three pillars, huge rooms, high ceilings, and charm galore. It needed work, but what fun we were going to have remodeling and revitalizing its grace.

As we were moving in, the child next door jumped the fence, beat up my son, and stole his bike! We could not believe it. We called 911 and were instructed to call Crime Check at 456-2233 because it was not a life-threatening emergency. I did and a lady began asking me questions. I told her we were just in the process of moving in when this happened. She asked from where we had moved and I told her from the west side of the state. She informed me that I had just moved into the worst neighborhood in Spokane. I said, "Lady, I don't want to hear that. . . . We just bought this house and the real estate agent assured my husband it was a nice older, quiet neighborhood." She replied, "Yeah, it is the twilight zone and felony flats. Get a lawyer and sue your agent!" I was astonished to hear this response from the police. I wanted help now, the kid was riding around on my son's bike, cussing out my husband, and had threatened to kill us all if we didn't leave him alone! The person on the phone informed me that the police would not be coming to our rescue over a bike dispute between kids! Needless to say, our first opinion of the Spokane Police Department was very negative.

In September 1990 I had hung clothes on the line to dry before I left for work. When I came home from work, the clothes were gone! All my son's Levis except the pair on his behind . . . *GONE!* I could not believe someone would come in my yard and steal our clothes right off the line! Again, I called the police and guess what . . . tooooooo bad for the Steele's! "You should know better than to hang your clothes out on a line living in felony flats," is what I was told. My dismay with the police was again reaffirmed. Life went on, however; our kids were in public school. We were living in a neighborhood where crime and poverty are daily experiences. Working a few hours while the kids were in school, remodeling the house, I was happier inside my soul than I had ever been! Even though it was the "zone" and "felony flats" we as a family were growing in ways that we did not know existed. Quantity time offered more for our spirit than quality time. The four of us were learning to be more than just four people living under one roof—*FAMILY* took on real meaning! Our extended family grew daily as our children made friends. It was not unusual to have 10 of God's little children at our dinner table and even tucked in our beds at night. The sounds of children penetrated our lives in every aspect. Our children were very happy. Our home was full of peace and security for all our neighborhood children. ☞

☞ Then one day it was all shattered.

Nikki Wood, the best friend of our daughter Lizi, was abducted with another friend, Rebecca West. This happened in broad daylight, approximately 4:00 P.M., at the local neighborhood convenience store. How could this be? The next night my husband and I heard on the late news that a body had been found under a burning bush. It was believed to be that of Nikki Wood. It was confirmed by morning that it was Nikki. I was sick that I had to tell my 10-year old daughter that her best friend, Nikki, would not be coming over anymore. The shock on her face when I told her I will never forget. It is an emotion Lizi feels to this day every time she thinks of Nikki. Nikki was a beautiful girl. Beautiful brown skin and lush, curly hair, with big brown eyes. She was so full of vision, hopes, and dreams. She would sit on our sofa for hours and tell us all about how her life was going to be when she grew up. She was going to be a doctor. She was going to take really good care of her brother and sisters. She was going to heal people. She was going to make all sickness go away and make sure we all stayed well. She and Lizi would laugh, plan, play, and roller skate the days away! They were not only playmates; they shared a kindred spirit.

After I told Lizi, I wondered how life got this way. What happened from the days when "community" mattered? How did we become this society of people who do not care for one another and look after one another? How could two children get abducted in broad daylight? Where was everyone? How could this not have been seen? What about her family? I really didn't know them. I knew Nikki lived with her mother. I knew there were problems at her house because she would spend days at our house without anybody ever asking where she was. I remember one day we were going to the local hardware store and Nikki wanted to ride along with us. I needed her mother's permission because I would not put children in my car or take them anywhere without the parents knowing. Nikki ran home to ask, five blocks away, and we drove over to meet her. It was a hot sunny day. Nikki was standing on the porch and I heard mother yelling at her, "Yeah just go, shut the f*(&^%$ door god dammit, get out of here!" Nikki looked at us, put a smile on her face, and bounced over to the car saying, "My mom said I could go!"

I thought then how awful this must have been for her sweet soul to bear those words and that rejection, but it was not uncommon for many of the children in my neighborhood. It was this exact situation, compounded by Nikki's death, that really made me take notice and commit myself to making a difference for my children and their generation. I carefully walked my daughter though the painful journey of loss. We attended the school memorial for Nikki and Rebecca. We visited the grave site. We attended a community meeting coordinated by our neighborhood community center director, Don Higgins.

At the neighborhood meeting I was astonished to see 260 neighbors who also felt anger and rage over this tragedy in our neighborhood. More important, we were all willing to do our part to correct the problems so this would never happen again in our city. With excellent professional facilitation by Mr. Higgins we formed a task force. Our mission was to take responsibility for the conditions in our neighborhood and make changes. We had five subcommittees to this task force. One was Police Community Relations, which I chaired as the citizen representative along with Officer Tim Conley from SPD and Mr. Higgins. We had 37 citizens on our committee. I learned at our first meeting that many citizens were mad at the police because they too got the responses I had received when I called for service. Officer Conley explained to us that we were not calling the "police." We were, in fact, calling an agency paid for by the county to take all calls for service, including police, sheriff, fire, medical, etc. This system agency had the task of determining needs and routing to the appropriate agency. Knowing that this county agency was not the "police" quickly dissipated all committee members' anger toward the police and at that instant created some leverage for the police with the citizens. I knew then the key was to educate people, motivate them to participate, help organize them, and then move out of their way! Our committee went on to define our priorities: (1) correct the lack of police presence in our neighborhood and (2) disseminate more effectively information regarding sex offenders living in our neighborhood. Priority one led to the opening of the first citizen-operated police substation in the city of ☞

❖ ❖ ❖ ❖

☞ Spokane. I chaired the process and was elected the first "volunteer president" in uncharted territory.

My journey as community activist began soon after Nikki was killed when I made a silent commitment to myself and children to change conditions for them in our community. It has become public because I have worked side-by-side with the police in developing the external component of community policing. I have been a voice to the systems in government for community. I have been an educator to the residents in my community about systems and how we as individuals must take responsibility for conditions and drive forward the necessary changes. This journey has affected the lives of my children in that they now know our "community" cares about them. They also have learned the importance of good citizenship, community values, and neighborhood responsibility. My son is now raising a family in our neighborhood because he knows the community and knows that his son is safe where we all know one another and look after each other. We have come full circle from this tragedy. Nikki has done more healing in this community than she could have ever done as a living doctor. Her death has healed an entire community, and this healing process has now spread to communities throughout this nation through replication.

I personally have pioneered some paths on this journey of community revitalization, community policing, and community governance. After four years of volunteering I was hired as program coordinator by Spokane COPS, the nonprofit umbrella organization for COP in Spokane. I have gone back to college, attended leadership classes in graduate training, and become a trainer for FLETC and our RCPI. My work has been honored with many awards, including the United Way Award and the JC Penny Golden Rule Award, the National Distinguished Leadership Award, YWCA Woman of the Year Award for Community Activism, AWC Municipal Achievement Award, and the IACP COP Award.

In 1998 Nikki's mother's boyfriend, Michael Tarbert, pleaded guilty to murdering the girls. Rebecca's body has still not been found. Tarbert plea bargained for a sentence of 10 years for each child for a total of 20 years. Lizi, I, and the community were outraged. We learned, however, through our network of system contacts that this was what Nikki's family wanted to end the ordeal. The prosecutor only had circumstantial evidence in the case because Nikki was burned up and Rebecca was never found. We learned to accept the situation in spite of our emotion. It has proven, however, that there is still plenty of work to be done. As a community leader, I plan to continue to create space for all to participate, blaze trails, and be a constant contender for change both in community and systems. This is a balancing act between citizens' needs and systems and laws! The balance comes from acknowledging opportunity, taking risks, building relationships, creating leverage, and working from a common ground. We must all do this because our children deserve no less from each of us!

---

Cheryl Ann Steele has a lengthy background in community service, both as a community activist and volunteer. She developed an all-volunteer-staffed police substation (COPS) in Spokane, Washington, that has been duplicated in 13 neighborhoods. The model was awarded the 1995 National League of Cities' Innovation Award for Rethinking Public Safety. She currently resides in Spokane and works for the Department of Corrections in Washington state. Steele is also a nationally certified community-mobilization trainer.

When police wait for serious crime to be reported before they take action, they tend to find that they have responded too late. By then, the mess that has to be cleaned has become nearly overwhelming. James Q. Wilson notes that

A public space—a bus stop, a market square, a subway entrance—is more than the sum of its human parts; it is a complex pattern of interactions that can become dramatically more threatening as the scale and frequency of those interactions increase. As the number of unconventional individuals increases arithmetically, the number of worrisome behaviors increases geometrically.[6]

Addressing problems at the front end before they can develop into full-scale crime waves requires better organization and swift action but much less resources over time than trying to fix some pattern of crime after it has become established.

Fourth, *how* does the department do its work? On the one hand, the strategic plan has to identify who among the employees and volunteers will be responsible for specific activities. On the other hand, the strategic plan must identify the types of programs and activities that it will attempt to deploy to achieve its mission.

Fifth, *when* is the strategic plan supposed to be made? Strategic planning usually unfolds over a period of several months. During this time the department will need to assess its strengths and weaknesses, reach consensus about its mission and what courses of action are desirable, and plan for the implementation process itself. Identifiable dates for completing each of these tasks serve as milestones for motivating progress and then charting success along the way.

## Features of the Strategic Plan

The strategic plan is a document produced by department leaders in collaboration with its own employees and the public. Drawing up such a plan includes the following steps: (1) acquiring support from the department's chief executive; (2) developing a vision, values, and mission statement; and (3) assembling a planning team composed of representatives from the department (both sworn and nonsworn personnel from all ranks) and from the community.

FLETC has identified several useful features of a strategic planning document. The first is a short summary of the entire document, prepared by the chief executive. The second is an introduction to the plan and a descriptive history of the community and the department's place in it.

The third feature of a strategic plan is a section on the department's mission and its values. The mission statement is an expression of the department's long-range commitment to transform itself into what it considers to be an ideal police department. The department's values reflect traits that the department considers desirable in its employees, such as honesty, fairness, and integrity. For example, consider the Tempe (AZ) Police Department's mission statement:

> The Tempe Police Department in partnership with the citizens of Tempe is committed to improving the quality of life in our city by identifying and resolving public safety concerns.

The fourth feature of a strategic plan is an organizational chart that depicts lines of authority within the department. The plan should also indicate how units and personnel are to be evaluated over time and identify both internal and external indicators of the department's success. Such evaluation includes measures for gauging the practice of community policing on an individual level and on a departmental level. Among these measures are crimes cleared by arrest or reductions in calls for services, as well as systematic feed-

❖ ❖ ❖ ❖ back from community members and businesses in the form of survey data and focus group interviews (discussed in greater detail in chapter 11).

The final feature of a strategic plan is detailed information on departmental goals and objectives. Goals are targets that the department wishes to attain, objectives are the specific steps used to reach a desired goal. For example, a goal may be to reduce fatalities from drunk driving in a particular part of town. An objective that may help reach this goal might be to step up enforcement of laws against driving while intoxicated in that part of town during the high risk hours. Another objective might be to seek an ordinance that requires servers of alcoholic beverages to get training to help them more effectively monitor the drinking behavior of high-risk drivers.

According to FLETC, some optional features of the strategic plan might include demographic data about the people who live in the community and how these numbers are expected to change over the next few years. There could also be important budgetary figures and other relevant information that the planning group believes might add to the presentation of the plan, such as references and indices.

## Barriers to Strategic Planning

Favorable organizational change can occur without the benefit of a formally recognized strategic plan or during the time that a strategic plan is being developed. Without such a document, however, change is not as predictable or as likely to be meaningful. Furthermore, it is the planning process itself that is at least as important as the document that results.

Despite the importance of strategic planning, there are inherent difficulties in achieving it. The chief barrier is resistance to change. Such resistance to change can slow or even stop the process of change when it is encountered in key leadership positions or at critical times when the direction for change is uncertain.

Resistance to organizational change comes in many forms. It may be of a general nature or more specific in origin. For example, although change is generally inevitable, people are naturally inclined toward stability and predictability. They are averse to change even if it means a better, more efficient and effective way of doing things. The old adage seems to apply here. We tend to be more comfortable with the "devil

*More senior members of the department are often reluctant to change to a new system. (Photo: Mark C. Ide)*

we know" than with risking change that could introduce us to the "devil we don't know."

More specifically, particular personality types may be opposed to change, as may personnel in particular positions in the department or at a particular point in their professional careers. For example, most employees tend to blame middle management for lack of support for changing policies or procedures. To some extent it is to be expected that those people who have succeeded in their careers based upon the old rules do not want to risk losing authority or having to face the challenges brought about by learning a new system. Similarly, senior people who are nearing retirement may not see value for them in engaging in a rather lengthy process of organizational change if they do not expect to be working for the department much longer.

One particular occupational group that tends to be highly resistant to community policing is the investigations unit. The rank of plain-clothes detective essentially is higher than that of a uniformed officer. Also, in larger departments, investigations are further organized by type of crime rather than by geographic location. Detectives are assigned to specific cases, a tradition that conflicts with community policing, where personnel engaged in community collaboration and problem solving tend to be assigned to specific neighborhoods. Detectives usually fail to see any direct benefit to themselves to support organizational changes that may mean they have to work in a different way.

## Community Assessment

The second of the four ingredients necessary for implementing community policing is community assessment. Community assessment is primarily discovering the community's needs, that is, identifying problems in need of a solution. Such assessment also involves identifying resources that can be brought into play to solve the problem. Thus community assessment is the process of identifying a community's needs and its resources.

---

### Police Making a Difference: Wichita's Cruise Control

#### *Lieutenant Darras L. Delamaide*

Call it what you will—dragging Broadway, dragging the strip, cruising the main drag, or just driving around—teenagers in cars looking for excitement and the chance to meet members of the opposite sex is part of American culture. Virtually everyone has cruised at some point as a teenager. And as long as there's motorized transportation at a reasonable cost, cruising is very likely to continue. But not everyone agrees that it's a harmless rite of passage that older citizens must learn to put up with.

When carried to an extreme, cruising can cause traffic congestion and accidents. It can lead to fights, vandalism, and even road rage. Some citizens complain that cruisers clog up the roads so local residents can't even get home, go out to rent a movie, or go to the grocery store on a Saturday night. It's not safe to be out on the streets, and it's not safe in the parking lots where cruisers gather. Cars dragging main are filled with rude and rowdy teenagers, many of whom are drinking, taking drugs, or both. Worse yet is the noise pollution that often goes along with cruising.

❖ ❖ ❖ ❖

☞ Motorcycles going from zero to a million miles an hour in under four seconds make an incredibly annoying wailing sound. Worse still, some stereos can rattle living room windows a full block or more away. Dawn arises to reveal trash and beer cans strewn about and the acrid odor of urine from front lawns used as bathrooms.

The cruising issue made for a tough assignment when Officer Lisa Rollins assumed her duties as a community police officer on 27 beat in South Wichita. One mile of asphalt in particular had become a magnet for cruisers from a six-county area. Every Friday and Saturday night it became clogged with literally thousands of cars and teenagers. Angry residents, many of them living only a few feet from the drag, were furious and fed up. They wanted Officer Rollins to do something about it.

Cruising wasn't always a problem in this part of town or elsewhere in the city. Until the early 1990s, most of the cruising done in Wichita was in the downtown business district on East Douglas. By day, downtown Wichita was frequented by mostly white-collar employees; by night, void of office workers, downtown was a well-lit strip that provided plenty of free parking, enough asphalt for even die-hard cruisers, no permanent residents, and a stoplight on every corner. The lights kept the traffic flow at a reasonable speed and provided both ample opportunity to visit with other cars at red lights and regular green lights for speed contests. This situation abruptly came to an end in the early 1990s when Old Town was born. Urban renewal meant overflow parking on Douglas Street, effectively blocking the heart of the strip and ending the possibility of cruising Douglas. And that's when the problems on Seneca Street began.

Seneca was just half a mile west and a mile south and filled all the cruisers' needs nicely. It had four lanes with a 40 mph speed limit and only two stoplights in the whole mile, plenty of fast-food places and gigantic, wide open parking lots for cruisers to gather.

There had always been a few southsiders cruising Seneca, but when the hordes of teens from Douglas descended on them, the neighborhood was quickly overrun. Seneca runs through the center of a residential area. With increased traffic congestion came a rise in street brawls as young cruisers from other neighborhoods tried to take over the southsiders' domain. Kids were getting hurt and it seemed out of control. Something had to be done.

The initial response was traditional law enforcement. Beat officers who patrolled the area were alerted to the problem and did their best to keep parking lots from becoming gathering spots since many of the fights would start when the cruisers parked. Radar-equipped patrol officers wrote greater numbers of speeding tickets in an effort to deter excessive speeding. Even businesses along the strip were asked to sign affidavits authorizing the police to issue tickets for loitering and after-hours parking; nearly every business owner or manager agreed to do so. The few businesses that were initially reluctant soon found that their lots were *THE* gathering spot since the police couldn't prevent cruisers from parking on their lots after hours. They too eventually agreed to sign affidavits.

In the end, however, traditional enforcement efforts, even with officers on special assignment dedicated to Seneca cruisers, fell far short of what the neighborhood had requested. Officer Rollins determined that a completely different approach was needed.

The first step was to identify the actual problems. A police presence was not going to stop cruising by itself, any more than the police alone can end homelessness or prostitution or similar vexing problems. The question to be answered was what specifically caused the cruising problem and what specifically the police could do about it. Officer Rollins conducted a survey of the business owners along Seneca as well as in the adjoining residential neighborhoods. She also attended many meetings of various neighborhood associations to hear and discuss in person their concerns about the cruisers. She learned that the neighborhood residents' main concerns were vandalism and loud stereos. The residents also feared large groups of teenagers gathering in the parking lots. Many residents simply would not go to the grocery store in the evening because of the cruisers. Traffic congestion was another concern. Those residents who did have to get out found themselves stuck in bumper-to-bumper traffic. ☞

Numerous residents complained about loud stereos. It seemed that people could not even enjoy sitting down and watching TV in their own homes because of the noise that came from the rolling boomboxes. The vibration from a booming bass would almost shake them out of their chairs. Calling 911 was of little help since many of the cars that created these problems would be several blocks away by the time police arrived. Unsurprisingly, these problems seemed unsolvable and strained the relationships between the cruisers, business employees and residents of the area, and the police.

Officer Rollins also conducted surveys with the cruisers themselves, assisted by members of Street Outreach, a program of the Wichita Children's Home. Free sodas were given to all the survey respondents. She was surprised to find that the cruisers included not only teenagers, but adults as well, with the range in ages being from 15 to about 25-years old. The cruisers came from all parts of Wichita and numerous small towns outside the city. Their main reason for cruising was to socialize. They told Office Rollins that cruising is a way of meeting new people and showing off their cars. It's also one of the few relatively inexpensive and fun things to do for teenagers in Wichita.

The cruisers identified some drawbacks to cruising on Seneca. They, too, were victims of crimes such as vandalism to their cars and personal assaults, with innocents sometimes being caught up in the brawls. (Generally, the "loser" of the fight would call the police and claim he or she had been assaulted, although quite often the complainant was initially willing to take part in the fight.) Of course, the cruisers complained about the police giving them tickets for having their stereos too loud or for loitering in the parking lots. The cruisers themselves voiced the opinion that only a handful of individuals were causing most of the problems on Seneca, and they would like to see the situation improve as well.

Unfortunately, the more the police increased traditional enforcement practices and upped the ticket count, the less cooperation they got from the cruisers. Traditional enforcement simply led to the cruisers developing an extremely negative attitude toward the police without any impact on crime control. It all had become a ridiculous game of chase.

Officer Rollins also gathered additional information from the department's Crime Analysis Unit regarding reported vandalisms, assaults, and citations issued. This information confirmed that although enforcement efforts had risen dramatically, they were not having any effect in reducing complaints or calls to 911.

The Southwest Neighborhood Association was one of the first groups to come forward and say they were concerned about the situation and wanted to be part of the solution. The association members handed out several hundred fliers to residents and businesses requesting their presence at a meeting on Seneca cruising. Several such meetings were held. Some of the ideas put forth were increased enforcement, neighborhood watches, and citizens on patrol. The area residents made it clear they wanted to reclaim their neighborhood.

As a result of this information gathering, it became obvious to Officer Rollins that the first order of business was to ease the strained relationship between the police and the cruisers. A pizza and soda party was held on Seneca, with donated pizza served up by the police officers themselves, assisted by Street Outreach. The cruisers were somewhat amazed to see police officers in this new role.

This interaction led to an idea for a car show, allowing the cruisers to show off their "rides." Officer Rollins contacted the owner of the shopping center whose lot served as the turnaround point for the cruisers and also a battleground between the police and cruisers. The owner was very leary of allowing the car show on his lot because of the amount of vandalism, loitering, and littering he'd had to deal with every weekend. He finally agreed, and because of his "gamble" and the cruisers' self-restraint (as well as the security effort by the community policing officers), the car show was a huge success. This success led to two more car shows that summer, with the 30 to 60 entries. The success of these events, and the positive impact they had on the whole situation, brought this property owner onto the bandwagon and he has since given time and considerable resources to the formation of a cruise control committee. Other business owners in the immediate area also donated prizes

❖ ❖ ❖ ❖
☞
to be awarded to the show winners, including fairly big-ticket items such as new chrome spoke wheels. During the shows, the officers continuously interacted with the cruisers, which eased tensions all the way around. They also handed out flyers noting the problem areas the cruisers could work on. The car show has continued to be the most popular event in the area.

Other events were held that first summer, sponsored by the community policing officers, the Southwest Neighborhood Association, and Street Outreach. These included a low-rider hydraulics demonstration and an end-of-the-summer party at a local park. Again, pizza and other refreshments were donated, as were prizes from area businesses. Once the tension between police and the cruisers eased, the kids were more amenable to taking and reading the nonstop stream of fliers that Officer Rollins and the other officers would pass out. These fliers contained information ranging from listing city ordinances that prohibited loud car stereos to listing the ages and hours for the curfew laws. They also offered tips on personal safety, how to avoid fights on the street, and other crime prevention ideas.

Traffic congestion was eased by putting up barricades at selected sites to control the flow of the cruisers, prevent crossing traffic, and keep the cruisers out of some of the neighborhoods. The officers experimented with the barricades, attempting to keep traffic flowing and eliminate congestion.

As the first summer progressed, the most noticeable result was the increased willingness of the community and cruisers to work together to solve their problems. As a result of the fliers and the interaction with the police and residents, the cruisers had a much better understanding of why the residents were so frustrated with the cruising taking place in their neighborhood. Likewise, the residents had a much better understanding of who the kids were and why they were cruising. It put faces on the kids in the cars, who were, for the most part, just being teenagers. It defused tensions among residents and reduced complaints to the police. The effort also resulted in decreased vandalism to businesses such as graffiti and broken plate glass. The number of assault reports also dropped as kids learned how to avoid fights and the importance of calling police when brawls did break out. Even a follow-up survey found that the residents felt much safer in their own neighborhood and many had willingly participated in the community events with the cruisers.

It is likely that the cruisers will stay on Seneca, at least for now, and the residents and businesses will remain there as well. Consequently, the cruise control committee remains active and has a big spring planning session to get ready for the busy summer. New activities have been added. One recent innovation was the volume control project. A decibel reader was put in the parking lot and the cruisers pulled up 50 feet away. The sound output was monitored by an officer who would tell the car owner when he or she exceeded legal limits. The decibel reader was also placed inside the car to monitor interior sound levels. Many of the cruisers were surprised to learn that their stereos were far above the level that caused permanent hearing loss. The volume control project had the effect of lowering the number of loud stereos, and the cruisers found out just how loud they could go without getting a ticket or permanently injuring themselves. Another community-building annual event that was added was the South Seneca Parade. The residents and business owners enter floats and the cruisers enter their cars. This continuous interaction and understanding has not eliminated all problems, but it does keep channels of communication open, and all sides now share something that was previously lacking—respect.

Darras L. Delamaide, a former cruiser himself, is a lieutenant with the Wichita Police Department and commander of the community policing/SCAT unit for the Patrol South Bureau. As a 17-year veteran he has served as a section watch commander for all four bureaus, in addition to spending eight years as a patrol officer and a master patrol officer in field services and planning and research. Delamaide recently completed an M.A. in criminal justice at Wichita State University and is studying for a doctoral degree in sociology at Oklahoma State University.

## A Variety of Perspectives                    ❖ ❖ ❖ ❖

A community's needs and resources can be viewed from various perspectives. These might include the perspective of the general business community or large corporation or public institution. Another perspective may be that of elected public officials, who supposedly represent the interests of their various constituencies. Public service providers, including the police, offer yet another perspective. Furthermore, citizens in general, as well as specific groups (e.g., senior citizens, parents, religious bodies, migrant workers, gays and lesbians, college students, etc.) may have distinct perspectives on what affects the quality of life in their community.

Considering all these perspectives yields several observations. First, some groups are good at voicing their concerns, and some have to be encouraged to speak out. Second, although many groups will have similar or even identical concerns, other groups will disagree. Third, to the extent that people share a common perspective about what is best for their community they also may be willing to join in partnerships with the police and other agencies to develop an effective approach to preserving or improving the quality of community life.

## Eight Steps of Assessment

According to the training guide prepared for FLETC's STAR CPTT program, there are eight steps to conducting a community assessment. The first involves interviewing people who represent the various perspectives in the community. Key here is the term *representative*. Most police executives and community leaders make the mistake of assuming they know what their community thinks based upon the people with whom they most frequently talk. However, research has shown that humans tend to remember and project information that fits well with their own beliefs and forget information that runs counter to what they think. Making sure that a wide spectrum of people are interviewed and their opinions noted will prove helpful for understanding various community perspectives and ensuring that solutions will have broad public appeal.

The second step in the community assessment process is to conduct a community survey or interviews with focus groups. Unlike interviews with a few people thought to represent varying points of view, community surveys can be sent to the vast majority of residents of an area who may only rarely get a chance to voice their opinions. Interviews with focus groups are particularly useful when information is needed quickly or where little money is available for collection of data on a larger scale. Examples of a community survey and a focus group interview schedule are found in Appendices C and D of *Community Policing in a Rural Setting* by Quint Thurman and Edmund McGarrell.[7]

In that same book, McGarrell and his colleagues, Socorro Benitez and Ricky Gutierrez, identify three reasons to conduct either a community survey or focus group interviews with community members.

> First, the information generated can assist in a performance appraisal of the organization. Traditional indicators of police performance, such as offenses known and arrests, have long been recognized as flawed, at least if considered uncritically. Do increased 'offenses known' indicate poor police perfor-

❖ ❖ ❖ ❖    mance or are the police being successful in convincing citizens to report their victimizations? Do increased arrests indicate good policing or rising crime? The community survey and focus group interview can provide direct information on police performance from the agency's customers. A second goal of the community survey and focus group interview is to support problem-solving activities within the community and to help set police priorities. Third, the community survey and focus groups can be used as part of an evaluation of specific programs.[8]

Data collection from focus group interviews typically involves group interviews from randomly selected members of a community, business, or other specialty groups. Similarly, random selection is the preferred method of choosing potential survey respondents rather than using convenience samples or snowball techniques (asking respondents to suggest names of others who might be willing to complete a survey). Either method should invite responses to questions that cover some or all of the following topical areas listed by McGarrell et al.:

- assessment of the level and quality of police services.

- fear of crime.

- victimization experience.

- neighborhood crime and disorder problems.

- police-public relations.

- assessment of and support for community policing.[9]

The third step in conducting a community assessment is to gather background information. Data here can come from a wide variety of sources. Census data on the population size and its composition in terms of age groups, housing types, ethnicity, and related variables can provide useful information. Other sources might include employment and health care data, as well as official crime report data obtained by the police department or the sheriff's office.

The fourth step in community assessment involves the review of public resources available locally. It is important to take a look at what kinds of government programs are in place in the community and how well they are being used.

The fifth step is to review the private services available in the community. At this point FLETC recommends using video cameras and narrative to record and then describe the community as it exists in its present form. These descriptions can then serve as a baseline from which to compare changes that occur over time as a strategic plan is implemented.

The sixth step in community assessment is to examine the various data that have been collected and make some preliminary judgments about the source of crime and crime-related problems and the extent to which they are negatively impacting the community's quality of life. It is at this point that the perceptions of the community and its strengths and weaknesses will become apparent.

The seventh step is prioritizing issues and problems in need of resolution. It is here that the need arises to bring together at a planning meeting a wide selection of people representing various perspectives so that they can identify what they see from the data as the top priorities and also help plan a course of action. Their interest and input may indicate their willingness to participate in police-community problem-solving partnerships.

The eighth and final step in the community assessment process is to summarize the events, findings, and conclusions from the previous seven steps in a report and make it available to all who are interested.

## Problem Solving

Problem solving, the third ingredient in implementing community policing, can take many forms. On an informal level, each of us engages in problem solving in our daily lives. For example, in order to get to class each day students and faculty have to solve a transportation problem, which may prove to be quite involved if the weather turns bad or traffic jams up. Similarly, for many students who work and go to school, prioritizing study time can prove problematic, especially if yet another dimension such as raising children must be addressed.

On a more formal level, organizations can develop systematic approaches to deal with problems. For example, Herman Goldstein introduced police departments to the idea of a systematic problem-solving approach some 20 years ago.[10] His views have since been elaborated in his book *Problem-Oriented Policing*.[11] Noted police researchers John Eck and William Spelman distinguish everyday problem solving from problem-oriented policing (POP). They see the latter as "an agency-wide strategy to encourage and guide all its members to engage in problem solving."[12]

Goldstein's important contribution to the idea of systematic problem solving in policing is primarily a response to five concerns. First, police departments tend to overemphasize the importance of internal management issues and underemphasize operational effectiveness outside the department. Second, police departments devote too little time to developing measures for reducing and preventing crime and instead tend to concentrate almost exclusively on reactive policing. Third, police departments largely ignore the wealth of community resources that is available to solve problems that eventually become matters for the police. Similarly, they tend to make poor use of a second important resource: "Within their agencies, police have readily available to them another huge resource: their rank-and-file officers, whose time and talent have not been used effectively."[13] Finally, Goldstein points out the need for organizational change and the fact that police departments will have to adapt if they are to change and improve.[14]

### The Importance of POP

Goldstein views POP as a key component in the development of an effective police department. He sees POP as

> a comprehensive plan for improving policing in which the high priority attached to addressing substantive problems shapes the police agency, influencing all changes in personnel, organization, and procedure. Thus, problem-oriented policing not only pushes policing beyond current improvement efforts, it calls for a major change in the direction of those efforts.[15]

❖ ❖ ❖ ❖    It is important to acknowledge Goldstein's emphasis on effectiveness and the role that POP plays in helping a department become more effective at problem solving. Effective problem solving is usually thought to mean eliminating a specific problem entirely. But problem-solving techniques can be effective in several ways. Eck and Spelman identify four of them. First, effectiveness can be seen as sufficiently attacking a problem so that the number of criminal incidents that the problem causes is reduced to some acceptable level. Second, effectiveness might be defined as significantly reducing the magnitude of harm that a problem generates. Third, effectiveness can mean improving the ability to handle efficiently the criminal incidents that the problem creates. Finally, effectiveness can be matching the problem with an appropriate solution that does not directly involve the police (e.g., mental health services, social welfare, animal control, etc.).[16]

To date, POP has been implemented successfully in several cities to address a variety of crimes ranging from prostitution to illegal drug sales. The

## A Problem-Solving Project to Reduce Public Fighting

### Aspen Police Department

The city of Aspen is a mountain resort community in western Colorado. According to the 1994 census, its population is 5,400. According to the Aspen Chamber Resort Association, the estimated population is 30,000 when visitors, seasonal workers, and a commuting workforce are taken into account.

The Aspen Police Department has 28 sworn officers, five nonsworn officers, and five administrative support staff. The annual operating budget is just over two million dollars. The department provides public-safety services in partnership with the community, including, but not limited to, customer service; problem solving; law education and enforcement; traffic safety; animal control; and involvement with a variety of youth programs, social services departments, nonprofit organizations, community action committees, neighborhood groups, and other public safety agencies such as the fire department, ambulance service, environmental health office, and liquor board.

*Aspen police officers check IDs in the central business district. Working with bar patrons and businesses is an important part of their public safety mission, which can be carried out through problem solving and crime prevention. (Photo: Courtesy of the Aspen Police Department)*

☞

❖ ❖ ❖ ❖

## The Problem

Aspen has 91 liquor-licensed establishments and a per capita county retail liquor sales of $5,209.00; the state average is $490.00 per capita. The destructive effects of alcohol abuse are enormous. Alcohol abuse is a major contributing factor in crime, domestic violence, child abuse, suicides, absenteeism, family breakdowns, and accidental deaths. It costs U.S. taxpayers over $240 billion annually, which is more than 3 percent of our Gross Domestic Product (3 percent is considered a healthy growth rate).

The Aspen Police Department responds to high number of calls about public fighting in the downtown area at night where most of the participants are intoxicated.

## 1995 Goals

In addition to patrol duties and responding to calls for service, the police planned to target problem areas and work with other departments to develop innovative responses to enhance the safety of the community and protect property. The police estimated they would reduce public fighting calls by 10 percent from the previous year by proactively addressing the problem with the bars and restaurants and the community.

*An Aspen Police Department patrol supervisor on a barcheck patrol. This Aspen problem-solving approach resulted in dramatic drops in assaults and public fighting by working together with businesses, the media, and other community partners to proactively address alcohol-related problems in the city. (Photo: Courtesy of the Aspen Police Department)*

## Responses

The Aspen Police made the following responses:

- The Aspen Liquor Board was established, which is comprised of five volunteer community members empowered by the Aspen City Council to review and approve or deny liquor license applications and renewals and conduct show-cause hearings regarding the revocation of liquor licenses.

- A partnership was created with the Aspen Liquor Board where police requested the responsible management of all liquor establishments by focusing on four problem areas: overserving, overcrowding, serving underage persons, and serving habitual drunkards.

- Three additional uniformed officers were hired so police could conduct consistent bar check patrols in which officers work with bar management to address the four problem areas. This increased opportunities for educational voluntary compliance and increased enforcement of the liquor code. TIPS training for bar and restaurant staff found in violation of the liquor code was made mandatory. (TIPS training teaches people the signs and symptoms of intoxication and how to conduct underage identification checks.)

- The police created a Chemical Dependency Task Force comprised of community members to enhance police detoxification services.

- The police developed a police substation at the Rubey Park Transit Station, which was a central location for the majority of calls about public fighting.

- The police worked with the print media and the Aspen Institute Community Health Forum on publicizing the negative impacts of alcohol abuse.

## Assessment

There was a 16 percent reduction in public fighting calls from 1994 to 1995. There continues to be a dramatic decrease in assaults and such calls—34 percent between 1995 and 1996.

Colorado West Recovery Center has increased its staffing service to the Aspen ☞

❖ ❖ ❖ ❖

☞

> area and established the Aspen Recovery Center with a community advisory board.
>    A partnership was established with Aspen Valley Hospital that resulted in the planning of a detox facility to be included in the new medical office building; construction began in the spring of 1999. The Aspen Valley Hospital emergency room staff is currently working in conjunction with the Colorado West Recovery Center on the detoxification of individuals who are a danger to themselves and others.
>    The Chemical Dependency Task Force participated on the Aspen Institute Community Health Forum, which discovered that alcohol and substance abuse was the number one community health problem. The task force is currently conducting community presentations to raise awareness of the destructive effects of alcohol and substance abuse and generate community support to address this problem. The Aspen Institute has pledged financial support to the task force in developing a marketing campaign.

most notable of these cities include Newport News, Virginia,[17] Madison, Wisconsin,[18] Tulsa, Oklahoma,[19] and San Diego[20] and Oakland, California.[21]

Goldstein identifies several commonly acknowledged features of modern-day policing that led to the development of POP:

- The police do much more than deal with crime; they deal with many forms of behavior that are not defined as criminal.

- The wide range of functions that police are expected to perform, including dealing with fear and enforcing public order, are appropriate functions for the police; from the perspective of the community, they may be as important as the tasks the police perform in dealing with behavior labeled criminal.

- Too much dependence in the past has been placed on the criminal law in order to get the police job done; arrest and prosecution are simply not an effective way to handle much of what constitutes police business. And even if potentially effective, it may not be possible to use the criminal justice system in some jurisdictions because it is so overloaded.

- Police use a wide range of methods—formal and informal—in getting their job done. 'Law enforcement' is only one method among many.

- Police, of necessity, must exercise broad discretion, including discretion in deciding whether to arrest and prosecute in situations in which there is ample evidence that a criminal law has been violated.

- The police are not autonomous; the sensitive function they perform in our society requires that they be accountable, through the political process, to the community.[22]

Goldstein recognizes that most "police problems" are really "community problems."[23] Therefore,

> The first step in problem-oriented policing is to move beyond just handling incidents. It calls for recognizing that incidents are often merely overt symptoms of problems. This pushes the police in two directions: (1) It requires that they recognize the relationships between incidents (similarities of behavior, location, persons involved, etc.); and (2) it requires that they take a more in-depth interest in incidents by acquainting themselves with some of the conditions and factors that give rise to them.[24]

POP is a problem-solving approach that is carried out following the principles of SARA (scanning, analysis, response, and assessment). During the *scanning* stage, an officer identifies an issue and determines whether it is really a problem. In the *analysis* stage, officers collect information from sources inside and outside their department in order to understand the scope, nature, and causes of the problem. In the *response* stage, this information is used to develop and implement solutions, using the assistance of other police units, other public and private organizations, and anyone else who can help. Finally, in the *assessment* stage, officers evaluate the effectiveness of the response and may use the results to revise the response, collect more data, or even to redefine the problem.[25]

## The Importance of CAPRA and SECAPRA

In more recent years, other varieties of the SARA approach to problem solving have emerged that are more explicitly linked to community policing. For example, the Royal Canadian Mounted Police (RCMP) developed CAPRA (clients, analysis, partnership, response, assessment), an approach that relies more heavily upon the role of the community in jointly identifying and solving local problems.[26]

CAPRA differs from SARA in four distinct ways. First, it was created in consort with a "training review" that examined information gathered from a variety of sources including trainers, academy graduates, and high-ranking management staff. Second, it was adopted by the RCMP as an institutionalized and advanced form of training that all cadets would receive, thereby signaling the start of significant organizational change to community policing. Third, the training itself is based upon an adult learning model that is "learner centered" rather than "instructor centered."[27] That is, instead of mainly relying on lectures to train a student audience, the instructor presents group problem-solving exercises that mirror realistic situations that students will likely face in the field. Fourth, CAPRA is "client centered," emphasizing "the importance of organizing policing around the needs of the community and individual clients rather than around policing disciplines or functions."[28]

The first of the five elements of CAPRA is the emphasis on clients, meaning the citizens whom a public police department is obligated to protect and serve. Frum Himelfarb notes that "Effective policing requires an understanding of the diverse and changing needs of the full range of clients in any particular situation and the ability to integrate or balance competing interests."[29]

The second element of CAPRA is the need to acquire and analyze information. Himelfarb points out that we live in an information-based society. "Problem solving for community policing requires an enhanced ability to acquire, organize, and analyze diverse data from diverse sources, identifying priorities and patterns, and creating and maintaining records in a manner compliant with both law and policy."[30]

The third element in CAPRA is for partnership. Good police officers learn, especially in rural areas, that it is extremely difficult to carry out the responsibilities associated with providing public safety all by themselves, without local support. Accordingly, Himelfarb notes that "in order to develop approaches that are effective and responsive to clients, it becomes increas-

❖ ❖ ❖ ❖    ingly important to develop partnerships that bring together the appropriate knowledge, skills, and resources for problem solving."[31] She points to the crucial need for police officers to develop "teamwork and negotiation"[32] in order to solve problems of crime and disorder more effectively.

The fourth element of CAPRA is response.

> Rather than simply asking what might be done given the law and police policy, the police also ask what might be done in partnership to meet clients' needs. The police mandate and powers are a resource for problem solving. Others in social services, health care or community leaders, can be instrumental as well.[33]

Finally, the fifth element of CAPRA is assessment for continuous improvement. Building effective partnerships to prevent and control crime is an essential feature of CAPRA. Beyond having such a structure in place is the idea that groups working together are involved in a long-term commitment to improve their community's quality of life. One important challenge for the group is to develop ways to chart their progress. Having indicators in place to measure change over time allows the partnership to view more objectively the impact of its actions to see what is working and what is not.

Training in problem solving developed at the Maryland State Police Academy by Captain Steve Rutzebeck and his colleagues represents an important modification of the CAPRA model. Following the lead of Himelfarb and her colleagues at the RCMP, Rutzebeck used the Canadian approach as a point of reference to develop SECAPRA. SECAPRA emphasizes two "filters" that are first applied to examine the problem and any related issues. The first is *scanning* for safety in order to assess any safety-related concerns that might affect the officer or the client. Involving the public in some problem-solving measures may place some citizens at risk of retaliation from a suspect or may compromise a covert investigation that already is underway.

The second filter is *ethics*. Not all problem solving is inherently ethical. Closing down a suspected crack house or a methamphetamine lab can be accomplished with a wrecking ball or explosives, but a more legally acceptable (and ethical) means might involve engaging neighbors in helping to document the extent and identity of illegal activity that goes on in the area and then obtaining arrest and search warrants. The application of the ethics filter ensures that decisions made are ethically appropriate for all of the parties involved in the action. For example, asking neighbors to use videocameras from a safe distance to keep tabs on suspected drug dealers operating on public streets and sidewalks is ethical; asking neighbors to collect physical evidence from the suspect's private property is not.

## Community Engagement

Once a police department has more complete information about community needs, either from community surveys or a focus group, it can proceed to the fourth ingredient of implementing community policing: engaging members of the community and community groups in developing and implementing solutions.

Although a police department will have sought input from the community at several points, step number seven in the community assessment process—bringing in community representatives to examine collected data in order to prioritize public safety needs and explore workable solutions—can be the point of emergence of formal police-community partnerships if they are not already in place.

Any experienced police chief or sheriff knows that public support is crucial to the successful leadership of an effective law enforcement agency. Public support creates a legitimate mandate for needed organizational change. It also provides a cushion of approval when disaster strikes. For example, when an officer has to use deadly force in the field or a financial crisis means severe budget cuts, a trusting public is much appreciated. Furthermore, the difficult job of policing can be made more manageable on a daily basis by public support. Citizen volunteers organized into block watch teams can be instrumental in preventing crime. Citizens in general can help to promote their community's public safety by willingly serving as the eyes and ears of their local police. Finally, as already noted, citizen support can help the police do a better job by helping to identify the specific crime problems that a community considers important enough for citizens to join with police to resolve.

*Outreaches like this crime prevention rally can help form the partnerships between police and citizenry necessary for successful community engagement. (Photo: Courtesy of the Omaha Police Department)*

FLETC identifies four conditions that must precede successfully engaging the community in policing partnerships:

- Frustration with the current way issues are being addressed.

- Information with which to get started on a new approach.

- One or more concerned people willing to act as leaders.

- The perception that things could change for the better.[34]

❖ ❖ ❖ ❖        FLETC also identifies four keys to building successful police-community partnerships: (1) meaningful community contact, (2) effective communication, (3) trust, and (4) information exchange. A meaningful contact refers to a favorable interaction between the police and members of the community that invites the latter to offer their input to police at a time and place that is not routine or taken for granted. Such contacts tell citizens that their input is really appreciated and that the police are listening to their concerns and suggestions for solutions. Similarly, good communication occurs when specific concerns are discussed in an open and sincere manner that engenders the third and fourth points, that is, trust and an open exchange of ideas and information.

Although the four conditions for community engagement are necessary, their presence does not guarantee that engagement will prove successful. Police departments have a tendency toward isolation that makes it difficult for them to truly engage the public in an equal and open partnership. Historically, during the professional era the police identified themselves as the experts on crime. Today, during the community era they realize that the public can play several important roles to help police professionals do their job. The challenge for the police is to recognize that civic groups, neighborhood associations, community alliances, the business community, residential associations, and other groups are willing to join the police in a broad-based mission that addresses the overall quality of life.

There are many barriers to building police-community partnerships. One is disorganized communities or apathetic public agencies who seem not to care about making their town or neighborhood a better place to live. Another is citizen fear of retaliation by criminal offenders if the citizens are involved with the police. Finally, there may be strong personalities or leaders who either want to drive a process along in a certain direction (contrary to where others think it should go) or block successful partnerships if they are not originally included.

These barriers notwithstanding, police executives and other personnel are encouraged to enlist broad-based support among those in the community who are willing to participate. The problem-identification stage of the community assessment is a good place to test the waters for those who might consider cooperating with the police. Prioritizing problems and brainstorming for potential solutions are naturally interactive exercises that encourage participation. The formation of effective partnerships is further enhanced by open town meetings with trained facilitators who can ensure that everyone in attendance has an equal voice. Success is further ensured by developing a shared vision for the community upon which all participants can agree. Although engaging the community is easier said than done, it is the process itself that is instrumental for bringing the police and their communities together.

## Conclusion

Community engagement is a natural follow-up to problem-solving partnerships, which grow out of community assessment, which in turn is an integral part of strategic planning. Although most police departments and sheriff's offices (still influenced by the calls-for-service emphasis of the professional era) do not realize it, the public is highly supportive of the police. Reactive policing means that the police usually meet the public only as complainants or suspects. Community policing means police will meet a much broader cross-section of people, most of them law-abiding citizens who ordinarily do not come in contact with the police. Ordinary citizens are a great untapped resource who tend to support good police work to control crime and disorder and stand ready to be invited into police-community partnerships. After all, who really wants to live in a society where crime and disorder are rampant? For the police to succeed, and ultimately for communities to succeed, all the police really have to do is ask citizens for their help.

## Study Questions

1. What is the purpose of a strategic plan? Describe its characteristics.

2. Identify and discuss the specific parts of a strategic plan in chronological order.

3. What is the purpose of a community assessment? Discuss the steps of the community assessment process according to the Federal Law Enforcement Training Center.

4. According to Goldstein, what are six commonly acknowledged features of modern-day policing that have led up to the development of problem-oriented policing (POP)?

5. How do problem solving and problem-oriented policing (POP) differ? What are three models of POP and how are they different from one another?

## Endnotes

1. Federal Law Enforcement Training Center, *Small Town and Rural Community Policing Train-the-Trainers*, training manual (Glynco, GA: State and Local Programs Division, 1999).
2. George Kelling and Catherine M. Coles, *Fixing Broken Windows: Restoring Order and Reducing Crime in Our Communities* (New York: Touchstone, 1997), p. 6.
3. *Ibid.*, p. 6.
4. *Ibid.*, p. 6.
5. *Ibid.*, p. 5.
6. James Q. Wilson, "Foreword," in *ibid.*, pp. xiii–xvi.
7. Quint C. Thurman and Edmund F. McGarrell, eds., *Community Policing in a Rural Setting* (Cincinnati: Anderson, 1997).
8. Edmund F. McGarrell, Socorro Benitez, and Ricky S. Gutierrez, "Getting to Know Your Community Through Citizen Surveys and Focus Groups," in *ibid.*, pp. 97–105 [p. 97].
9. *Ibid.*, p. 98.
10. Herman Goldstein, "Improving Policing: A Problem-Oriented Approach," *Crime and Delinquency* 25 (1979): 236–258.
11. Herman Goldstein, *Problem-Oriented Policing* (Philadelphia: Temple University Press, 1990).
12. John E. Eck and William Spelman, *Problem Solving: Problem-Oriented Policing in Newport News* (Washington, DC: Police Executive Research Forum, 1987).

❖ ❖ ❖ ❖    13. Goldstein, *Problem-Oriented Policing*.

14. *Ibid.*

15. *Ibid.*, p. 32.

16. John E. Eck and William Spelman, *Problem Solving: Problem-Oriented Policing in Newport News* (Washington, DC: Police Executive Research Forum, 1987).

17. *Ibid.*

18. Herman Goldstein and Charles E. Susmilch, *Experimenting with the Problem-Oriented Approach to Improving Police Service: A Report and Some Reflections on Two Case Studies* (Madison: University of Wisconsin Law School, 1982).

19. George E. Capowich, Janice A. Roehl, and Christine Andrews, *Evaluating Problem-Oriented Policing: Assessing Process and Outcomes in Tulsa and San Diego* (Washington, DC: National Institute of Justice, 1994).

20. *Ibid.*; George E. Capowich and Janice A. Roehl, "Problem-Oriented Policing: Actions and Effectiveness in San Diego," in *The Challenge of Community Policing: Testing the Promises*, ed. Dennis P. Rosenbaum (Newbury Park, CA: Sage, 1994), pp. 127–146.

21. Lorraine Green, *Policing Places With Drug Problems* (Newbury Park, CA: Sage, 1996).

22. Goldstein, *Problem-Oriented Policing*, p. 11.

23. *Ibid.*, p. 34.

24. *Ibid.*, p. 33.

25. Eck and Spelman, "Problem-Solving: Problem-Oriented Policing in Newport News,"in *Community Policing: Contemporary Readings*, eds. Geoffrey P. Alpert and Alex Piquero (Prospect Heights, IL: Waveland, 1998), pp. 63–77.

26. Frum Himelfarb, "RCMP Learning and Renewal: Building on Strengths," in *Community Policing in a Rural Setting*, eds. Quint Thurman and Edmund McGarrell (Cincinnati: Anderson, 1997), pp. 33–39.

27. *Ibid.*, p. 38.

28. *Ibid.*, p. 37.

29. *Ibid.*, p. 35.

30. *Ibid.*, p. 36.

31. *Ibid.*, p. 36.

32. *Ibid.*, p. 36.

33. *Ibid.*, p. 36.

34. Federal Law Enforcement Training Center, *Small Town and Rural Community Policing.* ✦

# Chapter Eleven

# Evaluating the Effectiveness of Community Policing

❖ ❖ ❖ ❖

> *'All there is to thinking,' he said, 'is seeing something noticeable which makes you see something you weren't noticing which makes you see something that isn't even visible.'*

> —Norman Maclean,
> *A River Runs Through It*

**M**any county and municipal police departments do community policing in one form or another. They must consider, however, not only the practical question of how best to do it but whether it is effective. Police administrators, line-level officers, public and private funding agencies, college professors, politicians, and private citizens have been asking whether or not community policing works. Evaluation research can help answer this question and related questions. Evaluation is a necessary step toward a better understanding of how changes in an organization might affect the environment in which they occur and the people who are asked to make changes. This chapter discusses the role of evaluation and suggests some specific ways to define and then measure the effectiveness of community policing.

## Why Evaluation?

What is evaluation research and what part does it play in community policing? The term *evaluation* in a broad sense is an assessment or appraisal process to determine the worth or quality of something. Although this definition is generally adequate, in the social sciences it has to be somewhat more specific. For the purposes of this chapter, *evaluation research* is the use of systematic research procedures to collect, analyze, and use information to answer questions about program effectiveness. Evaluation research is also useful if we indeed learn that something works and want to implement it again elsewhere. It is important to keep in mind that this definition of evaluation is somewhat narrow, since the term also includes scientific studies that assess the need for a program in the first place (needs assessments) and that examine the process of implementing the program (program monitoring), which was covered in the last chapter. It should also be noted that an evaluation is systematic to the extent that it uses accepted and consistent methods of collecting and analyzing information (data). Some of the accepted methods of data collection will be reviewed later in this chapter.

Evaluation research in its various forms has been conducted for hundreds of years. One often cited example, which dates from the 1700s, illustrates the complexity of any evaluation study. According to Peter Rossi and Howard Freeman, a British ship captain observed the lack of scurvy among sailors in Mediterranean countries compared to British sailors. He began to wonder what differences in the experiences of British sailors might account for the higher incidence of scurvy among his men. One obvious difference was the citrus fruits that the Mediterranean sailors were eating. The captain thought that perhaps if his men, too, ate citrus fruits, he might be able to prevent scurvy among his crew. But, because he was not sure that citrus fruits accounted for the difference, he made half of his crew eat limes and the other half maintain their regular diet. After some time, his hunch proved correct: those who ate limes were less likely to get scurvy than those who did not. Because of the results of this evaluation, eventually all British sailors were required to eat citrus fruit regularly in order to prevent scurvy (ultimately earning British sailors the nickname "limeys").[1]

The above example illustrates the usefulness of evaluation. The ship's captain used systematic procedures (selecting only half of the crew to eat limes) and accepted methods (observations) to determine program outcomes (the extent to which the treatment group differed from the comparison group succumbing to scurvy). Even so, determining the *validity*, or credibility, of the captain's research depends on factors unknown today. For example, how were sailors selected for the treatment and comparison groups? Were some more prone to get scurvy to begin with and to which group were they assigned? How much did the groups differ in outbreaks of scurvy? If there was a difference, to what extent was the captain confident that limes by themselves accounted for the difference?

It is enough to note here that credible evaluations of any program—especially community policing programs—can be complex. The credibility of an evaluation depends on the ability of the researcher to rule out alternative hypotheses that might explain what particular features of a program or policy really caused the change. Determining the reason for an outcome often depends on the research methods used to collect data and the design of the evaluation itself. In the scurvy experiment, it is now known that it was not the limes that prevented scurvy but rather the vitamin C found in limes. Vitamin C also is found in other citrus fruits such as oranges and lemons. Hence, vitamin C is the *mechanism* that further explains why those who ate limes were less likely to contract scurvy.

## The Nature of Evaluation

Asking the question, Does community policing work? means asking about specific program activities, objectives, and goals. Frank Levy, Arnold Meltsner, and Aaron Wildavsky highlight three important levels of assessment when conducting evaluations: outputs, outcomes, and impacts.[2]

### Outputs

According to Levy and his colleagues, outputs are the immediate services or goods that come about as a result of a policy change, program, or social intervention.[3] For example, a community policing program might request officers to initiate proactive contacts with community members. Therefore, "contacts with community members" is an output of the program. Outputs are usually the subject of process evaluations or implementation studies, as briefly discussed in the last chapter. In these kinds of evaluations, an evaluator would try to measure the extent to which implementation of the community policing program fits the original intent of the program. Although outputs are useful for monitoring the process of a program and whether or not it matches the program plan, they tell little about the *effects* of a program.

❖ ❖ ❖ ❖    ## Outcomes

Outcomes are the effects of a policy, program, or social intervention. They are program objectives, which are measured in a variety of ways according to the use of evaluation.[4] In the example above dealing with proactive police contacts with residents, one objective of the program might be to solve five neighborhood problems per month. The extent to which these problems were solved, then, is an outcome of the community policing program. According to William Johnson, outcomes are the intermediate result of implementing a program or policy.[5]

## Impacts

In general, there is considerable debate over the difference between outcomes and impacts. Outcomes may be more easily identifiable and immediately observable objectives. Impacts are longer-range and more broadly defined program goals—a long-term consequence of applying a particular policy or program. But the difference between the two is not always clear. For example, one goal of a community policing program might be to improve the quality of life for a neighborhood. In order to judge how much improvement a police department has made, an evaluator might consider several outcomes. Since one cannot directly measure "quality of life," the evaluator might look at related outcomes, such as the public's fear of crime. But there is considerable variation in the way evaluators define and measure impacts.

# Types of Evaluations

Johnson has outlined a number of approaches to evaluation research. For example, say that a local sheriff's department has set up a citizens' academy as part of its community policing initiative, in the belief that once citizens became aware of the nature of police work and the constraints under which police operate, citizens would be more likely than before to view police in a favorable light. A new sheriff is elected who wants to know whether the academy is favorably influencing citizen attitudes toward other departmental personnel. Several approaches might prove useful in evaluating the outcome, that is, favorable attitudes toward law enforcement.

## Intuitive Versus Scientific Evaluation

Evaluations can be intuitive or scientific. According to Johnson, intuitive evaluations are informal and occur during everyday interactions between the police and their clients.[6] In light of the previous definition of evaluation research, intuition by itself would be a less credible approach than a more formal evaluation because the intuitive method of collecting information is not necessarily systematic and depends on the beliefs, experiences, and perceptions of a single individual. In the citizens' academy example, an academy participant might be overheard telling another member that he has learned a great deal about police operations and now more readily appreciates the work that law enforcement officers do. This information might be passed on to program administrators, and ultimately to the new sheriff, as an indication

*Routinized police practices are difficult to evaluate but persist largely due to intuition and tradition. (Photo: Mark C. Ide)*

of program success. But use of this approach is only likely to confirm hunches on the part of administrators that the program does some good. Yet, because of the errors that might occur in using just one person's opinion as an indication of program success, it may do more harm than good.

The intuitive approach may be appropriate in many situations, such as when there is little time to do anything else or when there is little riding on the consequences of a judgment, but it is too limited in comparison to the scientific approach. Scientific evaluations can take many forms, depending largely on the importance of the questions asked and the resources available to arrive at answers. Nevertheless, despite variation in degree of sophistication and cost, they have in common the use of accepted methods of data collection and analysis. Because these methods are tried and true and lead to results that can be replicated by other evaluators, the findings of scientific evaluations are considered more credible than judgments based entirely on intuition.[7] In our citizens' academy example, a questionnaire to measure attitudes toward the sheriff's department might be administered to academy members both before and after their participation. Differences in attitudes would then be examined using accepted statistical procedures.

## Passive Versus Active

Evaluations can be passive or active. Passive evaluations, like intuitive evaluations, generally do not rely on the systematic collection of information. According to Johnson, passive evaluations rely on opinions and criticisms of program clients that are unsolicited by program administrators.[8] In the citizens' academy example, a recent woman graduate might call the sheriff's office to say that the presentations at the academy came off as demeaning to

❖ ❖ ❖ ❖    women and that her impression of the department continues to be unfavorable. The new sheriff might use this anecdotal information as evidence that the program should be fine-tuned or even terminated. But without such citizen input, the sheriff might justifiably continue to assume that the citizens' academy was attaining its objectives if she or he believed that public education about departmental activities was a good idea in the first place. By contrast, active evaluations are initiated by the evaluator rather than the citizen and involve the systematic collection of data, such as using a survey questionnaire before and after academy training.

## Narrow Versus Broad Evaluations

Evaluations also can be distinguished by their scope. Narrow evaluations focus on one program or part of a program in a specific location[9] and are usually less costly and require less time to conduct than broad ones. Broad evaluations assess the results of a variety of similar programs over a large geographic location, such as programs throughout a particular school system, county, state, or country. Because they tend to be more comprehensive (and typically, more expensive), they are more likely to provide information bearing directly on a fuller understanding of inputs and outcomes. Johnson notes that "the broader the study is, the more it can rise above variations in local leadership and economic conditions."[10] In short, from broader evaluations we can learn more about the unique qualities of a program, policy, or intervention that are linked to successful implementation and impact. Such information will prove helpful for developing similarly successful activities at other sites.

---

### South Central Prostitution Project

#### *Deputy Chief Steven Cole*

During the past 30 years, South Broadway Street in the heart of Wichita gained a reputation among residents as being the best place to pick up a street-walking prostitute. The typical response by the police department was a short-term approach to drive prostitutes out of sight. A couple of arrests would encourage prostitutes to be more discrete, resulting in fewer complaints from citizens, but doing little to reduce prostitution. The problem grew worse in early 1990 when prostitutes shared the streets with violent street gangs and drug dealers. It took three years to force these gangs to give up their stranglehold on the neighborhood and return it to its normal condition, which meant a number of pimps and prostitutes. Citizens, angrier than ever about the police department's inability to solve neighborhood problems, were becoming very vocal. They complained about used condoms and needles routinely found discarded in alleys and parking lots along South Broadway. Young women who lived in the area were afraid to walk down the street, because men mistook them for prostitutes.

In May 1994 the Wichita Police Department initiated community policing by assigning 17 specially trained community police officers to four high-crime target neighborhoods, one of which was South Central. There was no master plan or strategy established before the officers set up an office in a neighborhood strip mall. They were asked to work with the community to accomplish something that many officers felt was impossible. Where do we start? Could four officers really make a difference in South Central Wichita?    ☞

Public service messages like this one appearing on a billboard in South Central Wichita signal the arrival of change and serve to alert would-be violators that they are no longer welcome in the neighborhood. The police and residents have teamed up to make a difference. (Photo: Courtesy of the Wichita Police Department)

Police held meetings with neighborhood associations. Three goals were identified: reduce prostitution and crime, improve police-community cooperation through partnerships, and improve the appearance of the neighborhood. The neighborhood created a steering committee to guide the neighborhood initiative.

During the first six months of their assignment, officers learned as much as they could about the problems facing the neighborhood by utilizing existing research available through the Chamber of Commerce, Wichita State University, and the city of Wichita government. In addition, they conducted door-to-door surveys with businesses and residents to learn their concerns firsthand. This process turned out to be very time consuming and difficult but ultimately the most rewarding and beneficial. Through their daily contact with the community they saw the frustration and anger felt by citizens about prostitution. The officers could be seen walking the streets every day and soon became trusted members of the community. More important, the officers' commitment to improve the quality of life for residents intensified as a result of working so closely with residents. They collected crime statistics and asked other departments for ideas on how to combat prostitution. They also went to the source of the problem, developing and administering surveys to prostitutes and "johns" to gain insight. If they knew what motivated the offenders, they could develop strategies to reduce the activity.

Citizens blamed the motel managers and owners for catering to drug dealers, pimps, and prostitutes. Community police officers set up a private, nonthreatening meeting with motel owners and managers to address these matters. Motel owners did not want to be confronted by angry residents who were blasting them in the press. During the meeting, motel owners and government officials discussed neighborhood concerns. Everyone was surprised when motel owners expressed the same fears about the drug dealers, pimps, and prostitutes that other citizens did. The owners feared retaliation from pimps, prostitutes, and drug dealers if the motels refused their business. The owners were genuinely concerned for their own safety, but agreed to stop renting to offenders if they could get support from the police. As a result, the police gave names of convicted prostitutes to owners so they could screen customers before renting a room. In addition, police agreed to provide greater support to motel owners and managers. A motel association was created to provide a single voice to represent them when dealing with city government.

The police department also examined its own operation. Officers met with prosecutors and judges to familiarize them with the prostitution problem in the South Central neighborhood. Videotaping known prostitutes helped build the confidence of the prosecution in officer testimony during stings of johns and prostitutes. Two new ordinances were created and one was modified to help officers address prostitution. Prior to 1994, women could be arrested for loitering with the intent to commit an act of prostitution, but men could not be arrested for a similar offense of loitering for the purpose of patronizing a prostitute. The loophole was cleaned up so that men could also be arrested. Two more controversial ordinances were passed. The first increased penalties for prostitutes or johns arrested in a 12-by-22 block area along South Broadway. Officers used prostitution arrest data as the basis for setting the boundaries of the area. The second ordinance made it illegal for a con-

❖ ❖ ❖ ❖   ☞

*Just the simple improvement of the appearance of fire hydrants in a neighborhood can encourage resident ownership of an area and send a message to would-be offenders that criminal behavior will not be tolerated. (Photo: Courtesy of the Wichita Police Department)*

victed offender who was arrested in the neighborhood to return to the area within a year. Officers learned that 90 percent of the prostitutes did not live in the South Broadway area, but simply came to the area to conduct business. Preventing prostitutes from coming back to the neighborhood proved to be an effective strategy to reduce prostitution. In addition, arrests of johns increased from under 5 percent to over 50 percent.

Officers also followed every prostitution arrest through the courts to make sure cases were not plea-bargained. They stayed focused on the problem by creating a top 10 list of offenders who were the most criminally active in the area. Officers carried notebooks containing photographs and specific information on all prostitutes who worked in the neighborhood.

The physical environment started to change when several members of a local church painted neglected fire hydrants along South Broadway. This simple project encouraged business owners and residents to clean and paint their property. Citizens and officers worked side by side to clean vacant lots, mow yards, trim trees, and remove brush from alleys where prostitutes had previously performed sexual acts. The neighborhood association also paid for billboard messages denouncing prostitution using the acronym *STOP*, Stand Tough on Prostitution. These full-color billboards served as a daily reminder that the neighborhood was changing. A citizen-patrol group was also created to report crime and housing code violations. A second group of volunteers called Neighbor to Neighbor sought voluntary compliance with city housing codes through a peer notification process. If the code violations were not corrected, the group would notify city inspectors for follow-up.

The role of the media cannot be understated. On numerous occasions representatives attended community meetings, cleanups, and other activities where positive things were occurring. They reported on john stings and on one occasion participated in one.

The results were impressive. During a 20-week evaluation period, prostitution decreased 41 percent and prostitution-related crimes decreased 47 percent. In addition, 911 calls to the neighborhood decreased 16 percent. The average fine for prostitution-related offenses rose from $200 to $1,000.

---

Deputy Chief Stephen Cole has 21 years of law enforcement experience with the Wichita Police Department. Cole has an A.S. degree in administration of justice,   ☞

☞

❖ ❖ ❖ ❖

a B.A. in business administration, and recently finished an M.A. degree in criminal justice at Wichita State University. He has served as a patrol officer and worked as a detective. As a lieutenant he served as a patrol supervisor, commander of the auto theft section, recruit training supervisor, and preemployment supervisor. In 1994 he was selected as one of the first supervisors to command a newly created community policing unit. He also commanded the SWAT team for three years and served on the Wichita Police and Fire Pension Board. As a captain he saw assignments in Patrol West and Patrol South and served as an administrative assistant to the police chief. In May 1998 he was promoted to deputy chief and assigned to the Investigations Division. Here he comments on the experience:

> *Participating in the South Broadway project was one of the most rewarding experiences of my career, but also one of the most challenging. For the first time I truly felt that I was making a difference in the lives of the community I swore to serve. The move to community policing, however, was difficult to say the least. I was loved and respected by the community and loathed by fellow officers who feared the change to community policing. During the early days of the transition the unofficial slogan used by many officers to describe community policing was 'drop your gun and give me a hug.' Today, we are closer to being the department I envisioned 21 years ago when I became a police officer. I don't hear the negative comments anymore, and officers are seeing the real impact of community policing on our city. Officers are more involved with citizens then at any time in the last 30 years. Crime is down and confidence in our department has never been higher.*

In the citizens' academy example, any systematic attempt to determine the effects of a single program on citizens' attitudes toward law enforcement would be considered a narrow evaluation. In contrast, a broader evaluation might require the collection of data from citizens participating in citizens' academies across the United States. Compared to the results from a narrow evaluation of a single citizens' academy, collecting data more broadly from several academies operating under diverse conditions is more useful for understanding the potential influence of these academies. Such broad evaluations might also help to identify what specific features of several programs add the most to positive public perceptions of the police.

## Summative Versus Formative Evaluations

Summative and formative evaluations differ in purpose. Summative evaluations are concerned with a program's effectiveness as it relates to specific program objectives. They use accepted social science research methods and statistical techniques to discover whether or not the program succeeded.

Formative evaluations, on the other hand, focus on collecting data on program operations or objectives so that needed changes or modifications can be made. Formative evaluations focus either on the program's process or the program's outcomes for the purpose of making changes to the program before it is institutionalized. According to Johnson, formative evaluations require a judgment—based on some evidence—as to what needs to be changed and why.[11] Evaluators can disagree as to how they answer these questions.

In the citizens' academy example, a summative evaluation might present the findings from the systematic evaluation described above and conclude

❖ ❖ ❖ ❖   that the program either was effective (attitudes toward the police became positive) or ineffective (attitudes did not change or became negative). A formative evaluation might take the same information on attitudinal changes and other process components of the program, including academy modules, presentation style, and participant reactions, and make recommendations on how the program could be modified to better reach its goals.

### Insiders Versus Outsiders

Any of the evaluations described above may be carried out by people working inside the department or by evaluators hired from outside. Inside evaluations are desirable to some program managers because they are cheaper and rely on insiders who are most familiar with an identified program and have direct access to data.[12] But Johnson also notes that inside evaluations are limited because some inside evaluators may be tempted or pressured by managers to misrepresent their findings.[13] Outside evaluations are an obvious solution to this problem because independent evaluators are in a better position to use accepted scientific methods to gather data and then report their findings objectively.

Outside evaluations are typically conducted by college professors, private consultants, legislators, auditors, and others. Social scientists in an academic setting are particularly useful because of their knowledge of, and commitment to, the use of accepted research methods and practices. Although no evaluation can ever be considered completely objective, outside evaluations are believed to be the most objective and therefore invite greater consumer trust.

In the citizens' academy example, an assessment of attitudes toward law enforcement might be carried out by insiders (a program administrator or another member of the sheriff's department) or by someone outside the department. Which is more appropriate depends upon the reason for the evaluation. The need for objective and accurate information usually calls for an external evaluation by a highly skilled person. Urgent information to serve as an internal check that something indeed is getting done can often be more readily acquired by capable staff already employed at the department.

In summary, intuitive and passive evaluations often are used on an informal basis; scientific and active evaluations by independent outside evaluators are important resources for determining program effectiveness and allowing administrators to make any necessary modifications.

## Redefining Success: New Measures of Outcomes

Although many departments have started community policing, many have been slow to define what successful community is. Traditional measures of success deeply rooted in the professional style of policing, concerned with citations and crimes cleared by arrests, tend not to fit well with the reorientation of the police role in an era of community policing. Community policing expects personnel to subscribe to a much broader mission than law enforcement alone, including problem solving, community engagement, and community mobilization.

Measures of success associated with a professional model of policing depended on the *Uniform Crime Report*, a statistical summary of crimes based on voluntary reports to the FBI by federal, state, and local police departments. Crimes reported and crimes cleared by arrests were adopted as primary indicators of a police department's (or officer's) success or failure. According to Geoffrey Alpert and Mark Moore, traditional accounting practices eventually were institutionalized in policing and these sources of data became the key indicators of success.[14] These practices allowed police administrators to compare their own departments to other departments serving similar populations, or to compare one year to another in a single department in order to assess how well their department succeeded in controlling crime.

The problem with using traditional outcome measures as exclusive indicators of success or failure, however, is that these measures tap only an officer's success in enforcing the law. They deemphasize or ignore the functions of maintaining and delivering service. In community policing, the police mandate is broadened and tends to emphasize order maintenance and service. Therefore, new measures of outcome are needed.

As discussed earlier, program outcomes are equated with program objectives, and program impacts are equated with program goals. Administrators need to identify broad goals and, perhaps even more important, concrete objectives for particular programs so that they know what they are trying to evaluate. Establishing program goals, objectives, and activities should occur during a program's conceptualization and design phase.[15] It is important to state outputs and outcomes in terms that can be measured.

The various perspectives regarding community policing as offered by the Police Executive Research Forum were listed in chapter 1. From this chapter, students should be able to identify plausible outputs and outcomes for each perspective that would indicate community policing success. Plausible methods of evaluation, noted here, will be covered in more detail in a later section of this chapter.

## Deployment Perspective

From the deployment perspective, community policing is a way to bring officers closer to citizens on the streets whether by foot patrol, police substations, or some other means in order to make the officers more familiar with the persons and places they police. Getting to know each other better should help to build levels of trust between citizens and the police and lead to better sharing of information (see Table 11.1).

**Table 11.1  Plausible Outputs, Outcomes, and Methods of Evaluation**

| Outputs | Outcomes | Methods of Evaluation |
|---|---|---|
| Foot patrol | Changes in citizen familiarity with police officers | Citizen questionnaires |
| Bicycle patrol | Changes in officer familiarity with their surroundings | Officer questionnaires |
| Creating police substations | Changes in trust levels between officers and citizens | Personal interviews |
| Contacts with citizens | Amount and quality of information shared | Focus group interviews |

❖ ❖ ❖ ❖     ## Community Revitalization Perspective

From the community revitalization perspective, community policing is a set of strategies that focus on preventing neighborhood decay and fighting the fear of crime by eliminating those features of a neighborhood that cause residents to feel afraid. Efforts to turn a neighborhood or community around or prevent it from going downhill in the first place are important. Property must be kept up so that residents seem to be keeping a watchful eye on the area (see Table 11.2).

| Table 11.2  Plausible Outputs, Outcomes, and Methods of Evaluation | | |
|---|---|---|
| Outputs | Outcomes | Methods of Evaluation |
| Neighborhood clean-up efforts | Changes in fear of crime | Citizen questionnaires |
| Neighborhood action committees | Changes in signs of social disorder | Inventory of social and physical disorder |
| Police involvement in neighborhood committees | Changes in signs of physical disorder | Direct observation |
| Neighborhood watch programs | Extent of economic revitalization | Focus group interviews |
| Citizen social activities | | |

## Problem-Solving Perspective

From the problem-solving perspective, community policing is a focused approach by the police that involves the community in identifying a problem, analyzing its scope, developing a proactive response, and then assessing how well the response worked (see Table 11.3).

| Table 11.3  Plausible Outputs, Outcomes, and Methods of Evaluation | | |
|---|---|---|
| Outputs | Outcomes | Methods of Evaluation |
| Police involvement with neighborhood groups to solve a problem | Number of problems identified | Direct observation |
| Neighborhood resource officers assigned to solve a problem | Types of problems identified | Focus group interviews |
| Crime-prevention programs | Number of community problems solved | Official reports |
| Time and resources dedicated to problem solving | Neighborhood crime reductions | Official reports |

## Customer Perspective

In the customer perspective, listening to the needs of citizens is stressed. Police leadership places importance upon various crime and crime-related issues according to what the community would like addressed before any others. This perspective emphasizes open lines of communication with local residents, frequently involving citizen advisory groups and citizen surveys to provide feedback on police performance (see Table 11.4).

| Table 11.4 Plausible Outputs, Outcomes, and Methods of Evaluation | | |
|---|---|---|
| Outputs | Outcomes | Methods of Evaluation |
| Creation of citizen advisory groups | Police department responsiveness to citizen concerns and priorities | Direct observation |
| | | Police officer questionnaires |
| Implementation of citizen surveys | Extent to which police officers value citizen input | Citizen questionnaires |
| Newsletters | Accessibility of police department to citizens | Official reports |

## Legitimacy Approach

In the legitimacy perspective, the emphasis is on establishing the credibility of the police as an equitable public-service organization that dispenses resources evenly throughout the community. Of particular importance is the just treatment of the concerns of racial minorities and other groups that historically have suffered from poor police-community relations (see Table 11.5).

| Table 11.5 Plausible Outputs, Outcomes, and Methods of Evaluation | | |
|---|---|---|
| Outputs | Outcomes | Methods of Evaluation |
| Cultural diversity training for police officers | Citizen perceptions of police as equitable | Citizen questionnaires or interviews |
| Creating police substations | Citizen perceptions of how they are treated by police | Official records |
| | Number of complaints by racial minorities about the police | Direct observation |
| | Number of officers assigned to particular beats | Focus group interviews |
| | Responses toward concerns or ideas offered by racial minorities | |

## Common Outcomes in the Community Policing Literature

The following questions require sound answers that can only be supplied by evaluation:

- What effects will a community policing program have on residents' quality of life, including their perceptions of the amount of crime, disorder, and fear they experience?

❖ ❖ ❖ ❖

- What effects will a community policing program have on actual rates of crime and levels of disorder in a neighborhood?

- To what extent has community policing simply shifted crime and disorder problems from one area to another?

- To what extent does community policing facilitate the problem-solving efforts of the police and other service providers?

- How many neighborhood problems have been remedied through community policing efforts?

- What effect does community policing have on officers who practice it? Do they have high levels of motivation, low job stress, and high job satisfaction as compared to police who practice the professional style of policing?

- Is community policing an efficient use of police time and resources?

- Under community policing, to what extent are citizens truly equal under the law?

Evaluations of community policing efforts in the last decade have been numerous and diverse, primarily due to the scope of strategies and expected outcomes.[16] Some of the studies about community policing programs are reviewed below. Some of the more common outputs and outcomes mentioned earlier can be found in this brief review.

Some research has focused on the effectiveness of foot patrol in reducing crime and fear of crime and improving police-citizen relations. For example, in Newark, New Jersey, foot-patrol activities to maintain order had a significant impact—in a positive direction—on citizens' perceptions of safety and satisfaction with the police, but they did not affect crime rates.[17] In another widely cited study, Robert Trojanowicz and Dennis Banas found that foot patrol in Flint, Michigan, led to decreases in crime rates, increases in perceptions of safety, and improved police-citizen relations over a three-year evaluation period.[18]

Although William Spelman and John Eck have concluded that most foot-patrol programs tend to increase police-citizen contact and may lead to a reduction of fear and an increase in satisfaction with the police,[19] Lee Brown and Mary Ann Wycoff found that increasing the frequency of nonthreatening contacts between the police and the public through foot patrols in Houston reduced citizen fear only for white homeowners.[20] Their findings raise questions about whether the effects of foot patrol are always positive among all resident groups.[21]

Other evaluations of community policing initiatives have focused on the relationship between strategic problem-solving efforts and the fear of crime, crime rates, disorder, and satisfaction with the police. For example, Eck and Spelman found evidence that proactive problem-solving approaches in concert with community members and relevant city agencies can lead to a reduction in the incidence of specific crimes.[22] In addition, Hans Toch and James Grant found that a collaborative approach to problem solving involving the police, residents, and representatives of various city agencies can curtail neighborhood social and physical disorder.[23]

Community policing through collaborative problem-solving efforts involving citizens in partnership with the police also was assessed in Newark and Houston.[24] In Newark, collaborative problem solving to reduce disorder in an experimental area involved a variety of efforts, including opening a community service center, establishing citizen contact patrols, and initiating a neighborhood police newsletter. Also included was an intensive enforcement effort targeted at disorder problems. Wesley Skogan found that both physical and social disorder declined, fear of crime decreased, neighborhood satisfaction increased, and satisfaction with the police increased. In another area of Newark, however, where only intensive enforcement was used, social disorder decreased, but physical disorder increased; fear of crime, neighborhood satisfaction, and satisfaction with the police remained unchanged.[25]

❖ ❖ ❖ ❖

---

### Community-Police Anti-Drug Efforts
### Excerpted and Adopted From Case Studies of
### Community Anti-Drug Efforts

***Saul N. Weingart, Francis X. Hartmann, and David Osborne***

In response to the illicit drug trade that became especially troublesome in the late 1980s and early 1990s, a remarkable community anti-drug movement was formed, with groups becoming active in some of the most afflicted neighborhoods. Armed only with their courage and imagination, citizens devised a variety of clever strategies and tactics to reclaim their streets and parks from drug traffickers. This Research in Brief examines a number of factors that gave rise to these community anti-drug efforts and sustained them over time.

#### Historical Overview

Citizen anti-drug initiatives first came to the attention of the general public and to some policymakers through a collection of startling newspaper and magazine articles. Under dramatic headlines such as "Neighbors Fight to End Drug Plague," "Residents Fed up With Dope Dens, Prowlers," and "Neighbors' Fury Shakes Drug Ring," news reports of citizen drug fighters have revealed a number of surprises.

First, citizen activists deployed an array of anti-drug tactics and strategies. In addition to the block watch programs that police departments have promoted for many years, citizens developed a variety of creative responses aimed at reestablishing control over their neighborhoods. These included marches, innovative use of video cameras, street-corner vigils, public meetings, solidarity-building tactics, citizen foot patrols, and demonstrations at known drug houses. Other citizens initiated new partnerships with police departments, prosecutors' offices, and other city agencies to devise novel solutions to the illicit drug trade.

Second, innovative strategies flourished in desolate and seemingly disorganized neighborhoods—neighborhoods characterized by poverty and other disadvantages, with few apparent resources to draw upon. These neighborhoods had high levels of crime, violence, fear, and disorder.

Many researchers and community organizers believe that although crime may be an effective issue for organizing support, it has little value for sustaining citizen participation. Most believe that crime is a no-win issue, and few organizers would be willing to jeopardize their organization's survival by exclusively fighting crime. Because information about crime and crime prevention has often increased residents' fear of crime and of one another, some prevention programs have had the paradoxical effect of decreasing citizen participation. As a result, many scholars and organizers believe that it is necessary for a citizen anticrime group to broaden its agenda if it is to mount an effective response. Neighborhood groups involved in crime prevention have been shown to be more effective and able to maintain active support if they deal with a variety of neighborhood problems as well as crime. ☞

❖ ❖ ❖ ❖   ☞

Police researchers and police themselves have become increasingly aware of the importance of the community as a resource, especially within the context of community policing. This awareness stemmed in part from programs that demonstrated civic willingness to aid the police in crime control and prevention.

Also contributing to the idea that communities play a role in preventing crime was the strategy of "crime prevention through environmental design." It is based on the concept that the layout and management of buildings and neighborhoods can be changed to help citizens become more secure in their environments and make potential offenders less likely or able to commit criminal acts. Crime prevention through environmental design focuses on physical design in the context of the ways that residents think about and utilize the area in which they live.

## Summary of [Selected] Case Studies

*Fairlawn Coalition, Washington, D.C.* When a cocaine market took over the Washington, D.C., neighborhood of Fairlawn in the late 1980s and police seemed unable to mitigate the situation, residents responded by openly patrolling their streets.

An earlier experience with a police crime watch program had taught Fairlawn resident Edward Johnson two lessons: first, that citizens passively watching the street from inside their homes did little to deter crime in their neighborhood, and second, but more important, that it was the community's responsibility to help the police. With these lessons in mind, Johnson began organizing neighbors to take a sense of personal responsibility for their community, which in turn would motivate police to take a stronger interest in the community as well.

Following a kickoff anti-drug rally, a number of residents organized themselves into nightly patrol groups to walk the streets of Fairlawn and act as a deterrent to drug trafficking. Wearing their trademark bright orange hats, the members of the Fairlawn Coalition first drove drug dealers from their positions merely by standing out on the streets with them, and later by bringing in video cameras, still cameras, and the bright light of publicity. The local police district assigned a couple of officers to walk with the group, initially as protection. Then, as the police came to understand the dedication of the Coalition members, strong ties developed between the police and the neighborhood. The two patrol officers undertook creative problem-solving efforts to decrease criminal activity in the neighborhood, setting up roadblocks, tracking down outstanding warrants, and even knocking on doors of known drug dealers and asking them how business was. As the neighbors saw the commitment of the police to the neighborhood, they in turn began providing more useful information to aid in investigations. Soon a full-fledged police-community partnership was in place.

But the backbone of the Fairlawn Coalition's effort remained the nightly patrols. Through these patrols, residents felt safer walking the streets. The commitment of the Fairlawn Coalition to these patrols convinced police that a creative, fruitful partnership could in fact improve the quality of life in the neighborhood.

*Hill Street Crime Watch Committee, Boston, Massachusetts.* The Hill Street Crime Watch Committee was formed by residents of a troubled Boston neighborhood to help police crack down on the drug trade that was instilling fear and creating disorder there. The area, which one narcotics officer called "the worst section in the whole city," was well known to police as a major center for drug dealing.

Frustrated by conditions in her neighborhood, Hill Street resident Carmen Peralta called Christopher Hayes for help. Hayes, a civilian employee of the Boston Police Department who ran its neighborhood crime watch program, had already organized crime watch groups in about 100 Boston neighborhoods. After meeting with Peralta and other Hill Street residents and recognizing the extreme fear and danger present in the community, Hayes asked then Police Commissioner Francis (Mickey) Roache to meet the group. That meeting convinced the commissioner that drastic measures were needed.

To give the Hill Street neighborhood high priority, the police department established a special drug task force for that area. The Hill Street Crime Watch members were asked to participate in the drug reduction efforts by acting as informants, pro-   ☞

viding police with information that could lead to arrests and abatement of the problem.

After an intensive effort in the area, however, cooperation began to break down. The task force was transferred from the local police district to the department's citywide Drug Control Unit. The Hill Street Crime Watch Committee members felt abandoned, as they perceived that police efforts in the neighborhood waned while drug trafficking and related threats of violence continued. Intimidated relentlessly by drug dealers, the Crime Watch leader left the group and moved his family out of the country. Fear escalated among group members, and the effort fell apart.

***Stella Link Revitalization Coalition, Houston, Texas.*** Link Valley, once a comfortable neighborhood in the heart of Houston, had become an open-air, drive-through drug bazaar. Only one out of 10 available residential units was occupied, and the abandoned units, broken fences, litter, and disrepair made the area a convenient location for drug dealers and, in the eyes of the police, a dangerous site. In addition, Link Valley offered easy access for drug users. It was close to a highway, allowing consumers to drive in from other areas, make a purchase, and leave quickly.

Police efforts to control the rising tide of drugs in the area had not achieved the hoped-for impact. The many arrests, though substantial in number, did not make any headway with the problem. The police, such as Sergeant J. W. Collins, who was assigned to Link Valley, began to feel that a new strategy was necessary. It would be two-pronged, focusing on the buyers rather than the dealers themselves and addressing the physical decay that seemed to be contributing to the problems of the area.

The turning point was the murder of an elderly resident in 1988 in a neighborhood close to Link Valley and the arrest of her assailants soon after in a Link Valley drug den. Representatives of nine neighborhood associations organized themselves against drugs and formed the Stella Link Revitalization Coalition. After meeting with police, the coalition soon became committed to the new police strategy, offering to become an equal partner in cleaning up Link Valley.

With the support of superiors in the police department and the collaboration of the coalition, Houston police cordoned off Link Valley to prevent drive-through drug buys and conducted a 100-officer sweep of abandoned buildings to look for squatters and drug traffickers. At the same time, the coalition coordinated a massive cleanup of the area, picking up trash, cutting down weeds, and hauling out garbage. Coalition members also worked with city agencies to facilitate the enforcement of health and housing ordinances. As a result of these efforts—keeping drug customers away and making drug dealing less convenient—the Link Valley cocaine market vanished.

## Key Findings

From these case studies a number of findings emerged.

- Effective community anti-drug efforts show wide variations in institutional robustness and in breadth of approach. In general, the researchers recommend that citizens be encouraged and helped to address drug problems from a perspective broader than that of drugs alone. Community efforts that provide a comprehensive approach to drugs and crime are more likely to be sustained.

- Policymakers need to appreciate and support community efforts focused primarily on drugs. Although some of these efforts were found to be fragile and tenuous, such informal associations can be an effective means of combating drug problems.

- Useful forms of citizen anti-drug efforts have emerged in a variety of neighborhoods, including those seriously afflicted by crime and violence that were previously not considered likely to engage in this form of community action.

- Citizen drug fighters emerge from a variety of backgrounds and experiences. They need and appropriately use both conventional and unconventional resources to meet their objectives.

❖ ❖ ❖ ❖   ☞

- Policymakers should consider carefully the broad scope of help they can provide citizens, ranging from financial help to granting citizens access to decision makers, from providing a meeting room to offering technical assistance on organizing and implementing program activities.

- Police play a particularly pivotal role in citizens' assault on drugs. Many citizens initially regard the drug problem as one of obtaining adequate police protection, but, in general, partnerships involving citizens, police, and other agencies provide useful strategies to combat drugs.

- To forge productive relationships between police and citizens, police executives should actively support local patrol officers in working with citizen groups. Police officers should be encouraged to respond to all interested citizens, even those who initially may be rancorous and complain, because these individuals often evolve into hardworking partners with the police. Since no single community response to drugs can be considered the best, research should continue to identify approaches that work best under specific conditions and in various neighborhood settings.

### Conclusion

Because there is a variety of community responses to drugs it is important to appreciate and cultivate variability and innovation. Different citizen initiatives have evolved to address different problems in different environments. Before specifying one or several model programs, it is essential first to identify what works best under what conditions. If social scientists can evaluate community drug-fighting efforts and assess the kinds of interventions that work best in particular drug markets, then they can offer concrete, practical advice to citizens, police officials, and policymakers for the most effective strategy to defeat drugs, neighborhood by neighborhood.

U.S. Department of Justice, Office of Justice Programs, National Institute of Justice, Research in Brief, October 1994. NCJ 149316. The research for the study was funded by the National Institute of Justice, Office of Justice Program, U.S. Department of Justice, grant 90-IJ-CX-0033. Findings and conclusions of the research reported here are those of the authors and do not necessarily reflect the official position or policies of the U.S. Department of Justice. The National Institute of Justice is a component of the Office of Justice Programs, which also includes the Bureau of Justice Assistance, Bureau of Justice Statistics, Office of Juvenile Justice and Delinquency Prevention, and the Office for Victims of Crime.

In another approach tried in Houston, the community policing problem-solving effort included opening a storefront police-community station where police could meet citizens and engage in problem-solving planning, creating a community-organizing response team to mobilize citizens into neighborhood organizations that could work with the police in solving neighborhood problems, and initiating a citizen-contact patrol to increase interaction between the police and residents. According to Skogan, these projects led to decreases in physical and social disorder, decreases in fear of crime, and increases in satisfaction with one's neighborhood and with the police. However, similar to the findings of Wycoff and Brown, the most positive program findings of Skogan, in terms of disorder, fear, and satisfaction, tended to be confined to white residents and homeowners; there was little evidence of program effects on African Americans, Hispanics, or renters.[26]

# Common Methods of Data Collection

❖ ❖ ❖ ❖

Methods of data collection are the specific techniques used to collect useful information about program outputs, outcomes, and impacts. Social scientists use a variety of methods to collect data and sometimes use more than one method in a single study. Some of the common research methods used in evaluations of community policing are direct observation, focus group interviews, survey research, official records, and disorder inventories.

## Direct Observation

Direct observation involves one or more researchers watching the behavior of others and systematically recording what they see. Arnold Binder and Gilbert Geis describe four types of systematic observation: (1) the "complete participant" who conceals his or her identity from those who are being studied and participates in the activities being monitored; (2) the "participant as observer" who is involved in the activities being monitored but makes his or her role known as a researcher; (3) the "observer as participant" who makes himself or herself known to the participants as an observer and interacts with participants sporadically, but makes no formal attempt at actual participation; and (4) the "complete observer" who only passively observes the activities without becoming part of them.[27]

Although it remains unclear which type of observation is best, direct observation as a research tool has its limitations. First, in the case of the complete participant there are potential ethical issues concerning concealing the researcher's true identity. Second, in all four types of observations, there is the potential for the researcher knowingly or unknowingly to alter the behavior of the participants, thereby limiting the validity of the study. As Peter Rossi and Howard Freeman have noted, observational methods are a preferable source of data for monitoring programs as long as the observer is not obtrusive.[28] Third, direct observations are subject to the perceptions of the researcher and as a result may not be consistent among all observers.

Despite these limitations, systematic observations are useful in drawing conclusions about the everyday world.[29] Although direct observations may not by themselves completely eliminate alternative hypotheses (because social science research rarely produces a perfect experiment), the gradual accumulation of knowledge in social science research "can be gained by good observational procedures."[30]

## Focus Group Interviews

Focus group interviews are designed to record the perceptions or opinions of individuals in a group setting of eight to 10 people. According to David Stewart and Prem Shamdasani, focus group interviews are an ideal way to collect qualitative data, that is, information that is difficult to measure in numerical terms, such as whether feelings of personal safety have improved. Other advantages of focus group interviews include the following: (1) they allow the researcher to interact directly with the program recipients; (2) they allow the researcher to obtain large amounts of data in the respondents' own words; and (3) they allow the researcher to ask respondents additional,

❖ ❖ ❖ ❖   related questions that build upon responses to more basic questions.[31] Furthermore, Albert Reiss notes that interviewing in general can help researchers better understand direct observations.[32]

Despite the many advantages of focus group interviews, they also have several limitations. One noted in the discussion of systematic observations is the potential for the researcher to influence the behavior—and in this case, the responses—of subjects. In addition, any given focus group has the potential to be dominated by one or more individuals; the result may be the researcher's reliance on information that may not be representative of the entire group. Similarly, some participants may be less willing to talk openly than others, also resulting in data that may not be representative of the entire group. It should be noted, however, that the role of the focus group moderator is important with respect to these limitations. A variety of techniques help a well-trained interviewer to casually acquire responses from all (or most) focus group participants.[33]

## Survey Research

Survey research, a widely used data collection method in the social sciences, is an observational approach that attempts to determine attitudes, values, perceptions, feelings, and beliefs of individuals.[34] The survey method is used extensively in assessing community policing and crime-prevention programs and at times is the sole source of data for determining the effectiveness of these programs.[35]

Although widely used already, the use of survey research is increasing, especially as a tool for local government accountability. According to Chava Frankfort-Nachmias and David Nachmias, roughly half of cities with populations over 100,000 have used some form of survey at some time. This popularity is probably the result of wide experimentation with the idea of "reinventing government," in which community input and "customer satisfaction" are considered vital components in determining the effectiveness of governmental services.[36]

However, there also are well-documented criticisms of relying on survey research to determine attitudes and beliefs. First, and perhaps foremost, is the question of whether surveys truly reveal the actual attitudes, beliefs, and values of the respondent. "Center of attention" effects come into play when respon-

*Survey data from the community can be quite helpful to strategic planning and evaluation. (Photo: Mark C. Ide)*

dents do not accurately depict their attitudes, beliefs, or values.[37] Other notable limitations to survey research include interviewer bias, question bias, and low response rates.

There are two basic forms of survey research: personal interviews and survey questionnaires. Both are widely used in community policing evaluations. Of the various forms that personal interviews can take, the *schedule-structured interview* is most often used. Schedule-structured interviews are fixed in their questions, wording, and sequence, and are identical for each respondent.[38] According to Frankfort-Nachmias and Nachmias, schedule-structured interviews are preferable to other approaches in that they allow the researcher to reduce the risk that differences in the wording of questions and in the sequence of questions might result in variations in responses.[39] There are two important limitations to using face-to-face interviews as a method of data collection: interviewer bias and lack of anonymity. Although interviewers are supposed to remain objective, there is the potential for them to give both verbal and nonverbal cues that can influence a respondent's answers. Also, because respondents are not anonymous in face-to-face interviews, some respondents may feel intimidated or threatened by some questions.[40]

Mail questionnaires are a more impersonal method of data collection than face-to-face interviews. They increase anonymity and are rather inexpensive compared to the costs of personal interviews. But there are a number of disadvantages to mail questionnaires, including: (1) mail questionnaires require simple questions comprehensible on the basis of printed instructions; (2) there is no opportunity for additional probing once an answer has been given; (3) there is no control over who actually completes the questionnaire; and (4) it often is difficult to elicit an adequate response rate.[41] Despite these limitations, however, survey research (and mail questionnaires in particular) remains an important data collection method in the social sciences.

## Official Records

As Binder and Geis note, much criminal justice research revolves around the use of official statistics to determine the extent and form of criminal activity.[42] And as Arthur Lurigio and Dennis Rosenbaum point out, many past evaluations of community policing and crime prevention have used police statistics in determining the outcomes of these programs.[43]

Although official statistics are useful to the researcher because they generally are easily obtainable at low or no cost, they have some well-noted limitations as measures of any particular program's outcomes. The first concerns the "dark figure of crime."[44] Official police statistics, in the form either of reported crime or official arrests, do not take into account the large number of crimes that never come to the attention of police. At best, then, official statistics are a conservative estimate of the incidence of crime, and at worst, they can reflect an unrealistic picture of the extent of crime.

The second, and perhaps more important, limitation of police statistics (especially as it relates to community policing research) concerns the interpretation of these data with regard to measures of success. It generally is assumed that any *reduction* in the incidence of crime attributable to a specific intervention can be considered a positive program outcome. However, this

❖ ❖ ❖ ❖   assumption may not be valid. The very nature of community policing programs requires citizen mobilization and increased involvement with the police. Citizens typically become more involved in reporting crime in their particular neighborhood, a practice that, if effective, could result in *increases* in reports of crime and, at least theoretically, increases in arrests. In this situation, increases in the number of reported crimes or arrests can be considered a positive program impact. Because of these limitations to the use of official police statistics, analysis of these data should be undertaken with caution. It also can show positive program impacts regardless of the direction of any noted changes. Due to this inherent limitation, official police statistics are usually only one of several sources of data used to address questions of community policing program effectiveness.

## Social and Physical Disorder Inventory

Although evaluations of community policing programs frequently measure residents' perceptions of social and physical disorder, rarely do evaluations attempt to objectively measure these variables. Social and physical inventories have been constructed to more objectively measure disorder in neighborhoods. These inventories then allow evaluators to measure any changes in physical and social disorder and to determine if any associations exist between residents' subjective perceptions of disorder and the objective measures of disorder.

Following Douglas Perkins and his colleagues' research in Baltimore and Poplar Grove, Utah, block-level environmental inventories typically consist of two parts: (1) a social environment inventory used to determine the number of individuals present on any given block, their gender, their approximate age, and their behavior, and (2) a physical environment inventory used to determine property types: the amount of litter, broken glass, and potholes present on the block; guardianship items such as the presence of barriers, personalizations on property, windows with security bars or gates, surveillance cameras, signs of security or alarms, places to sit outside, crime watch signs, plantings in public domain, and plantings on individual properties; lighting items such as the number of broken and unbroken public lights and the number of broken and unbroken private lights; and disorder items such as the number of abandoned cars on the street, damage on public property, graffiti both on public and private property, and broken windows and other fixtures.[45]

According to Perkins et al., items reflected in a social environment inventory try to gauge the extent of social incivility at the block level.[46] These include signs of loitering youths, panhandlers, open prostitution, open drug sales, and public drunkenness. According to James Q. Wilson and George Kelling and Perkins et al., social incivilities, as well as physical incivilities, send powerful messages about how much tolerance there is for lawlessness by the people who live and work in a given area.[47]

In addition, as Perkins et al. notes, the items in the physical environment inventory reflect both the transient and built environment at the block-level.[48] The transient environment includes both territorial markers (e.g., plantings and decorations) and physical incivilities (e.g., broken glass, litter, and graffiti), which send symbolic messages regarding the extent of control and privacy found in a particular area. The built environment consists of architectural and urban planning features that are "defensible space," including barriers around individual properties, public and private lighting, outdoor seating, and bars on windows.[49]

## Multiple Sources of Evidence: Triangulation

As Lurigio and Rosenbaum note, any of the above sources of data have been used as the sole source of data for past studies of community policing and crime prevention studies.[50] According to Robert Yin, investigators in the past often relied primarily on crime data as a major outcome measure to evaluate community anticrime efforts.[51] The isolated use of data sources is probably because researchers tend to choose the data source with which they are most familiar; therefore, they not only announce which problem they will study but only select a *single* source of data.[52] Given the inherent limits of single research methods, the triangulation method of combining multiple sources of information seems to offer the best potential for measuring the effectiveness of community policing programs. An illustration of the use of multiple sources of evidence follows.

# Outcome Evaluation in the El Paso Police Department

Under the direction of Chief Russ Leach, the El Paso Police Department's commitment to policing innovations and the broader philosophy of community policing was clearly evident by late 1995. The department's mission embodied the community policing philosophy—working in partnership with the community to enhance the quality of life in El Paso. In the spirit of that mission, the police department and citizens initiated a number of community policing programs: a citizens on patrol program, a citizens' police academy, a youth police academy, collaborative programs involving the El Paso Housing Authority and City of Juarez (Mexico), crisis response teams to console victims of crimes, neighborhood pride days in an effort to reduce physical disorder in El Paso's neighborhoods, police drop-in centers, and others.

In addition, the concept of the regional command center (RCC) was adopted as part of the police department's decentralization effort in 1995. Each of five RCCs serves as a full-service facility for the citizens of El Paso, providing them with all services offered by the department without having to leave their region. In addition, a police area representative (PAR) was assigned to most neighborhood districts within each RCC. PAR officers are patrol officers who are responsible for addressing the problems and concerns brought to their attention by the officers and citizens who work and live within their police district. Their major responsibility is to keep issues from becoming problems that may require police action.

Problem solving was fueled by the RCCs' advisory boards, groups of representatives of residents, and businesses within the jurisdiction of each RCC. Their composition reflected the diversity of the particular region. The groups provided commanders of the RCCs with constructive input regarding the concerns or problems found in their community.

❖ ❖ ❖ ❖     ## Was the PAR Program a Success?

El Paso's PAR program is an example not only of a community policing initiative, but also an example of a community policing program that has been evaluated using multiple methods of research and of the complexity of such program evaluation. By 1997, the El Paso Police Department and city politicians wanted to know whether the PAR program was a success or failure. This wish led to a formal inside evaluation (a formative evaluation) of the program by the department's Planning, Research, and Development Office. As noted earlier, formative evaluations collect data on program outputs and outcomes in an effort to provide feedback to staff so that changes to the program may be made at the program's early stages.[53]

The PAR evaluators relied upon survey research in the form of self-administered questionnaires completed by PAR officers and their sergeants, face-to-face interviews with neighborhood residents and business owners, and direct observations of program activities. The findings indicated that the PAR program was essential to an overall community policing strategy in El Paso, but fell short of reaching its full potential. The following are among a number of recommendations made by evaluators for improving the PAR program:

- PAR operations should be better integrated with those of patrol officers.

- The department should more clearly define and separate the community services functions from PAR's main focus on problem-solving activities.

- The department should establish and publish guidelines and standards of performance and evaluation for PAR officers.

- Communication, both internal and external, should be improved within the PAR program.

Although decentralization is a common component of community policing, the PAR program in El Paso was difficult to evaluate because of the lack of measurable program objectives. Richard Berk and Peter Rossi note that one of the most important steps before a program is carried out is the formation of program goals and measurable objectives.[54] Without program goals and objectives, the evaluator is left wondering how to determine whether or not a program is a success. Law enforcement agencies interested in knowing with any certainty whether they have achieved their goals need to clearly define what their goals are and then employ systematic evaluation techniques to measure program success and shortcomings.

## Conclusion

This chapter focused on the importance of evaluation for community policing. Although many departments have implemented community policing, fewer have conducted systematic evaluations to find out if particular initiatives actually work. Of the variety of approaches and methods of evaluation, triangulation proves to be the most fruitful—albeit costly—way to confidently determine program outputs, outcomes, and impacts.

## Study Questions

❖ ❖ ❖ ❖

1. Discuss outputs, outcomes, and impacts as they relate to program evaluation.

2. Compare and contrast the approaches to evaluation discussed in this chapter.

3. Identify the strengths and weaknesses of the common methods of data collection described in this chapter.

## Endnotes

1. Peter Rossi and Howard Freeman, *Evaluation: A Systematic Approach*, 4th ed. (Newbury Park, CA: Sage, 1989).
2. Frank S. Levy, Arnold J. Meltsner, and Aaron Wildavsky, *Urban Outcomes: Schools, Streets, and Libraries* (Berkeley: University of California Press, 1974).
3. *Ibid.*
4. *Ibid.*
5. William C. Johnson, *Public Administration: Policy, Politics, and Practice* (Guilford, CT: Dushkin Publishing Group, 1992).
6. *Ibid.*
7. *Ibid.*
8. *Ibid.*
9. *Ibid.*
10. Ibid, page 470.
11. *Ibid.*
12. *Ibid.*
13. *Ibid.*
14. Geoffrey Alpert and Mark H. Moore, "Measuring Police Performance in the New Paradigm of Policing," in *Performance Measures for the Criminal Justice System*, ed. U.S. Department of Justice (Washington, DC: U.S. Government Printing Office, 1993).
15. Richard Berk and Peter Rossi, *Thinking About Program Evaluation* (Newbury, CA: Sage, 1990).
16. Jack R. Greene and Robert B. Taylor, "Community-Based Policing and Foot Patrol: Issues of Theory and Evaluation," in *Community Policing: Rhetoric or Reality?*, eds. Jack R. Greene and Stephen D. Mastrofski (New York: Praeger, 1988).
17. George Kelling, *Conclusions From the Newark Foot Patrol Experiment* (Washington, DC: The Police Foundation, 1981); George Kelling, *Foot Patrol* (Washington, DC: National Institute of Justice, 1986); Anthony M. Pate, *Reducing Fear of Crime in Houston and Newark: A Summary Report* (Washington, DC: The Police Foundation and National Institute of Justice, 1986).
18. Robert Trojanowicz, *An Evaluation of the Neighborhood Foot Patrol Program in Flint Hills, Michigan* (East Lansing: Michigan State University, National Neighborhood Foot Patrol Center, 1982); Robert Trojanowicz and Dennis W. Banas, *A Comparison of Foot Patrol Versus Motor Patrol Officers* (East Lansing: Michigan State University, 1985).
19. William Spelman and John E. Eck, *Problem-Oriented Policing* (Washington, DC: National Institute of Justice, 1987).
20. Lee Brown and Mary Ann Wycoff, "Policing Houston: Reducing Fear and Improving Service," *Crime & Delinquency* 33 (1987): 71–89.
21. *Ibid.*
22. John E. Eck and William Spelman, *Problem Solving: Problem-Oriented Policing in Newport News* (Washington, DC: Police Executive Research Forum, 1987).

❖ ❖ ❖ ❖    23. Hans Toch and James D. Grant, *Police as Problem Solvers* (New York: Plenum, 1991).

24. Wesley Skogan, *Disorder and Decline: Crime and the Spiral of Decay in American Neighborhoods* (Berkeley: University of California Press, 1990).

25. *Ibid.*

26. *Ibid.*

27. Arnold Binder and Gilbert Geis, *Methods of Research in Criminology and Criminal Justice* (New York: McGraw Hill, 1983).

28. Rossi and Freeman, *Evaluation.*

29. Binder and Geis, *Methods of Research.*

30. *Ibid.*, p. 132.

31. David W. Stewart and Prem N. Shamdasani, *Focus Groups: Theory and Practice* (Newbury Park, CA: Sage, 1990).

32. J. J. Reiss, Jr. *The Police and the Public* (New Haven, CT: Yale University Press, 1971).

33. Stewart and Shamdasani, "Focus Groups."

34. Binder and Geis, *Methods of Research*; Chava Frankfort-Nachmias and David Nachmias, *Research Methods in Social Sciences*, 4th ed. (New York: St. Martin's, 1992).

35. Arthur Lurigio and Dennis Rosenbaum, "Evaluation Research in Community Crime Prevention: A Critical Look at the Field," in *Community Crime Prevention: Does It Work?*, ed. Dennis Rosenbaum (Beverly Hills, CA: Sage, 1986).

36. Frankfort-Nachmias and Nachmias, *Research Methods.*

37. Binder and Geis, *Methods of Research.*

38. Frankfort-Nachmias and Nachmias, *Research Methods.*

39. *Ibid.*

40. Binder and Geis, *Methods of Research*; Frankfort-Nachmias and Nachmias, *Research Methods.*

41. Frankfort-Nachmias and Nachmias, *Research Methods.*

42. Binder and Geis, *Methods of Research.*

43. Lurigio and Rosenbaum, "Evaluation Research in Community Crime Prevention."

44. George F. Cole and Christopher E. Smith, *The American System of Criminal Justice*, 8th ed. (Pacific Grove, CA: Wadsworth, 1992).

45. Douglas D. Perkins, John W. Meeks, and Ralph B. Taylor, "The Physical Environment of Street Blocks and Resident Perceptions of Crime and Disorder: Implications for Theory and Measurement," *Journal of Environmental Psychology* 12 (1992): 21–34; Douglas D. Perkins, Abraham Wandersman, Richard C. Rich, and Ralph B. Taylor, "The Physical Environment of Street Crime: Defensible Space, Territoriality and Incivilities, " *Journal of Environmental Psychology* 13 (1993): 29–49.

46. Douglas D. Perkins, Abraham Wandersman, Richard C. Rich, and Ralph B. Taylor, "The Physical Environment of Street Crime: Defensible Space, Territoriality and Incivilities, " *Journal of Environmental Psychology* 13 (1993): 29–49.

47. James Q. Wilson and George Kelling, "Broken Windows," *The Atlantic Monthly* 249 (1982): 29–38; Douglas D. Perkins, John W. Meeks, and Ralph B. Taylor, "The Physical Environment of Street Blocks and Resident Perceptions of Crime and Disorder: Implications for Theory and Measurement," *Journal of Environmental Psychology* 13 (1993): 29–49.

48. Douglas D. Perkins, Abraham Wandersman, Richard C. Rich, and Ralph B. Taylor, "The Physical Environment of Street Crime: Defensible Space, Territoriality and Incivilities," *Journal of Environmental Psychology* 13 (1993): 29–49.

49. Oscar Newman, *Defensible Space: Crime Prevention Through Urban Design* (New York, NY: Macmillan, 1972).

50. Lurigio and Rosenbaum, "Evaluation Research in Community Crime Prevention."

51. Robert K. Yin, "What Is Citizen Crime Prevention?" *Review of Criminal Justice Evaluation* (Washington, DC: Law Enforcement Assistance Administration, 1979).

52. Robert K. Yin, *Case Study Research: Design and Methods* (Newbury Park, CA: Sage, 1989).

53. U.S. Department of Housing and Urban Development, *A Guide to Evaluating Crime Control Programs in Public Housing* (Washington, DC: KRA Corp., 1997).

54. Berk and Rossi, *Thinking About Program Evaluation.* ✦

❖ ❖ ❖ ❖

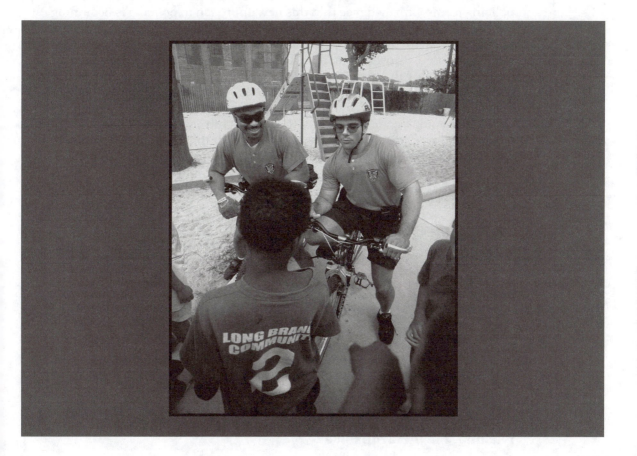

# Chapter Twelve

# Institutionalizing Community Policing

❖ ❖ ❖ ❖

*I find that the great thing in the world is not so much where we stand, as
in what direction we are moving. To reach the port of heaven, we must
sail sometimes with the wind and sometimes against it, but we must sail,
and not drift, nor lie at anchor.*

—Oliver Wendell Holmes

At the beginning of the twenty-first century, the literature on community
policing teems with evidence that this new approach to policing is beginning
to achieve its objectives. In neighborhoods across the nation, residents are
joining forces with the police in a collaborative partnership to solve problems
related to crime, disorder, and fear. The Federal Crime Bill of 1994 allocated
funds to cities for the hiring and training of 100,000 new community police
officers. Records abound of dramatic improvements in the quality of neighborhood life for many of America's poorest communities.

This chapter organizes some of the themes introduced in previous chapters around the changes that must occur if community policing is to achieve
long-term success. It argues that community policing must be brought about
by internal changes in both the culture of policing and police operations. It
then describes the complementary external changes that must occur among
citizens. In combination, these internal and external changes offer the best
hope for promoting the long-term success of a collaborative partnership
between citizens and police.

## The Success of Community Policing in Four Cities

As a preliminary to the discussion of the internal and external dimensions of community policing, its effects may be studied in four, geographically diverse cities: Nashua, New Hampshire; Charleston, South Carolina;
San Jose, California; and Spokane, Washington. Each case study raises the
question how it was possible for community policing to have achieved what it
did.

### Nashua, New Hampshire

Nashua is home to approximately 80,000 residents and recently was
named one of America's most livable cities. The Nashua Police Department
has a number of programs consistent with the philosophy of community
policing, including a Police Athletic League, bike patrols, and neighborhood
community policing offices. In addition, it instituted a problem-oriented
policing unit that assists patrol officers and community groups with neighborhood problem solving.

According to A. Yost, local community groups have been enthusiastic
about the police department's willingness to forge police-community relationships. The department has several police substations throughout the city,
including one in the local shopping mall. In fact, Neighborhood Housing Services (NHS), a nonprofit organization created in the 1980s, purchased a

building in one area of the city and invited the police department to open
another police substation in one of its offices. Local residents also are pleased
to see that the police department, the Police Athletic League, and NHS are
working collaboratively on converting a lot that was the site of a double murder in 1987 to a "tot lot" with playground equipment.[1]

## Charleston, South Carolina

Charleston's North Central Neighborhood of 500 residents, located in the
downtown core of the city, demonstrates the success of community policing.
Yost reports that the department's "Take Back Our Streets" philosophy has
resulted in positive impacts for the residents. With some seed money from
the U.S. Department of Justice and the Community Foundation Serving
Coastal South Carolina (CFSCSC), neighborhood residents and police officers have been working collaboratively to improve the neighborhood.[2]

Police officers in the area make an effort through the department's foot-
patrol initiatives to become familiar with residents and their problems, to
organize neighborhood watch programs, and to work with other city agencies to control stray animals and board up vacant buildings. Residents have
used the funds from the CFSCSC to repair and expand a neighborhood playground and have organized a schedule for playground supervision. Yost
reports that residents perceive a decrease in crime in the neighborhood and
an overall increase in the quality of their neighborhood life.[3]

## San Jose, California

Community policing is well established at the San Jose Police Department, as attested by its mission and vision statements, as well as a number of
innovative community policing programs and its emphasis on working with
community residents in an effort to prevent crimes. The San Jose Police
Department serves an estimated population of 850,000.

According to Yost, San Jose's Mayfair neighborhood, which includes
many single-parent families and retirees of Latino descent, had been experiencing high levels of social and physical disorder in the form of open-air drug
dealing and vandalism. Residents, fed up with the situation, joined the Association of Community Organizations for Reform Now (ACORN), surveyed
other residents to discover what concerned them, and ultimately established
a community policing center in the neighborhood. The center has become a
hub for community activity: Resident volunteers take police reports, San
Jose police officers make daily contacts with citizens, and neighborhood
meetings are conducted. Mayfair residents in cooperation with the police
and other city officials have had a number of successes, including improved
lighting in the area, the addition of a stop sign at a busy intersection, and
increased mobilization of residents to look after one another.[4]

## Spokane, Washington

In Spokane, a city of about 180,000 people, the community policing philosophy was galvanized into action in the fall of 1991 after the abduction of
two preteenage girls in west central Spokane in broad daylight. The ensuing

❖ ❖ ❖ ❖ community activism led to the creation of a neighborhood task force that began to examine policing resources in the city, how public safety information was shared with citizens, and what residents might do to help the police solve crime and related problems.

Spokane developed a community policing vision of an integrated community where citizens would form partnerships with the police to help reduce crime and solve problems to improve the quality of life. Under the leadership of Spokane Police Chief Terry Mangan, Administrative Service Director Dave Ingle worked behind the scenes with community activist Cheryl Steele (featured in chapter 10) to establish neighborhood-

*Bike patrols promote favorable interactions between citizens and patrol officers, especially among young Americans. (Photo: corbisimages.com)*

driven COPS (Community-Operated Police Substations) shops that would be staffed by over 800 trained volunteers. These shops resulted in the delivery of over 160 different programs throughout 25 different areas of the city and the eventual formation of a community-driven nonprofit organization overseen by a community mobilization board to help administer operations.

Key developments in Spokane include the creation of school and neighborhood-based community policing officers and neighborhood-based investigators, prosecutors, and probation officers (both adult and juvenile).[5] Citizen volunteers have made major contributions to the public safety effort by organizing neighbors-on-patrol units and implementing the Safe Streets Now! program. Citizen volunteers are schooled in the broken-windows theory and are trained to scan the community for problems ranging from graffiti to abandoned cars and drug trafficking. As a result of its successes, Spokane COPS was named a national demonstration center for training police departments around the world in community mobilization and system partnerships; the Spokane Police Department received the 1998 Community Policing Award from the International Association of Chiefs of Police (IACP) and ITT Night Vision, topping some 192 entries from across the United States and six foreign countries.

## Internal Changes Necessary for the Long-Term Success of Community Policing

Police departments must make a number of changes to achieve successes such as those in the case studies above and to ensure that they continue.

## An Organizational Culture That Fosters Community Policing

❖ ❖ ❖ ❖

Although many community policing programs have been recognized for their diversity and creativity, the various forms of community policing have not always been appreciated. For example, the long list of programs embodying community policing has generated strong criticism from some social scientists who contend that the lack of common features makes it difficult to test whether community policing really works; such lack also promotes the use of the term "community policing" simply as a slogan for enhancing a police department's public image.[6]

Furthermore, although community policing has emerged as the dominant philosophy in policing today, Dennis Rosenbaum and Arthur Lurigio argue that for it to be sustained over time depends upon overcoming difficulties in changing the organization of police departments from the philosophy of the professional era.[7] They suggest that effective community policing requires an organizational commitment to problem solving, customer satisfaction, and decentralized decision making, a commitment that is reflected in changes in mission and values statements and organizational structure.[8] The importance of organizational change was discussed in chapters 4 and 5. Here the authors want to emphasize the importance of this process and the barriers that must be overcome.

According to Malcolm Sparrow, one of the biggest barriers toward real change in policing deals with the general reluctance among police personnel to actually *change*. When the change represents a complete redefinition of a police officer's role in society—as in changing from professional-style to community policing—the change process often is slow and turbulent. Sparrow also notes that smooth police administration, with little or no external pressure to change, makes the change process particularly problematic. If the perception among police personnel is that "nothing's broken," then it is reasonable to ask why someone is trying to fix it.[9] Conversely, organizational change inspired by a critical incident or low external confidence in the police may result in a climate that is more supportive of change.

As noted in earlier chapters, effective organizational change typically begins with considerable planning. Chapter 10 discussed strategic planning as a critical component of any organizational change. Here, mission, values, and vision statements guide organizational goals, objectives, and operational strategies reflective of a community policing philosophy.[10] Sparrow maintains that organizational communication is of extreme importance during the change process, and leaders in the organization must not only preach the values of the department but also practice them in their day-to-day actions.[11] Participative management strategies, discussed in chapter 9, are an ideal way both to enhance communication within a police department and to allow employees at all levels of the organization to have some input into the change process.

The general reluctance to change to community policing reflects the existing professional police subculture. This view is contrary to community policing, which suggests that citizens are equal partners with the police in the effort to improve the quality of their neighborhood life. The idea that police officers work with citizens in an effort to solve neighborhood problems is contrary to the traditional opinion, which holds that citizens should do noth-

❖ ❖ ❖ ❖   ing more than serve as witnesses to crimes and report them to the police. The long-term success of community policing depends upon the creation of a new police subculture that values the participation of other service providers and citizens as problem-solving partners. But changing a subculture is difficult and slow. Although many departments have successfully changed mission and values statements, the statements themselves do little in the way of changing culture. Communicating a mission and values, leading by example, implementing training initiatives that emphasize the value of police-community partnerships, and publicizing behaviors consistent with the philosophy of community policing are just some of the ways that police leaders are beginning to address subcultural resistance to community policing.

Other departments are attempting to recruit and select police officers who embrace the ideals of community policing in the first place. For example, during a recent recruiting drive, the Portland (Oregon) Police Bureau emphasized its community orientation:

> Become a Community Police Officer with the Portland Police Bureau! Our mission is to work with all citizens to preserve life, maintain human rights, protect property and promote individual responsibility and community commitment.[12]

But perhaps of greatest importance in changing the professional-style police subculture is the ability of police departments to become "learning organizations" and to alter their ways of appraising police performance. This aspect of subcultural change is briefly discussed below.

## Police Departments as Learning Organizations

According to Peter Senge, a learning organization is one that expands "its capacity to create its future."[13] William Geller notes that learning organizations collect information on programs, strategies, and tactics and use it to learn what works, what does not, and what should be done to achieve an organizational objective. In an era of community policing, which requires constant innovative problem solving, it is a necessity for a police department to become a learning organization, learning to measure important outcomes and use the information for constant improvement.[14]

As Geller notes, however, it should not be assumed that police departments can easily become learning organizations. A variety of obstacles often stand in the way. For example, the fear of meaningful change in police departments and clinging to more traditional (professional-style) beliefs about crime, its control, and the role of police will hinder learning.[15] In addition, long-held skepticism about research and researchers impedes the creation of a learning organization. A police indoctrination process that discourages critical thinking and self-appraisal also tends to threaten the ability of police departments to learn from the past and reinvent themselves.

Despite these obstacles, if community policing is to succeed in the long term, police departments must foster an organizational subculture that supports continual learning, self-criticism, and change.[16] Geller offers some suggestions for the long-term success of community policing:

***Establish a research and development unit that really does research and development***. Although many police departments currently have a research and development unit, Geller suggests that these units often are

*Storefront 'copshops' like this one are examples of notable changes ushered in during the community era of policing. Usually staffed by volunteers, copshops make convenient stopping-by points for officers and citizens to exchange information and engage in problem solving and planning. (Photo courtesy of the Spokane (WA) Police Department)*

underused because of small budgets and personnel who have neither the capacity nor the resources to carry out the unit's mandate.

*Create talent inventories of organizational employees, community groups, and community institutions*. Both civilian and sworn employees have a variety of skills—research, public speaking, writing, and others—that can be used to foster organizational learning. Community group members and employees in external organizations also have these skills and often are willing to donate them if asked.

*Organize police work around problem solving*. In the right organizational environment, problem-solving groups involving departmental employees and interested outsiders can not only help build trust but also improve quality of life. However, Geller suggests that problem-solving procedures need to be created and implemented, and regular problem-solving brainstorming sessions need to be part of the process. Problem-solving training both for employees and external constituents also must be institutionalized, and performance appraisal systems, which typically fail to reward problem-solving activities, need to be altered.

*Foster critical thinking*. Long-held assumptions about what works, what is right, and what is wrong should be replaced with a process of constant questioning. In short, *groupthink* needs to be replaced by *synergism*. Geller suggests that middle managers take the lead in fostering critical thinking in police departments because of their unique organizational position between those who make policy and those who carry it out.

*Implement an employee suggestion program and take it seriously*. Geller cites the success of employee suggestion programs in private industry and suggests that in police departments they would have the dual benefit of empowering line-level employees to think critically about their work processes and improving work processes by carrying out their suggestions. The key to the success of these programs, according to Geller, is the timely consid-

❖ ❖ ❖ ❖   eration of the suggestion by managers, the timely response to the suggestion by the employee, and if reasonable, the timely implementation of the suggestion.

*Foster organizational research.* Research conducted on police department programs, policies, and other initiatives can be used to guide organizational efforts but only if it is used in such a capacity. Geller notes that "learning" police departments may have to convince managers and subordinates about the value and practical application of police research by showing the benefits of past research. To accomplish this and aid in future research, police-researcher partnerships should be established or expanded.

"Police departments as learning organizations" is one of the first steps toward ensuring the success of community policing. In the absence of a subculture that fosters learning, police departments are reluctant to stray too far away from business as usual, making only slight changes in the professional police role. Creativity, innovation, and problem solving must be viewed by the police as legitimate activities that are likely to have a positive effect on the quality of neighborhood life.

## Performance Measures of Community Policing

Yet another barrier to the long-term success of community policing is the police performance appraisal system characteristic of the professional era. To what extent do such systems need to change under community policing? Mary Wycoff and Timothy Oettmeier, who were involved in the Houston Police Department's creation of an experimental evaluation process designed to support community policing, note that employee performance evaluations should meet five, at times overlapping, standards:

1. *Validity.* Does the evaluation accurately reflect job content and expected quality of work?

2. *Reliability.* Does the evaluation result in similar job performances being given similar ratings even if the evaluators are different people? Will similar job performances across time by the same employee result in similar ratings?

3. *Equity.* Do employees who do the same or similar work receive equal evaluations of their performance?

4. *Legality.* Are the evaluation results used to determine rewards or punishments for employees? If so, to what extent does the evaluation reflect performance?

5. *Utility.* Is there an underlying purpose for evaluating an employee's performance?[17]

At the Houston Police Department, the evaluation instruments assessed officers' performance from a variety of perspectives, including officers' immediate supervisors and citizens whom the officers served. In general, the evaluation instruments pointed toward a more comprehensive and meaningful evaluation that was more commensurate with the actual activities of police officers than were professional-style evaluations that counted arrests or computed response times. The following are examples of the types of evaluation instruments used in the Houston experiment:

- **Patrol Officer's Biannual Assessment Report.** Twenty-two criteria were used here to assess a police officer's performance. The criteria were consistent with the department's expectations concerning officer responsibilities under a community policing framework.

- **Patrol Officer's Monthly Worksheet.** Officers would identify various projects on which they were working and report the progress they were making.

- **Community Information Form.** This form allowed citizens who worked on projects with police officers to assess an officer's performance through a series of open-ended questions centered on police-community communications, relationships, and problem solving.

- **Calls for Service—Citizen Feedback Form.** Sergeants would use this instrument to obtain information about the nature and quality of interactions between a particular police officer and citizens.

- **Investigator Questionnaire.** This instrument allowed a sergeant to assess an officer's knowledge and performance in handling investigations.

- **Officer's Immediate Supervisor Assessment Form.** An officer was given the opportunity on this form to provide lieutenants with information on a variety of dimensions about the officer's sergeant.[18]

Changes in performance appraisal systems that reflect the scope of community policing activities, along with meaningful assessment procedures, are likely to send messages regarding the true mission of a police department. Police officers who break from the mold of the professional-style subculture will be rewarded, while those resistant to change will find their goals in conflict with the new ones.

## Reallocating Resources to Community Policing

It would be a mistake to overlook one of the most frequently mentioned internal barriers to community policing. The conventional wisdom of many police executives is that their "share" of the 100,000 additional community police officers funded by the 1994 Federal Crime Act falls short if community policing is to be fully implemented in their department. Very often, these are the same departments that have created specialized community policing units, solely dedicated to working with residents at the neighborhood level.

This specialized-unit approach to community policing has resulted in some positive changes in the quality of neighborhood life but also has its limitations.[19] First, the approach tends to feed the argument that community policing cannot be accomplished by "regular" patrol officers, that is, specialized problem-solving officers must be hired and trained to do community policing. This, of course, comes back to the problem of scanty resources. Second, the specialized-unit approach gives patrol officers, detectives, and other police personnel the impression that community policing does not necessarily concern them but is a program implemented by the community policing people. Third, the approach does little in the way of changing an organizational culture; in fact, it might create an "us (the *real* police officers) versus them (the *community* police officers)" mentality.

❖ ❖ ❖ ❖        But one should remember that community policing is both a management approach and a philosophy that guides the actions of *all* individuals in a department—both sworn and nonsworn. Therefore, the change process must include plans to train all personnel in community policing from the civilian records clerk to the chief of police. It is not necessary, however, to disband specialized problem-solving units, so long as it is clearly communicated that all members of the department are expected to embrace the ideals of community policing.

Even if those police executives acknowledge the necessity of a department-wide commitment to community policing, some are skeptical of the ability of line-level police officers to engage in meaningful problem solving in concert with citizens *and* also respond to radio calls. Such ability is, indeed, problematic. However, a thorough analysis of calls for service often uncovers considerable uncommitted time that officers can spend discussing problems with citizens, mobilizing community groups, or engaging in problem solving. Finally, if community policing helps mobilize citizens, increases informal control mechanisms, and eventually reduces crime and disorder problems at the neighborhood level, limited resources eventually may be a less important issue.

## External Changes Necessary for the Long-Term Success of Community Policing

If the essence of community policing is a true collaborative partnership between police and citizens in an effort to solve problems and improve quality of life, then clearly the ability of police departments to change internally is not enough by itself. External factors are also important. By the 1960s, the role of citizens in professional-style police departments was well entrenched: Citizens were of little value to professional crime fighters beyond their ability to report crimes, to describe suspects, and to testify in court. As the popular television show *Dragnet* illustrated, police professionals were interested in "just the facts."

But as departments turned toward community policing in the 1980s, a much larger role for citizens was envisioned. John J. DiIulio has clearly shown that the role of citizens in the police process is far greater than simply reporting crime to the police. He maintains that it is unrealistic for the formal agents of government to have a measurable, positive impact on the quality of neighborhood life without the active assistance, cooperation, and participation of residents formally outside of government. In this newer spirit of community-police collaboration, the older ideas that judges, prosecutors, or the police could and should solve society's problems without the assistance of citizens is unrealistic. DiIulio suggests that citizens have a large role in ensuring that justice is done, in promoting secure communities, in restoring victims of crime, and in promoting noncriminal options for offenders.[20]

According to Dallin Oakes, the ability of citizens to rise to the occasion and assume some responsibility for the quality of their neighborhood life at least partly depends on their ability to move away from the current "rights-oriented society," as touched on in chapter 3. Oakes notes that citizens tend to emphasize their rights over their responsibilities. For example, Americans value the right to vote over the *duty* to vote and the right to a jury as a criminal defendant over the *duty* to serve as a juror. Oakes maintains that there is a fundamental difference between rights and responsibilities: Rights can be enforced by law, while most responsibilities only can be encouraged.[21] Therein, perhaps, lies the problem. A citizen cannot be forced to participate in a neighborhood watch program sponsored by a local community group and the police department. A citizen cannot be forced to look after a neighbor's home while the neighbor is on vacation.

If community policing is to succeed in the long term, citizens must assume responsibility for the quality of their neighborhood life. How will that happen? Oakes suggests that responsibilities can be encouraged by making positive examples more visible through rewards or media coverage. In addition, there could be a renewed emphasis on responsibilities in the institutions that promote moral development, such as churches, schools, and family.[22]

Taking seriously responsibility for one's community may be a first step in an effort to mobilize residents for community policing. But, as discussed later in this chapter, there are other—perhaps even more profound—stumbling blocks to be overcome.

## Community Policing Among America's Poor

It is somewhat ironic that community policing is most difficult to implement and institutionalize in those areas most in need of effective responses to crime, disorder, and quality-of-life problems. Impoverished areas of American cities illustrate both the difficulty of implementing community policing and the hope that it can be successful. Is it possible for community policing to succeed in high-crime and disorderly neighborhoods? If so, what must occur? The following sections will discuss these questions.

*Crime and the urban poor.* According to actual crime trends over the last 15 years, serious crime across the nation seems to be slightly decreasing.[23] These trends hold true for both reporting and arrest data from the *Uniform Crime Reports* and victimization data from the National Crime Victimization Survey. Decreases in crime rates and victimization, however, are dependent upon who you are and where you live. In cities of more than half a million residents, serious crime continues to increase. Although only approximately 18 percent of the population live in such cities, they account for more than 50 percent of all reported index crimes against persons and almost 33 percent of all reported crimes against property.[24]

Within these larger cities, crime rates tend to rise the closer they are to the city's urban core. In what Clifford Shaw, Henry McKay, and Ronald Burgess call the "zone in transition," a city's inner core typically is characterized by high crime, poor housing, social and physical disorder, fear of crime, transiency, and heterogeneity in terms of race and ethnicity.[25]

Although poor economic conditions combined with a high incidence of street crime in the inner cities may lead one to wonder if "being poor" indeed leads to crime and victimization, it is the conventional wisdom of students of crime that there is no direct causal relationship between unfavorable economic conditions and the likelihood of committing street crime.[26] Instead, a variety of ecological conditions combine to make the urban core an attractive area to commit crime, including the physical condition of the area, the opportunities to commit crime, and low levels of social control.[27]

❖ ❖ ❖ ❖     William Julius Wilson describes a subset of individuals within the urban core who are at the very bottom of the economic hierarchy: the urban underclass.[28] This group, primarily African American and Hispanic, is characterized by poverty, unemployment, criminal victimization, drug use, and welfare dependency.[29] According to Wilson, many members of the urban underclass typically have few direct ties to family or social institutions and rely mostly on crime to make a living.[30]

Even though the urban core includes those who routinely engage in criminal activity and disorderly conduct on a routine and ongoing basis, the vast majority of urban-core residents are law-abiding citizens. Furthermore, these residents are at some considerable risk for becoming "victims" of both crimes and fear of crime. Lacking the resources to move elsewhere, the alternative for many residents is to remain isolated and withdrawn from any semblance of community life. These individuals, unable to move into safer areas, suffer the most from inner-city street crime. Since they typically have little personal property or real income, a theft or robbery can have devastating consequences for them. Indeed, as DiIulio points out, crime itself may actually cause poverty in inner-city areas.[31]

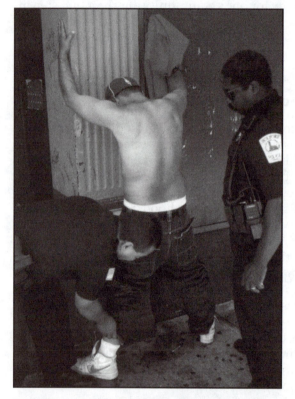

The urban underclass neighborhood often lacks ties to community institutions, making it difficult for police to establish positive relationships. (Photo: Mark C. Ide)

***Crime in and around public housing.*** The vast majority of research dealing with crime in public housing has come from some of the largest housing developments and yields disturbing evidence of crime and disorder. For example, William Brill, studying public housing units in Washington, Baltimore, Los Angeles, and Boston, found higher rates of crime in large public housing units than in neighborhoods in their immediate vicinity.[32]

In a more recent analysis of crime in public housing, Terence Dunworth and Aaron Saiger studied offense rates in Washington, Phoenix, and Los Angeles from 1986 to 1989. In all three sites, drug and violent offense rates were "severe problems in housing developments."[33] Although property offense rates did not show this same pattern, drug and violent offense rates in each of the cities were greater in the public housing developments when compared both to the city as a whole and to surrounding neighborhoods. Nevertheless, to say that all public housing units are "crime infested" would be inaccurate. In fact, Dunworth and Saiger themselves assert that serious offenses appear to be more prevalent in some public housing facilities than in others. The serious offense rate within the public housing facilities in Los Angeles and Washington was lower than the rate for the cities as wholes.[34]

Important contextual variables might lead to the variation in offense rates between public housing sites. These variables may include size of the facility, resident makeup, location, and existing levels of physical disorder. Indeed, Dennis Roncek et al. and John Farley, in contrast to Dunworth and Saiger, found that levels of crime did not significantly vary when comparing public housing facilities to their surrounding neighborhoods.[35]

Although public housing facilities across the United States vary considerably in terms of size and resident composition, particular attention has been

---

## Crime Prevention Through Environmental Design and Community Policing

Crime Prevention Through Environmental Design (CPTED) and community policing are overlapping and complementary strategies that can be used to improve the quality of neighborhood life. According to Dan Fleissner and Fred Heinzelmann, CPTED and community policing can be considered a comprehensive approach to community crime prevention.

. . . [H]ere's what both police and residents can do to improve neighborhoods.

**The Police Can. . .**

- Conduct security surveys for residents and provide security improvements such as adequate lighting and locks.

- Conduct park patrols and patrols of other public spaces to eliminate crime and drug use.

- Use their substations to inform residents of high-risk locations in the neighborhood.

- Work with urban planners and architects to review the designs and plans in order to enhance community security.

- Prepare educational materials for building owners and managers to deal with problem tenants and improve the livability and security of rental units. These materials are useful because they address not only the manner in which the physical environment is designed but also how it can be managed more effectively to enhance public safety.

- Control traffic flow to reduce the use of streets by criminals and enhance neighborhood cohesion and resident interaction. Streets can be closed or traffic diverted to create residential enclaves that give residents greater control of their living environment.

**Residents Can. . .**

- Engage in cleanup programs to remove trash or graffiti.

- Carry out programs to improve the appearance, safety, and use of public spaces.

- Conduct their own patrols to identify neighborhood problems.

- Join an organized block watch program.

---

This essay is excerpted from Dan Fleissner and Fred Heinzelmann, "Crime Prevention Through Environmental Design and Community Policing," *National Institute of Justice: Research in Action*, August 1996.

❖ ❖ ❖ ❖ given to those located in or near inner-city cores.[36] Crime rates in these areas have increased during the late 1980s and early 1990s, in sharp contrast to the decreases in national crime trends.[37] Strategies to combat violent crime and disorder in and around public housing have been numerous and diverse—from more traditional suppression activities primarily involving local police, to better screening and eviction policies initiated by some public housing authorities, to community building often initiated by public housing residents. In some locations, these strategies have been combined in an effort to reduce crime, disorder, and fear.[38]

## Successful Community Efforts to Improve Quality of Life

*Crime prevention through environmental design.* Recent efforts to improve the quality of life for America's poor include Crime Prevention Through Environmental Design (CPTED) and community building through local community policing initiatives. CPTED is based on Oscar Newman's work concerning defensible space, suggesting that offenders operate with some degree of rationality.[39] Changing the physical environment to clearly establish public versus private space is one of many ways to send the real or symbolic message to the potential offender that residents care about their surroundings.[40] Ralph Taylor and Adele Harrell suggest four broad approaches to make particular areas more resistant to crime and related problems: (1) addressing housing design or block layout, (2) altering land-use and circulation patterns, (3) erecting territorial markers, and (4) controlling physical deterioration.[41]

Empirical research in this area is somewhat contradictory. For example, Henry Cisneros reports that defensible-space strategies "have had considerable success in several smaller scale [public housing] developments, and they have made at least some dent in the crime problems of certain high-rise developments."[42] However, Langley Keyes and Harold Holzman et al. provide evidence suggesting that levels of community safety may not be enhanced with CPTED techniques.[43] Taylor and Harrell suggest that the implementation of CPTED may simply displace crime and disorder problems to surrounding areas.[44]

Steven Lab notes, however, that CPTED is probably most effective when used in combination with other strategies relevant to a particular neighborhood's problems, including community policing and community crime-prevention programs that emphasize collaborative partnerships in an effort to solve problems and build "sense of community" among residents.[45] Although there are many obstacles to mobilizing residents (discussed in the next section), effective community building appears to hold promise for reducing crime and disorder problems in and around public housing developments.[46] In fact, in an evaluation of HUD's Public Housing Drug Elimination Program, Abt Associates found that programs involving resident empowerment in collaboration with police and service agencies were important components to a successful drug-crime elimination program.[47]

*Community crime-prevention programs.* Throughout recent history, crime prevention has taken a variety of forms. For example, team policing, which appeared in the late 1960s, is now viewed as more of a community-relations gimmick used by the police to try to improve their image than anything else. In the mid-1970s, crime prevention took two other forms, first in training individuals in protecting themselves and their property, then in promoting collective community crime-prevention measures such as BlockWatch and Neighborhood Watch.[48] According to Paul Lavrakas, it was not until the late 1970s that the community began to play a major role in shaping and defining its own crime-prevention initiatives.[49]

Most current community crime-prevention programs follow one of two approaches: the opportunity-reduction approach and the social-problems approach.[50] Programs following the opportunity-reduction approach attempt to remove or reduce the opportunities available for committing crimes.[51] They include deterring potential offenders by altering the physical environment, patrolling the streets, and promoting individual or collective activities that may reduce the possibility of people becoming victims. Such activities include target-hardening efforts and educational crime-prevention programs such as block or neighborhood watches.[52] According to Lurigio and Rosenbaum, efforts to develop closer and more meaningful working relationships between the police and neighborhood residents also serve to deter potential offenders and fall under the opportunity-reduction approach.[53]

The social-problems approach seeks to identify and remedy underlying social conditions—the root causes—that lead to criminal activity.[54] Crime prevention efforts might take the form of providing opportunities for youth to engage in constructive activities.[55] According to S. F. Bennett and Paul Lavrakas, such activities may include police athletic leagues, drug-prevention programs, and job training programs.[56] Other programs attempt to have residents enforce social norms[57] and to increase interactions and develop sense of community.[58] These programs appear to be particularly relevant in light of James Q. Wilson and George Kelling's broken-windows hypothesis.[59]

In the 1970s, with urban crime rates and fear of crime on the rise, community efforts to prevent crime (mainly burglaries and personal robberies) continued to increase.[60] Several federally funded community anticrime demonstration projects were implemented in the early 1970s, and by the mid-1970s the Law Enforcement Assistance Administration (LEAA) funded several national evaluations to determine the effectiveness of specific programs such as citizen patrols and security surveys.[61] Perhaps the greatest boost to community crime-prevention activities in the 1970s occurred as a result of Congress' authorization of LEAA's Anti-Crime Program, which allocated $30 million to community groups to become more involved in preventing crime, reducing fear, and contributing to neighborhood revitalization.[62] Although this funding led to the design and implementation of many community crime-prevention programs, the effectiveness of such efforts remained in question.

Two key findings from evaluation research on community crime-prevention programs suggest that media accounts of "successful" community anticrime activities of the 1970s may have been overly generalized. Researchers concluded that: (1) collective community crime-prevention activities are unlikely to develop in poor, high-crime areas, and (2) these efforts require the involvement of many residents in order to be successful.[63]

Since the early 1980s, however, researchers have learned that crime-prevention activities can be successfully implemented in poor, high-crime areas (although it is more difficult than in well-to-do areas) and that the involve-

## Every Community Has Its Challenges

### *Sergeant Darrell Atteberry*

It was never supposed to be a permanent community. Built in the 1940s as temporary housing for people working for the war effort against Nazi Germany, the simple wooden residences comprising the Hilltop area of south Wichita became a thriving residential area during the 1940s, 1950s, and 1960s. Eventually, as the city grew, Hilltop residences were bought up by investors bent on leasing them. Over time, however, absentee landlords let their property fall into disrepair and decay and the Hilltop area deteriorated much as Wilson and Kelling's broken-window theory might predict. By the late 1980s, gangs and crack cocaine had gained a foothold in the area and physical decay had increased, causing the area to decline even further.

A feeling of separation from the rest of the city took hold as the neighborhood grew older and tenants of the cheap housing tended to be underemployed or unemployed. Crime flourished without any coordinated effort to fight it. Not trusting the government to do anything positive in the area, or even to show much concern, residents had low expectations for improvement. Even the police saw little hope for the area and seemed resigned to practice only a reactive, traditional style of policing.

*Wichita's Hilltop neighborhood recreation center before the police and citizens joined together to attract city support to tear the structure down and rebuild on the same site. Run-down municipal properties can send a message that citizen needs in a neighborhood are not a high priority of local government. (Photo: Courtesy of the Wichita Police Department)*

Little changed in the Hilltop area until 1993, when the Wichita Police Department began a transition to community policing. A community that had for decades been stigmatized by its record-high levels of crime, drive-by shootings, homicides, rapes, robberies, burglaries, larcenies, and auto thefts was viewed as ripe for intervention. Especially challenging beyond the poor living and economic conditions in the area were tensions between the police and residents. Officers called into the Hilltop area felt that they always had to be on their guard and tended to distrust the people. Even good citizens believed the police were unapproachable. As the number of crimes increased, residents began to feel as if they were being treated as second-class citizens. The situation got so bad that some residents threatened to kill officers who worked there.

From all indications it seemed that the many problems associated with the Hilltop area appeared insurmountable. If community policing could be made to work in Hilltop, it could work anywhere. However, several long-term projects would have to be undertaken. To begin with, many of Hilltop's problems were the result of poor environmental design. The area has 557 dwellings with only six streets running through them. The dwellings, mostly duplexes, line the alleys running back from the street. In most situations, the dwellings are three deep, with a fourth house at the end of the alley. In one area there are as many as 120 residences bounded by four streets. Most of the residences have limited direct access to the street. Additionally, only a few have posted addresses, and nearly all suffer from poor lighting at night. As a result, emergency response to the area is difficult, further signaling to the residents the lack of the city's regard for their public safety.

Unfortunately, the philosophy of community policing in place at the end of 1993 was not well understood and its practices were untested. Although the police department recognized the need for dramatic change in the Hilltop area, it chose a very traditional approach to begin with and committed Special Community Action Teams (SCAT) to initiate the effort. SCAT, the enforcement arm of the newly formed

☞ community policing units, took a proactive approach toward gangs, gang houses, and drug interdiction. They closed gang houses in one part of Hilltop, but the unintended result was displacement. Drug traffickers would simply move to nearby locations, reopen their drug houses, and continue their criminal activities. The SCAT solution by itself seemed to hold little or no motivation for officers to find solutions to the underlying problems of the area.

A survey was conducted by the St. Joseph Hospital group. The hospital is located just west of the Hilltop neighborhood and sees many of the Hilltop residents as patients. It was determined by the survey that the median income for the residents in the area was approximately $15,000. Such poverty helped fuel the crime problem and contributed to a lost sense of community. In addition, the old recreation center in the heart of the Hilltop area had been abandoned. The city had taken over the building and boarded it up in order to avoid the cost of operation, maintenance,

A Wichita Police Department officer receives congratulations from a citizen for the department's involvement in mustering support for a new neighborhood recreation center. Partnerships with communities can make a noticeable and permanent impression on quality-of-life issues in a neighborhood. (Photo: Courtesy of the Wichita Police Department)

and repair. Those residents in Hilltop who still had a sense of community felt disenfranchised with no good place to meet and work out their problems. To them, the abandoned recreation center symbolized a city government that did not care.

The traditional approach to crime having failed, the door was open for a more innovative, community-driven response. Local clergy, the police, and citizens organized a town meeting to discuss neighborhood problems, police actions, and how the city might help. A neighborhood association was formed, along with key police-community partnerships. Businesses, organizations, and agencies around Hilltop helped to work on solutions. The Via Christi-St. Joseph Hospital, Sedgwick County Extension Office, First Evangelical Church, Wichita Independent Neighborhoods, South-Oliver Business Association, Wichita Police Department, and others all joined together to study the problems plaguing Hilltop.

A broad range of possible solutions was considered. Not only was attention given to larger (macro) needs of the area but also to the smaller (micro) needs. Some of the problem-oriented projects started by the police department were geared towards law enforcement, and some were structured to help build a sense of community and address the quality of life. It became clear that a crucial first step was to build a positive relationship with the local government and with the police, who now had access to resources to combat many of the environmental problems.

A community policing officer was assigned to the Hilltop area to coordinate community activities with his beat team and the neighborhood. He was instructed to work with the Hilltop neighborhood and the Hilltop-Jefferson Neighborhood Association to clean up the area physically and to identify projects for further improvement. Several cleanups were conducted to remove many years worth of accumulated trash, and large numbers of abandoned vehicles were impounded. The community policing officer and the beat-team officers worked to repair the relationship between the police and the residents by resolving large and small problems. In the process, they established mutual trust.

As SCAT continued to focus on gangs and drug houses in professional police fashion, the community police officer and beat officers called on the landlords and persuaded them to evict the drug dealers and other people involved in criminal activity. They told landlords what the renters were doing and asked the landlords to be part of the solution to the crime problems. The landlords were responsive.

☞

❖ ❖ ❖ ❖   ☞

The community police officer and the beat officers attended regular meetings of the Hilltop-Jefferson Neighborhood Association. They listened to their concerns and acted to resolve problems. The citizens began to trust the police much more than they had in the past and no longer feared to call in criminal complaints. This new trust allowed the police and the community to continue working on special projects in an effort to build the sense of community that Hilltop needed.

A response plan was initiated with the partners in the project so that community problems could be collectively resolved. The plan called for acquiring a much needed community building as a base for important services for the area. The plan recognized a need to reduce crime in the area and improve the delivery of city and agency services. It also recognized the importance of finding activities for the youth of the area and building relationships between them and responsible adults.

For many years there had been no youth activities in the Hilltop area, and the community center, also used for games, had long been closed. A city councilman was taken on a tour of the area. He asked the community policing officer to give a speech before the city council requesting that the old center be demolished and a new one built in its place. The community policing officer helped put together a partnership between key people in the community and the city to accomplish this task. For a year and a half several brainstorming sessions and planning meetings took place to ensure the building would meet the needs of the Hilltop community. In 1998 the abandoned center was demolished to make room for a new center to house a Head Start program with two classrooms, a large multipurpose room, community policing office space, and a neighborhood association office.

Four at-risk teens were recruited to help coach T-ball, a simplified form of baseball. As an incentive they were offered a membership to a health club. Two Patrol East officers donated their off-duty time to mentor the teen coaches and volunteers from Via-Christi Sports Medicine donated time as senior coaches. An ambulance from Via-Christi was used as a portable recruitment station to sign up players. Neighborhood volunteers came out to the baseball field to clean it up, paint the backstop, and cut a baseball diamond into the grass. Entrance fees for the city league, mitts, bats, tennis shoes, and other equipment were all given by private donors. The community policing officer also obtained a $10,000 donation from a local businessman who had grown up in the Hilltop area; that money also was used to buy sports equipment for youth.

Progress in the Hilltop area instilled public confidence in the police and also encouraged an awareness of other needs in the community. In spring 1998 Community Policing Officer James Bratt was notified by the pastor of a Hilltop church that a family was living in the Hilltop area in a house without electricity or running water. Bratt paid a visit and found that the house wasn't fit to be inhabited. It had numerous code violations and was infested by roaches. To complicate matters, the woman had costly medical problems, which had caused the family to lose their former home to the bank. The woman had to be hooked up to an expensive breathing machine at night and constantly monitored. The breathing machine was very costly and its consumption of electricity was high. The local electric company had shut off service because of an overdue bill of $2000.

Bratt was able to convince the family to let a housing inspector come in and document the code violations. The family was hesitant at first because they feared that the landlord would evict them. Bratt assured them that a new place for them to live would be found. The housing inspector documented the code violations and the property was condemned. That made the family eligible for assistance. The man, who had been employed by the city for 19 years, was eligible for free financial counseling through the Employee Assistance Program. The Mennonites helped them find a new house. A payment plan was worked out with the electric company so that service could be started there. The Friendship Fund, a fund operated by the city to assist employees, paid the family's overdue electric bill, and they were able to maintain electric service at their new home. The family eventually had to file for bankruptcy in order to have their medical bills forgiven.

Responsiveness to the problems in the Hilltop area were dictated by the needs of the community. A multilevel approach to problem solving was taken by a police-citizen partnership to rebuild a sense of community and improve the quality of life. This was accomplished through the neighborhood association networking with ☞

☞

❖ ❖ ❖ ❖

the business community and building a working relationship among the police, community residents, and other local businesses and groups. The partnership rallied behind the call for a new neighborhood center as a foundation upon which to build a renewed sense of community.

Several keys to this successful partnership were evident. One was focusing on the youth. The T-Ball project developed relationships between the community and the police and the benefits are expected to improve communication in the future. Another key was individual citizen response. Many landlords are remiss in keeping their properties in livable condition. Families move into neglected homes and then have problems getting relief from the landlords. The police department took an active role in mediating disputes between renters and landlords, and helping renters who had received no redress.

The Hilltop Community Project continues to succeed. Ground was broken for a new $375,000 Hilltop Neighborhood Center, city services are being delivered more quickly than before, crime has been reduced, and youth programs have helped build bridges between youths and the police department. Individuals continue to assist in efforts to improve quality of life.

The police department, the business community, governmental agencies, not-for-profit organizations, community block grant funds, and private donations all provided resources. No roadblocks encountered along the path were so large as not to be overcome. Police officers have bought in, and many attend the neighborhood association meetings on their own time because they feel ownership in the neighborhood. The officers have also donated time to coach the T-Ball program and mentor other youth. Citizen buy-in, once a problem, is now a much appreciated asset.

---

Sgt. Darrell G. Atteberry is a community policing supervisor and an 18-year veteran of the Wichita Police Department. His current assignment includes overseeing the Patrol East Bureau Community Policing Unit and the Patrol East School Resource Officers. He has a B.A. in economics and an M.A. in public administration from Wichita State University.

---

ment of large segments of community residents—although desired—is not necessary to success. There are documented successes at reducing some street crimes such as burglaries[64] and at discouraging open-air drug dealing and prostitution.[65]

According to Wilson and Kelling and later Wesley Skogan, the nature of many "victimless crimes" such as street-walking prostitution and drug dealing tend to contribute to the overall social disorder of particular communities.[66] As Barbara Smith and Robert Davis contend, these crimes are markedly different from street crimes such as burglaries and robberies, which often target unknown persons or establishments at random. Prostitution and drug dealing, by contrast, require some degree of visibility in rather stationary locations.[67]

The nature of drug dealing makes both sellers and buyers easy targets to spot, even by small numbers of citizens who may wish to become involved in community anticrime activities. In addition, there has been ample, although nonscientific, evidence that community antidrug efforts have had some success in poorer, high-crime neighborhoods owing to residents' frustration at neighborhood disorder and crime. Residents have begun to mobilize and work with the police to rebuild neighborhoods and fight drug activity.[68]

***Collaborative efforts between the police and citizens.*** Rosenbaum contends that "There has been a steady and growing recognition that the police and the citizenry are on the front line of this battle and must do more than

❖ ❖ ❖ ❖     just react to the problem after the fact."[69] In fact, criminal justice scholars, policymakers, and lay persons have come to realize that effective crime control entails much more than a government response to offenders after a crime has been committed. Instead, they urge multilevel, collaborative partnerships between citizens and the formal system of justice at the neighborhood level as offering the most potential for reducing crime, fear of crime, and social and physical disorder and enhancing the overall quality of life for those who find themselves not only talking about crime, but also as victims.

Although scholars in the early 1980s began to focus almost exclusively on effective community mobilization as the key variable for successful community anticrime efforts and virtually discounted the role of the criminal justice system,[70] there has been growing evidence that the police-citizen collaborative partnership may be the key to effective community crime prevention.[71] According to Susan Popkin et al. and T. M. Hammett et al., the most successful community anticrime programs to date have reflected "comprehensive" efforts that include law enforcement activities, community involvement, and situational crime-prevention efforts.[72]

Such "law enforcement activities" might include professional-style suppression tactics as well as more innovative police programs that may be considered community policing. *Community involvement* typically includes a variety of resident activities that can increase informal social control, an important variable that has been related to crime, fear of crime, and neighborhood social and physical disorder.[73] Finally, "situational crime-prevention efforts" seek to limit the opportunities for committing criminal acts in specific locations.[74] Such efforts include physical design features that denote defensible space, the increased use of surveillance, and target-hardening efforts.

## External Obstacles to Overcome

The chief external obstacle to the effectiveness of community policing efforts in any form has been the long-standing difficulty of community mobilization, especially in the most economically disadvantaged neighborhoods of cities and towns.[75] Ironically, it is those neighborhoods that are most in need of effective community-based responses to crime. In addition, crime-prevention efforts that involve only citizens have been relatively ineffective at creating neighborhood-level change.[76]

Accordingly, as several researchers contend, collaborative partnerships between communities and the formal system of justice offer the most potential for defining and administering community crime-prevention undertakings.[77] As community policing becomes more dominant, true collaboration between community residents and the police may prove to be one telling solution in the effort to prevent and control crime and to stem the tide of neighborhood decay in those neighborhoods most in need of such responses.

Although Oakes maintains that the ability of citizens to assume some responsibility for the quality of their neighborhood life is at least partially dependent on their ability to move away from the present "rights-oriented society,"[78] Randolph Grinc suggests related obstacles that must be overcome if community policing is to succeed in the long term.[79]

## Implementation Challenges in Community Policing

### *Excerpted From Susan Sadd and Randolph Grinc*

The external obstacles discussed in this text come from a larger study on the implementation challenges of community policing by Susan Sadd and Randolph M. Grinc. They were the principal evaluators of Innovative Neighborhood-Oriented Policing (INOP) programs, established with Bureau of Justice Assistance funding in eight jurisdictions across the United States. INOP programs are grounded in the assumption that crime and drug problems can best be addressed by communities working with the police, rather than relying solely on the police. Each INOP site was awarded between $100,000 and $200,000 for first-year activities. The sites were Hayward, California; Houston, Texas; Louisville, Kentucky; New York City; Norfolk, Virginia; Portland, Oregon; Prince George's County, Maryland; and Tempe, Arizona.

The following are the key findings of the evaluation as reported by Sadd and Grinc.

- The major implementation challenges were resistance by police officers to community policing and the difficulty of involving other public agencies and of organizing the community.

- With the exception of one site, the involvement of other public agencies was limited.

- Police officers generally did not understand community policing; saw INOP assignments as conferring an elite status; perceived INOP as less productive, more time-consuming, and more resource-intensive than traditional policing; and felt their powers, particularly to enforce the law, were restrained.

- Average citizens had less knowledge than community leaders about INOP and were reluctant to participate; their reasons included fear of drug dealers, fear of retaliation, and cynicism about the perceived short duration of the project.

- The perceived effects of INOP on drug trafficking were mixed; they resulted in geographic and temporal displacement of markets. In the sites where people thought INOP had reduced crime, fear of crime declined.

- Most site residents believed their relationship with the police had improved, even where the effect on drugs, crime, and fear was believed to be minimal.

- INOP's limited success in reducing drug crime and fear may be related to the obstacles generally encountered in transforming program ideas into action, especially within the short timeframe of the evaluation.

---

Excerpted from Susan Sadd and Randolph M. Grinc, "Implementation Challenges in Community Policing: Innovative Neighborhood-Oriented Policing in Eight Cities," *National Institute of Justice: Research in Brief*, February, 1999, pp. 1–2.

## Fear of Retaliation

If the essence of community policing is the collaborative problem-solving partnership between police and citizens, fear may be a formidable barrier to

❖ ❖ ❖ ❖   such a partnership. Fear can vary from a rather diffuse feeling of being unsafe to fear of being a victim to fear of retaliation for reporting offenses. Any of these forms of fear can result in low levels of community participation in community policing endeavors.

This barrier is not easily overcome. If, according to the broken-windows hypothesis, disorder truly causes a considerable amount of fear among neighborhood residents, one strategy might be to have the police, at least initially, take the lead in dealing with disorder. As fear decreases over time, perhaps more residents would participate in community policing. Other community policing programs have attempted to deal with fear of becoming a victim by providing facts about an individual's true risk of being victimized, which is lower than many people think. Still other community policing programs have emphasized discrete methods of reporting offenses, which decrease the chances of victimization out of retaliation.[80]

## Historically Poor Relationship Between the Police and the Community

Although there is growing evidence that police-citizen partnerships at the neighborhood level may be the key to effective responses to crime and disorder, police partnerships with the poor, members of minority groups, and public housing residents is usually difficult to initiate and maintain. Long histories of police discrimination toward the poor and racial minorities have led many members of these groups to distrust the police.[81] Public housing residents are particularly problematic because police officers often are suspicious and fearful of them, and they rarely receive cooperation from them in solving crimes, especially the drug crimes in large housing projects.[82] Public housing residents are no different from residents of "ordinary poor and minority neighborhoods."[83] Many public housing residents have the same negative attitudes toward the police as other poor and minority groups. Community policing—based on collaborative problem solving, mutual respect, and officer and citizen empowerment—may offer the best hope for breaking down the barriers between the police and those groups who traditionally have questioned the motivations, authority, and professionalism of the formal agents of the law.

## Apathy

Grinc notes that although apathy or "laziness" may be a one explanation for achieving low levels of participation in community policing programs, a more likely explanation stems from "rational" reasons, such as mistrust of the police.[84] Although Grinc's assertion is relevant to those who historically have had negative relations with the police, it may be less relevant for those who hold the police in high regard. The apathy explanation may apply to them. Quite simply, people have other things to do—for themselves or their immediate family—which may cause them to have no interest in the proposition of working with other neighborhood residents to solve community, not necessarily individual, problems.

Continued efforts at community policing attempt to mobilize neighborhood residents by sending the message that they are responsible for the quality of their neighborhood life.[85] These efforts continue despite much difficulty. But it should not be forgotten that high rates of neighborhood participation are not essential for the long-term success of community policing.[86] For example, in Spokane a small group of public housing residents working with community police officers contributed to substantial improvements in the social and physical environment. Although relatively few did the work, all the residents reaped the benefits.[87]

## The Fleeting Nature of Projects to Help Poor Communities

Grinc notes that economically disadvantaged residents are likely to be skeptical about government-sponsored programs.[88] Based on very real experiences, they tend to view programs as temporary, typically disappearing once external funding has been depleted. It makes little sense to them to participate in programs that are here today, gone tomorrow. If community policing is to succeed over time, especially in impoverished areas of cities, residents must be convinced that community policing itself is not a temporary fix.

Even in areas where community policing has been implemented, some residents believe that community policing is somewhat fleeting.[89] This is especially true of highly publicized programs that begin with a high level of police service and then are scaled back once conditions in the neighborhood improve. Even though such programs may have been planned, effective communication between residents and the police at times is lacking.

## Residents' Failure to Understand Their Role in Community Policing

There is little doubt that most police today understand the philosophy of community policing. But the same may not be true for citizens. They may be confused about their role in the community-policing partnership. Do ordinary residents assume the duties of commissioned police under community policing? While this example may seem far-fetched, it was the understanding of one community group in the Northwest several years ago. Residents would routinely attempt to make traffic stops along their neighborhood streets until the police told them not to do so.

Grinc suggests starting training programs that focus on the principles of community policing, including the community's role in such efforts.[90] Such training may be carried out on an individual basis between a resident and a community police officer, through established community crime-prevention programs, or by citizens' academies at local police departments.

## Heterogeneity, Disorganization, and Intragroup Conflict

Grinc notes that intragroup conflict among community leaders and residents may result in a lack of involvement by some individuals. He discusses this problem not only in terms of "battling" personalities but also in terms of values. In heterogeneous communities, a lack of shared values and experiences combined with differing opinions on what problems need to be solved

❖ ❖ ❖ ❖

*Poverty and homelessness tend to indicate communities with a higher incidence of crime. (Photo: Mark C. Ide)*

and how to solve them can lead to conflict. In some communities, individuals may not even welcome police action.[91] This problem manifests itself in relatively homogeneous neighborhoods as well.

The highly disorganized nature of some communities, combined with few shared values, makes mobilization efforts particularly difficult. According to Grinc, areas characterized by poverty and unemployment also tend to lack organized community associations that might partner with police.[92] Consequently, the task of organizing residents may fall on the shoulders of police officers, who may or may not be successful in this endeavor. Although there is no easy way to overcome all these obstacles, some community groups have received training in resolving intragroup conflict, and some police officers have received training in effective strategies for mobilizing the population.[93]

## Conclusion

This chapter has attempted to glimpse the future of community policing based on a growing body of evidence suggesting that substantial internal changes from the professional style of policing are necessary to make community policing an established institution. The chapter has also discussed that these internal changes by themselves are not enough to ensure the success of community policing.

If community policing truly represents a collaborative partnership between police and citizens—and the authors think it does—then external changes are necessary. Residents in neighborhoods throughout the country must come to the realization that they, too, are accountable for the quality of their neighborhood life. In addition to following the advice of Oakes and DiIulio to begin to think in terms of "we" rather than in terms of "I," communities must overcome many more obstacles if community policing is ultimately to succeed. Collaborative partnerships between citizens, the police, and other service providers at the neighborhood level have been recommended as offering great potential for reducing crime, fear of crime, and social and physical disorder, and enhancing the overall quality of life of citizens. Documented successes in many American cities include Nashua, Charleston, San Jose, and Spokane. However, we believe that longer term positive effects of community policing are dependent upon the ability of police departments to progress through innovative internal changes and upon the response of citizens to actively participate in community policing and problem solving.

## Study Questions

1. To what extent is the professional police subculture a barrier to the long-term success of community policing? What specifically can be done to foster an organizational subculture of community policing?

2. What is a "learning organization"? How might police departments transform themselves into learning organizations? How does the idea of a learning organization relate to the success of community policing?

3. What specific community strategies might be used in an effort to improve the quality of life of the urban poor?

4. Grinc discusses a variety of external obstacles that threaten the long-term success of community policing. Which barrier is the most difficult to overcome and why? What ideas do you have to overcome this problem?

## Endnotes

1. A. Yost, "Community Policing: Enforcing Law Through Building Relationships," *Neighbors* (August, 1996): 12.
2. *Ibid.*
3. *Ibid.*
4. *Ibid.*
5. Edmund F. McGarrell, Andrew L. Giacomazzi, and Quint C. Thurman, "Neighborhood Disorder, Integration, and the Fear of Crime," *Justice Quarterly* 14 (1997): 479–500; Andrew L. Giacomazzi and Quint C. Thurman, "Cops and Kids Revisited: A Second Year Evaluation of a Community Policing and Delinquency Prevention Innovation," *Police Studies* 17 (1995): 1–20; Quint Thurman and Phil Bogen, "Research Note: Spokane Community Policing Officers Re-Visited," *American Journal of Police* 15 (1996): 97–116; Quint Thurman, Phil Bogen, and Andrew Giacomazzi, "Program Monitoring and Community Policing: A Process Evaluation of Community Policing Officers in Spokane, Washington," *American Journal of Police* 12 (1993): 89–114; Quint Thurman, Andrew Giacomazzi, and Phil Bogen, "Research Note: Cops, Kids, and Community Policing—An Assessment of a Community Policing Demonstration Project," *Crime & Delinquency* 39 (1993): 554–564.

❖ ❖ ❖ ❖    6. David Bayley, "Community Policing: A Report from the Devil's Advocate," in *Community Policing: Rhetoric or Reality?*, eds. Jack R. Greene and Stephen D. Mastrofski (New York: Praeger, 1988); Jack R. Greene and R. B. Taylor, "Community-Based Policing and Foot Patrol: Issues of Theory and Evaluation," in *ibid.*; Mollie Weatheritt, "Community Policing: Rhetoric or Reality?" in *ibid.*; Carl B. Klockars, "The Rhetoric of Community Policing," in *ibid.*; Stephen Mastrofski, "Community Policing as a Reform: A Cautionary Tale," in *ibid.*

7. Dennis P. Rosenbaum and Arthur J. Lurigio, "An Inside Look at Community Policing Reform: Definitions, Organizational Changes, and Evaluation Findings," *Crime and Delinquency* 40 (1994): 299–314.

8. *Ibid.*

9. Malcolm K. Sparrow, "Implementing Community Policing," *Perspectives on Policing* (Washington, DC: U.S. Department of Justice, Office of Justice Programs, November, 1988).

10. Robert Denhardt, *Public Administration: An Action Orientation*, 2nd ed. (Belmont, CA: Wadsworth, 1995).

11. Sparrow, "Implementing Community Policing."

12. Portland (Oregon) Police Bureau Recruiting Flyer (November, 1998).

13. Peter M. Senge, *The Fifth Discipline: The Art and Practice of Learning Organization* (New York: Currency Doubleday, 1994), p. xv.

14. William A. Geller, "Suppose We Were Really Serious About Police Departments Becoming Learning Organizations?" *National Institute of Justice Journal* 237 (December, 1997): 2–7.

15. *Ibid.*

16. *Ibid.*

17. Mary A. Wycoff and Timothy Oettmeier, "Evaluating Patrol Officer Performance Under Community Policing: The Houston Experience," *National Institute of Justice Research Report* (Washington, DC: U.S. Department of Justice, Office of Justice Programs, 1994).

18. *Ibid.*, pp. 7–8.

19. Andrew Giacomazzi, Edmund McGarrell, and Quint Thurman, *Reducing Disorder, Fear, and Crime in Public Housing: An Evaluation of a Drug Crime Elimination Program in Spokane, Washington. A Final Report to the National Institute of Justice* (Unpublished report, 1998).

20. John J. DiIulio, "Rethinking the Criminal Justice System: Toward a New Paradigm," in *Performance Measures for the Criminal Justice System, Discussion Papers from the BJS-Princeton Project* (Washington, DC: U.S. Department of Justice, Office of Justice Program, 1993).

21. Dallin H. Oakes, "Rights and Responsibilities," in *Rights and the Common Good: The Communitarian Perspective*, ed. Amitai Etzioni (New York: St. Martin's, 1995).

22. *Ibid.*

23. Samuel Walker, *Sense and Nonsense About Crime and Drugs: A Policy Guide*, 3rd ed. (Belmont, CA: Wadsworth, 1994).

24. George F. Cole and Christopher E. Smith, *The American System of Criminal Justice*, 8th ed. (Pacific Grove, CA: Wadsworth, 1998).

25. Clifford Shaw and Henry McKay, *Juvenile Delinquency and Urban Areas* (Chicago: University of Chicago Press, 1942); Ronald Burgess, "The Growth of a City," in *The City*, eds. Robert E. Park and Ernest Burgess, (Chicago: University of Chicago Press, 1925).

26. Rodney Stark, "Decent Places: A Theory of the Ecology of Crime," *Criminology* 25 (1987): 893–909.

27. *Ibid.*

28. William Julius Wilson, "Inner City Dislocation," *Society* 21 (November-December, 1983): 80.

29. Cole and Smith, *The American System of Criminal Justice.*

30. Wilson, "Inner City Dislocation."

31. DiIulio, "Rethinking the Criminal Justice System."

32. William H. Brill, *Victimization, Fear of Crime, and Altered Behavior: A Profile of Four Public Housing Projects in Boston* (Washington, DC: Department of Housing and Urban Development, 1975); William H. Brill, *Victimization, Fear of Crime, and Altered Behavior: A Profile of the Crime Problem in William Nickerson, Jr. Gardens, Los Angeles, California* (Washington, DC: U.S. Department of Housing and Urban Development, 1976); William H. Brill, *Millvale Safety and Security Evaluation* (Cincinnati: Cincinnati Housing Authority, 1976); William H. Brill, *Victimization, Fear of Crime, and Altered Behavior: A Profile of the Crime in Capper Dwellings, Washington, DC* (Washington, DC: U.S. Department of Housing and Urban Development, 1977): William H. Brill, *Victimization, Fear of Crime, and Altered Behavior: A Profile of the Crime Problem in Murphy Homes, Baltimore Maryland* (Washington, DC: U.S. Department of Housing and Urban Development, 1977).

33. Terence Dunworth, and Aaron Saiger, *Drugs and Crime in Public Housing: A Three-City Analysis* (Los Angeles: Rand, 1994), xi.

34. *Ibid.*

35. Dennis W. Ronceck, Ralph Bell, and Jeffrey M. A. Francik, "Housing Projects and Crime: Testing a Proximity Hypothesis," *Social Problems* 29 (2)(1981): 151–166; John E. Farley, "Has Public Housing Gotten a Bum Rap? The Incidence of Crime in St. Louis Public Housing Developments," *Environment and Behavior* 14 (1982): 442–477.

36. Harold Holzman, "Criminological Research on Public Housing: Toward a Better Understanding of People, Places, and Spaces," *Crime and Delinquency* 42(3) (1996): 361–378.

37. Jack R. Greene, "Crime Control in Public Housing: What Do We Know?" Paper prepared for the National Institute of Justice Planning Conference on Policing Public Housing, Washington, DC (1997).

38. Susan J. Popkin, Lynn M. Olson, Arthur J. Lurigio, Victoria E. Gwiasda, and Ruth G. Carter, "Sweeping Out Drugs and Crime: Residents' Views of the Chicago Housing Authority's Public Housing Drug Elimination Program," *Crime and Delinquency* 41 (1995): 73–99.

39. Oscar Newman, *Defensible Space: Crime Prevention Through Urban Design* (New York, NY: Macmillan, 1972).

40. Henry G. Cisneros, *Defensible Space: Deterring Crime and Building Community: Second in a Series of Essays* (Washington, DC: U.S. Government Printing Office, 1995).

41. Ralph B. Taylor and Adele V. Harrell, *Physical Environment and Crime* (Washington, DC: U.S. Department of Justice, Office of Justice Programs, 1996).

42. Cisneros, *Defensible Space.*

43. Langley Keyes, *Strategies and Saints: Fighting Drugs in Subsidized Housing* (Washington, DC: Urban Institute, 1992); Harold Holzman, Carl Roger Kudrick, and Kenneth Voytek, "Revisiting the Relationship Between Crime and Architectural Design: An Analysis of HUD's 1994 Survey of Public Housing Residents," *Cityscape: A Journal of Policy Development and Research* 2 (1996): 107–126.

44. Taylor and Harrell, *Physical Environment and Crime.*

45. Steven Lab, "Neighborhood Crime Prevention," in *Crime Prevention: Approaches, Practices and Evaluations* (Cincinnati: Anderson, 1988).

46. Greene, "Crime Control in Public Housing."

47. Theodore M. Hammett, Judith D. Fins, Theresa Mason, and Ingrid Ellen, *Public Housing Drug Elimination Program Evaluation. Vol. 1 Findings* (Cambridge, MA: Abt Associates, 1994).

48. Dennis Rosenbaum, "Community Crime Prevention: A Review and Synthesis of the Literature," *Justice Quarterly* 5 (1988): 323–95.

❖ ❖ ❖ ❖

❖ ❖ ❖ ❖    49. Paul J. Lavrakas, "Citizen Self-Help and Neighborhood Crime Prevention Policy," in *American Violence and Public Policy*, ed. L. A. Curtis (New Haven, CT: Yale University Press, 1985).

50. Aaron Podolefsky and Fred Dubow, *Strategies for Community Crime Prevention* (Springfield, IL: Charles C. Thomas, 1981); Aaron Podolefsky, *Case Studies in Community Crime Prevention* (Springfield, IL: Charles C. Thomas, 1983).

51. Rosenbaum, "Community Crime Prevention."

52. Fred Heinzelmann, "Crime Prevention from a Community Perspective," in *Community Crime Prevention* (Washington, DC: Center for a Responsive Governance, 1983); Douglas D. Perkins, John W. Meeks, and Ralph B. Taylor, "The Physical Environment of Street Blocks and Resident Perceptions of Crime and Disorder: Implications for Theory and Measurement," *Journal of Environmental Psychology* 12 (1992): 21–34; Douglas D. Perkins, Abraham Wandersman, Richard C. Rich, and Ralph B. Taylor, "The Physical Environment of Street Crime: Defensible Space, Territoriality and Incivilities," *Journal of Environmental Psychology* 13 (1993): 29–49; Cisneros, *Defensible Space*.

53. Arthur J. Lurigio and Dennis Rosenbaum, "Evaluation Research in Community Crime Prevention: A Critical Look at the Field," in *Community Crime Prevention: Does It Work?*, ed. Dennis Rosenbaum (Beverly Hills, CA: Sage, 1986).

54. Podolefsky and Dubow, *Strategies*.

55. *Ibid.*

56. S. F. Bennett and Paul J. Lavrakas, *Evaluation of the Planning and Implementation of the Neighborhood Program, Final Process Report to the Eisenhower Foundation* (Evanston, IL: Northwestern University, Center for Urban Affairs and Policy Research, 1988).

57. Stephanie Greenberg, William Rohe, and Jay Williams, "Neighborhood Conditions and Community Crime Control," in *Community Crime Prevention* (Washington, DC: Center for Responsive Governance, 1983).

58. Fred Dubow and David Emmons, "The Community Hypothesis," in *Reactions to Crime*, ed. Dan Lewis (Beverly Hills, CA: Sage, 1981).

59. James Q. Wilson and George Kelling, "Broken Windows," *Atlantic Monthly*, March, 1982, 29–38.

60. Barbara E. Smith and Robert C. Davis, "Successful Community Anticrime Programs: What Makes Them Work," in *Drugs and the Community: Involving Community Residents in Combating the Sale of Illegal Drugs*, eds. Robert C. Davis, Arthur J. Lurigio, and Dennis P. Rosenbaum (Springfield, IL: Charles C. Thomas, 1993).

61. Dennis Rosenbaum, "The Problem of Crime Control," in *Community Crime Prevention: Does it Work?* ed. Dennis P. Rosenbaum (Beverly Hills, CA: Sage, 1986).

62. U.S. Department of Justice, Law Enforcement Assistance Administration, *Got a Minute? You Could Stop Crime* (Washington, DC: Ad Council, 1978).

63. Smith and Davis, "Successful Community Anticrime Programs," p. 124.

64. Anne L. Schneider, "Neighborhood-Based Anti-Burglary Strategies: An Analysis of Public and Private Benefits From the Portland, Oregon Program," in *Community Crime Prevention: Does it Work?* ed. Dennis Rosenbaum (Beverly Hills, CA: Sage, 1986).

65. Smith and Davis, "Successful Community Anticrime Programs."

66. Wilson and Kelling, "Broken Windows;" Wesley Skogan, *Disorder and Decline: Crime and the Spiral of Decay in American Neighborhoods* (Berkeley: University of California Press, 1990).

67. Smith and Davis, "Successful Community Anticrime Programs."

68. *Ibid.*

69. Rosenbaum, "The Problem of Crime Control."

70. Dennis Rosenbaum, "Community Crime Prevention."

71. Wesley Skogan, "Community Organizations and Crime," in *Crime and Justice: A Review of Research*, eds. Albert J. Reiss, Jr. and Michael Tonry (Chicago, IL: University

of Chicago Press, 1987); Dan A. Lewis, J. A. Grant, and Dennis Rosenbaum, *The Social Construction of Reform: Community Organizations and Crime Prevention* (New Brunswick, NJ: Transaction, 1988); J. A. Roehl and R. F. Cook, *Evaluation of the Urban Crime Prevention Program* (Washington, DC: U.S. Department of Justice, National Institute of Justice, 1984); Robert K .Yin, "Community Crime Prevention: A Synthesis of Eleven Evaluations," in *Community Crime Prevention: Does It Work?* ed., Dennis Rosenbaum (Beverly Hills, CA: Sage, 1986).

72. Susan J. Popkin, et al., "Sweeping Out Drugs and Crime: Residents;" T. M. Hammett et. al. *Public Housing Drug Elimination.*

73. Wesley Skogan, *Disorder and Decline: Crime and the Spiral Decay in American Neighborhoods* (Berkeley: University of California Press, 1990); L. Schuerman and S. Kobrin, "Community Careers in Crime," in *Communities and Crime*, eds. Albert J. Reiss and Michael Tonry (Chicago: University of Chicago Press, 1986).

74. Ronald V. Clarke, *Situational Crime Prevention: Successful Case Studies* (New York: Harrow & Heston, 1992).

75. Greenberg, Rohe, and Williams, "Neighborhood Conditions"; Richard P. Taub, D. Garth Taylor, and Jan Dunham, "Neighborhoods and Safety," in *Reactions to Crime*, ed. Dan A. Lewis (Newbury Park, CA: Sage, 1981).

76. J. Garofalo and M. McLeod, *Improving the Effectiveness and Utilization of Neighborhood Watch Programs*, (Unpublished report to the National Institute of Justice from the State University of New York at Albany, Hindelang Criminal Justice Research Center, 1986).

77. Dan A. Lewis, Jane A. Grant, and Dennis Rosenbaum, *The Social Construction of Reform: Community Organizations and Crime Prevention* (New Brunswick, NJ: Transaction, 1988); J. A. Roehl and R. F. Cook, *Evaluation of the Urban Crime Prevention Program* (Washington, DC: U.S. Department of Justice, National Institute of Justice, 1984); Robert K. Yin, "Community Crime Prevention: A Synthesis of Eleven Evaluations," in *Community Crime Prevention: Does it Work?*, ed. Dennis P. Rosenbaum (Beverly Hills, CA: Sage, 1986).

78. Oakes, "Rights and Responsibilities."

79. Randolph Grinc, "Angels in Marble: Problems in Stimulating Community Involvement in Community Policing," *Crime and Delinquency* 40 (1994): 437–468.

80. Giacomazzi, McGarrell, and Thurman, *Reducing Disorder, Fear, and Crime.*

81. Wesley Skogan and S. Annan, "Drug Enforcement in Public Housing," in *Drugs and the Community: Involving Community Residents in Combating the Sale of Illegal Drugs*, eds. Robert C. Davis, Arthur Lurigio, and Dennis Rosenbaum (Springfield, IL: Charles C. Thomas, 1993).

82. Deborah L. Weisel, *Tackling Drug Problems in Public Housing: A Guide for Police* (Washington, DC: Police Research Forum, 1990).

83. Skogan and Annan, "Drug Enforcement in Public Housing."

84. Grinc, "Angels in Marble."

85. DiIulio, "Rethinking the Criminal Justice System."

86. Smith and Davis, "Successful Community Anticrime Programs."

87. Giacomazzi, McGarrell, and Thurman, *Reducing Disorder, Fear, and Crime.*

88. Grinc, "Angels in Marble."

89. *Ibid.*, p. 453.

90. *Ibid.*

91. *Ibid.*

92. *Ibid.*

93. *Ibid.*; Giacomazzi, McGarrell, and Thurman, *Reducing Disorder, Fear, and Crime.* ✦

# Chapter Thirteen

# The Future of Community Policing

❖ ❖ ❖ ❖

*Twenty years from now you will be more disappointed by the things that you didn't do than the ones you did do. So throw off the bowlines. Sail away from the safe harbor. Catch the trade winds in your sails. Explore dreams. Discover.*

—Mark Twain

**W**hat is the direction of community policing in the twenty-first century? A similar question was asked at the start of the twentieth century when modern policing was in its infancy. Predicting the future of any occupation or organization is a formidable task that is fraught with difficulty. For example, many innovations in the criminal justice system that once were predicted to have far-reaching effects have failed to do so. In his book, *Sense and Nonsense About Crime*, noted scholar Samuel Walker studied the impact of 20 such innovations proposed by either liberals or conservatives and found that very few of them met with expectations.[1]

In that light, it might be wiser not to speculate about the future of American policing. However, aside from the fact that the authors find the challenge irresistible, two other reasons for doing so are compelling. First, we believe that a fairly accurate forecast of police departments over the next five years is possible because community policing is well underway as a new style of policing. The concept of community policing and its implementation has a history that spans two decades if the pilot studies on foot patrol in Flint, Michigan, and Newark, New Jersey, are considered.[2]

A second reason that we believe that prediction is warranted is that the implementation of community policing has been accompanied by a strong emphasis on research evaluation, especially over the past five years. As discussed in previous chapters, we can draw on the results from several studies to inform our predictions based upon information that is both theoretical and practical.

## Where Community Policing Is Now and Where It Is Going

Before any prediction can be made, it is important to know what is the pattern of change in community policing. In chapter 4, three stages of organizational change proposed by Robert Yin were introduced.[3] The first stage involved initiation, that is, the implementation of innovative activities. In this stage an organization tries a variety of innovations and then assesses their respective utility. Effective innovations are retained, while ineffective ones are discontinued.

James Thompson noted that during the initiation stage, these innovative programs are isolated from the core of an operation.[4] This means that innovations are not deliberately integrated into the formal organizational structure. In addition, they are evaluated by organizational rationality based upon social recognition rather than by technical rationality based on a cost-and-benefit analysis, even though the latter is more certain.

The pattern of change in community policing is similar to what Thompson predicted about the initiation stage of organizational change. As discussed in the previous chapters, the change process always starts with the adoption of innovative programs. The number of programs will differ depending on the size and location of the police department. The New York Police Department, for example, may implement more programs than a medium-sized police department because it is much larger and is located in a very dynamic environment.

Innovative programs such as foot patrols and storefront police substations are generally set up by a designated unit, which, to a large extent, is isolated from core police operations such as patrol and criminal investigations. This isolation allows police administrators to have better control of new programs before they can decide to expand the scope, change the focus, or even terminate the programs without disturbing the normal operations of the department.

A review of the literature on community policing suggests that a majority of innovative programs are rarely implemented more widely than by a special unit.[5] The primary means of evaluating innovative programs is customer satisfaction. This evaluation is usually done by conducting a variety of citizen surveys and interviews about their contacts with beat police officers. The effectiveness of these programs is then determined according to organizational rationality. Does this program generate social recognition? Do residents like the program?

After 20 years of community policing, there has been no unrefutable evidence that it significantly reduces crime in a community. This means that technical rationality based upon a cost and benefits analysis cannot be applied to community policing innovations. The bottom line is this—despite

*Positive interactions with key members of a community—its children—help to build public trust among the police and future generations.*

❖ ❖ ❖ ❖    some 20 years of efforts, community policing as a form of organizational change still remains largely at the initiation stage.

Most of the research in policing suggests that community policing is the future model for American policing in the twenty-first century. Consequently, community policing should progress naturally toward the second stage identified by Yin, the institutionalization of change.

Institutionalization has several important aspects. The first concerns organizational structure. To institutionalize community policing, the structure of police departments needs to be modified so that innovations may be integrated. Innovative units must become a formal part of patrol operations or criminal investigations rather than remain as isolated units. The second is that evaluation of community policing should move beyond simply measuring citizen satisfaction. Although it is extremely valuable to learn what local communities think of a police program, technical rationality must be achieved, and clearly defined measures to facilitate institutionalization should be developed. The third aspect, as discussed in earlier chapters, concerns the culture of police departments, which must be altered in a direction consistent with community policing.

The next sections present the positive, negative, and uncertain forces that affect the institutionalization of community policing. The purpose is to examine the feasibility of community policing in the near future.

## Positive Forces

In order to predict whether or not the institutionalization of community policing will be the future of American policing, it is necessary to examine the competing forces of change and evaluate the possible outcomes. Four specific forces seem to favor the change to community policing.

### More Community Policing Programs

First, community policing programs are very popular with police executives, other community leaders, and the public as evidenced by the considerable increase in these programs over the past five years. Recent studies show that community policing is widespread, having been adopted not only in a few large police departments but also in medium and small departments that traditionally have followed the winds of change.[6] In addition to the expansion of community policing, there also is a wider variety of community policing programs in place compared to the previous five years.

In the 1980s, the primary focus of community policing programs was to reduce citizen fear of crime and social disorder. For example, an important factor behind the implementation of the foot-patrol program in the Houston Police Department was to reduce the fear of crime; an evaluation of the program found that it was effective in reducing public fear of crime.[7] At that time, only a handful of community policing programs were identified as such, including foot patrol, special units, and neighborhood watch.[8] Recent developments have substantially expanded the variety of programs available.[9] The Resolving Conflict Creatively Program (RCCP) implemented in the New York City and the Boston Police Youth Corps are examples.[10]

The expansion of community policing programs makes organizational change in policing more visible to the public and the news media. It seems fair to say that the longer police departments can keep up the momentum of innovation, the more likely it is that innovations will be institutionalized.

## Strong Support From the Federal Government Since 1994

The second positive force behind institutionalization of community policing has been the very strong endorsement of the federal government after the passage of the Violent Crime Control and Law Enforcement Act in 1994. This statute represents "an investment of more than $30 billion over six years. . . . [It] is the largest Federal anti-crime legislation in the Nation's history."[11] As a direct result of this legislation the federal government is actively involved in the national implementation of community policing. In addition, this act subsidized the hiring of an additional 100,000 officers who must promote community policing goals in their departments. A key example of this effort includes the establishment of COPS. A primary goal of COPS is to ensure the institutionalization of community policing innovations in police departments across the country. COPS coordinates and supervises federally subsidized community policing programs and oversees evaluations. The creation of 35 community policing regional training institutes across the nation is another important step taken to expand the scope of implementation.[12]

Similarly, as a direct result of the 1994 Crime Act there has been more money available for research and evaluation than at any other time in the history of American policing. Many of COPS' grants to local departments, for example, include provisions for research and evaluation. There has been a substantial increase in research activities to document the progress of community policing. In sum, the direct involvement of the federal government, particularly the Clinton administration, provides much needed funding and technical support for the implementation of community policing.

## The Use of Technology

A third positive force for change is the increase in the use of advanced technology in community policing. Since the early 1990s, community policing innovations have extended to the use of hi-tech tools for combating urban crimes and reducing social disorder. Computerized statistics (CompStat) is a good example of this development. Police departments in several large cities such as Boston, Indianapolis, and Chicago have used CompStat and computer-mapping technology to disseminate information to all the ranks of officers to make them all accountable for fighting crime. The best-known use of CompStat was in New York in 1993 under the leadership of then police commissioner William Bratton. During his brief tenure, Bratton chided his sworn personnel: "No one ever lost his job over not having the right answers. No one gets into trouble for crime being up in their precinct. People got in trouble if they didn't know what the crime was and had no strategy to deal with it."[13]

As the first step in CompStat, personnel from each of the 76 New York City precincts, nine police service areas, and 12 transit districts compiled a statistical summary of the week's crime incidents. Next, the information on arrests, summons activity, use of firearms, and victims was forwarded to cen-

❖ ❖ ❖ ❖    tral headquarters. These data included the specific times, locations of the crimes, and police activities. The CompStat unit in the department loaded the information into a citywide database for an analysis of crime patterns. A weekly CompStat report was then generated to present a concise summary of crime incidents and other important performance indicators.

The next step in CompStat involved crime strategy meetings attended by senior administrators, all the precinct commanders, and supervisors of specialized investigative units. These meetings were usually convened every two weeks from 7 A.M. to 10 A.M. in the command and control center. Every commander was expected to be called on at random to make his or her presentation approximately once a month. During the presentation, the commander had to analyze the pattern of crime incidents in the area, potential problems, and the strategies adopted or planned to deal with them. The presentation was aided with a computerized "pin mapping" technology that displayed crimes, arrests, and quality-of-life data in a series of visual formats including charts, graphs, and tables. During the presentation, the senior administrators frequently asked commanders questions and looked for solutions.[14]

The significance of using CompStat is that the precinct commanders and supervisors were held accountable for an increase or decrease in local crimes and social disorder. Therefore, they were forced to develop new strategies to reduce neighborhood crimes. At the same time, the lower level of management also was held responsible for their respective areas because the "pin mapping" was able to display crime patterns at the street level. CompStat became the crucial link that demanded accountability at every level of the department.

*The use of high technology promises greater coordination of police resources, as well as more systematic tracking and evaluation of a department's effectiveness. (Photo: Mark C. Ide)*

New York City mayor Rudolph Giuliani observed that                    ❖ ❖ ❖ ❖

CompStat transformed the Department from an organization that reacted to crime to a Department that actively works to deter offenses. Before CompStat, the Department's 76 precinct commanders were isolated from the Department's top executives. Under the CompStat system, precinct commanders meet with the Police Commissioner and other high-ranking members of the Department at semi-weekly meetings to identify local crime patterns, select tactics, and allocate resources. Arrests are no longer the measure of effective policing—commanders are now responsible for deterring crime.[15]

Similarly, the Chicago Police Department adopted the Information Collection for Automated Mapping (ICAM) computer program. This program has two primary features. First, it can produce a map of reported offenses of a particular type in an area, or it can generate a list of the 10 most frequently reported offenses in a patrol beat. Second, it can generate a map and conduct a search of a particular type of offense. The unique part of the ICAM program is that the computer terminals can be installed at the district level, and supervisors and patrol officers can have access to ICAM. In essence, the availability of this high-tech program facilitates the problem-solving efforts in the department. The ICAM program has been well received in Chicago. It is estimated that 20 percent of all officers use ICAM regularly, and 60 percent use it occasionally. From June 26 to July 25, 1995, a total of 6,689 queries were requested in the department, or 223 queries per day.[16]

## The Crime Rate Is Down

The fourth positive force for change is that crime rates are down. No matter what happens, police departments are essentially evaluated by the local crime rate because the public believes that crime is the most important component of their job description. It is one thing for a police department to establish a few outreach programs and improve the quality of life in a community, but it is another if the crime rate remains the same or rises; then pressure falls on the police to respond appropriately.

As discussed in chapter 5, a primary reason for the police to move toward community policing is that, for most of the 1960s and 1970s, the rates for both violent and property crimes were up significantly. Since the early 1990s, however, the crime rate has been declining. According to the *Uniform Crime Report*, for example, the crime index rate fell for the sixth straight year in 1997 and was down almost 17 percent from 1991. In addition, the violent crime rate declined 7 percent, continuing the downward trend since 1994.[17] In nearly all major cities, including New York, Los Angeles, and Chicago, the number of murders has dropped significantly. In turn, the continuing decline of crime rates has captured the attention of almost all major news networks and received extensive coverage. American cities are becoming safer.

Who should be given the credit for this declining crime rate? Unquestionably, the implementation of community policing has received much of the praise. In a recent public address, President Clinton stated, "In 1997, crime decreased for the sixth straight year thanks in part to community policing. Our commitment to American's law enforcement officers is working to keep our streets and communities safe."[18] To date, law enforcement agencies have

❖ ❖ ❖ ❖    added more than 88,000 community policing officers to patrol the streets, and the public seems to have responded favorably to this trend. Although other factors, such as the aging of the baby boomer generation, might also account for declining crime rates, community policing is widely perceived to be at least partially responsible.[19]

Even at the local level, the reduction of crime has been attributed to community policing innovations. Since 1993, overall crime was down more than 43 percent in New York City. The city's murder rate at the time was at its lowest level since the late 1960s, and Mayor Giuliani gave much of the credit to the NYPD and its new methods for dealing with crime and incivilities: "A very critical component of the success of the New York City Police Department has been an innovative style of police management called CompStat."[20] Although some might debate whether or not CompStat and community policing are synonymous, this New York style of meeting the public-safety needs of its citizens has been credited with achieving miraculous results.

Similarly, in Boston, the police and juvenile probation officers joined hands and created an innovative program, Operation Night Light, to prevent juvenile probationers from getting into trouble again and again. At night, police and juvenile probation officers visited each probationer's residence to make sure the person stayed at home. Since the inception of the program, the number of juveniles killed by gunfire has greatly diminished. In fact, from July 1995 to December 1997, not a single boy or girl in the city was murdered. Much of this success has been attributed to Operation Night Light.

In sum, the decline of crime has provided the police with a favorable external environment. They can show the nation that community policing is working and that people are benefiting from these innovative programs. All four of these positive forces keep the momentum of community policing moving forward toward institutionalization.

## Negative Forces

### Ambiguity About COP

The first negative force that impedes change concerns the ambiguity surrounding the definition of community policing. What is community policing anyway? As discussed in the first chapter, questions remain. Police administrators and quite a few scholars have a hard time defining the term despite the popularity of community policing across the nation. John Eck and Dennis Rosenbaum argue that, "One reason for its popularity is that community policing is a plastic concept, meaning different things to different people."[21] Furthermore, Mark Moore has suggested that, "It is important that the concept mean something, but not something too specific . . . the ambiguity is a virtue."[22] However, it is exactly the virtue of looseness as a concept that may act as an impediment to its institutionalization.[23]

Today, it is difficult to reject community policing as a welcome reform because every program implemented in a police department can be labeled a community policing innovation of one type or another. At the same time, it is difficult to accept it as a legitimate reform movement as long as its definition remains largely elusive. For example, after almost two full decades of imple-

mentation, there is not a single department that can claim to have implemented community policing completely, to have institutionalized its principles throughout the department. Community policing remains a loosely
defined concept, with definitions that vary from broad abstraction to narrow
specificity.

As discussed in an earlier chapter, three distinctive theories might
explain the institutionalization of the police during the professional era.
They are: (1) scientific management articulated by Taylor, focusing on one
best way and technical rationality; (2) the "ideal-type" of bureaucracy suggested by Weber, emphasizing the structural rationality of management; and
(3) Gulick's organizational-supervision approach that proposes a chain of
command and span of control. As previously suggested, the institutionalization of the bureaucratic style of policing was guided by a clearly developed
theoretical framework for a specific structural arrangement.

Community policing, however, lacks this theoretical refinement. The theoretical framework continues to remain relatively undefined or "plastic," as
more new programs labeled community policing are added nearly every day.
The authors believe that this confusion at the theoretical level threatens to
impede the institutionalization of community policing.

## The Largely Unchanged Organizational Structure

The second negative force that impedes the institutionalization of community policing concerns structural change in police departments. In general, organizational structure can be defined as "the enduring characteristics
of an organization reflected by the distribution of units and positions within
the organization and their systematic relationships with each other."[24] This
definition suggests that an organizational structure is relatively permanent.
Unlike innovative programs that can easily be modified or dropped, the
structure of an organization, especially the core structure, is not very easy to
change over a short period of time.

Peter Blau identified two dimensions of organizational structure based
on a study of 53 public employment security agencies.[25] As discussed in an
earlier chapter, the horizontal dimension has two components: spatial differentiation and occupational differentiation. Spatial differentiation is the
extent to which an organization's tasks are divided among subordinate units,
for example, the number of different units in a police department. Occupational differentiation is the number of different specialties available in an
organization, that is, the extent of the division of labor. The number of specialists (e.g., crime lab specialists and computer analysts) is greater in the
New York Police Department, for example, than in the Omaha Police Department.

The vertical dimension, or hierarchy, concerns the distribution of authority, reflecting the degree of managerial control. In a police department, organizational hierarchy can be assessed by the number of ranks from police officer at the bottom to the chief at the top. It is assumed that the more levels in
the hierarchy, the more formalized the organizational structure. The more
formal the structure, the less likely it is to institutionalize innovations.

As previously mentioned, three anthologies published since 1994 focus
on community policing.[26] They contain many influential research studies,

❖ ❖ ❖ ❖    but only a few of them refer to the relationship between structural change and the institutionalization of community policing. Among these few, there is a consensus that organizational hierarchy impedes innovations.[27] Little research is available on the relationship between reducing organizational hierarchy and community policing innovations. Research is very limited on how to incorporate community policing programs into the formal structure of a police department. Very little has been written on the need to increase the horizontal structure of a police department and flatten the vertical structure if community policing is to be institutionalized. Studies on this topic tend to focus on evaluation of community policing programs.

## Uncertain Forces

### The Increase in Paramilitary Policing Units

About three decades ago, Egon Bittner argued that the use of force is the defining feature of American police.[28] Therefore, he argued, crime control will always be the core function of police work. This view of American policing seems to rule out any substantial deviation from the bureaucratic or professional model because community policing promotes the idea of police-community partnerships to produce order. In addition, community policing recommends a reprioritization of police functions to make controlling social disorder and provision of services more important.

The purpose of a paramilitary policing unit (PPU) or Special Weapons and Tactics (SWAT) unit in a police department is straightforward. These highly trained law enforcement bodies can be swiftly deployed with an impressive use of force. During the last 10 years when students of American policing were focusing mostly on an expansion of community policing, there also has been a less noticeable trend toward the militarization of some components of the American police. Peter Kraska and Louis Cubellis conducted a survey of police departments serving small jurisdictions of 25,000 to 50,000 citizens.[29] The 40 items of the survey were designed to collect data on the formation, prevalence, and activities of PPUs in small cities that had not previously had a paramilitary emphasis. More than half of the departments completed and returned the survey. Kraska and Cubellis noted three important findings. First, they found a rapid expansion of PPUs in these departments between 1985 and 1995 (an increase of 157 percent). More and more departments have established PPUs to call on for hostage situations, acts of terrorism, civil disturbances, and high-risk search and arrests—infrequent activities in small cities. Second, the establishment of a PPU was not linked to worsening conditions because there was no increase in crime rates, drug use, fear of crime or the economic problems in these small cities. Third, in Kraska and Cubellis' opinion, the emergence of the PPU represents a pent-up desire to return to an earlier era that was characterized by the war on drugs and crimes. In the light of these findings, one might conclude that rather than becoming more open and progressive, the police culture may be returning to a more paramilitaristic orientation and one that proved largely ineffective in dealing with the conditions and causes of crime in the 1970s as discussed in chapter 5.

The authors believe that the growth of PPUs constitutes an uncertain force affecting the institutionalization of community policing, because any incident involving the police use of force can lead to conflict between police and residents in a community, particularly minority residents. The history of police-community relations in this country is replete with examples of peaceful demonstrations turning violent because of an inappropriate police action or because a controversial court decision appeared to exonerate police misconduct. The fact that PPUs are being established in small cities not as a result of an increase in crimes or social disorder but as an appeasement to a paramilitary culture suggests a grave error may be in the making. It could force a showdown between factions who embrace a community problem solving approach and factions who wish to return to the narrower mission of law enforcement and reactive policing.

## The Role of the Police Unions

Research in community policing is almost completely silent on the relationship between police unions and organizational change. Police unions have played an important role in the history of American policing. In general, unions are not advocates for change. Unions tend more toward fighting for the benefits of ordinary employees and for power sharing with management.[30]

Unions operating in the public sector have similar interests to those in the private sector. Labor relations often take on the character of intense and tough "battles" with management to settle a host of issues connected primarily to the economic interests of employees.[31] In the recent history of police

*There has been a marked increase in paramilitary police units in cities of all sizes, even without a justifying increase in crime. (Photo: Mark C. Ide)*

❖ ❖ ❖ ❖  unions in America, there has been a tough "war" between the management and unions concerning economic benefits and management discretion.[32] Recent research confirms that the collective bargaining by police unions does produce economic benefits for police officers.

In police departments that use collective bargaining, a number of management issues such as the allocation of manpower and structural change need the approval of police unions. In addition, any new department policies concerning disciplinary actions and employee benefits usually involve the participation of police unions. If unions are to play an important role in such managerial issues, then they might be expected to be heavily involved in the process of structural and operational changes brought about by community policing. For example, community policing encourages police officers to know their beats and interact with local residents, which could mean a longer shift assignment for individual officers. At this point, however, there is little information about the role of police unions in the implementation of community policing. The role of PPUs and police unions in the institutionalization of community policing will be determined over time.

## The Future Direction of Community Policing

If organizational change is represented as a continuum between the bureaucratic style of policing during the professional era at one end and the community policing style of the community era at the other end, American policing might be described as making some progress away from the bureaucratic style toward the community policing style. Movement in such a direction does not mean, however, that community policing has been fully institutionalized.

Considering the positive, negative, and uncertain forces affecting the institutionalization of community policing, the authors predict that in the next five years community policing will neither be institutionalized in all American police departments nor abandoned. Probably, it will continue to be somewhere in the middle. The following text suggests what students of policing might expect to see over the next few years:

*Community policing innovations will continue to expand in police departments across the United States.* Police departments will continue to explore new ways of doing things as long as the external environment remains dynamic, which is likely. More demands concerning crime, social disorder, and quality of life will force police departments and their leaders to respond and change. Community policing innovations are a good way to demonstrate that police departments are responsive to the needs of the community. There is little to risk for a local chief of police to implement outreach programs such as citizen academy, block watch, and storefront stations. These programs have been around for several years, and the public seems to like them. Programs that target crime reduction, such as weed and seed programs, also are well received. *Weed and seed* is a federally funded program that is divided into two parts. The *weed* part is strong law enforcement. Police target high-crime areas and officers intensify their law enforcement activities. The *seed* part focuses on community rebuilding, crime prevention, etc. The popularity of two types of program—crime-focused or prevention-focused—may depend on local crime trends. If the crime rate in a community has increased significantly, the crime-focused program will be given a high priority and vice-versa. Either way, the police stand to lose little and gain the support of the public by trying innovative solutions.

The authors also expect that *change in the organizational structure of police departments will occur at a very slow pace.* Structural changes involve greater risks than programmatic changes because of the high investment of personnel in the current way of doing things. For example, to reduce the rank structure by eliminating the rank of lieutenant would take some time to get through city politics, rewrite job descriptions for sergeants and captains, develop new policies, and relocate the lieutenants. Modifying the span of organizational control and chain of command is always perceived as risky. Throughout police history, the structural arrangements in police departments have been relatively stable. Consequently, there is little reason to believe that substantial structural change will take place at a rapid pace any time in the near future.

Nevertheless, it is important to acknowledge the necessity of change. American society is changing and so are other public-service agencies. Seen

## Noble-Cause Corruption and the Future of American Policing

### John P. Crank

Phrases such as "Fort Apache," the "choir boys," and the "thin blue line" have been used in American literature at various times to paint a compelling portrait of the police subculture in our country's largest cities. This subculture, defined partly by the unique work of the police and partly by the unique workers themselves who find themselves isolated from the mere civilians who have never worn the badge, is comprised of those persons who have answered a call to protect and serve. Unfortunately, taken to an extreme, this calling can have drawbacks that continue to threaten the legitimacy of the profession and test the morality of individual police officers. A case in point is unethical or illegal behavior that appears justifiable under special circumstances, otherwise referred to as noble-cause corruption.

Noble-cause corruption is ignoble behavior committed in the name of good ends. It is corruption committed in order to get the bad guys off the streets at all costs, to protect the innocent and the children from the predators that inflict pain and suffering on them. It occurs when officers do questionable or even harmful things because they believe that the outcomes ultimately will be good. But in today's world of intricate social and legal complexity, there has to be a limit on the zeal police show for their work. All too often, there is not.

Americans live in a country where the authority of the police to intervene in the affairs of the citizenry is on the rise. Traditional due-process restrictions of police authority are being relaxed. Citizens, other justice professionals, and legislators inadvertently encourage illegal police conduct by challenging cops to "do something about crime." Amid such an environment, opportunities for noble-cause corruption will prove difficult to resist. The power of the police to intervene in citizen's lives stems directly from the courts, whose legal opinions are in turn driven by public opinion favorable to stern justice. It is a power that can be used for good or evil. It has enormous power to corrupt individual police officers.

To understand how police can be corrupted by their work, we need to first recognize that most police officers strongly believe in the "core" activity of their work, doing something about crime. Sometimes the public thinks of uniformed police as automatons in blue, without feelings, dispensing law in a "just the facts, ma'am" style of police work. Police personnel, however, believe in their work, and they carry it out passionately. They care about getting "bad guys" off the streets, and they are morally committed to this task. For the police, good and evil are concrete

❖ ❖ ❖ ❖   ☞

notions practiced in their daily world. The police see themselves on the side of the angels. And they deal with bad guys and "assholes," who, they firmly believe, are associates of the non-angelic crowd. But it is precisely this—the nature of good and evil, and who decides which is which—that is up for grabs in the times we live in.

The central theme in my book *Police Ethics: The Corruption of Noble Cause*, co-authored by Michael Caldero, is that the police subculture is intensely moral, and members of the subculture use the law to enforce that morality on the street. When an officer makes a questionable arrest, or when an "asshole" is thumped, or when an officer tells lies on the witness stand to protect another officer or put away a "bad guy," the police are acting out of strongly held moral beliefs. These are all examples of noble-cause corruption, corruption in the name of the moral rightness of good ends. Noble cause corruption is consequently about how police can be corrupted while they are carrying out their firmest beliefs. In a dark way, it is the police's strongly felt desire to protect the innocent from cruelty that sometimes carries the seeds of the police's own undoing.

A commitment to noble cause is pervasive in police practice. Officers are selected, in large part, because of their commitment, and many aspects of police work reinforce it. Police hiring, police discretion, administrative oversight, and community policing all need to be rethought in terms of the noble cause and its consequences. The hiring process, for example, reinforces the noble cause in important ways. Police departments seek a particular kind of officer, and extensive screening ensures that police officers think a particular, moral way. Those that don't think the right way—that is, those who don't share a commitment to the noble cause—are unlikely to be invited to join the force.

Noble-cause corruption is a form of what ethicists call a means-ends dilemma. Hubert Packer shows how the justice system creates pressure to deemphasize police concerns over the due process laws and administrative guidelines and emphasize criminal justice "ends" such as the accumulation of arrest statistics.[1] But police work is focused too much on ends. The police sense of identity is bound up in the achievement of order. They tend to believe that there are ends so noble, so right, that sometimes it's okay to bend the rules a bit. Sometimes they end up bending the rules a lot. Ends-oriented thinking is pervasive to professional era policing. The challenge to community policing is to prevent it from becoming central there as well. An officer who believes that he or she is the guardian of neighborhood order is simply exchanging ends-oriented law enforcement for ends-oriented order maintenance. The problems of noble-cause corruption are left unaddressed and may in fact increase if police are not careful.

In our book Caldero and I argue for a means-oriented ethic of negotiated order that will prepare police for America's future. The United States is in the midst of profound demographic changes, in rural as well as urban areas. The population is radically diversifying in ethnicity and racial character, and economic growth is creating crime and disorder pressures in traditionally rural areas. The reality we confront of this as a nation is a polyglot of ethnic, religious, racial, age, and income groups. For the most part, they don't live in enclaves but mix and mingle in heterogeneous neighborhoods. Policing, in order to adapt to the needs of the twenty-first century, requires a refocusing from moral ends to negotiated ends. Order is not to be asserted but negotiated.

Today, the police are responding to changes in the urban and rural American landscape by implementing what is commonly called community policing. What will the role of a community police officer be in the twenty-first century? The idea that the future will be full of neighborhoods of like-minded individuals is false. We don't need police to be guardians of some sort of moral order that exists only mythically in neighborhoods and certainly doesn't describe the way in which the country is becoming increasingly diversified along religious, ethnic, and income lines. To respond to the dramatic changes in American society, the country needs police to be *negotiators of public order*. Skills at negotiating will be the tools police will use to enable people to get along. Ends-oriented thinking cannot do the job. Means-oriented thinking, Caldero and I believe, can.

Noble-cause corruption is particularly difficult to deal with because it involves ☞

☞

behaviors consistent with the beliefs of many police officers. Their identification with victims and stern determination to get criminals off the street are powerful and admirable elements of police work, and they provide the core elements of the noble cause. But they also foster a psychology that justifies corruption for noble causes. Noble-cause corruption will pose a challenge in the future for community policing just as it has throughout the previous eras of American policing. The motivation to make the right things happen has to be tempered by the commitment to do things the right way.

---

John Crank received his Ph.D. from the University of Colorado and currently is an associate professor of criminal justice at Boise State University. Dr. Crank continues to study police organizations and police subculture and has published dozens of articles on these and related subjects. He is author of *Understanding Police Culture* (1998) and coauthor with Michael Caldero of *Police Ethics: The Corruption of Noble Cause* (1999).

### Endnote

1. Packer, Hubert. 1968. *The Limits of the Criminal Justice Sanction.* Stanford, CA: Stanford University Press.

---

in this perspective, community policing is a part of broader social change. The current round of change in public-service agencies began in the late 1980s. The National Commission on the Public Service highlights the need for organizational change in public service by calling for a return to a public-service ethic:

> The central message of this report of the Commission on the Public Service is both simple and profound, both urgent and timeless. In essence, we call for a renewed sense of commitment by all Americans to the highest traditions of the public service—to a public service responsive to the political will of the people and also protective of our constitutional values.[33]

As we discussed in chapter 9, some scholars emphasize the need to change public-service practices—a theme commonly referred to as "reinventing government." In their book, David Osborne and Ted Gaebler provide a forceful argument that American public service is in crisis and that a fundamental change is essential for its survival:

> And then, in 1990, the bottom fell out. It was as if all our government had hit the wall, at the same time. Our states struggled with multibillion-dollar deficits. Our cities laid off thousands of employees. Our federal deficit ballooned toward $350 billion.[34]

The economic turnaround in the 1990s has changed much of the political landscape in America. Municipal governments have enjoyed a considerable economic surplus, and the economy remains strong across the country. Change is continuous and will surely affect police departments.

Crises like social turmoil and rising crime rates breed change in policing. This was the case for American policing during the late 1960s and 1970s when crime rates rose to an astonishing level, and the professional-style means to control crime proved to be ineffective. Today, police departments across the nation are in a much better position than they were 25 years ago. Seen from this perspective, there really is no compelling reason why police departments should make broad and sweeping organizational changes, as long as external sources are not beckoning their leadership to do so.

❖ ❖ ❖ ❖

*The concerns and future of a community should be reflected in the practices and goals of its police department. (Photo: Mark C. Ide)*

Unless police executives and employees share the same vision for how organizational change can serve both police personnel and the public, the future of substantial organizational change in American policing is likely to be slow. The future of community policing remains uncertain, at least in terms of the important dimension of organizational change. The authors think that although police departments will continue to make programmatic responses to the need for change that the external environment demands, community policing still has a way to go before it is institutionalized. But, we do think it is headed in a forward direction.

## Study Questions

1.  What forces seem to indicate that community policing will probably be institutionalized in the next few years? Identify and briefly discuss each.

2.  What forces could impede the institutionalization of community policing? Identify and briefly discuss each.

3.  Identify and briefly discuss the two forces that make predicting the success of community policing difficult.

4.  What are PPUs and what does their popularity in police departments say about the police culture of those departments?

## Endnotes

1.  Samuel Walker, *Sense and Nonsense About Crime* (Monterey, CA: Brooks/Cole, 1985).
2.  Robert Trojanowicz and Bonnie Bucqueroux, *Community Policing: A Contemporary Perspective* (Cincinnati: Anderson, 1990). For a discussion of theoretical framework, see Herman Goldstein, *Policing a Free Society* (Cambridge, MA:

Ballinger, 1977); John Angell, "Toward an Alternative to the Classic Police Organizational Arrangement: A Democratic Model," *Criminology* 8 (1971): 185–206.

3. Robert Yin, *Changing Urban Bureaucracies* (Lexington, MA: Lexington Books, 1979).

4. James Thompson, *Organizations in Action* (New York: McGraw-Hill, 1967).

5. There is very little research on the relationship between a change in organizational structure and COP innovations. To a large extent, there has been limited effort to change the structural arrangements of a police department in order to make COP programs permanent. Please also see, Jack Greene, William Bergman, and Edward McLaughlin, "Implementing Community Policing: Cultural and Structural Change in Police Organizations," in *The Challenge of Community Policing: Testing the Promises*, ed. Dennis Rosenbaum (Thousand Oaks, CA: Sage, 1994), pp. 92–109.

6. Please see two books on this topic: Dennis Rosenbaum, *The Challenge of Community Policing: Testing the Promises* (Thousand Oaks, CA: Sage, 1994); and Quint Thurman and Edmund McGarrell, *Community Policing in a Rural Setting* (Cincinnati, OH: Anderson, 1997).

7. Mary Ann Wycoff, "The Benefits of Community Policing: Evidence and Conjecture," in *Community Policing: Rhetoric or Reality?* eds. Jack Greene and Stephen Mastrofski (New York: Praeger, 1988), pp. 103–120.

8. Please see the discussion in Jack Greene and Stephen Mastrofski, *Community Policing: Rhetoric or Reality?* (New York: Praeger, 1988). The programs were the early phase of implementation of community policing.

9. Please read in chapter 10, which focuses on the implementation of community policing.

10. William DeJong, *Building the Peace: The Resolving Conflict Creatively Program (RCCP)* (Washington, DC: National Institute of Justice, 1994).

11. National Institute of Justice, *Criminal Justice Research Under the Crime Act—1995 to 1996* (Washington, DC: U.S. Department of Justice, 1997), p. 2.

12. Office of Community Oriented Policing Services, *Community Cops* (Washington, DC: U.S. Department of Justice, February/March, 1997).

13. William Bratton, *Turnaround: How America's Top Cop Reversed the Crime Epidemic* (New York: Random House, 1998), p. 239.

14. The above information is obtained on the website of the New York Police Department at (www.ci.nyc.ny.us/html/nypd/html/).

15. New York Police Department News Release #268-97 (May 13, 1997). "Mayor Giuliani Delivers Keynote Address at the International CompStat Conference."

16. The discussion about the ICAM program is adapted from Thomas Rich, "The Chicago Police Department's Information Collection for Automated Mapping (ICAM) Program," *Program Focus* (Washington, DC: National Institute of Justice, 1996).

17. Bureau of Justice Statistics, *Crime and Victims Statistics* (1998). The above data were obtained from the Bureau of Justice Statistics website at www.ojp.usdoj.gov/bjs/cvict.htm.

18. The Office of Community Oriented Policing Services, "American's Law Enforcement to Receive Community Policing Boost," *Press Release* (Wednesday, November 25, 1998).

19. Please see chapter 5 for a discussion. Also see Alfred Blumstein and Richard Rosenfeld, "Assessing the Recent Ups and Downs in U.S. Homicide Rates," *National Institute of Justice Journal* (Washington, DC: U.S. Department of Justice, October, 1998).

20. "Mayor Giuliani Delivers Keynote Address at the International CompStat Conference."

21. John Eck and Dennis Rosenbaum, "The New Police Order: Effectiveness, Equity, and Efficiency in Community Policing," in *The Challenge of Community Policing*, ed. Dennis Rosenbaum (Thousand Oaks, CA: Sage, 1994), pp. 3–26.

❖ ❖ ❖ ❖    22. Mark Moore, "Research Synthesis and Policy Implications," in *The Challenge of Community Policing*, ed. Dennis Rosenbaum (Thousand Oaks, CA: Sage, 1994), pp. 285–299.

23. Jayne Seagrave, "Defining Community Policing," *American Journal of Police* 15 (1996): 1–22.

24. Lawrence James and Allan Jones, "Organizational Structure: A Review of Structural Dimension and Their Conceptual Relationships With Individual Attitudes and Behavior," *Organizational Behavior and Human Performance* 16 (1976): 74–113.

25. Peter Blau, "A Formal Theory of Differentiation in Organizations," *American Sociological Review* 35 (1970): 201–218.

26. The three books are Dennis Rosenbaum, *The Challenge of Community Policing: Testing the Promises* (Thousand Oaks, CA: Sage, 1994); Peter Kratcoski and D. Dukes, *Issues in Community Policing* (Cincinnati: Anderson, 1995); and Geoffrey Alpert and Alex Piquero, *Community Policing: Contemporary Readings* (Prospect Heights, IL: Waveland, 1998).

27. For a discussion see: Farimorz Damanpour, "Organizational Innovation: A Meta-Analysis of Effects of Determinants and Moderators," *Academy of Management Journal* 34 (1991): 555–590.

28. Egon Bittner, *The Functions of Police in Modern Society* (Washington, DC: National Institute of Mental Health, 1970).

29. Peter Kraska and Louis Cubellis, "Militarizing Mayberry and Beyond: Making Sense of American Paramilitary Policing," *Justice Quarterly* 14 (1997): 607–629.

30. Samuel Walker, *A Critical History of Police Reform* (Lexington, MA: D. C. Heath, 1977).

31. T. Chandler and R. Gely, "Union and Management Organizational Structure for Bargaining in the Public Sector," in *Handbook of Public Sector Labor Relations*, eds. Jack Rabin, Thomas Vocino, W. Bartley Hildreth, and Gerald Miller (New York: Marcel Dekker, 1994).

32. For a discussion on the history of police unions and management relations please see International Association of Chiefs of Police, *Critical Issues in Police Labor Relations* (Gaithersburg, MD: IACP, 1974); Steven Rynecki and Michael Morse, *Police Collective Bargaining Agreements: A National Management Survey* (Washington, DC: Police Executive Research Forum, 1981); and David Carter and Allen Sapp, "A Comparative Analysis of Clauses in Police Collective Bargaining Agreements as Indicators of Change in Labor Relations," *American Journal of Policing* 12 (1992): 17–46.

33. Volcker Commission, "Leadership for America: Rebuilding the Public Service," cited in *Classics of Public Personnel Policy*, ed. Frank Thompson, (Pacific Grove, CA: Brooks/Cole, 1991), pp. 386–390.

34. David Osborne and Ted Gaebler, *Reinventing Government: How the Entrepreneurial Spirit Is Transforming the Public Sector, From Schoolhouse to City Hall to the Pentagon* (Reading, MA: Addison-Wesley, 1992), p. 1. ✦

# Author Index

# Subject Index